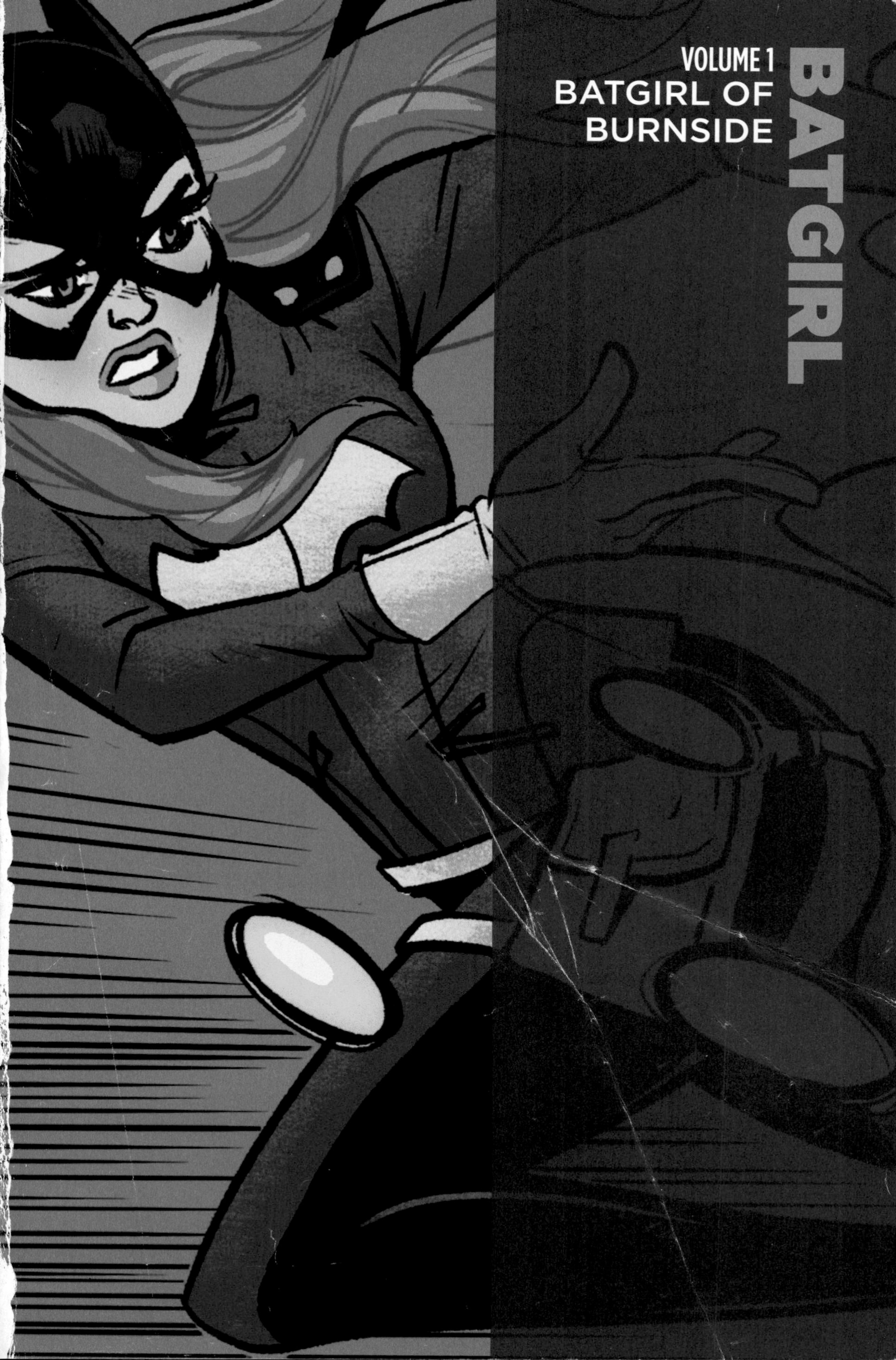

BATGIRL

VOLUME 1

BATGIRL OF BURNSIDE

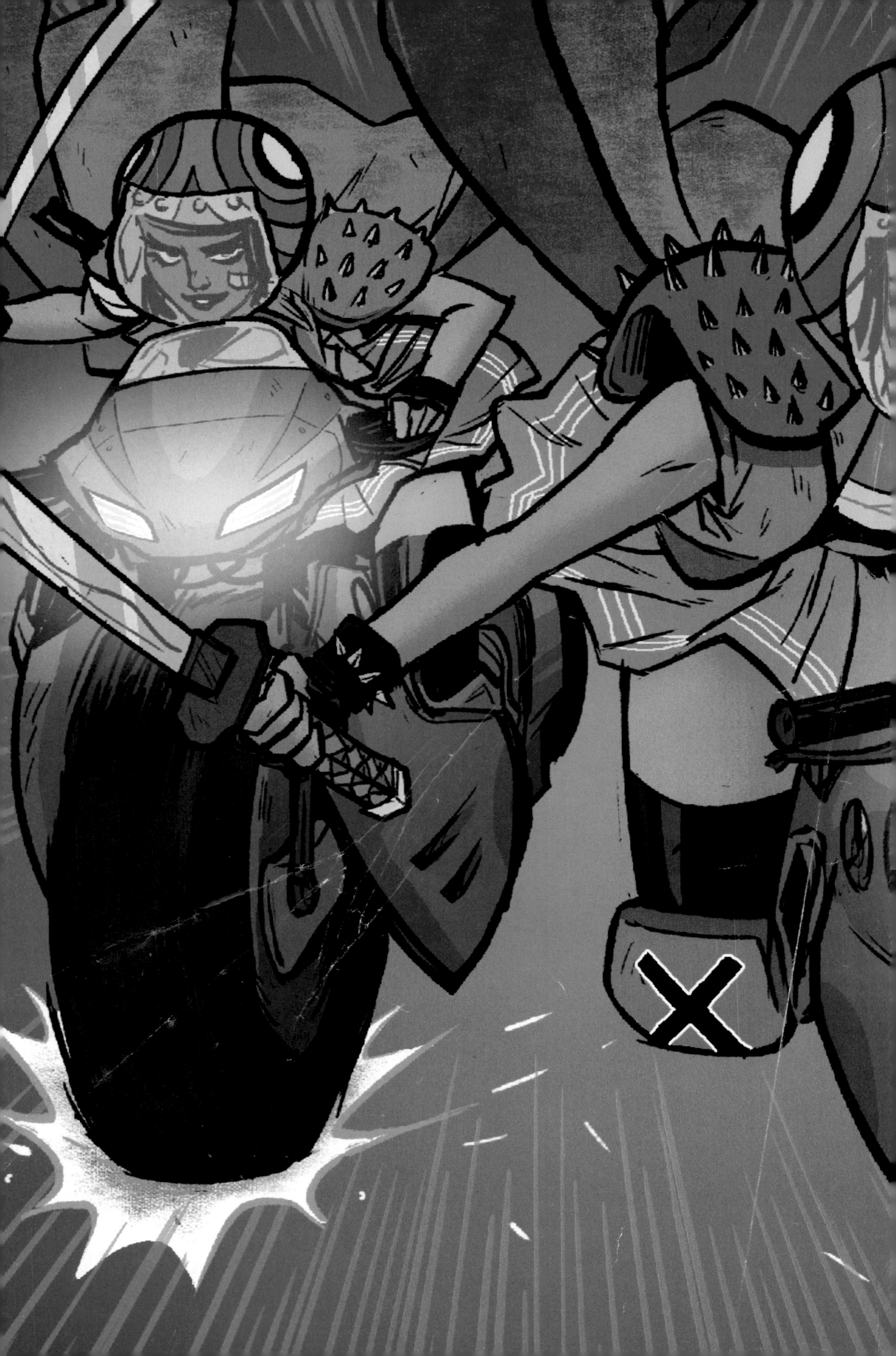

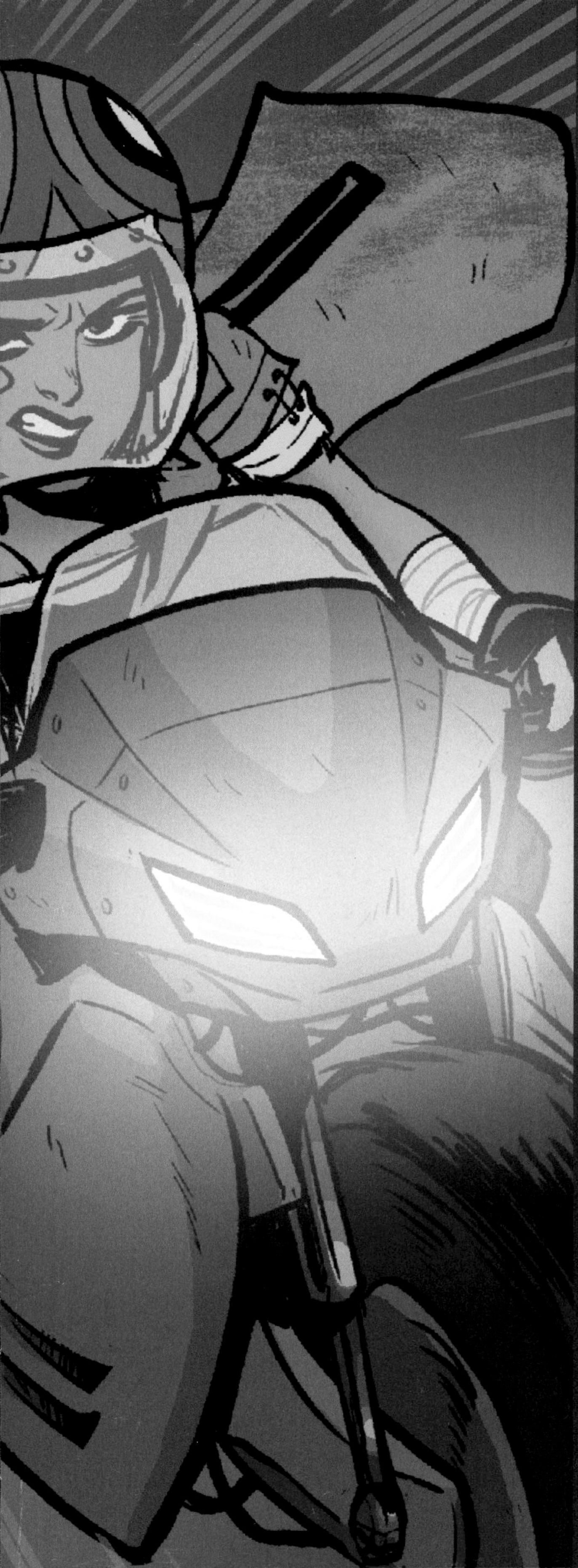

BATGIRL

VOLUME 1
BATGIRL OF BURNSIDE

WRITTEN BY
CAMERON STEWART
& BRENDEN FLETCHER

ART BY
BABS TARR

BREAKDOWN ART BY
CAMERON STEWART

SECRET ORIGIN ART BY
IRENE KOH

SECRET ORIGIN COLOR BY
HI-FI

COLOR BY
MARIS WICKS

LETTERS BY
JARED K. FLETCHER

ORIGINAL SERIES &
COLLECTION COVER ART BY
CAMERON STEWART

SECRET ORIGIN COVER BY
BRYAN HITCH

BATMAN CREATED BY
BOB KANE

CHRIS CONROY Editor – Original Series
DAVE WIELGOSZ Assistant Editor – Original Series
ROBIN WILDMAN Editor
ROBBIN BROSTERMAN Design Director – Books
DAMIAN RYLAND Publication Design

BOB HARRAS Senior VP – Editor-in-Chief, DC Comics

DIANE NELSON President
DAN DIDIO and JIM LEE Co-Publishers
GEOFF JOHNS Chief Creative Officer
AMIT DESAI Senior VP – Marketing & Franchise Management
AMY GENKINS Senior VP – Business & Legal Affairs
NAIRI GARDINER Senior VP – Finance
JEFF BOISON VP – Publishing Planning
MARK CHIARELLO VP – Art Direction & Design
JOHN CUNNINGHAM VP – Marketing
TERRI CUNNINGHAM VP – Editorial Administration
LARRY GANEM VP – Talent Relations & Services
ALISON GILL Senior VP – Manufacturing & Operations
HANK KANALZ Senior VP – Vertigo & Integrated Publishing
JAY KOGAN VP – Business & Legal Affairs, Publishing
JACK MAHAN VP – Business Affairs, Talent
NICK NAPOLITANO VP – Manufacturing Administration
SUE POHJA VP – Book Sales
FRED RUIZ VP – Manufacturing Operations
COURTNEY SIMMONS Senior VP – Publicity
BOB WAYNE Senior VP – Sales

BATGIRL VOLUME 1: BATGIRL OF BURNSIDE

DC Comics, 4000 Warner Blvd., Burbank, CA 91522
A Warner Bros. Entertainment Company.
Printed by RR Donnelley, Salem, VA, USA. 5/8/15.
First Printing.
ISBN: 978-1-4012-5332-5

Library of Congress Cataloging-in-Publication Data

Stewart, Cameron, 1976- author.
Batgirl. Volume 1, The Batgirl of Burnside / Cameron Stewart, Brenden Fletcher, Babs Tarr.
pages cm. — (The New 52!)
ISBN 978-1-4012-5332-5 (hardback)
1. Graphic novels. I. Fletcher, Brenden, author. II. Tarr, Babs, illustrator. III. Title. IV. Title: Batgirl of Burnside.
PN6728.B358S74 2015
741.5'973—dc23
2015006319

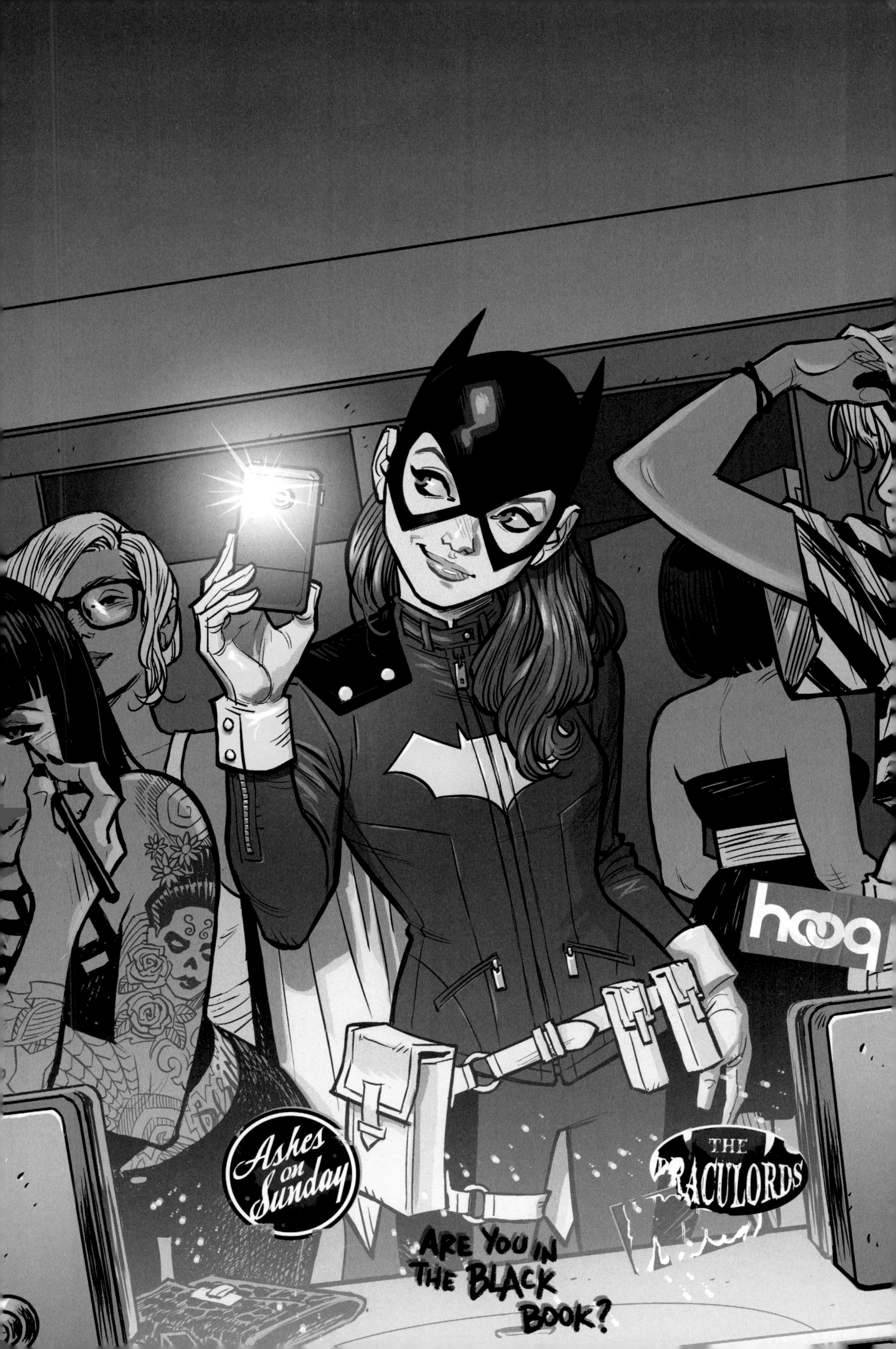
hoop
Ashes on Sunday
THE DRACULORDS
ARE YOU IN THE BLACK BOOK?

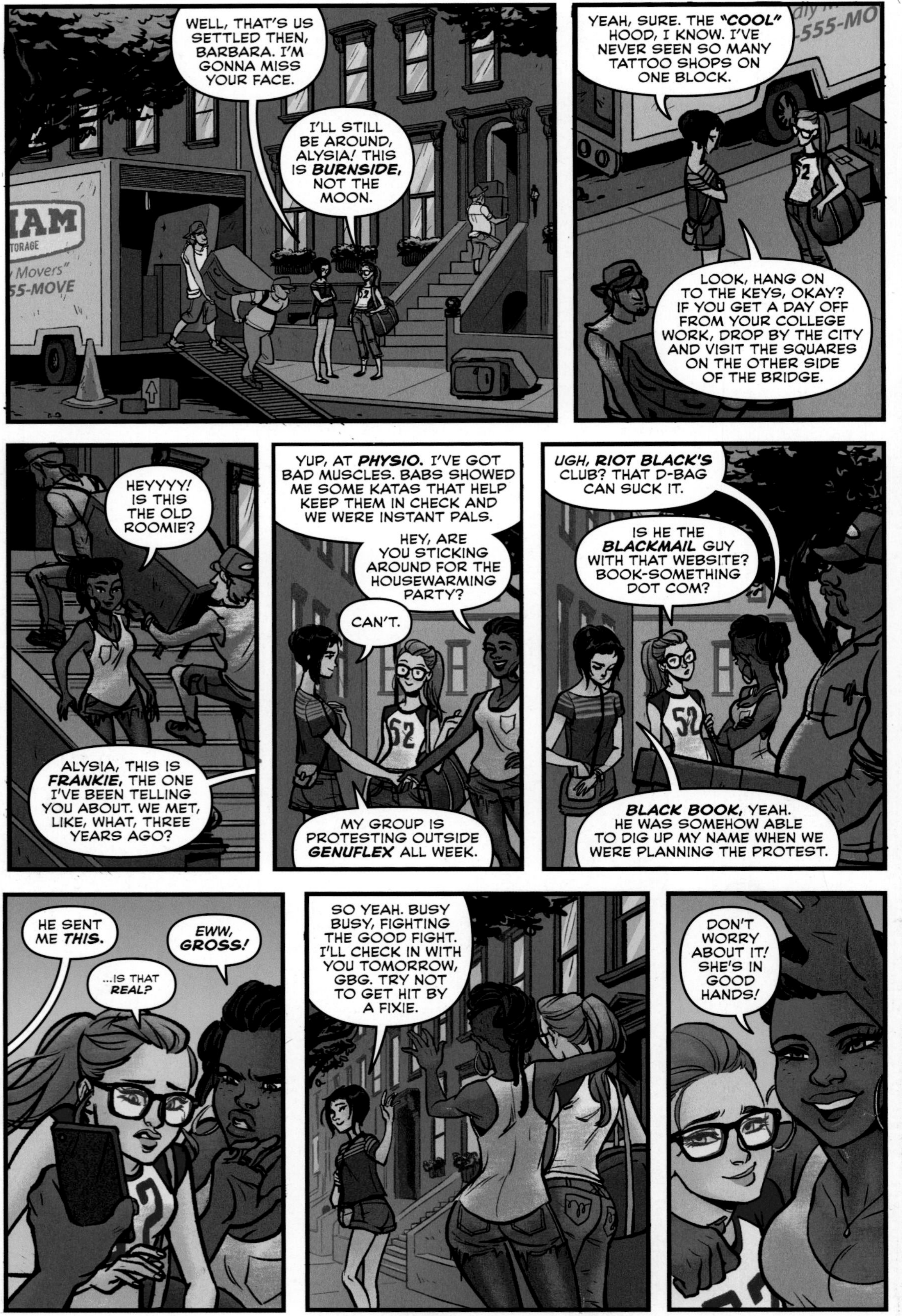
WELL, THAT'S US SETTLED THEN, BARBARA. I'M GONNA MISS YOUR FACE.
I'LL STILL BE AROUND, ALYSIA! THIS IS *BURNSIDE,* NOT THE MOON.
YEAH, SURE. THE "*COOL*" HOOD, I KNOW. I'VE NEVER SEEN SO MANY TATTOO SHOPS ON ONE BLOCK.
LOOK, HANG ON TO THE KEYS, OKAY? IF YOU GET A DAY OFF FROM YOUR COLLEGE WORK, DROP BY THE CITY AND VISIT THE SQUARES ON THE OTHER SIDE OF THE BRIDGE.
HEYYYY! IS THIS THE OLD ROOMIE?
ALYSIA, THIS IS *FRANKIE,* THE ONE I'VE BEEN TELLING YOU ABOUT. WE MET, LIKE, WHAT, THREE YEARS AGO?
YUP, AT *PHYSIO.* I'VE GOT BAD MUSCLES. BABS SHOWED ME SOME KATAS THAT HELP KEEP THEM IN CHECK AND WE WERE INSTANT PALS.
HEY, ARE YOU STICKING AROUND FOR THE HOUSEWARMING PARTY?
CAN'T.
MY GROUP IS PROTESTING OUTSIDE *GENUFLEX* ALL WEEK.
UGH, RIOT BLACK'S CLUB? THAT D-BAG CAN SUCK IT.
IS HE THE *BLACKMAIL* GUY WITH THAT WEBSITE? BOOK-SOMETHING DOT COM?
BLACK BOOK, YEAH. HE WAS SOMEHOW ABLE TO DIG UP MY NAME WHEN WE WERE PLANNING THE PROTEST.
HE SENT ME *THIS.*
...IS THAT *REAL?*
EWW, GROSS!
SO YEAH. BUSY BUSY, FIGHTING THE GOOD FIGHT. I'LL CHECK IN WITH YOU TOMORROW, GBG. TRY NOT TO GET HIT BY A FIXIE.
DON'T WORRY ABOUT IT! SHE'S IN GOOD HANDS!

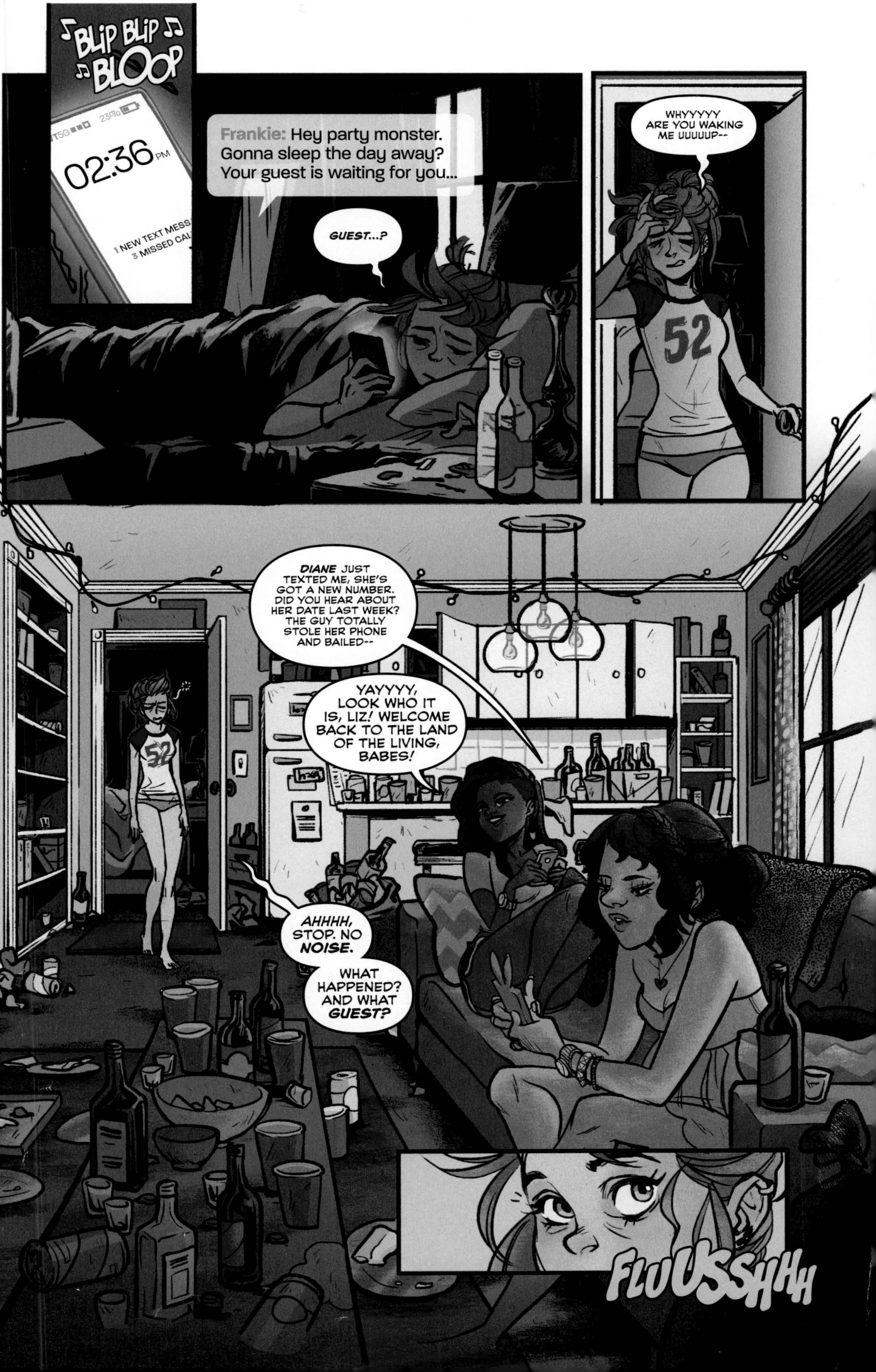
BLIP BLIP BLOOP
02:36 PM
23%
1 NEW TEXT MESS
3 MISSED CAL
Frankie: Hey party monster. Gonna sleep the day away? Your guest is waiting for you...
GUEST...?
WHYYYYY ARE YOU WAKING ME UUUUUP--
DIANE JUST TEXTED ME, SHE'S GOT A NEW NUMBER. DID YOU HEAR ABOUT HER DATE LAST WEEK? THE GUY TOTALLY STOLE HER PHONE AND BAILED--
YAYYYY, LOOK WHO IT IS, LIZ! WELCOME BACK TO THE LAND OF THE LIVING, BABES!
AHHHH, STOP. NO NOISE.
WHAT HAPPENED? AND WHAT GUEST?
FLUUSSHHH

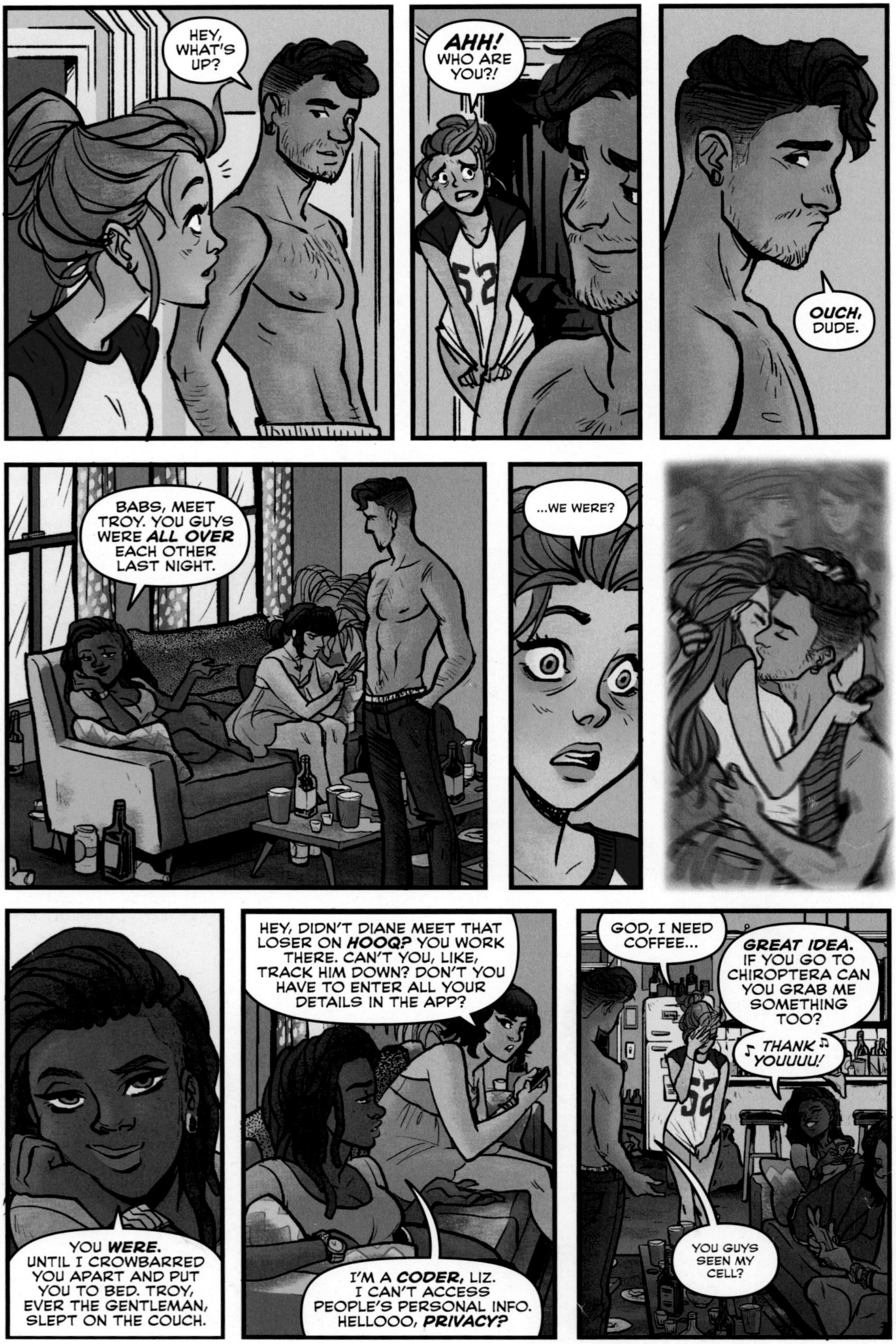
HEY, WHAT'S UP?
AHH! WHO ARE YOU?!
OUCH, DUDE.
BABS, MEET TROY. YOU GUYS WERE ALL OVER EACH OTHER LAST NIGHT.
...WE WERE?
YOU WERE. UNTIL I CROWBARRED YOU APART AND PUT YOU TO BED. TROY, EVER THE GENTLEMAN, SLEPT ON THE COUCH.
HEY, DIDN'T DIANE MEET THAT LOSER ON HOOQ? YOU WORK THERE. CAN'T YOU, LIKE, TRACK HIM DOWN? DON'T YOU HAVE TO ENTER ALL YOUR DETAILS IN THE APP?
I'M A CODER, LIZ. I CAN'T ACCESS PEOPLE'S PERSONAL INFO. HELLOOO, PRIVACY?
GOD, I NEED COFFEE...
GREAT IDEA. IF YOU GO TO CHIROPTERA CAN YOU GRAB ME SOMETHING TOO?
♪ THANK YOUUUU! ♪
YOU GUYS SEEN MY CELL?

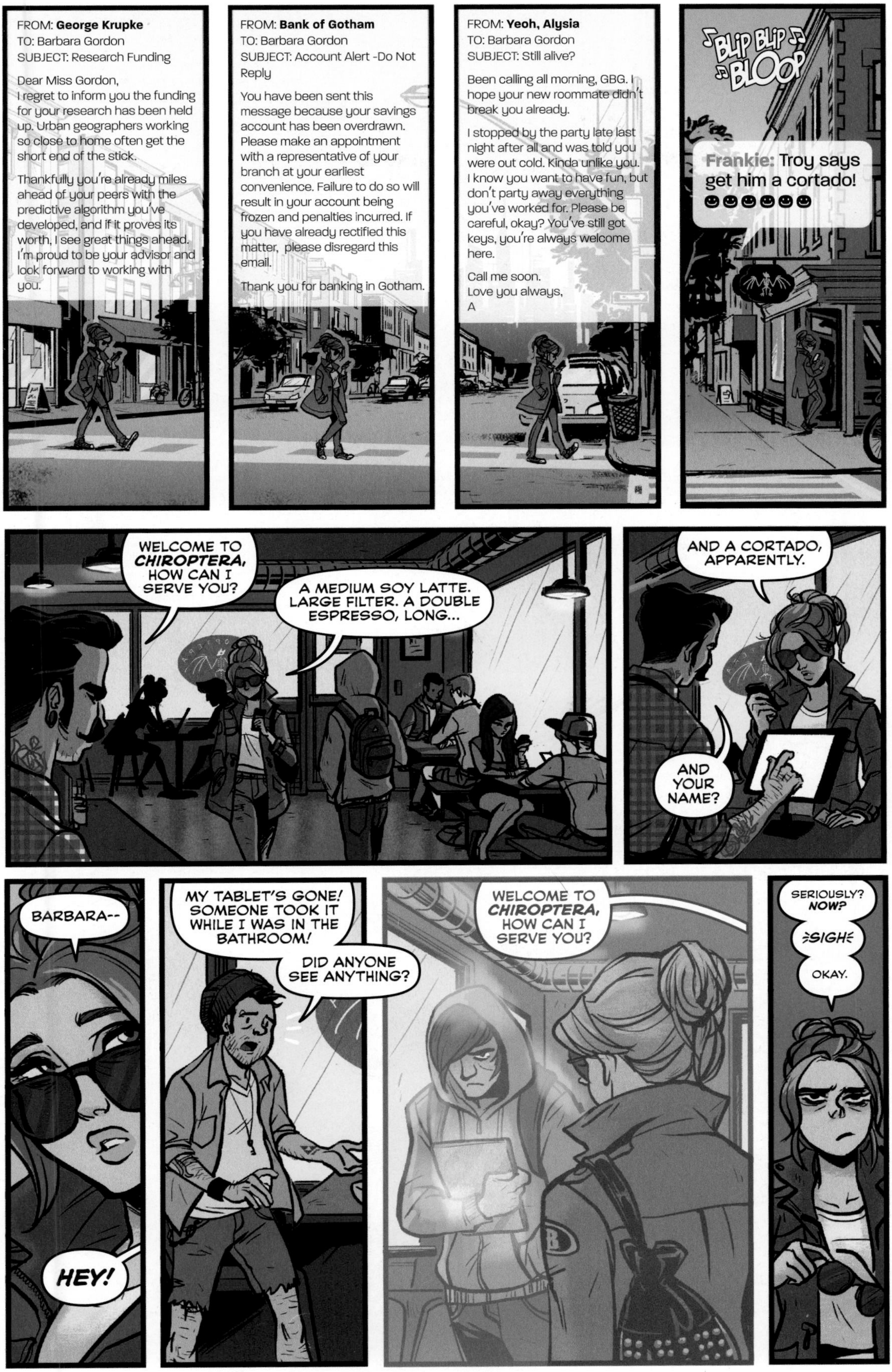
FROM: George Krupke
TO: Barbara Gordon
SUBJECT: Research Funding
Dear Miss Gordon,
I regret to inform you the funding for your research has been held up. Urban geographers working so close to home often get the short end of the stick.
Thankfully you're already miles ahead of your peers with the predictive algorithm you've developed, and if it proves its worth, I see great things ahead. I'm proud to be your advisor and look forward to working with you.
FROM: Bank of Gotham
TO: Barbara Gordon
SUBJECT: Account Alert -Do Not Reply
You have been sent this message because your savings account has been overdrawn. Please make an appointment with a representative of your branch at your earliest convenience. Failure to do so will result in your account being frozen and penalties incurred. If you have already rectified this matter, please disregard this email.
Thank you for banking in Gotham.
FROM: Yeoh, Alysia
TO: Barbara Gordon
SUBJECT: Still alive?
Been calling all morning, GBG. I hope your new roommate didn't break you already.
I stopped by the party late last night after all and was told you were out cold. Kinda unlike you. I know you want to have fun, but don't party away everything you've worked for. Please be careful, okay? You've still got keys, you're always welcome here.
Call me soon.
Love you always,
A
BLIP BLIP BLOOP
Frankie: Troy says get him a cortado!
WELCOME TO CHIROPTERA, HOW CAN I SERVE YOU?
A MEDIUM SOY LATTE. LARGE FILTER. A DOUBLE ESPRESSO, LONG...
AND A CORTADO, APPARENTLY.
AND YOUR NAME?
BARBARA--
HEY!
MY TABLET'S GONE! SOMEONE TOOK IT WHILE I WAS IN THE BATHROOM!
DID ANYONE SEE ANYTHING?
WELCOME TO CHIROPTERA, HOW CAN I SERVE YOU?
SERIOUSLY? NOW?
SIGH
OKAY.

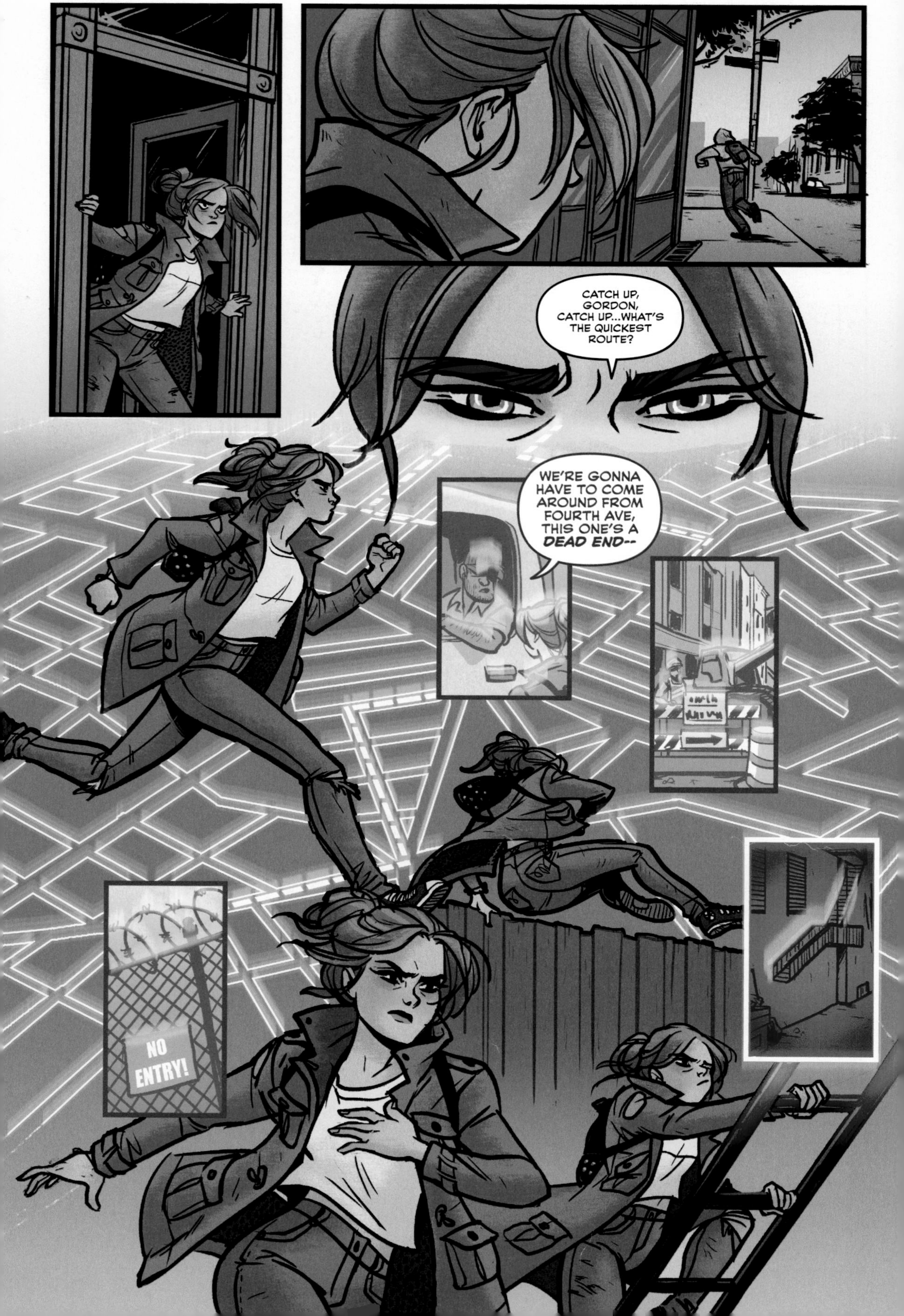
CATCH UP, GORDON, CATCH UP...WHAT'S THE QUICKEST ROUTE?
WE'RE GONNA HAVE TO COME AROUND FROM FOURTH AVE, THIS ONE'S A DEAD END--
NO ENTRY!

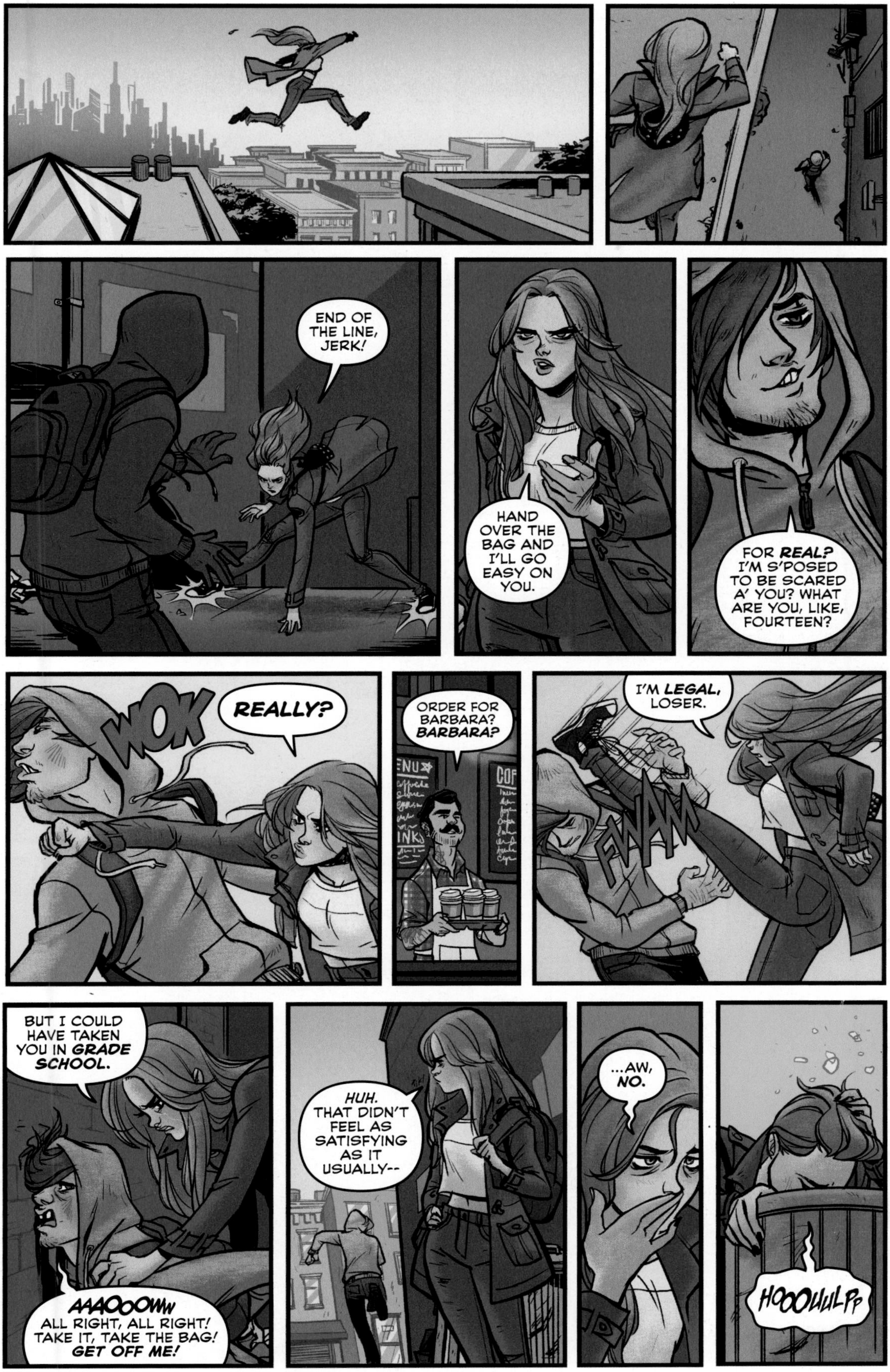

END OF THE LINE, JERK!
HAND OVER THE BAG AND I'LL GO EASY ON YOU.
FOR **REAL?** I'M S'POSED TO BE SCARED A' YOU? WHAT ARE YOU, LIKE, FOURTEEN?
WOK
REALLY?
ORDER FOR BARBARA? **BARBARA?**
I'M **LEGAL,** LOSER.
FWAM
BUT I COULD HAVE TAKEN YOU IN **GRADE SCHOOL.**
AAAOOOWW
ALL RIGHT, ALL RIGHT! TAKE IT, TAKE THE BAG! **GET OFF ME!**
HUH. THAT DIDN'T FEEL AS SATISFYING AS IT USUALLY--
...AW, **NO.**
HOOOULLPP

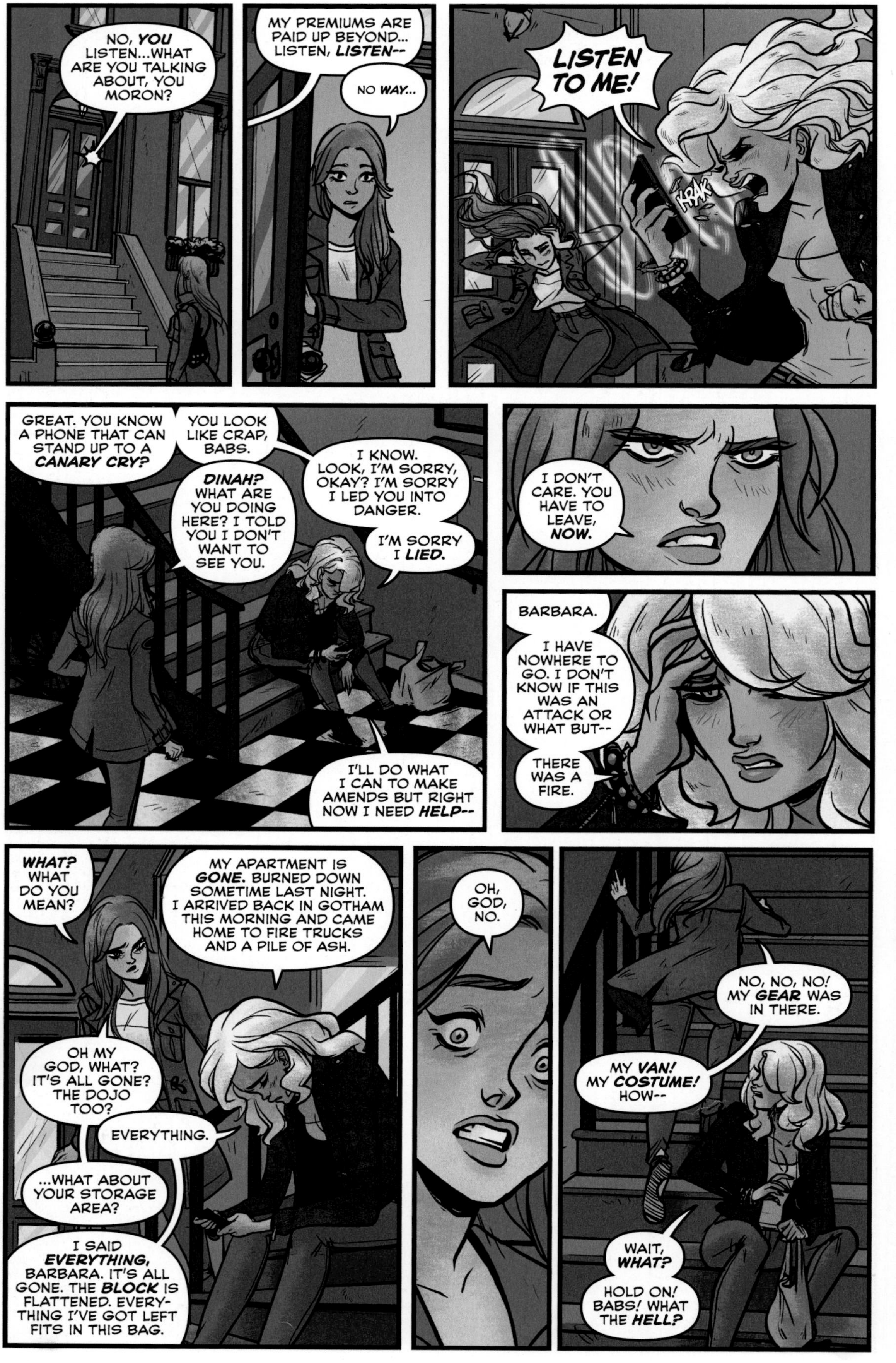
NO, YOU LISTEN...WHAT ARE YOU TALKING ABOUT, YOU MORON?
MY PREMIUMS ARE PAID UP BEYOND... LISTEN, LISTEN--
NO WAY...
LISTEN TO ME!
KRAK
GREAT. YOU KNOW A PHONE THAT CAN STAND UP TO A CANARY CRY?
YOU LOOK LIKE CRAP, BABS.
DINAH? WHAT ARE YOU DOING HERE? I TOLD YOU I DON'T WANT TO SEE YOU.
I KNOW. LOOK, I'M SORRY, OKAY? I'M SORRY I LED YOU INTO DANGER.
I'M SORRY I LIED.
I'LL DO WHAT I CAN TO MAKE AMENDS BUT RIGHT NOW I NEED HELP--
I DON'T CARE. YOU HAVE TO LEAVE, NOW.
BARBARA.
I HAVE NOWHERE TO GO. I DON'T KNOW IF THIS WAS AN ATTACK OR WHAT BUT--
THERE WAS A FIRE.
WHAT? WHAT DO YOU MEAN?
MY APARTMENT IS GONE. BURNED DOWN SOMETIME LAST NIGHT. I ARRIVED BACK IN GOTHAM THIS MORNING AND CAME HOME TO FIRE TRUCKS AND A PILE OF ASH.
OH MY GOD, WHAT? IT'S ALL GONE? THE DOJO TOO?
EVERYTHING.
...WHAT ABOUT YOUR STORAGE AREA?
I SAID EVERYTHING, BARBARA. IT'S ALL GONE. THE BLOCK IS FLATTENED. EVERYTHING I'VE GOT LEFT FITS IN THIS BAG.
OH, GOD, NO.
NO, NO, NO! MY GEAR WAS IN THERE.
MY VAN! MY COSTUME! HOW--
WAIT, WHAT?
HOLD ON! BABS! WHAT THE HELL?

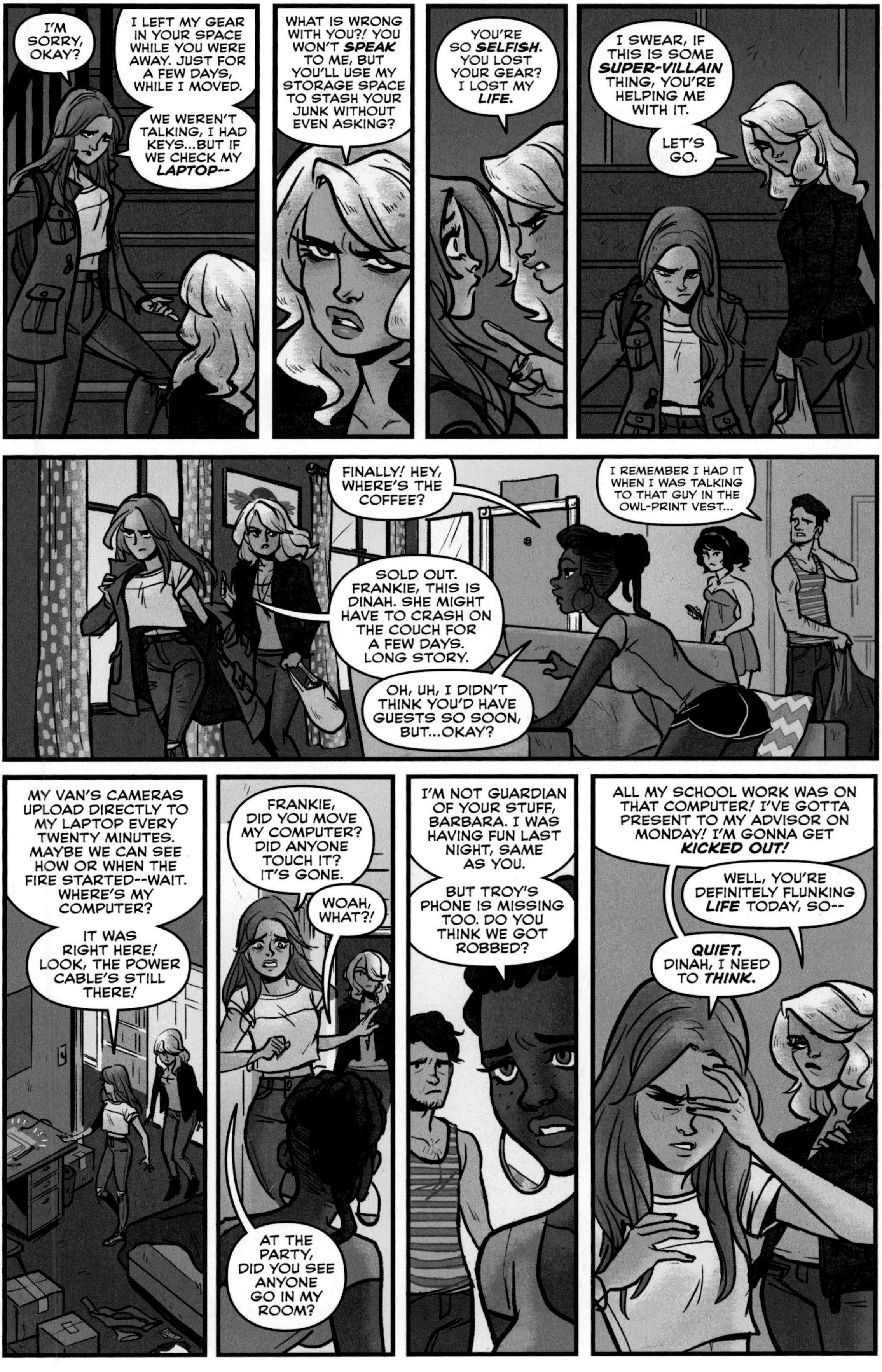
I'M SORRY, OKAY?
I LEFT MY GEAR IN YOUR SPACE WHILE YOU WERE AWAY. JUST FOR A FEW DAYS, WHILE I MOVED.
WE WEREN'T TALKING, I HAD KEYS...BUT IF WE CHECK MY LAPTOP--
WHAT IS WRONG WITH YOU?! YOU WON'T SPEAK TO ME, BUT YOU'LL USE MY STORAGE SPACE TO STASH YOUR JUNK WITHOUT EVEN ASKING?
YOU'RE SO SELFISH. YOU LOST YOUR GEAR? I LOST MY LIFE.
I SWEAR, IF THIS IS SOME SUPER-VILLAIN THING, YOU'RE HELPING ME WITH IT.
LET'S GO.
FINALLY! HEY, WHERE'S THE COFFEE?
I REMEMBER I HAD IT WHEN I WAS TALKING TO THAT GUY IN THE OWL-PRINT VEST...
SOLD OUT. FRANKIE, THIS IS DINAH. SHE MIGHT HAVE TO CRASH ON THE COUCH FOR A FEW DAYS. LONG STORY.
OH, UH, I DIDN'T THINK YOU'D HAVE GUESTS SO SOON, BUT...OKAY?
MY VAN'S CAMERAS UPLOAD DIRECTLY TO MY LAPTOP EVERY TWENTY MINUTES. MAYBE WE CAN SEE HOW OR WHEN THE FIRE STARTED--WAIT. WHERE'S MY COMPUTER?
IT WAS RIGHT HERE! LOOK, THE POWER CABLE'S STILL THERE!
FRANKIE, DID YOU MOVE MY COMPUTER? DID ANYONE TOUCH IT? IT'S GONE.
WOAH, WHAT?!
AT THE PARTY, DID YOU SEE ANYONE GO IN MY ROOM?
I'M NOT GUARDIAN OF YOUR STUFF, BARBARA. I WAS HAVING FUN LAST NIGHT, SAME AS YOU.
BUT TROY'S PHONE IS MISSING TOO. DO YOU THINK WE GOT ROBBED?
ALL MY SCHOOL WORK WAS ON THAT COMPUTER! I'VE GOTTA PRESENT TO MY ADVISOR ON MONDAY! I'M GONNA GET KICKED OUT!
WELL, YOU'RE DEFINITELY FLUNKING LIFE TODAY, SO--
QUIET, DINAH, I NEED TO THINK.

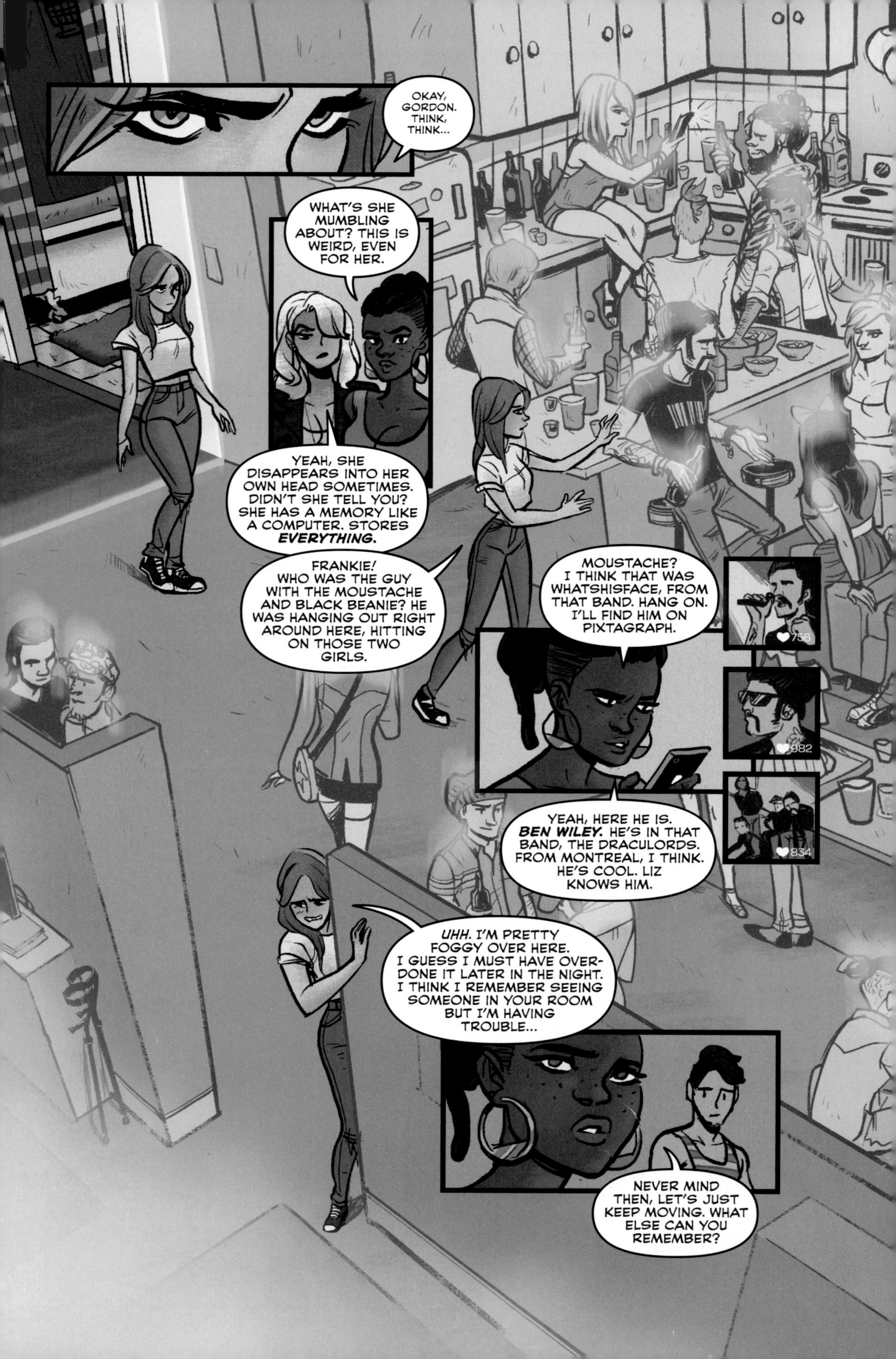
OKAY, GORDON. THINK, THINK...
WHAT'S SHE MUMBLING ABOUT? THIS IS WEIRD, EVEN FOR HER.
YEAH, SHE DISAPPEARS INTO HER OWN HEAD SOMETIMES. DIDN'T SHE TELL YOU? SHE HAS A MEMORY LIKE A COMPUTER. STORES *EVERYTHING.*
FRANKIE! WHO WAS THE GUY WITH THE MOUSTACHE AND BLACK BEANIE? HE WAS HANGING OUT RIGHT AROUND HERE, HITTING ON THOSE TWO GIRLS.
MOUSTACHE? I THINK THAT WAS WHATSHISFACE, FROM THAT BAND. HANG ON. I'LL FIND HIM ON PIXTAGRAPH.
756
982
834
YEAH, HERE HE IS. ***BEN WILEY.*** HE'S IN THAT BAND, THE DRACULORDS. FROM MONTREAL, I THINK. HE'S COOL. LIZ KNOWS HIM.
UHH. I'M PRETTY FOGGY OVER HERE. I GUESS I MUST HAVE OVERDONE IT LATER IN THE NIGHT. I THINK I REMEMBER SEEING SOMEONE IN YOUR ROOM BUT I'M HAVING TROUBLE...
NEVER MIND THEN, LET'S JUST KEEP MOVING. WHAT ELSE CAN YOU REMEMBER?

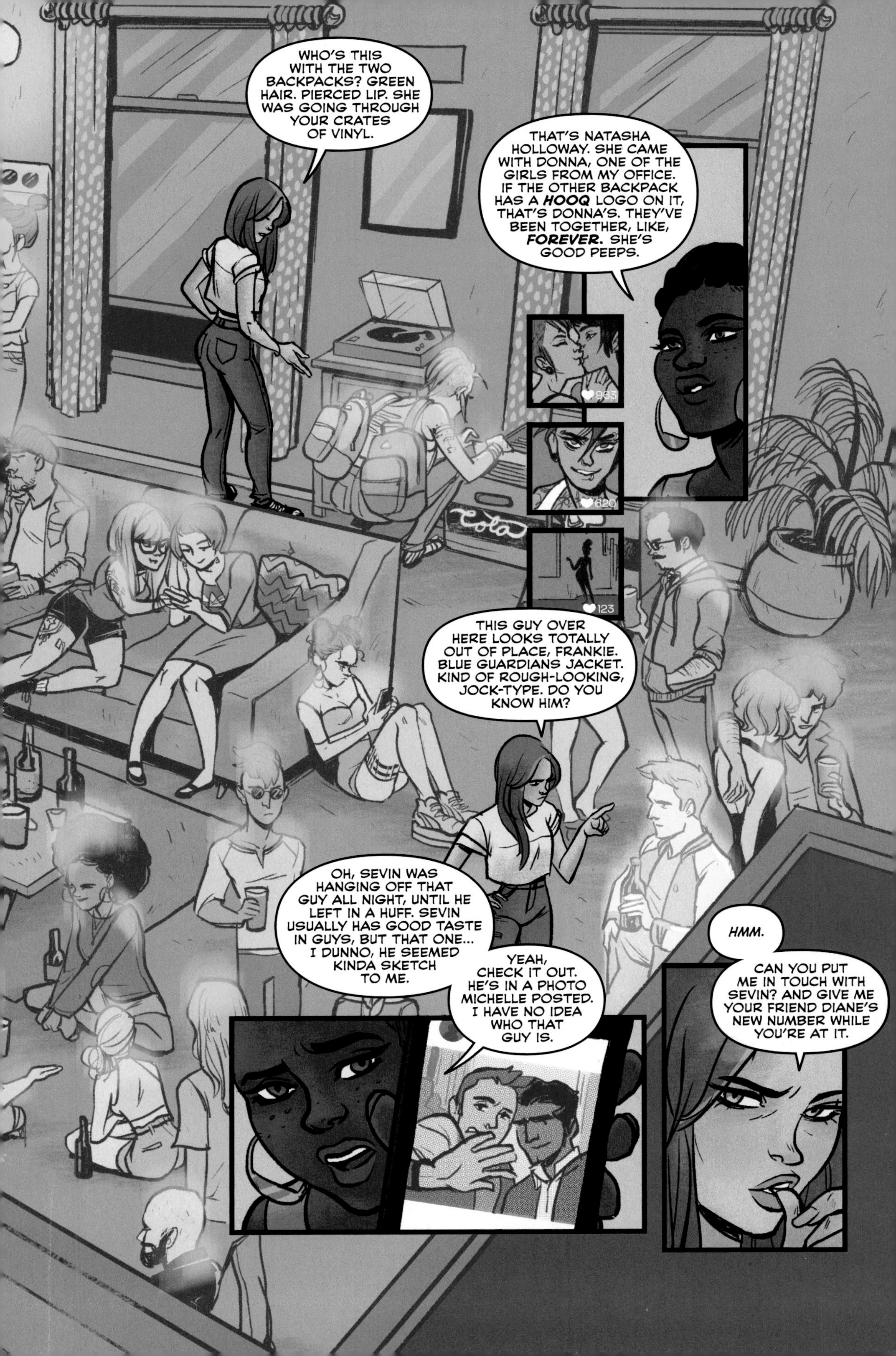
WHO'S THIS WITH THE TWO BACKPACKS? GREEN HAIR. PIERCED LIP. SHE WAS GOING THROUGH YOUR CRATES OF VINYL.
THAT'S NATASHA HOLLOWAY. SHE CAME WITH DONNA, ONE OF THE GIRLS FROM MY OFFICE. IF THE OTHER BACKPACK HAS A **HOOQ** LOGO ON IT, THAT'S DONNA'S. THEY'VE BEEN TOGETHER, LIKE, **FOREVER.** SHE'S GOOD PEEPS.
963
620
123
THIS GUY OVER HERE LOOKS TOTALLY OUT OF PLACE, FRANKIE. BLUE GUARDIANS JACKET. KIND OF ROUGH-LOOKING, JOCK-TYPE. DO YOU KNOW HIM?
OH, SEVIN WAS HANGING OFF THAT GUY ALL NIGHT, UNTIL HE LEFT IN A HUFF. SEVIN USUALLY HAS GOOD TASTE IN GUYS, BUT THAT ONE... I DUNNO, HE SEEMED KINDA SKETCH TO ME.
YEAH, CHECK IT OUT. HE'S IN A PHOTO MICHELLE POSTED. I HAVE NO IDEA WHO THAT GUY IS.
HMM.
CAN YOU PUT ME IN TOUCH WITH SEVIN? AND GIVE ME YOUR FRIEND DIANE'S NEW NUMBER WHILE YOU'RE AT IT.

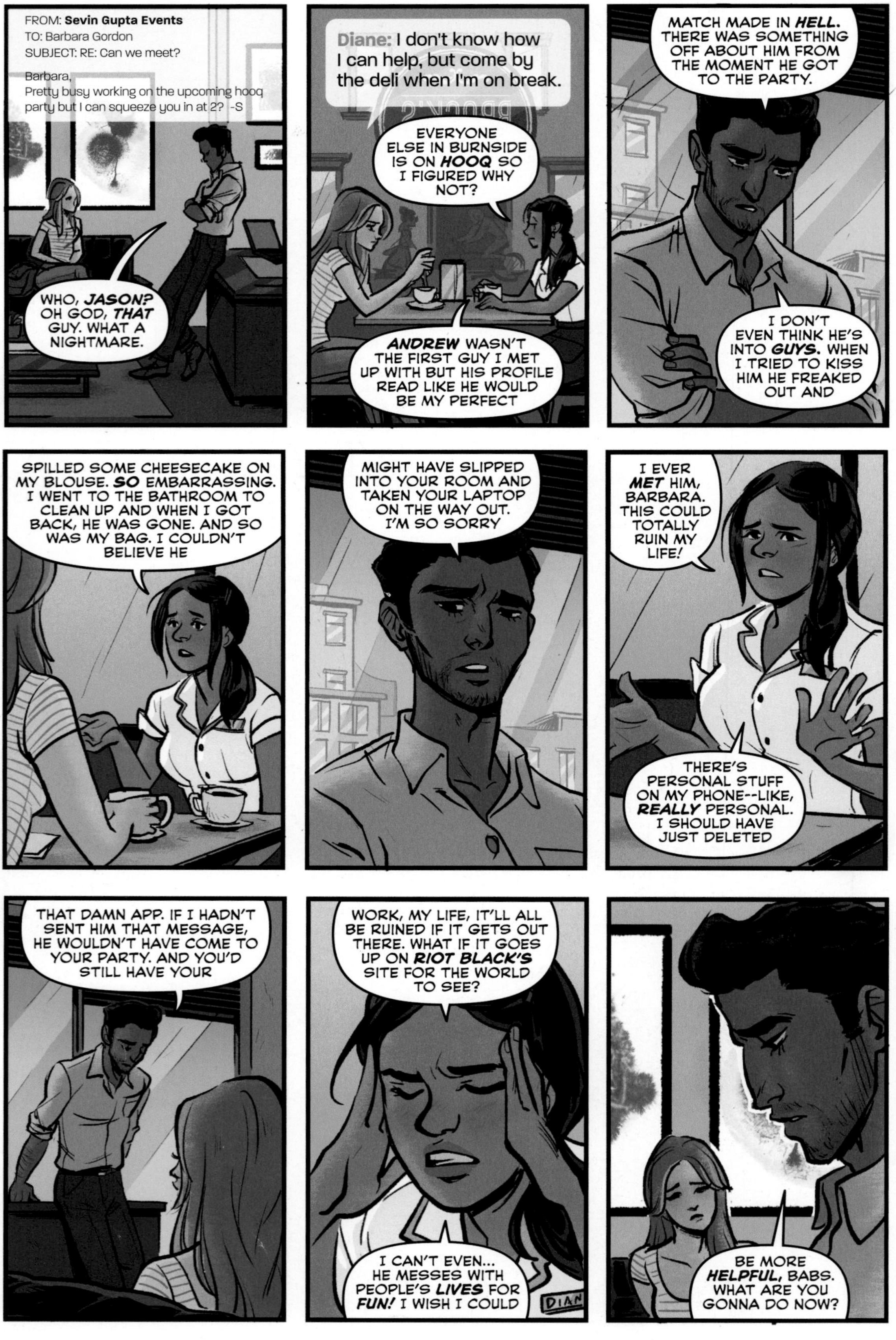
FROM: Sevin Gupta Events
TO: Barbara Gordon
SUBJECT: RE: Can we meet?
Barbara,
Pretty busy working on the upcoming hooq party but I can squeeze you in at 2? -S
WHO, JASON? OH GOD, THAT GUY. WHAT A NIGHTMARE.
Diane: I don't know how I can help, but come by the deli when I'm on break.
EVERYONE ELSE IN BURNSIDE IS ON HOOQ SO I FIGURED WHY NOT?
ANDREW WASN'T THE FIRST GUY I MET UP WITH BUT HIS PROFILE READ LIKE HE WOULD BE MY PERFECT
MATCH MADE IN HELL. THERE WAS SOMETHING OFF ABOUT HIM FROM THE MOMENT HE GOT TO THE PARTY.
I DON'T EVEN THINK HE'S INTO GUYS. WHEN I TRIED TO KISS HIM HE FREAKED OUT AND
SPILLED SOME CHEESECAKE ON MY BLOUSE. SO EMBARRASSING. I WENT TO THE BATHROOM TO CLEAN UP AND WHEN I GOT BACK, HE WAS GONE. AND SO WAS MY BAG. I COULDN'T BELIEVE HE
MIGHT HAVE SLIPPED INTO YOUR ROOM AND TAKEN YOUR LAPTOP ON THE WAY OUT. I'M SO SORRY
I EVER MET HIM, BARBARA. THIS COULD TOTALLY RUIN MY LIFE!
THERE'S PERSONAL STUFF ON MY PHONE--LIKE, REALLY PERSONAL. I SHOULD HAVE JUST DELETED
THAT DAMN APP. IF I HADN'T SENT HIM THAT MESSAGE, HE WOULDN'T HAVE COME TO YOUR PARTY. AND YOU'D STILL HAVE YOUR
WORK, MY LIFE, IT'LL ALL BE RUINED IF IT GETS OUT THERE. WHAT IF IT GOES UP ON RIOT BLACK'S SITE FOR THE WORLD TO SEE?
I CAN'T EVEN... HE MESSES WITH PEOPLE'S LIVES FOR FUN! I WISH I COULD
BE MORE HELPFUL, BABS. WHAT ARE YOU GONNA DO NOW?

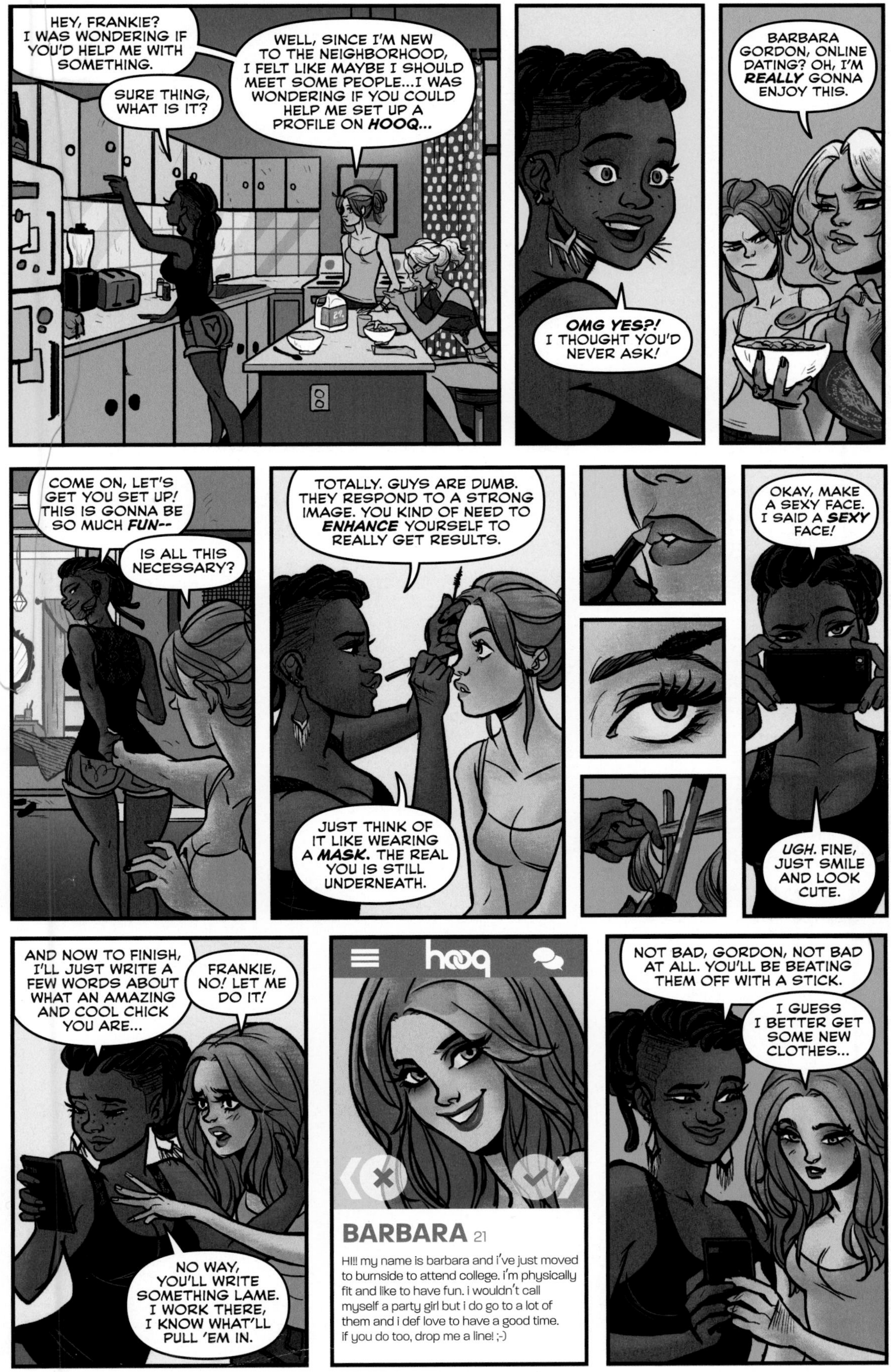
HEY, FRANKIE? I WAS WONDERING IF YOU'D HELP ME WITH SOMETHING.
SURE THING, WHAT IS IT?
WELL, SINCE I'M NEW TO THE NEIGHBORHOOD, I FELT LIKE MAYBE I SHOULD MEET SOME PEOPLE...I WAS WONDERING IF YOU COULD HELP ME SET UP A PROFILE ON HOOQ...
OMG YES?! I THOUGHT YOU'D NEVER ASK!
BARBARA GORDON, ONLINE DATING? OH, I'M REALLY GONNA ENJOY THIS.
COME ON, LET'S GET YOU SET UP! THIS IS GONNA BE SO MUCH FUN--
IS ALL THIS NECESSARY?
TOTALLY. GUYS ARE DUMB. THEY RESPOND TO A STRONG IMAGE. YOU KIND OF NEED TO ENHANCE YOURSELF TO REALLY GET RESULTS.
JUST THINK OF IT LIKE WEARING A MASK. THE REAL YOU IS STILL UNDERNEATH.
OKAY, MAKE A SEXY FACE. I SAID A SEXY FACE!
UGH. FINE, JUST SMILE AND LOOK CUTE.
AND NOW TO FINISH, I'LL JUST WRITE A FEW WORDS ABOUT WHAT AN AMAZING AND COOL CHICK YOU ARE...
FRANKIE, NO! LET ME DO IT!
NO WAY, YOU'LL WRITE SOMETHING LAME. I WORK THERE, I KNOW WHAT'LL PULL 'EM IN.
hooq
BARBARA 21
HI!! my name is barbara and i've just moved to burnside to attend college. i'm physically fit and like to have fun. i wouldn't call myself a party girl but i do go to a lot of them and i def love to have a good time. if you do too, drop me a line! ;-)
NOT BAD, GORDON, NOT BAD AT ALL. YOU'LL BE BEATING THEM OFF WITH A STICK.
I GUESS I BETTER GET SOME NEW CLOTHES...

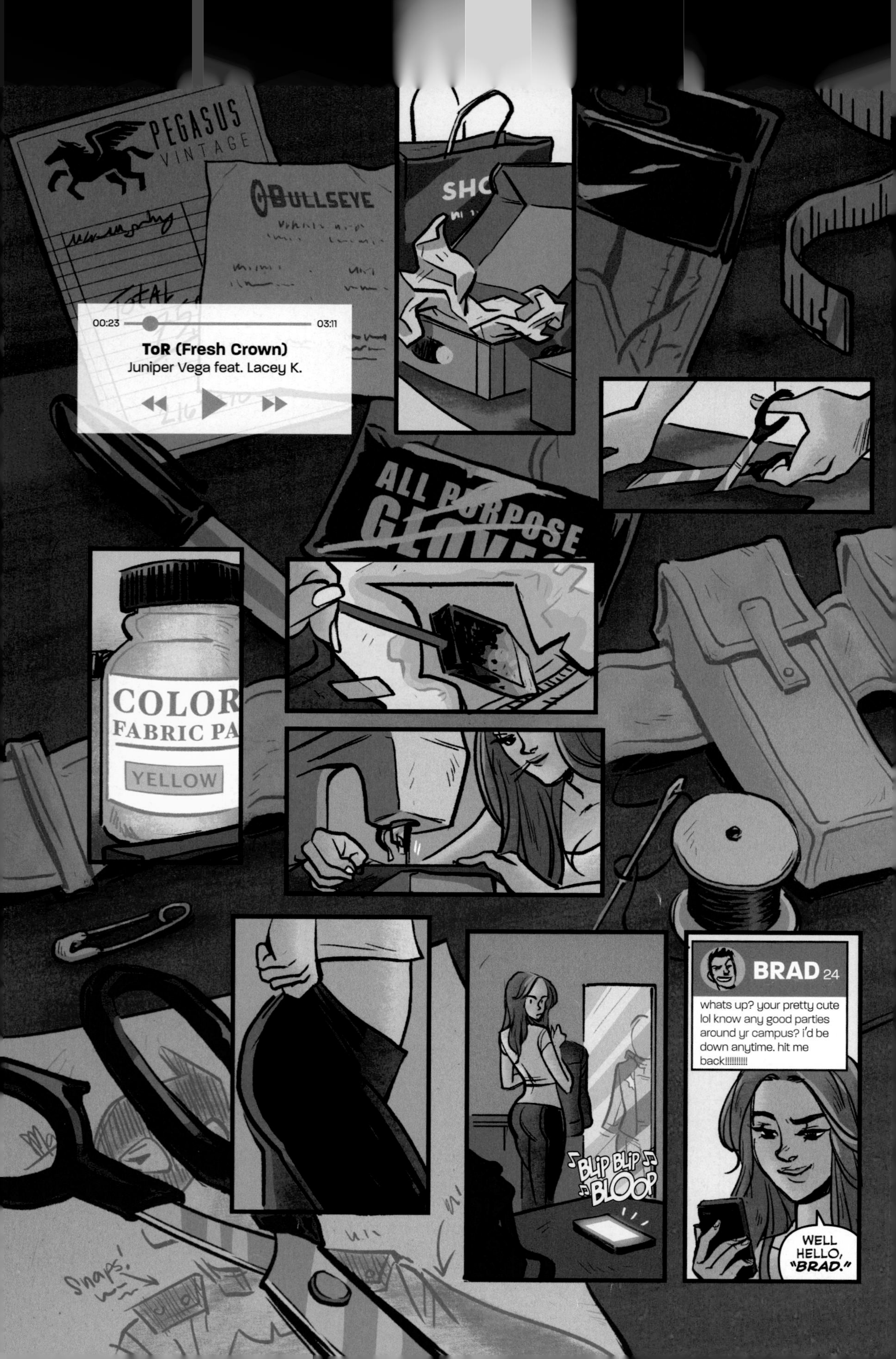
PEGASUS VINTAGE
BULLSEYE
00:23
03:11
ToR (Fresh Crown)
Juniper Vega feat. Lacey K.
ALL PURPOSE GLOVES
COLOR FABRIC PA
YELLOW
BRAD 24
whats up? your pretty cute lol know any good parties around yr campus? i'd be down anytime. hit me back!!!!!!!!!!
BLIP BLIP BLOOP
WELL HELLO, "BRAD."
Snaps!

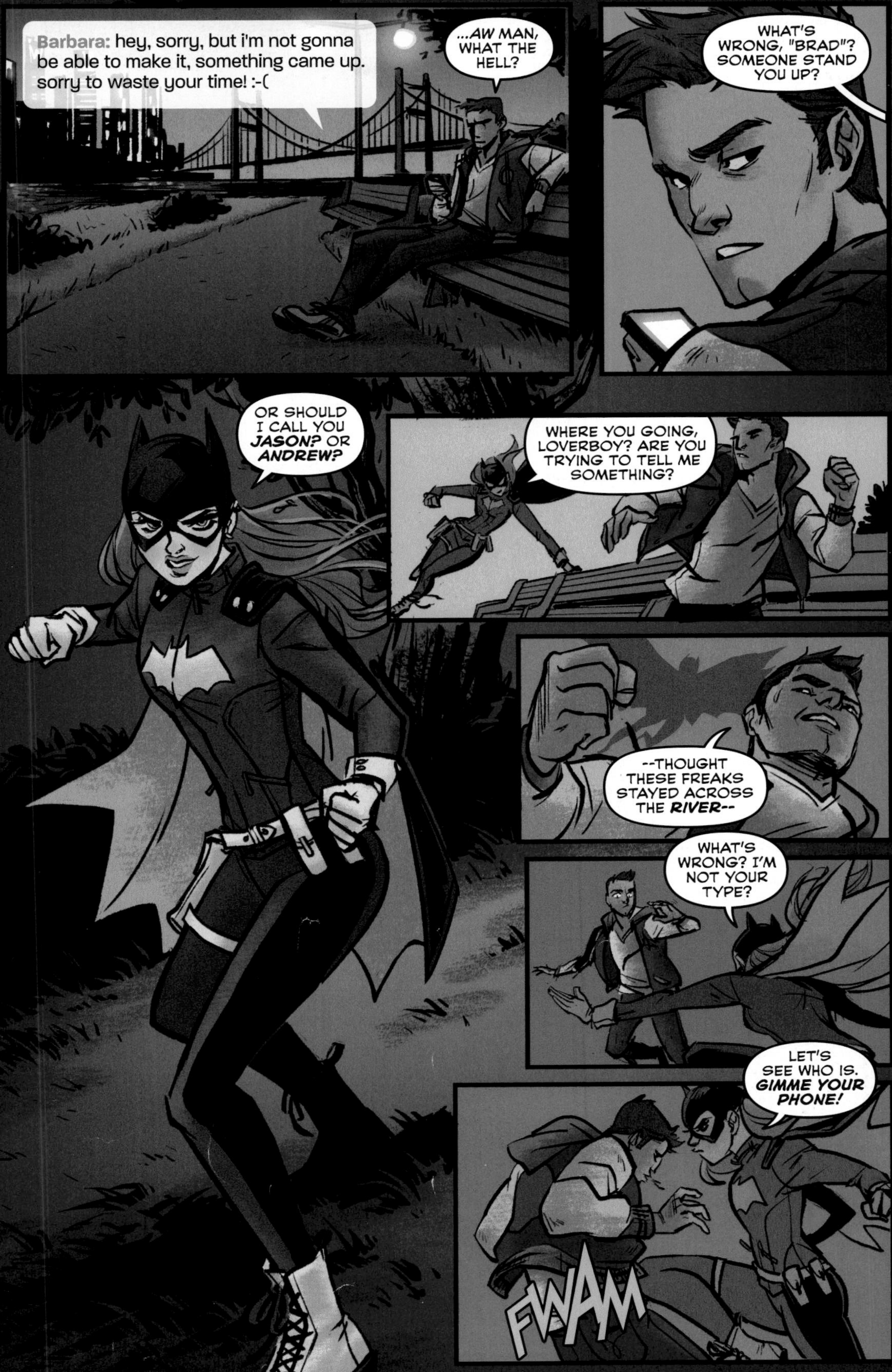

Barbara: hey, sorry, but i'm not gonna be able to make it, something came up. sorry to waste your time! :-(
...AW MAN, WHAT THE HELL?
WHAT'S WRONG, "BRAD"? SOMEONE STAND YOU UP?
OR SHOULD I CALL YOU JASON? OR ANDREW?
WHERE YOU GOING, LOVERBOY? ARE YOU TRYING TO TELL ME SOMETHING?
--THOUGHT THESE FREAKS STAYED ACROSS THE RIVER--
WHAT'S WRONG? I'M NOT YOUR TYPE?
LET'S SEE WHO IS. GIMME YOUR PHONE!
FWAM

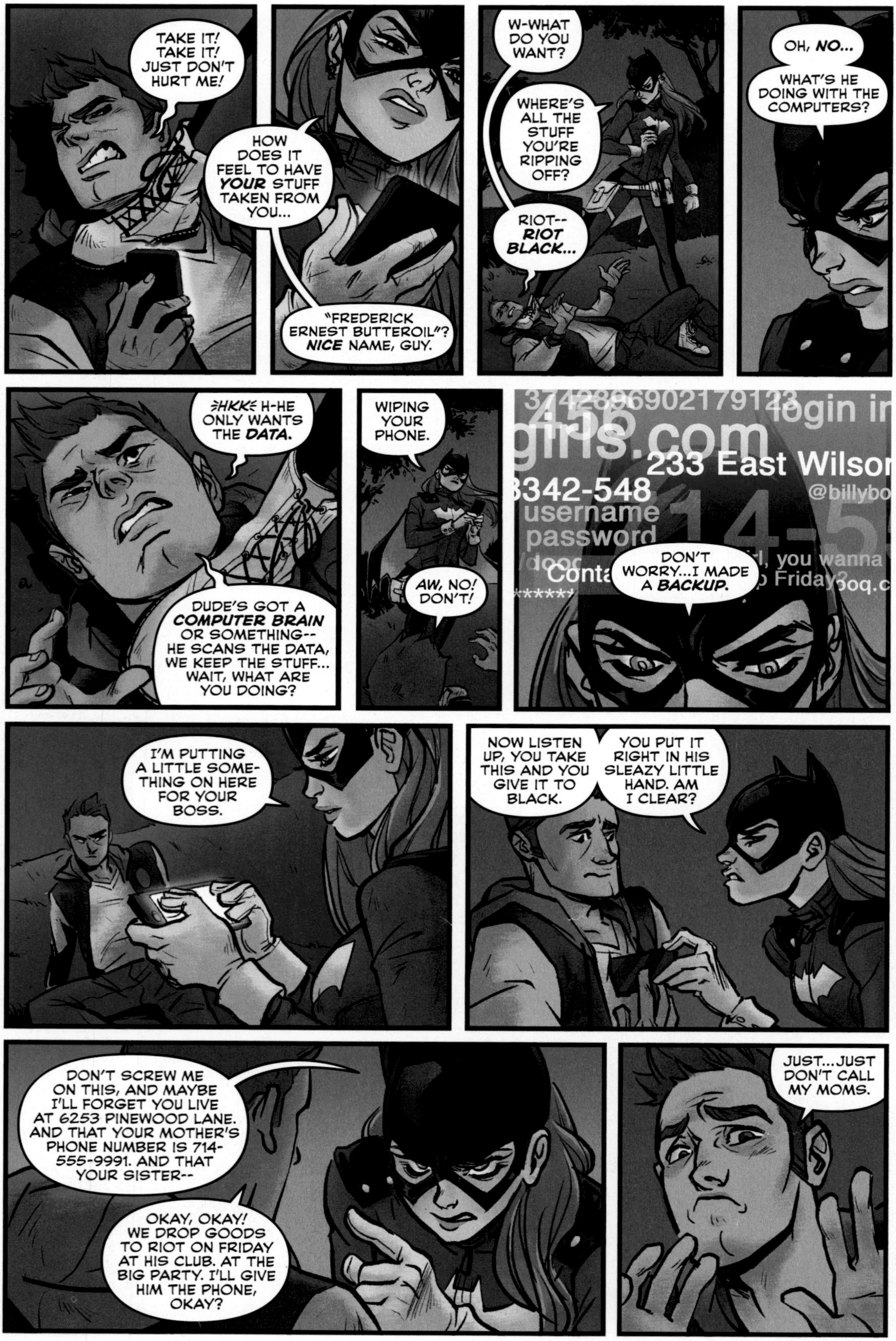
TAKE IT! TAKE IT! JUST DON'T HURT ME!
HOW DOES IT FEEL TO HAVE YOUR STUFF TAKEN FROM YOU...
"FREDERICK ERNEST BUTTEROIL"? NICE NAME, GUY.
W-WHAT DO YOU WANT?
WHERE'S ALL THE STUFF YOU'RE RIPPING OFF?
RIOT-- RIOT BLACK...
OH, NO...
WHAT'S HE DOING WITH THE COMPUTERS?
HKK H-HE ONLY WANTS THE DATA.
DUDE'S GOT A COMPUTER BRAIN OR SOMETHING-- HE SCANS THE DATA, WE KEEP THE STUFF... WAIT, WHAT ARE YOU DOING?
WIPING YOUR PHONE.
AW, NO! DON'T!
233 East Wilson
username
password
DON'T WORRY...I MADE A BACKUP.
I'M PUTTING A LITTLE SOME-THING ON HERE FOR YOUR BOSS.
NOW LISTEN UP, YOU TAKE THIS AND YOU GIVE IT TO BLACK.
YOU PUT IT RIGHT IN HIS SLEAZY LITTLE HAND. AM I CLEAR?
DON'T SCREW ME ON THIS, AND MAYBE I'LL FORGET YOU LIVE AT 6253 PINEWOOD LANE. AND THAT YOUR MOTHER'S PHONE NUMBER IS 714-555-9991. AND THAT YOUR SISTER--
OKAY, OKAY! WE DROP GOODS TO RIOT ON FRIDAY AT HIS CLUB. AT THE BIG PARTY. I'LL GIVE HIM THE PHONE, OKAY?
JUST...JUST DON'T CALL MY MOMS.

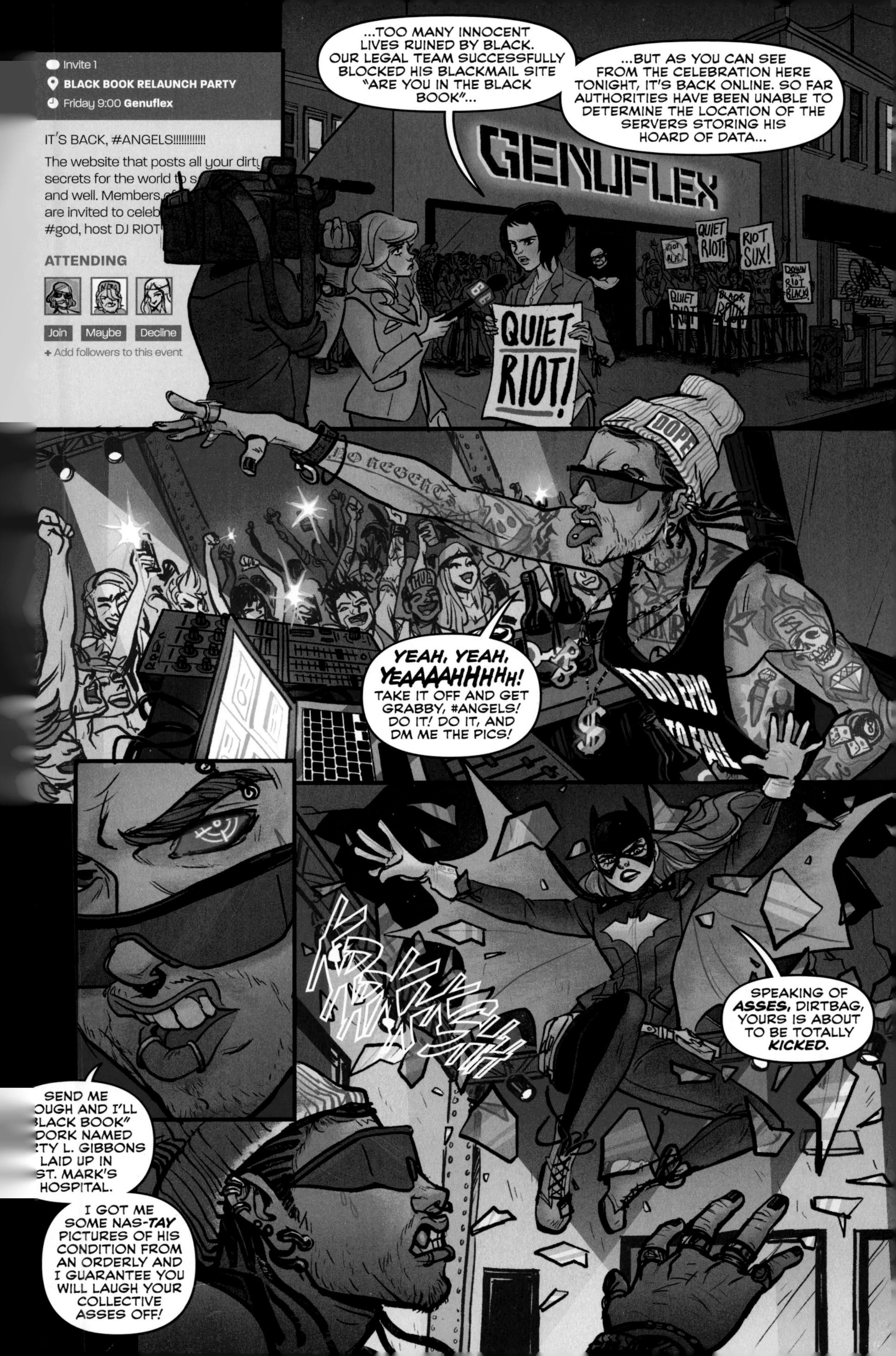
Invite 1
BLACK BOOK RELAUNCH PARTY
Friday 9:00 Genuflex
IT'S BACK, #ANGELS!!!!!!!!!!!!
The website that posts all your dirty secrets for the world to s and well. Members are invited to celeb #god, host DJ RIOT
ATTENDING
Join
Maybe
Decline
+ Add followers to this event
...TOO MANY INNOCENT LIVES RUINED BY BLACK. OUR LEGAL TEAM SUCCESSFULLY BLOCKED HIS BLACKMAIL SITE "ARE YOU IN THE BLACK BOOK"...
...BUT AS YOU CAN SEE FROM THE CELEBRATION HERE TONIGHT, IT'S BACK ONLINE. SO FAR AUTHORITIES HAVE BEEN UNABLE TO DETERMINE THE LOCATION OF THE SERVERS STORING HIS HOARD OF DATA...
GENUFLEX
QUIET RIOT!
RIOT SUX!
QUIET RIOT!
DOPE
NO REGRETS
YEAH, YEAH, YEAAAAHHHHH! TAKE IT OFF AND GET GRABBY, #ANGELS! DO IT! DO IT, AND DM ME THE PICS!
TOO EPIC TO FAIL
KRAKKASSHH
SPEAKING OF ASSES, DIRTBAG, YOURS IS ABOUT TO BE TOTALLY KICKED.
SEND ME OUGH AND I'LL BLACK BOOK" DORK NAMED TY L. GIBBONS LAID UP IN ST. MARK'S HOSPITAL.
I GOT ME SOME NAS-TAY PICTURES OF HIS CONDITION FROM AN ORDERLY AND I GUARANTEE YOU WILL LAUGH YOUR COLLECTIVE ASSES OFF!

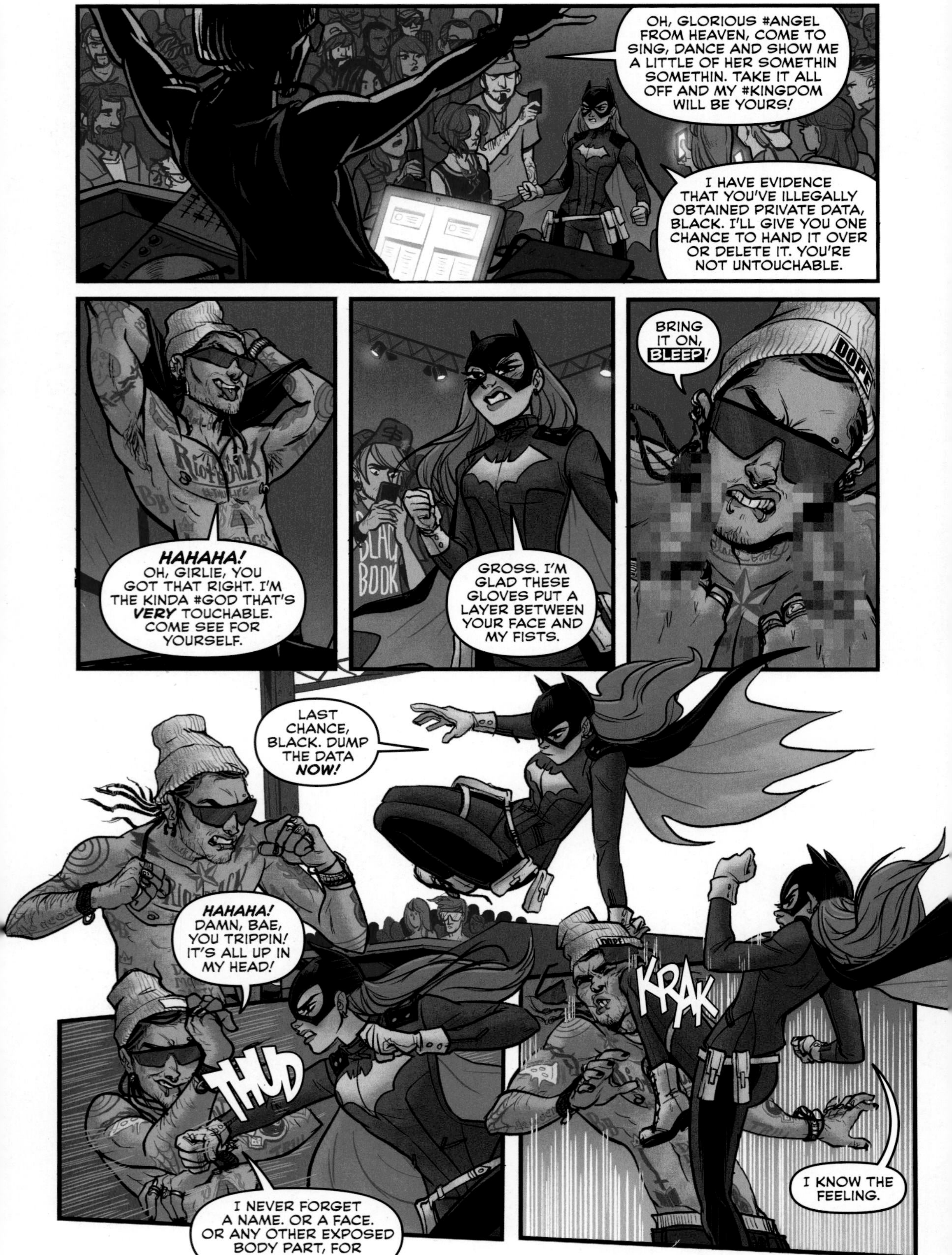

OH, GLORIOUS #ANGEL FROM HEAVEN, COME TO SING, DANCE AND SHOW ME A LITTLE OF HER SOMETHIN SOMETHIN. TAKE IT ALL OFF AND MY #KINGDOM WILL BE YOURS!
I HAVE EVIDENCE THAT YOU'VE ILLEGALLY OBTAINED PRIVATE DATA, BLACK. I'LL GIVE YOU ONE CHANCE TO HAND IT OVER OR DELETE IT. YOU'RE NOT UNTOUCHABLE.
HAHAHA! OH, GIRLIE, YOU GOT THAT RIGHT. I'M THE KINDA #GOD THAT'S VERY TOUCHABLE. COME SEE FOR YOURSELF.
BLACK BOOK
GROSS. I'M GLAD THESE GLOVES PUT A LAYER BETWEEN YOUR FACE AND MY FISTS.
BRING IT ON, BLEEP!
DOPE
LAST CHANCE, BLACK. DUMP THE DATA NOW!
HAHAHA! DAMN, BAE, YOU TRIPPIN! IT'S ALL UP IN MY HEAD!
THUD
KRAK
I NEVER FORGET A NAME. OR A FACE. OR ANY OTHER EXPOSED BODY PART, FOR THAT MATTER!
I KNOW THE FEELING.

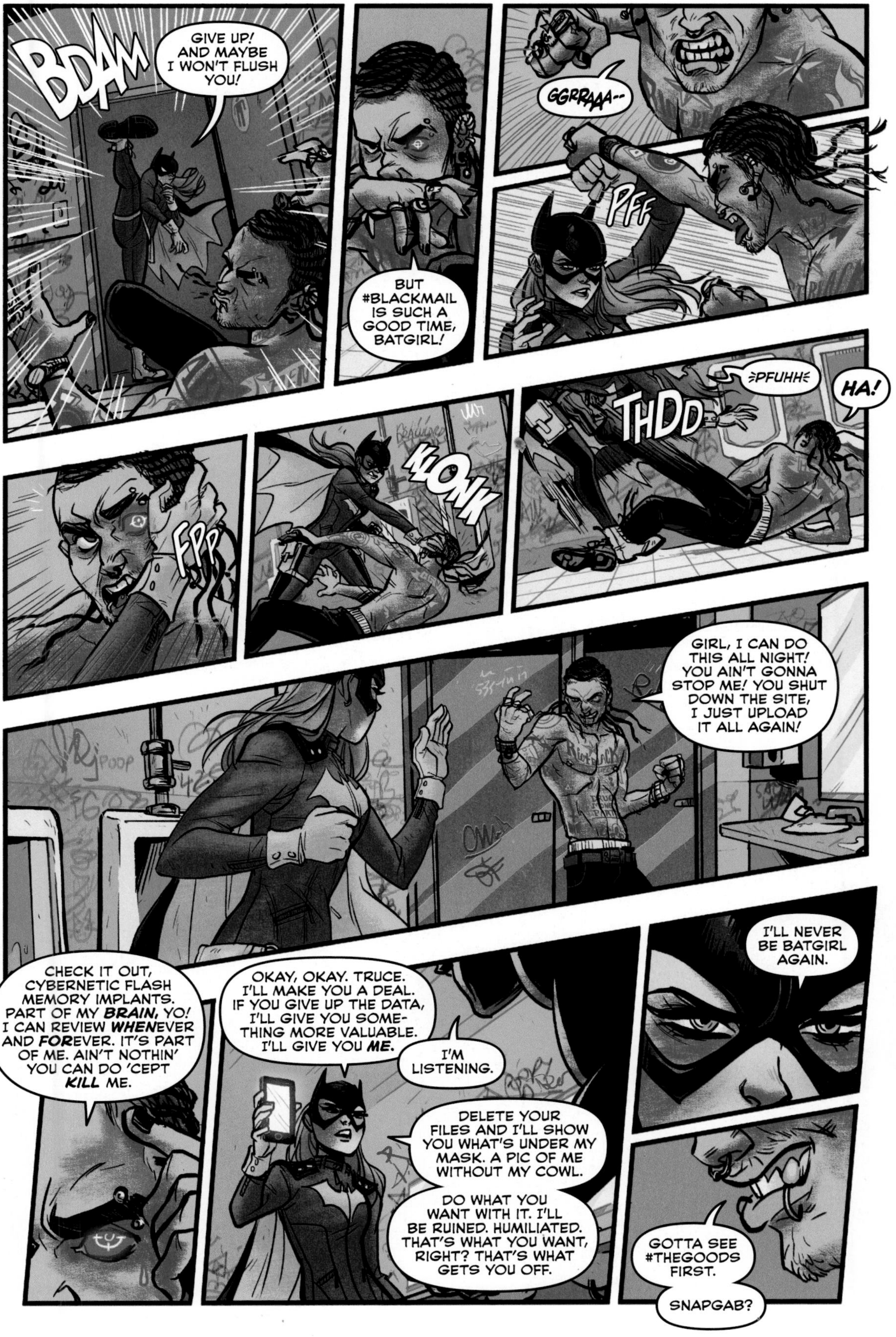
BDAM
GIVE UP! AND MAYBE I WON'T FLUSH YOU!
BUT #BLACKMAIL IS SUCH A GOOD TIME, BATGIRL!
GGRRAAA--
PFF
PFUHH
HA!
THDD
FPP
KLONK
GIRL, I CAN DO THIS ALL NIGHT! YOU AIN'T GONNA STOP ME! YOU SHUT DOWN THE SITE, I JUST UPLOAD IT ALL AGAIN!
CHECK IT OUT, CYBERNETIC FLASH MEMORY IMPLANTS. PART OF MY BRAIN, YO! I CAN REVIEW WHENEVER AND FOREVER. IT'S PART OF ME. AIN'T NOTHIN' YOU CAN DO 'CEPT KILL ME.
OKAY, OKAY. TRUCE. I'LL MAKE YOU A DEAL. IF YOU GIVE UP THE DATA, I'LL GIVE YOU SOMETHING MORE VALUABLE. I'LL GIVE YOU ME.
I'M LISTENING.
DELETE YOUR FILES AND I'LL SHOW YOU WHAT'S UNDER MY MASK. A PIC OF ME WITHOUT MY COWL.
DO WHAT YOU WANT WITH IT. I'LL BE RUINED. HUMILIATED. THAT'S WHAT YOU WANT, RIGHT? THAT'S WHAT GETS YOU OFF.
I'LL NEVER BE BATGIRL AGAIN.
GOTTA SEE #THEGOODS FIRST.
SNAPGAB?

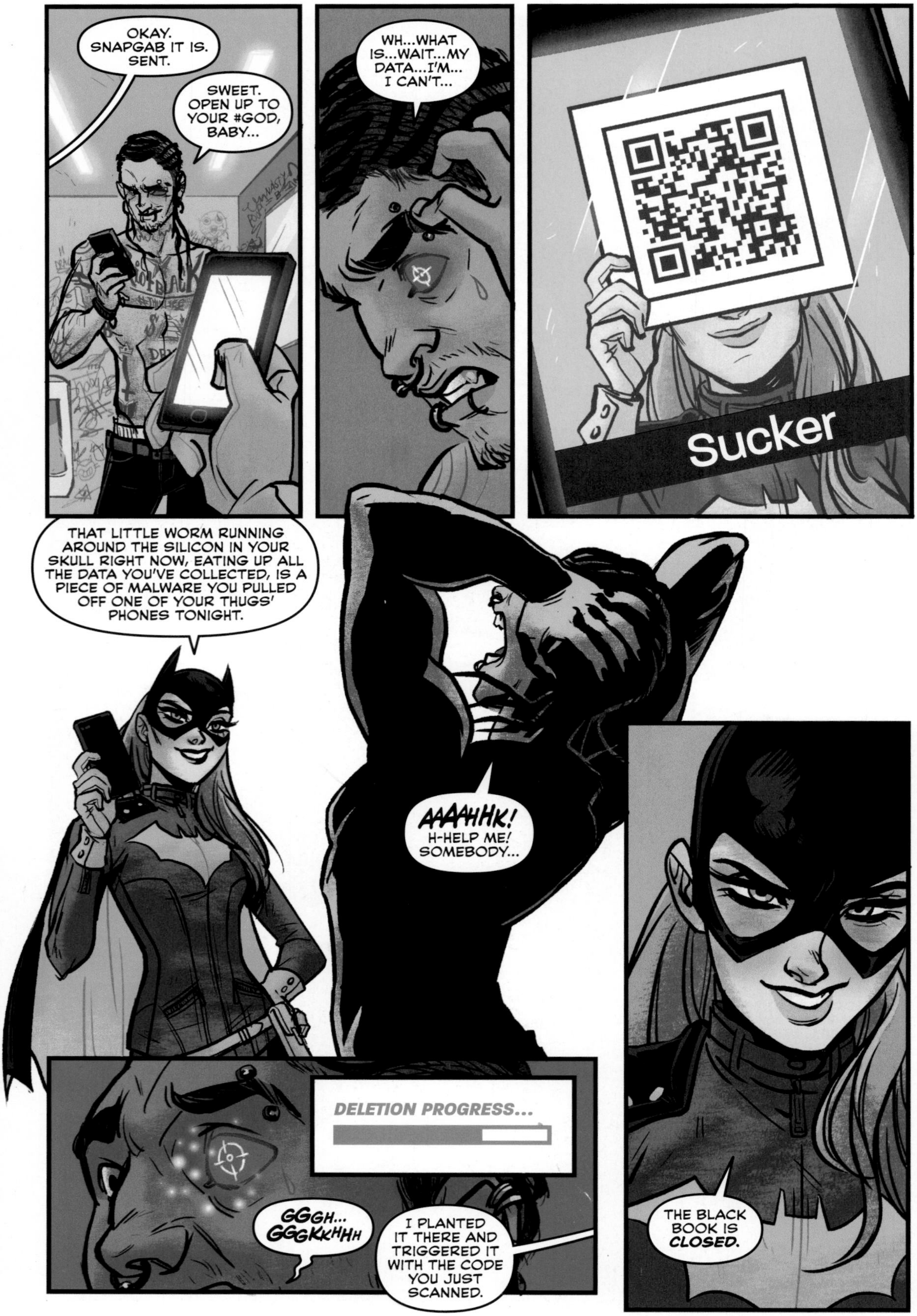
OKAY. SNAPGAB IT IS. SENT.
SWEET. OPEN UP TO YOUR #GOD, BABY...
WH...WHAT IS...WAIT...MY DATA...I'M... I CAN'T...
Sucker
THAT LITTLE WORM RUNNING AROUND THE SILICON IN YOUR SKULL RIGHT NOW, EATING UP ALL THE DATA YOU'VE COLLECTED, IS A PIECE OF MALWARE YOU PULLED OFF ONE OF YOUR THUGS' PHONES TONIGHT.
AAAAHHK! H-HELP ME! SOMEBODY...
DELETION PROGRESS...
GGGH... GGGKKHHH
I PLANTED IT THERE AND TRIGGERED IT WITH THE CODE YOU JUST SCANNED.
THE BLACK BOOK IS CLOSED.

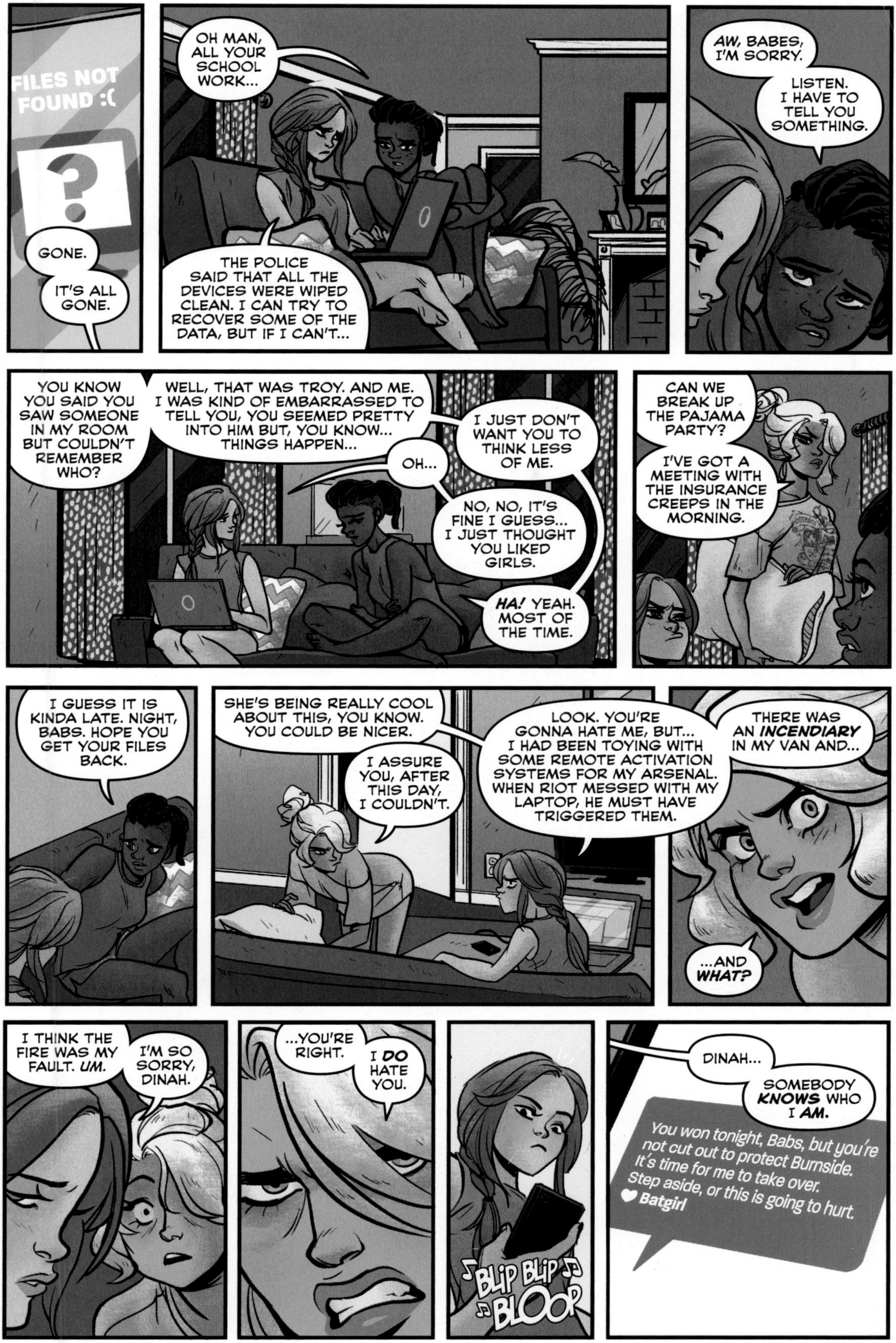
FILES NOT FOUND :(
?
GONE.
IT'S ALL GONE.
OH MAN, ALL YOUR SCHOOL WORK...
THE POLICE SAID THAT ALL THE DEVICES WERE WIPED CLEAN. I CAN TRY TO RECOVER SOME OF THE DATA, BUT IF I CAN'T...
AW, BABES, I'M SORRY.
LISTEN. I HAVE TO TELL YOU SOMETHING.
YOU KNOW YOU SAID YOU SAW SOMEONE IN MY ROOM BUT COULDN'T REMEMBER WHO?
WELL, THAT WAS TROY. AND ME. I WAS KIND OF EMBARRASSED TO TELL YOU, YOU SEEMED PRETTY INTO HIM BUT, YOU KNOW... THINGS HAPPEN...
I JUST DON'T WANT YOU TO THINK LESS OF ME.
OH...
NO, NO, IT'S FINE I GUESS... I JUST THOUGHT YOU LIKED GIRLS.
HA! YEAH. MOST OF THE TIME.
CAN WE BREAK UP THE PAJAMA PARTY?
I'VE GOT A MEETING WITH THE INSURANCE CREEPS IN THE MORNING.
I GUESS IT IS KINDA LATE. NIGHT, BABS. HOPE YOU GET YOUR FILES BACK.
SHE'S BEING REALLY COOL ABOUT THIS, YOU KNOW. YOU COULD BE NICER.
I ASSURE YOU, AFTER THIS DAY, I COULDN'T.
LOOK. YOU'RE GONNA HATE ME, BUT... I HAD BEEN TOYING WITH SOME REMOTE ACTIVATION SYSTEMS FOR MY ARSENAL. WHEN RIOT MESSED WITH MY LAPTOP, HE MUST HAVE TRIGGERED THEM.
THERE WAS AN INCENDIARY IN MY VAN AND...
...AND WHAT?
I THINK THE FIRE WAS MY FAULT. UM.
I'M SO SORRY, DINAH.
...YOU'RE RIGHT.
I DO HATE YOU.
BLIP BLIP BLOOP
DINAH...
SOMEBODY KNOWS WHO I AM.
You won tonight, Babs, but you're not cut out to protect Burnside. It's time for me to take over. Step aside, or this is going to hurt.
Batgirl

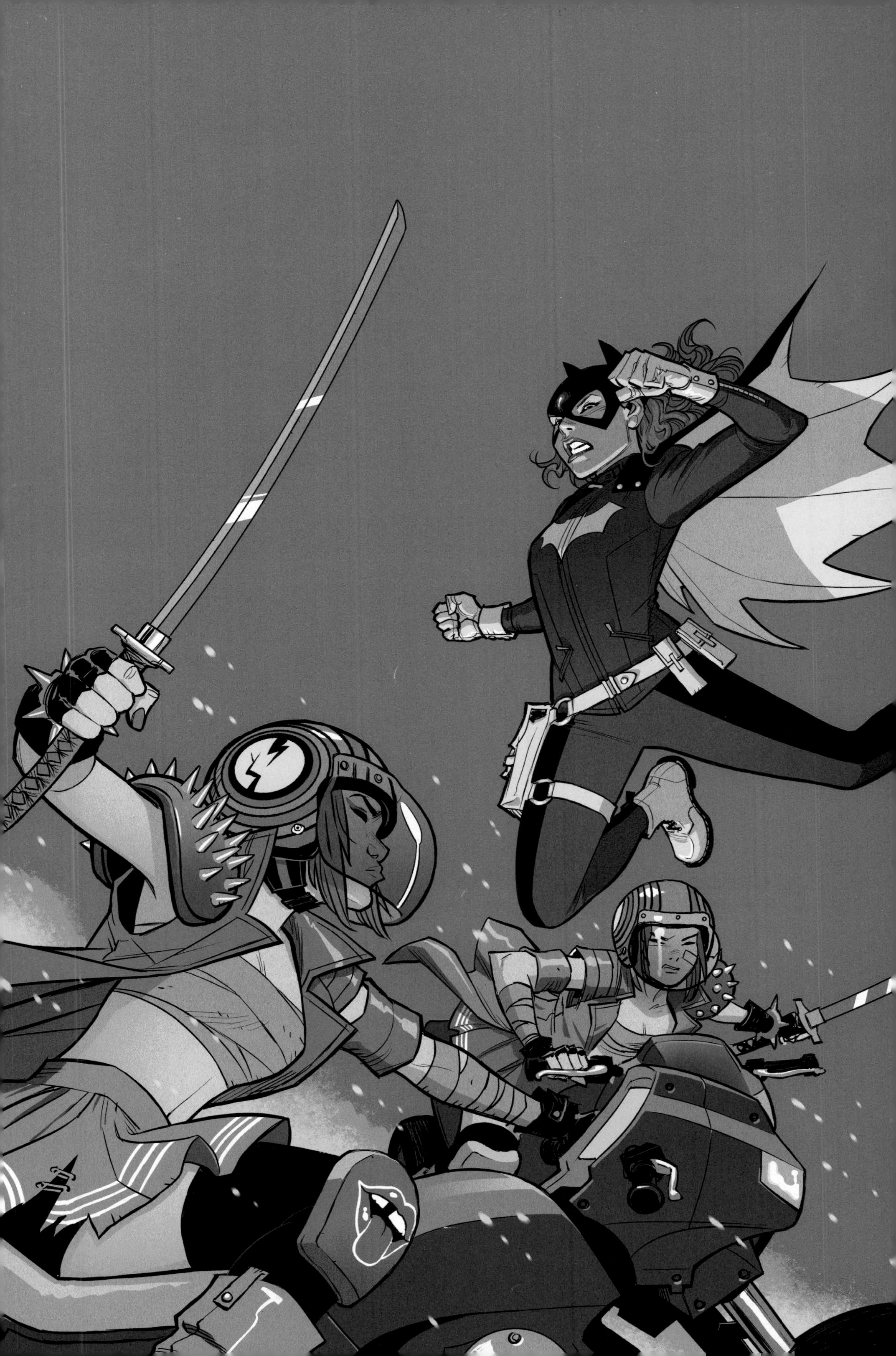

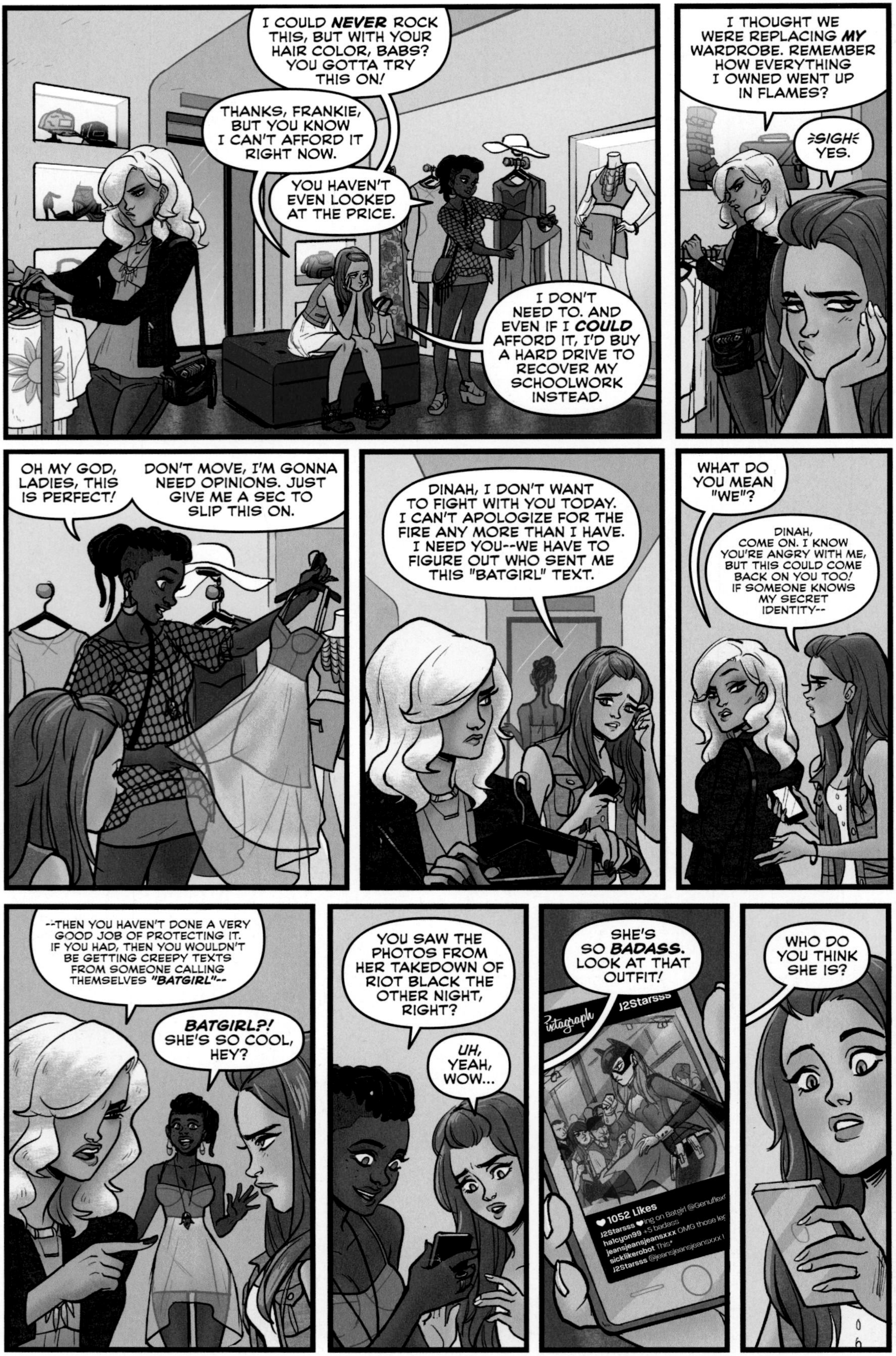
I COULD NEVER ROCK THIS, BUT WITH YOUR HAIR COLOR, BABS? YOU GOTTA TRY THIS ON!
THANKS, FRANKIE, BUT YOU KNOW I CAN'T AFFORD IT RIGHT NOW.
YOU HAVEN'T EVEN LOOKED AT THE PRICE.
I DON'T NEED TO. AND EVEN IF I COULD AFFORD IT, I'D BUY A HARD DRIVE TO RECOVER MY SCHOOLWORK INSTEAD.
I THOUGHT WE WERE REPLACING MY WARDROBE. REMEMBER HOW EVERYTHING I OWNED WENT UP IN FLAMES?
SIGH YES.
OH MY GOD, LADIES, THIS IS PERFECT!
DON'T MOVE, I'M GONNA NEED OPINIONS. JUST GIVE ME A SEC TO SLIP THIS ON.
DINAH, I DON'T WANT TO FIGHT WITH YOU TODAY. I CAN'T APOLOGIZE FOR THE FIRE ANY MORE THAN I HAVE. I NEED YOU--WE HAVE TO FIGURE OUT WHO SENT ME THIS "BATGIRL" TEXT.
WHAT DO YOU MEAN "WE"?
DINAH, COME ON. I KNOW YOU'RE ANGRY WITH ME, BUT THIS COULD COME BACK ON YOU TOO! IF SOMEONE KNOWS MY SECRET IDENTITY--
--THEN YOU HAVEN'T DONE A VERY GOOD JOB OF PROTECTING IT. IF YOU HAD, THEN YOU WOULDN'T BE GETTING CREEPY TEXTS FROM SOMEONE CALLING THEMSELVES "BATGIRL"--
BATGIRL?! SHE'S SO COOL, HEY?
YOU SAW THE PHOTOS FROM HER TAKEDOWN OF RIOT BLACK THE OTHER NIGHT, RIGHT?
UH, YEAH, WOW...
SHE'S SO BADASS. LOOK AT THAT OUTFIT!
Instagraph
J2Starsss
1052 Likes
WHO DO YOU THINK SHE IS?

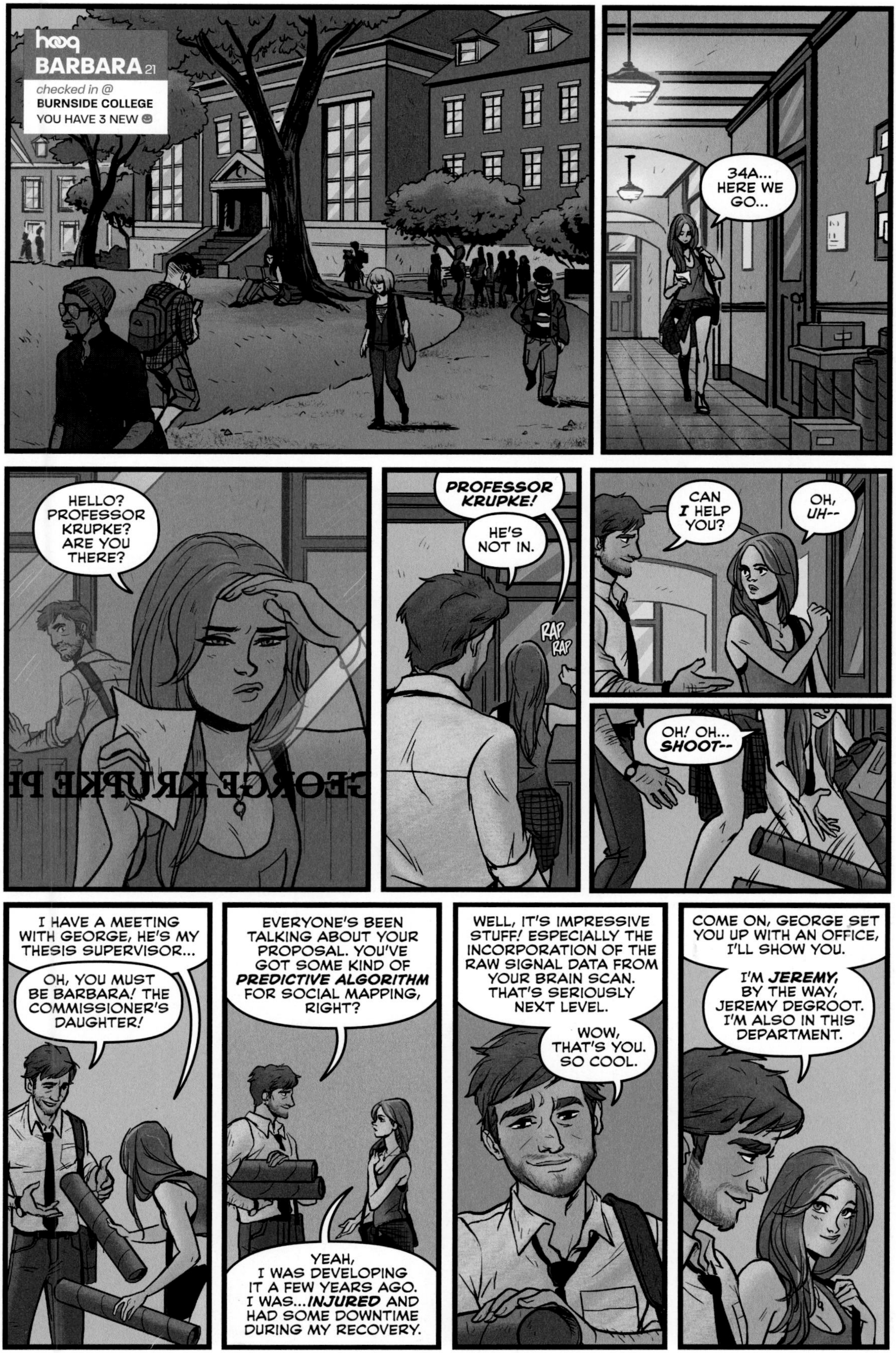
hooq
BARBARA 21
checked in @
BURNSIDE COLLEGE
YOU HAVE 3 NEW ☻
34A... HERE WE GO...
HELLO? PROFESSOR KRUPKE? ARE YOU THERE?
PROFESSOR KRUPKE!
HE'S NOT IN.
RAP RAP
CAN *I* HELP YOU?
OH, *UH--*
OH! OH... ***SHOOT--***
I HAVE A MEETING WITH GEORGE, HE'S MY THESIS SUPERVISOR...
OH, YOU MUST BE BARBARA! THE COMMISSIONER'S DAUGHTER!
EVERYONE'S BEEN TALKING ABOUT YOUR PROPOSAL. YOU'VE GOT SOME KIND OF ***PREDICTIVE ALGORITHM*** FOR SOCIAL MAPPING, RIGHT?
YEAH, I WAS DEVELOPING IT A FEW YEARS AGO. I WAS...***INJURED*** AND HAD SOME DOWNTIME DURING MY RECOVERY.
WELL, IT'S IMPRESSIVE STUFF! ESPECIALLY THE INCORPORATION OF THE RAW SIGNAL DATA FROM YOUR BRAIN SCAN. THAT'S SERIOUSLY NEXT LEVEL.
WOW, THAT'S YOU. SO COOL.
COME ON, GEORGE SET YOU UP WITH AN OFFICE, I'LL SHOW YOU.
I'M ***JEREMY,*** BY THE WAY, JEREMY DEGROOT. I'M ALSO IN THIS DEPARTMENT.

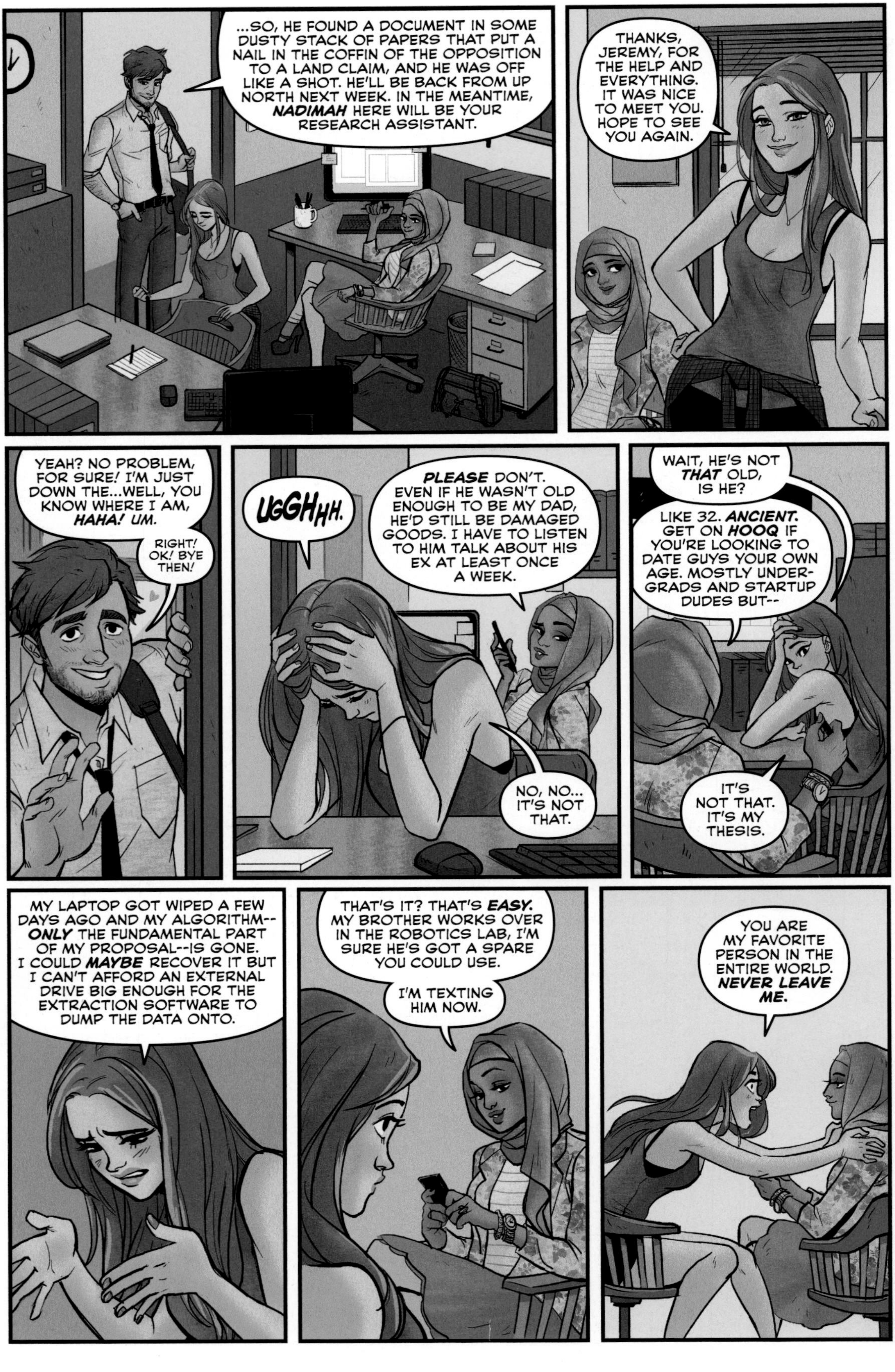
...SO, HE FOUND A DOCUMENT IN SOME DUSTY STACK OF PAPERS THAT PUT A NAIL IN THE COFFIN OF THE OPPOSITION TO A LAND CLAIM, AND HE WAS OFF LIKE A SHOT. HE'LL BE BACK FROM UP NORTH NEXT WEEK. IN THE MEANTIME, NADIMAH HERE WILL BE YOUR RESEARCH ASSISTANT.
THANKS, JEREMY, FOR THE HELP AND EVERYTHING. IT WAS NICE TO MEET YOU. HOPE TO SEE YOU AGAIN.
YEAH? NO PROBLEM, FOR SURE! I'M JUST DOWN THE...WELL, YOU KNOW WHERE I AM, HAHA! UM.
RIGHT! OK! BYE THEN!
UGGHHH.
PLEASE DON'T. EVEN IF HE WASN'T OLD ENOUGH TO BE MY DAD, HE'D STILL BE DAMAGED GOODS. I HAVE TO LISTEN TO HIM TALK ABOUT HIS EX AT LEAST ONCE A WEEK.
NO, NO... IT'S NOT THAT.
WAIT, HE'S NOT THAT OLD, IS HE?
LIKE 32. ANCIENT. GET ON HOOQ IF YOU'RE LOOKING TO DATE GUYS YOUR OWN AGE. MOSTLY UNDERGRADS AND STARTUP DUDES BUT--
IT'S NOT THAT. IT'S MY THESIS.
MY LAPTOP GOT WIPED A FEW DAYS AGO AND MY ALGORITHM--ONLY THE FUNDAMENTAL PART OF MY PROPOSAL--IS GONE. I COULD MAYBE RECOVER IT BUT I CAN'T AFFORD AN EXTERNAL DRIVE BIG ENOUGH FOR THE EXTRACTION SOFTWARE TO DUMP THE DATA ONTO.
THAT'S IT? THAT'S EASY. MY BROTHER WORKS OVER IN THE ROBOTICS LAB, I'M SURE HE'S GOT A SPARE YOU COULD USE.
I'M TEXTING HIM NOW.
YOU ARE MY FAVORITE PERSON IN THE ENTIRE WORLD. NEVER LEAVE ME.

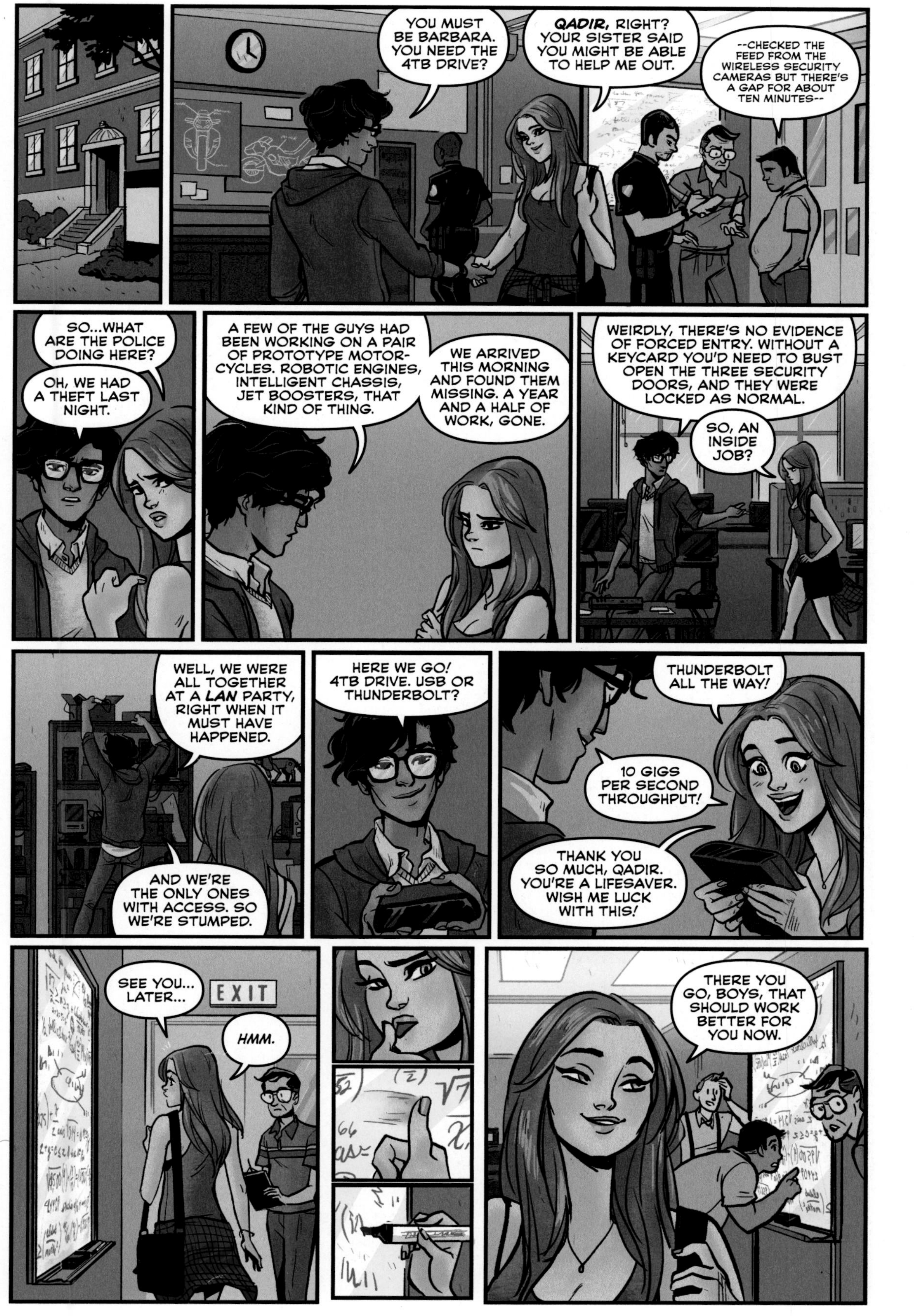
YOU MUST BE BARBARA. YOU NEED THE 4TB DRIVE?
QADIR, RIGHT? YOUR SISTER SAID YOU MIGHT BE ABLE TO HELP ME OUT.
--CHECKED THE FEED FROM THE WIRELESS SECURITY CAMERAS BUT THERE'S A GAP FOR ABOUT TEN MINUTES--
SO...WHAT ARE THE POLICE DOING HERE?
OH, WE HAD A THEFT LAST NIGHT.
A FEW OF THE GUYS HAD BEEN WORKING ON A PAIR OF PROTOTYPE MOTOR-CYCLES. ROBOTIC ENGINES, INTELLIGENT CHASSIS, JET BOOSTERS, THAT KIND OF THING.
WE ARRIVED THIS MORNING AND FOUND THEM MISSING. A YEAR AND A HALF OF WORK, GONE.
WEIRDLY, THERE'S NO EVIDENCE OF FORCED ENTRY. WITHOUT A KEYCARD YOU'D NEED TO BUST OPEN THE THREE SECURITY DOORS, AND THEY WERE LOCKED AS NORMAL.
SO, AN INSIDE JOB?
WELL, WE WERE ALL TOGETHER AT A *LAN* PARTY, RIGHT WHEN IT MUST HAVE HAPPENED.
AND WE'RE THE ONLY ONES WITH ACCESS. SO WE'RE STUMPED.
HERE WE GO! 4TB DRIVE. USB OR THUNDERBOLT?
THUNDERBOLT ALL THE WAY!
10 GIGS PER SECOND THROUGHPUT!
THANK YOU SO MUCH, QADIR. YOU'RE A LIFESAVER. WISH ME LUCK WITH THIS!
SEE YOU... LATER...
EXIT
HMM.
THERE YOU GO, BOYS, THAT SHOULD WORK BETTER FOR YOU NOW.

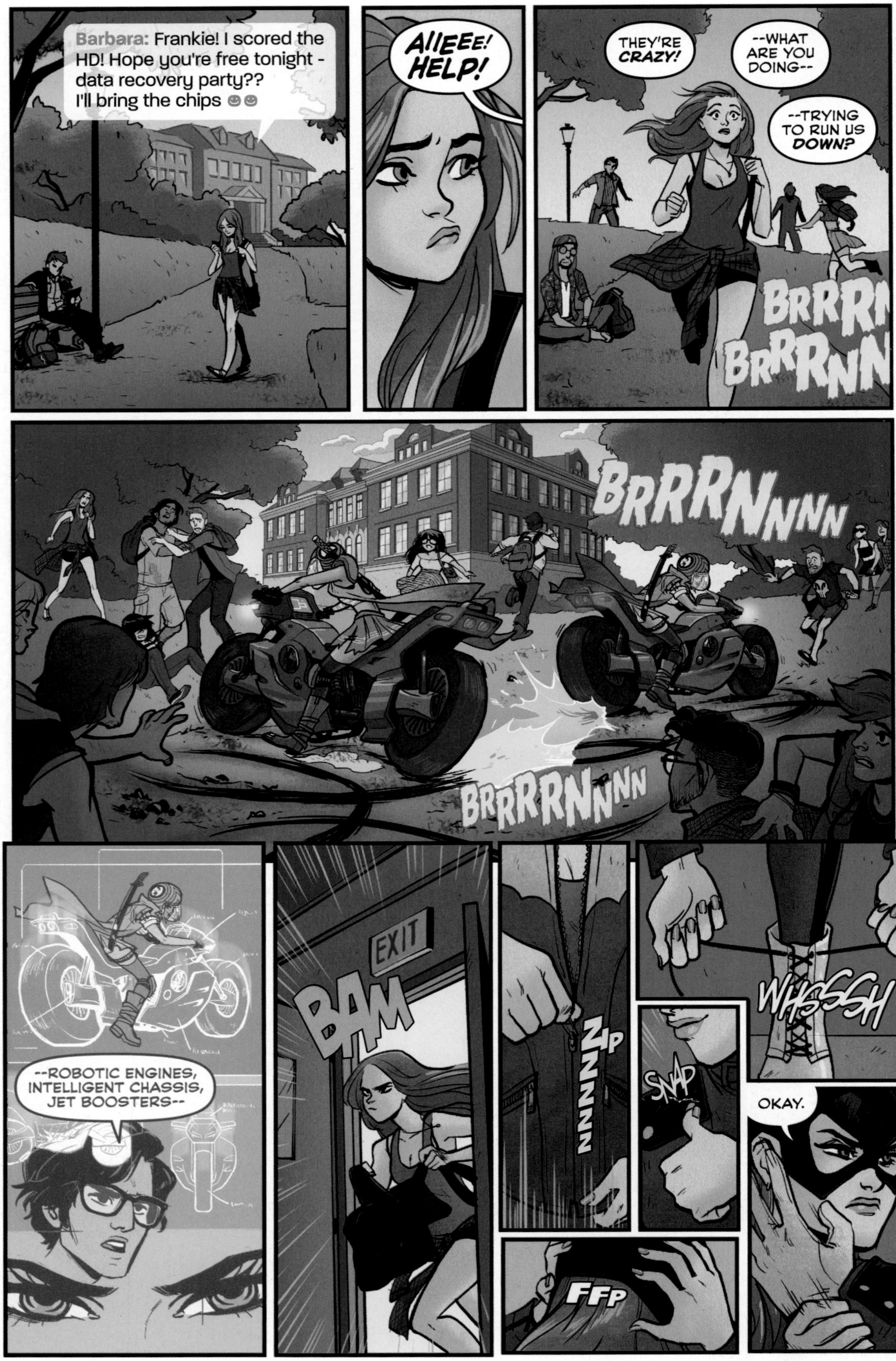
Barbara: Frankie! I scored the HD! Hope you're free tonight - data recovery party?? I'll bring the chips ☻☻
AIIEEE! HELP!
THEY'RE CRAZY!
--WHAT ARE YOU DOING--
--TRYING TO RUN US DOWN?
BRRRN BRRRNN
BRRRNnnn
BRRRNnnn
--ROBOTIC ENGINES, INTELLIGENT CHASSIS, JET BOOSTERS--
EXIT
BAM
ZIP
ZNNNN
WHSSSH
SNAP
OKAY.
FFP

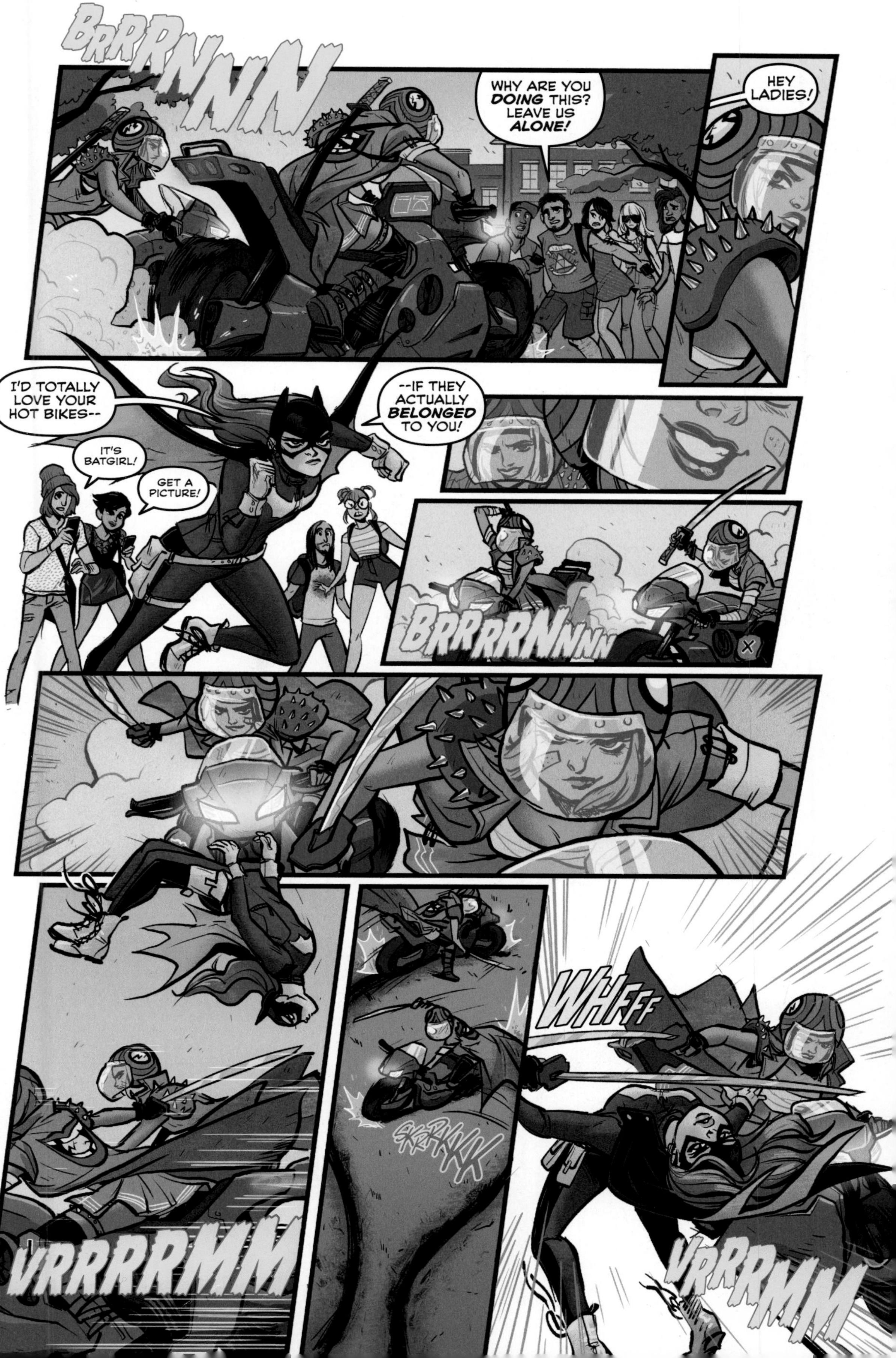
BRRRNNNN
WHY ARE YOU DOING THIS? LEAVE US ALONE!
HEY LADIES!
I'D TOTALLY LOVE YOUR HOT BIKES--
--IF THEY ACTUALLY BELONGED TO YOU!
IT'S BATGIRL!
GET A PICTURE!
BRRRRNNNN
VRRRRMM
SKRRKKK
WHFFF
VRRRMM

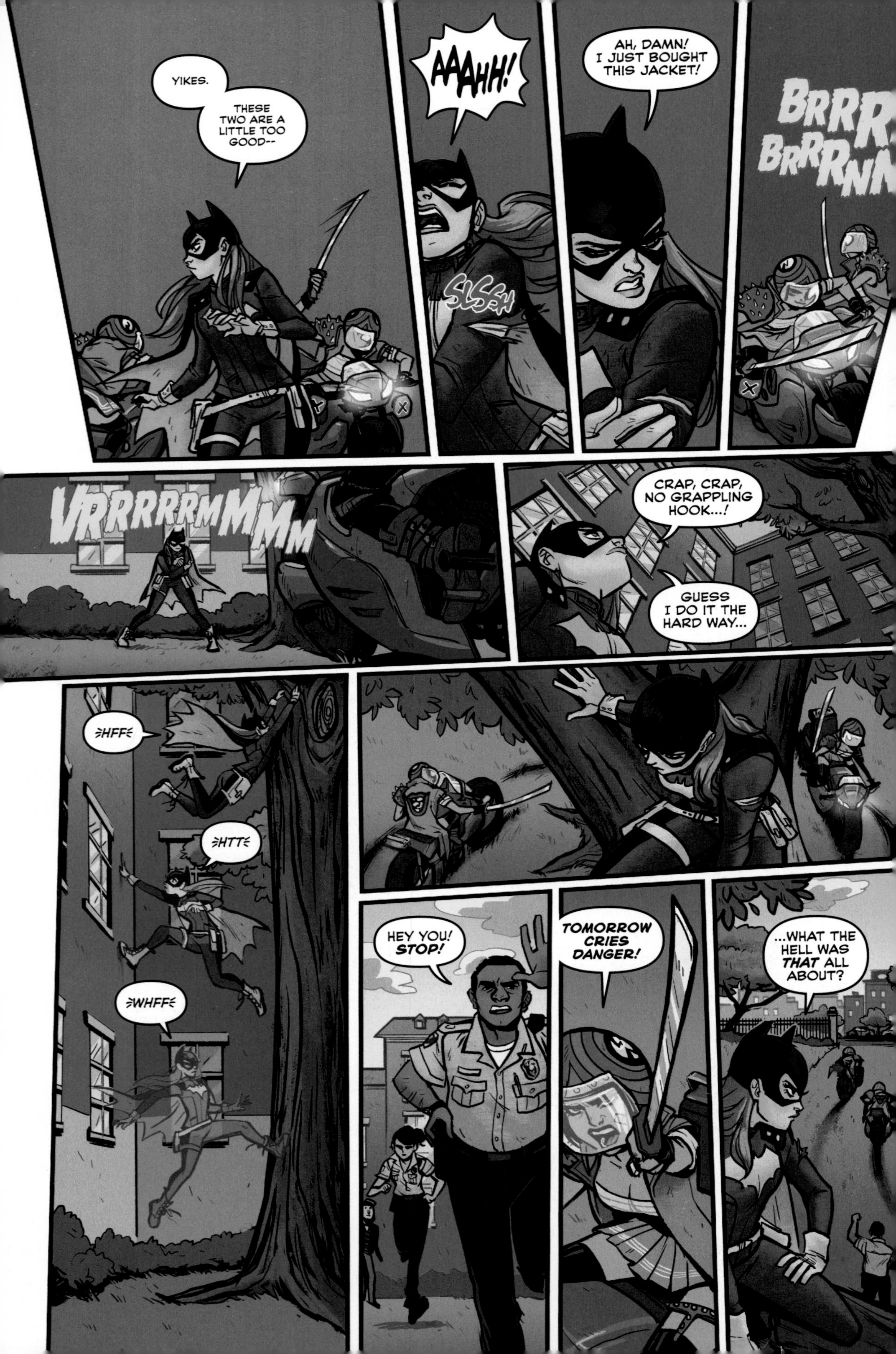
YIKES.
THESE TWO ARE A LITTLE TOO GOOD--
AAAHH!
SLSSH
AH, DAMN! I JUST BOUGHT THIS JACKET!
BRRRR BRRRRNN
VRRRRRMMMM
CRAP, CRAP, NO GRAPPLING HOOK...!
GUESS I DO IT THE HARD WAY...
HFF
HTT
WHFF
HEY YOU! STOP!
TOMORROW CRIES DANGER!
...WHAT THE HELL WAS THAT ALL ABOUT?

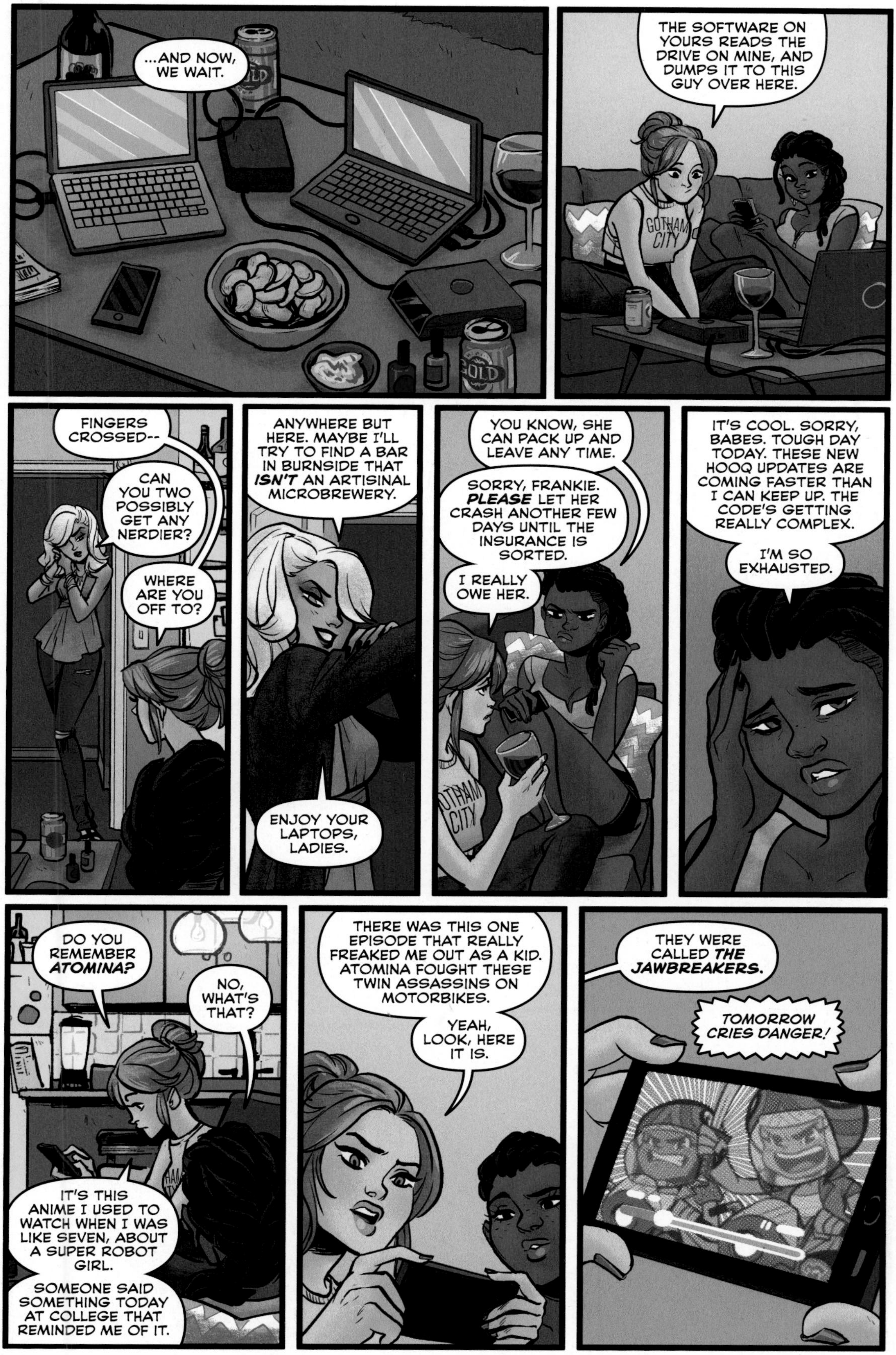
...AND NOW, WE WAIT.
THE SOFTWARE ON YOURS READS THE DRIVE ON MINE, AND DUMPS IT TO THIS GUY OVER HERE.
FINGERS CROSSED--
CAN YOU TWO POSSIBLY GET ANY NERDIER?
WHERE ARE YOU OFF TO?
ANYWHERE BUT HERE. MAYBE I'LL TRY TO FIND A BAR IN BURNSIDE THAT *ISN'T* AN ARTISINAL MICROBREWERY.
ENJOY YOUR LAPTOPS, LADIES.
YOU KNOW, SHE CAN PACK UP AND LEAVE ANY TIME.
SORRY, FRANKIE. ***PLEASE*** LET HER CRASH ANOTHER FEW DAYS UNTIL THE INSURANCE IS SORTED.
I REALLY OWE HER.
IT'S COOL. SORRY, BABES. TOUGH DAY TODAY. THESE NEW HOOQ UPDATES ARE COMING FASTER THAN I CAN KEEP UP. THE CODE'S GETTING REALLY COMPLEX.
I'M SO EXHAUSTED.
DO YOU REMEMBER ***ATOMINA?***
NO, WHAT'S THAT?
IT'S THIS ANIME I USED TO WATCH WHEN I WAS LIKE SEVEN, ABOUT A SUPER ROBOT GIRL.
SOMEONE SAID SOMETHING TODAY AT COLLEGE THAT REMINDED ME OF IT.
THERE WAS THIS ONE EPISODE THAT REALLY FREAKED ME OUT AS A KID. ATOMINA FOUGHT THESE TWIN ASSASSINS ON MOTORBIKES.
YEAH, LOOK, HERE IT IS.
THEY WERE CALLED ***THE JAWBREAKERS.***
TOMORROW CRIES DANGER!

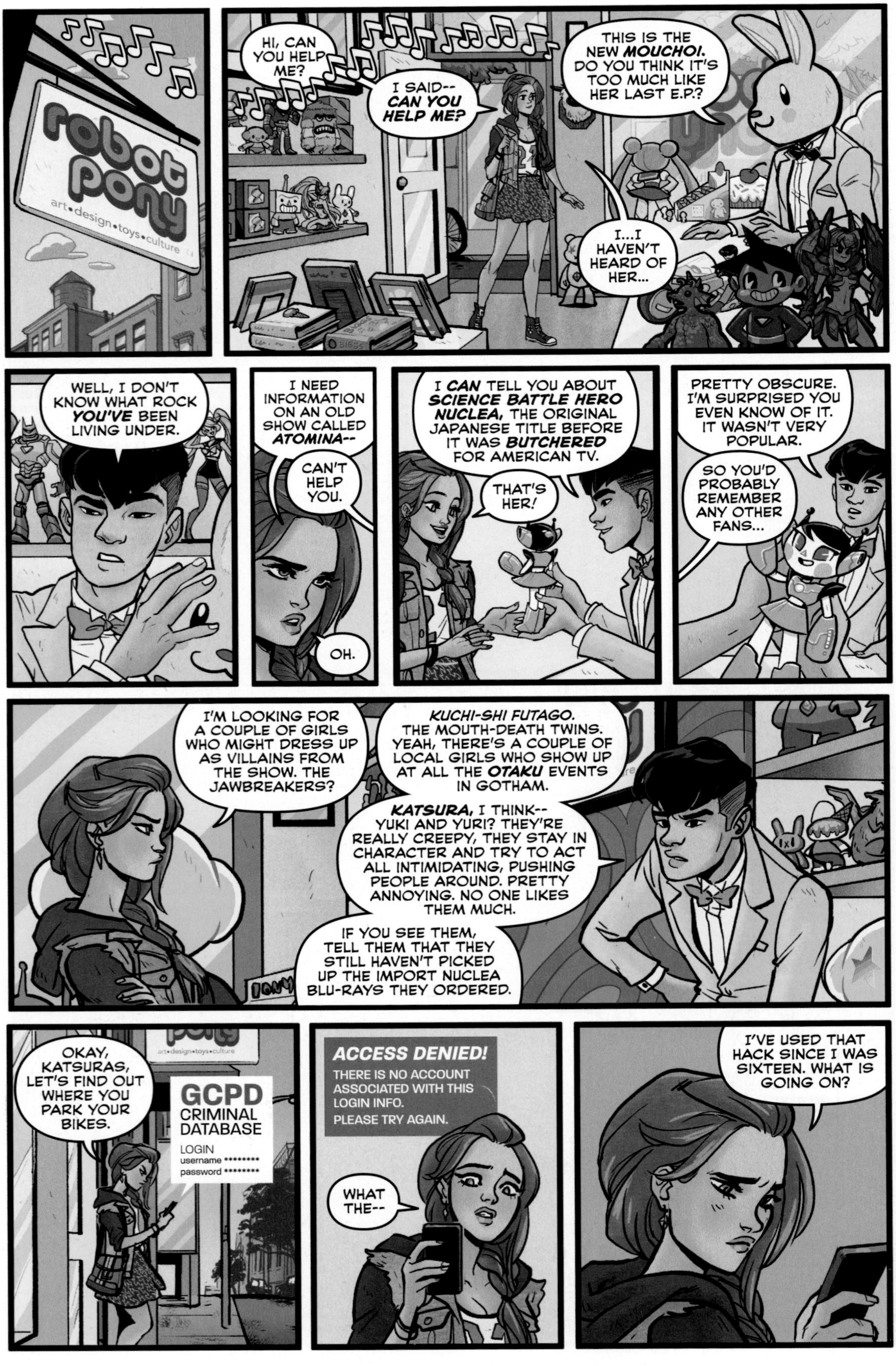
robot pony
art•design•toys•culture
HI, CAN YOU HELP ME?
I SAID-- CAN YOU HELP ME?
THIS IS THE NEW MOUCHOI. DO YOU THINK IT'S TOO MUCH LIKE HER LAST E.P.?
I...I HAVEN'T HEARD OF HER...
WELL, I DON'T KNOW WHAT ROCK YOU'VE BEEN LIVING UNDER.
I NEED INFORMATION ON AN OLD SHOW CALLED ATOMINA--
CAN'T HELP YOU.
OH.
I CAN TELL YOU ABOUT SCIENCE BATTLE HERO NUCLEA, THE ORIGINAL JAPANESE TITLE BEFORE IT WAS BUTCHERED FOR AMERICAN TV.
THAT'S HER!
PRETTY OBSCURE. I'M SURPRISED YOU EVEN KNOW OF IT. IT WASN'T VERY POPULAR.
SO YOU'D PROBABLY REMEMBER ANY OTHER FANS...
I'M LOOKING FOR A COUPLE OF GIRLS WHO MIGHT DRESS UP AS VILLAINS FROM THE SHOW. THE JAWBREAKERS?
KUCHI-SHI FUTAGO. THE MOUTH-DEATH TWINS. YEAH, THERE'S A COUPLE OF LOCAL GIRLS WHO SHOW UP AT ALL THE OTAKU EVENTS IN GOTHAM.
KATSURA, I THINK-- YUKI AND YURI? THEY'RE REALLY CREEPY, THEY STAY IN CHARACTER AND TRY TO ACT ALL INTIMIDATING, PUSHING PEOPLE AROUND. PRETTY ANNOYING. NO ONE LIKES THEM MUCH.
IF YOU SEE THEM, TELL THEM THAT THEY STILL HAVEN'T PICKED UP THE IMPORT NUCLEA BLU-RAYS THEY ORDERED.
OKAY, KATSURAS, LET'S FIND OUT WHERE YOU PARK YOUR BIKES.
GCPD CRIMINAL DATABASE
LOGIN
username ********
password ********
ACCESS DENIED!
THERE IS NO ACCOUNT ASSOCIATED WITH THIS LOGIN INFO.
PLEASE TRY AGAIN.
WHAT THE--
I'VE USED THAT HACK SINCE I WAS SIXTEEN. WHAT IS GOING ON?

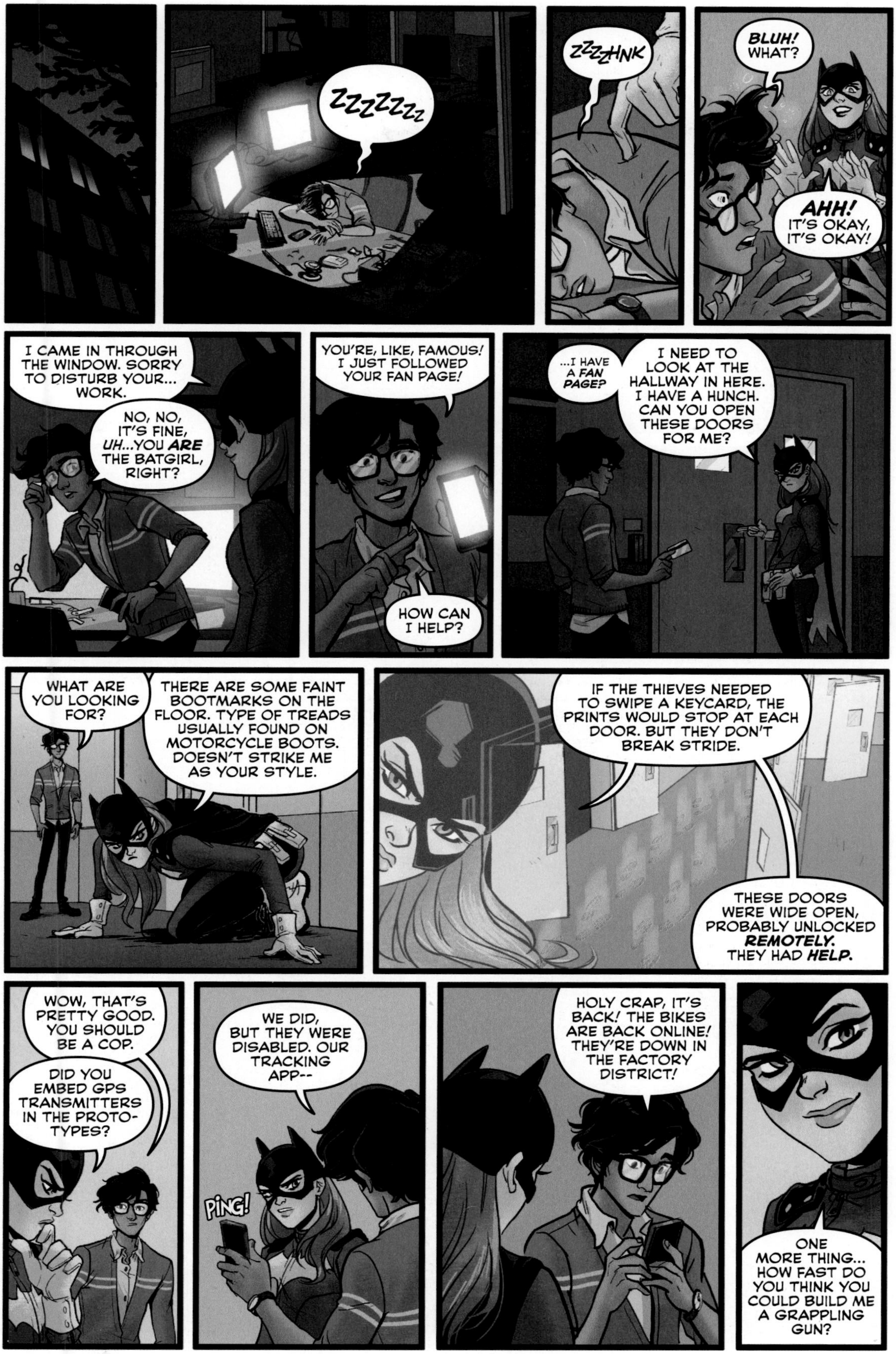
ZZZZZZZ
ZZZZHNK
BLUH! WHAT?
AHH! IT'S OKAY, IT'S OKAY!
I CAME IN THROUGH THE WINDOW. SORRY TO DISTURB YOUR... WORK.
NO, NO, IT'S FINE, UH...YOU ARE THE BATGIRL, RIGHT?
YOU'RE, LIKE, FAMOUS! I JUST FOLLOWED YOUR FAN PAGE!
HOW CAN I HELP?
...I HAVE A FAN PAGE?
I NEED TO LOOK AT THE HALLWAY IN HERE. I HAVE A HUNCH. CAN YOU OPEN THESE DOORS FOR ME?
WHAT ARE YOU LOOKING FOR?
THERE ARE SOME FAINT BOOTMARKS ON THE FLOOR. TYPE OF TREADS USUALLY FOUND ON MOTORCYCLE BOOTS. DOESN'T STRIKE ME AS YOUR STYLE.
IF THE THIEVES NEEDED TO SWIPE A KEYCARD, THE PRINTS WOULD STOP AT EACH DOOR. BUT THEY DON'T BREAK STRIDE.
THESE DOORS WERE WIDE OPEN, PROBABLY UNLOCKED REMOTELY. THEY HAD HELP.
WOW, THAT'S PRETTY GOOD. YOU SHOULD BE A COP.
DID YOU EMBED GPS TRANSMITTERS IN THE PROTO-TYPES?
WE DID, BUT THEY WERE DISABLED. OUR TRACKING APP--
PING!
HOLY CRAP, IT'S BACK! THE BIKES ARE BACK ONLINE! THEY'RE DOWN IN THE FACTORY DISTRICT!
ONE MORE THING... HOW FAST DO YOU THINK YOU COULD BUILD ME A GRAPPLING GUN?

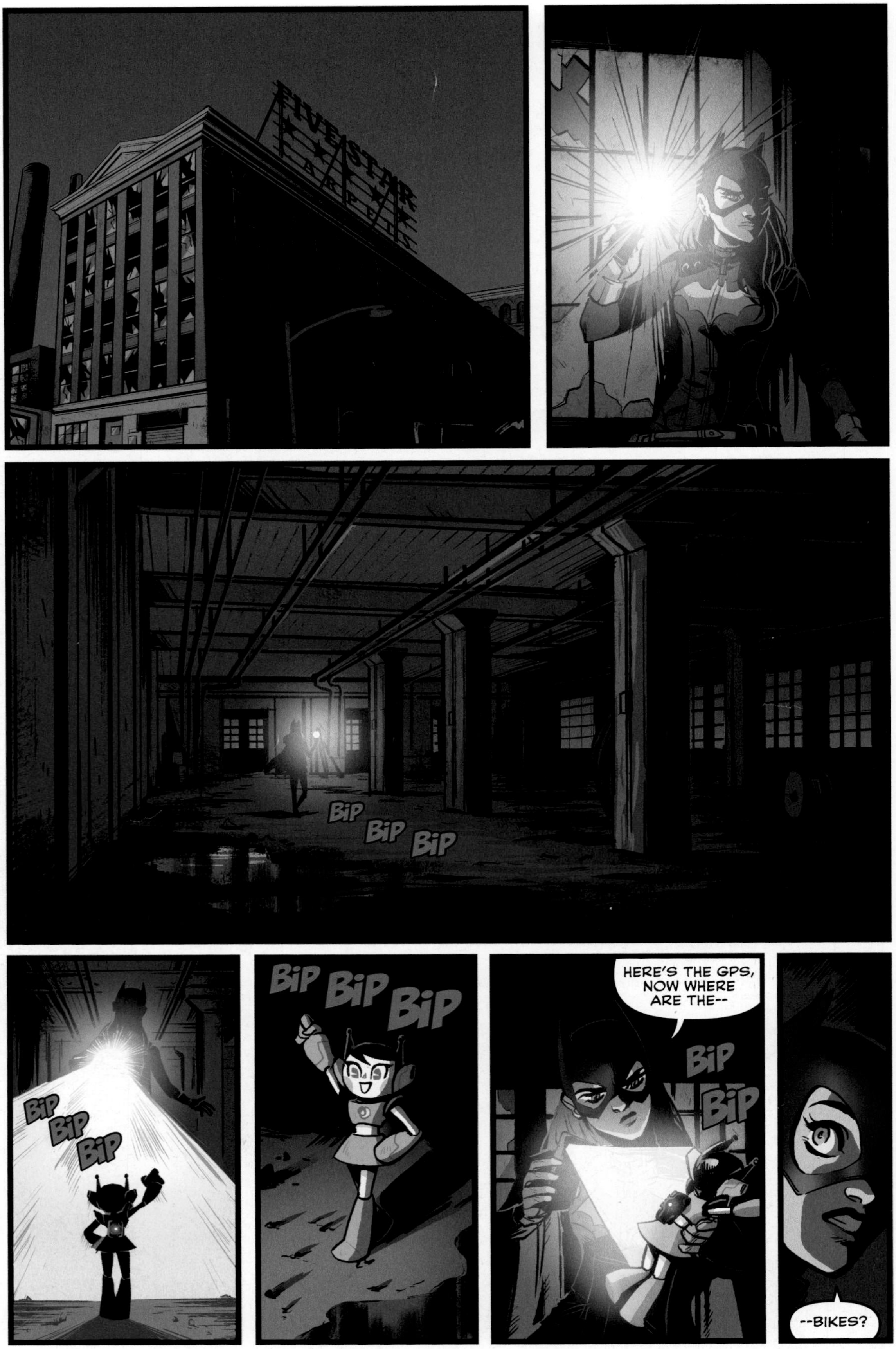
FIVE STAR CARPETS
BIP BIP BIP
BIP BIP BIP
BIP BIP BIP
HERE'S THE GPS, NOW WHERE ARE THE--
BIP BIP
--BIKES?

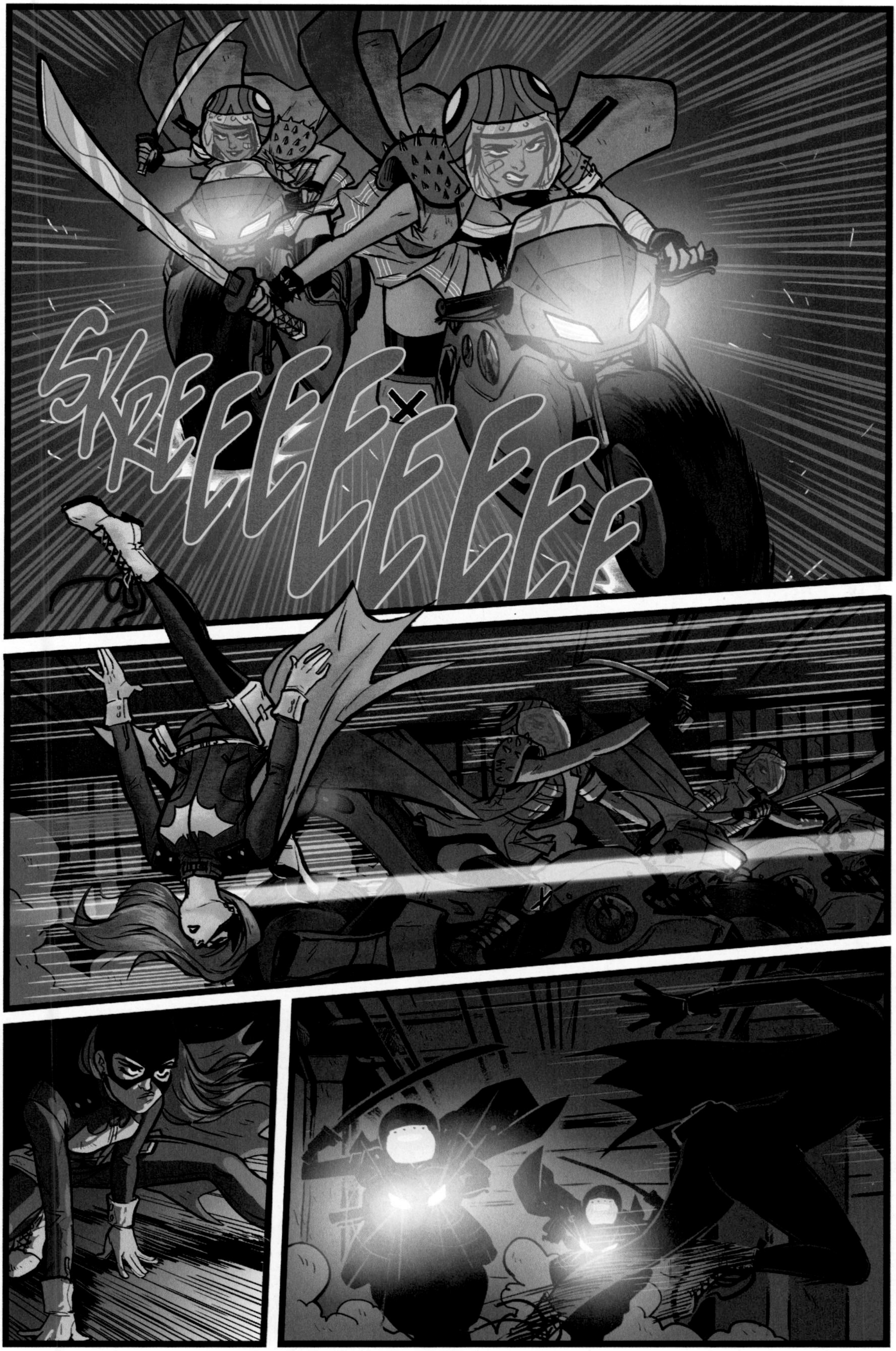
SKREEEEEEEEEE

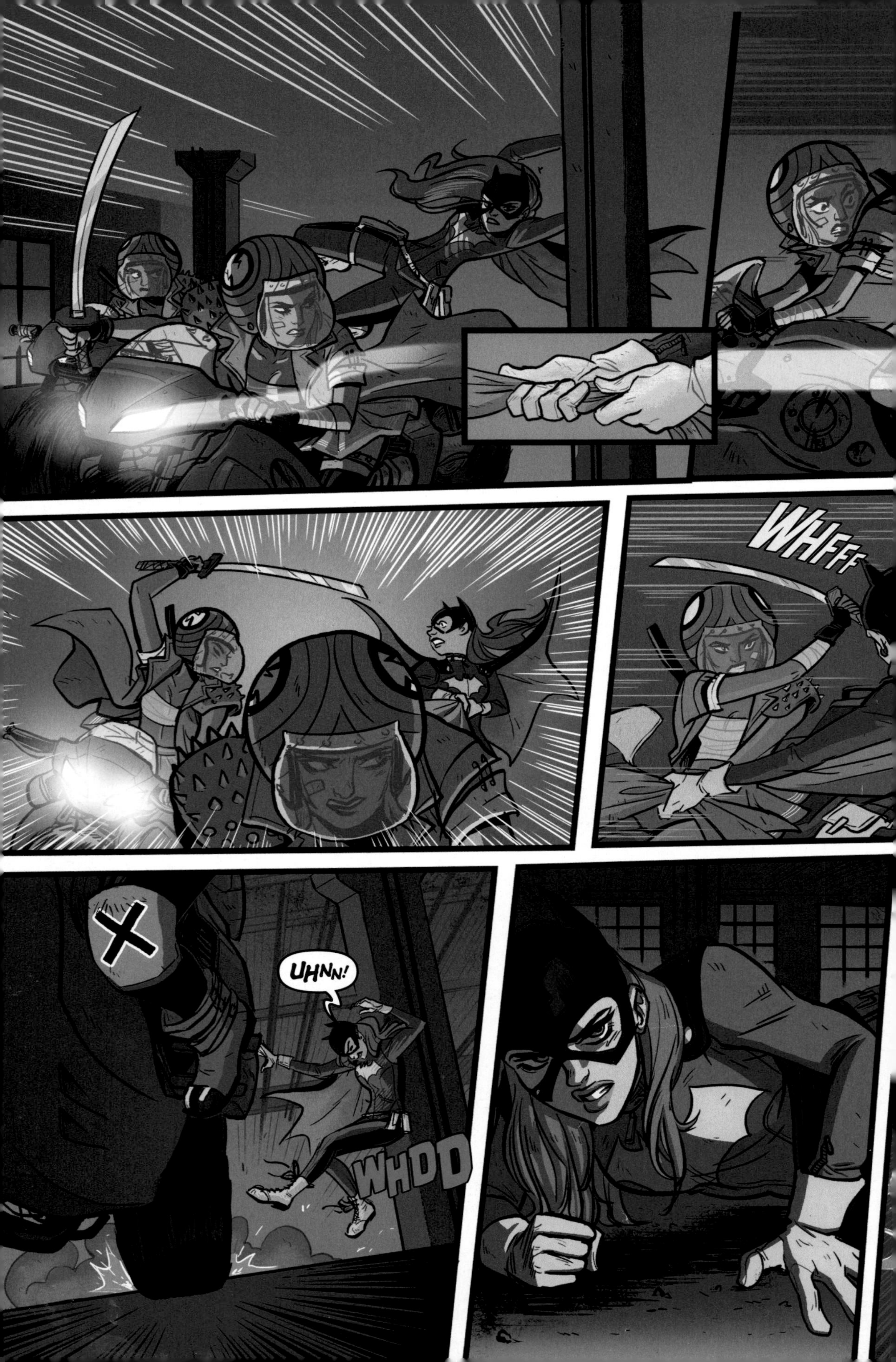
WHFFF
UHNN!
WHDD

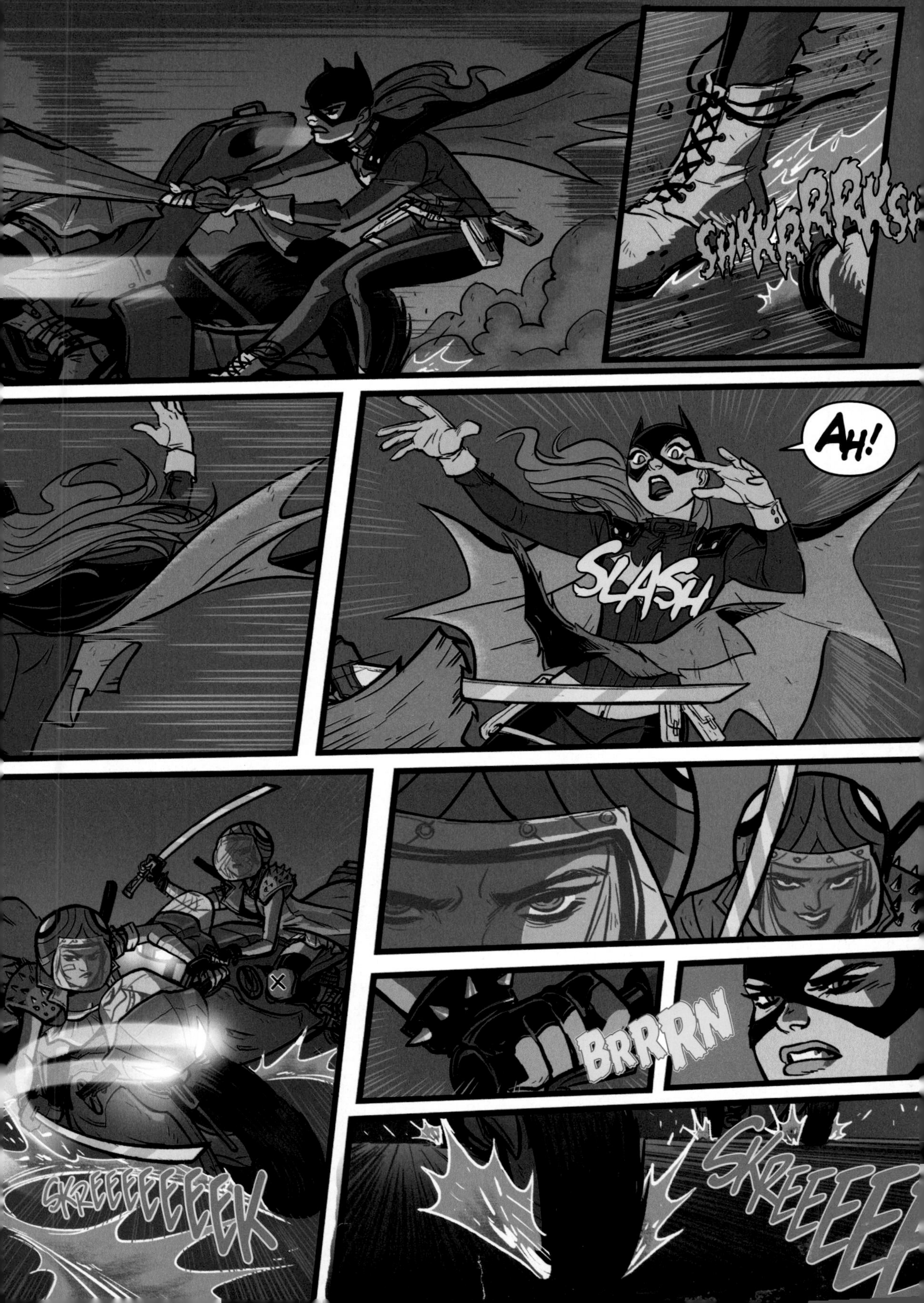
SHKKRRRKSH
AH!
SLASH
BRRRN
SKREEEEEEEEK
SKREEEEE

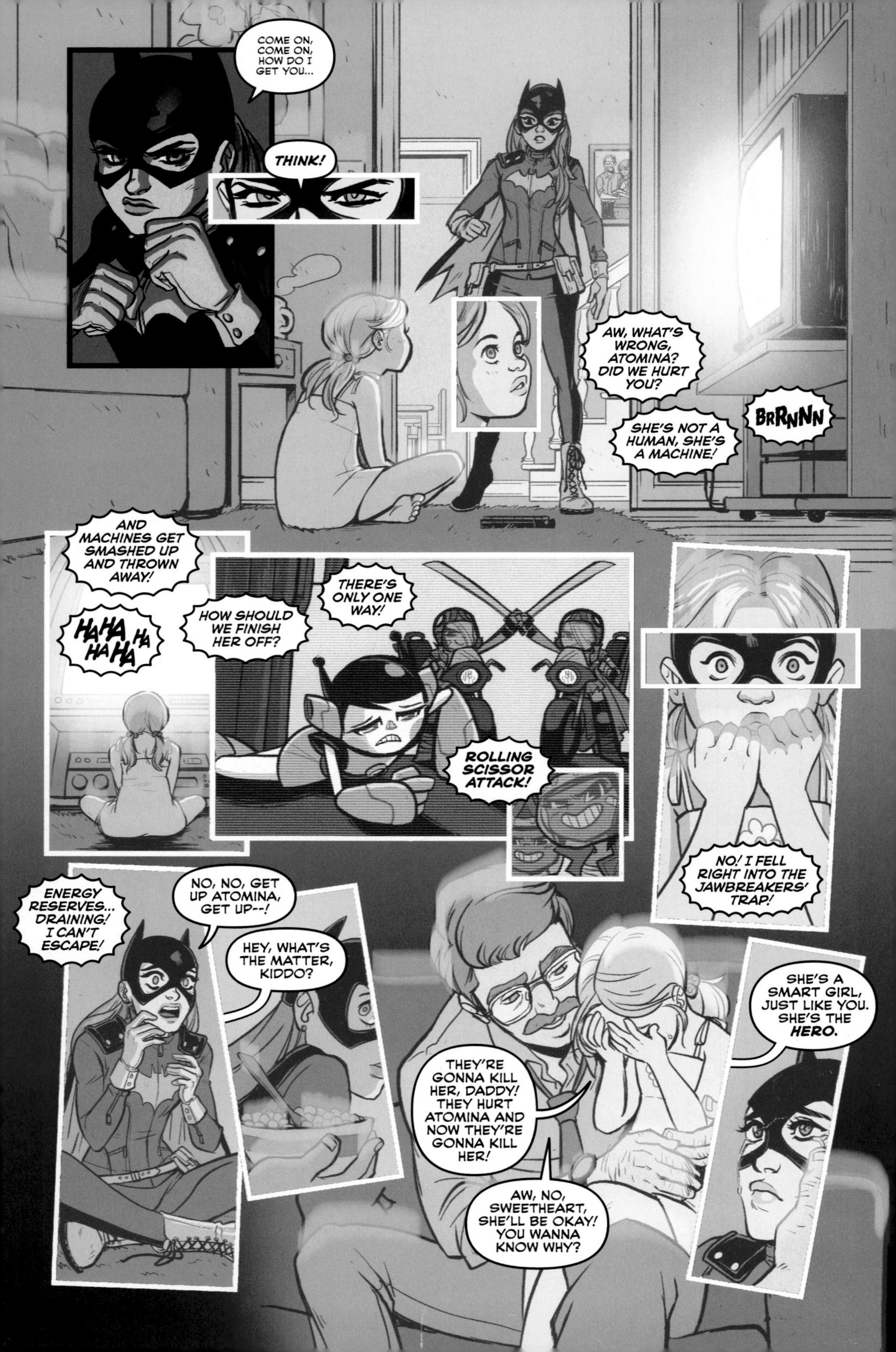
COME ON, COME ON, HOW DO I GET YOU...
THINK!
AW, WHAT'S WRONG, ATOMINA? DID WE HURT YOU?
SHE'S NOT A HUMAN, SHE'S A MACHINE!
BRRNNN
AND MACHINES GET SMASHED UP AND THROWN AWAY!
HAHA HA HAHA HA
HOW SHOULD WE FINISH HER OFF?
THERE'S ONLY ONE WAY!
ROLLING SCISSOR ATTACK!
NO! I FELL RIGHT INTO THE JAWBREAKERS' TRAP!
ENERGY RESERVES... DRAINING! I CAN'T ESCAPE!
NO, NO, GET UP ATOMINA, GET UP--!
HEY, WHAT'S THE MATTER, KIDDO?
THEY'RE GONNA KILL HER, DADDY! THEY HURT ATOMINA AND NOW THEY'RE GONNA KILL HER!
AW, NO, SWEETHEART, SHE'LL BE OKAY! YOU WANNA KNOW WHY?
SHE'S A SMART GIRL, JUST LIKE YOU. SHE'S THE HERO.

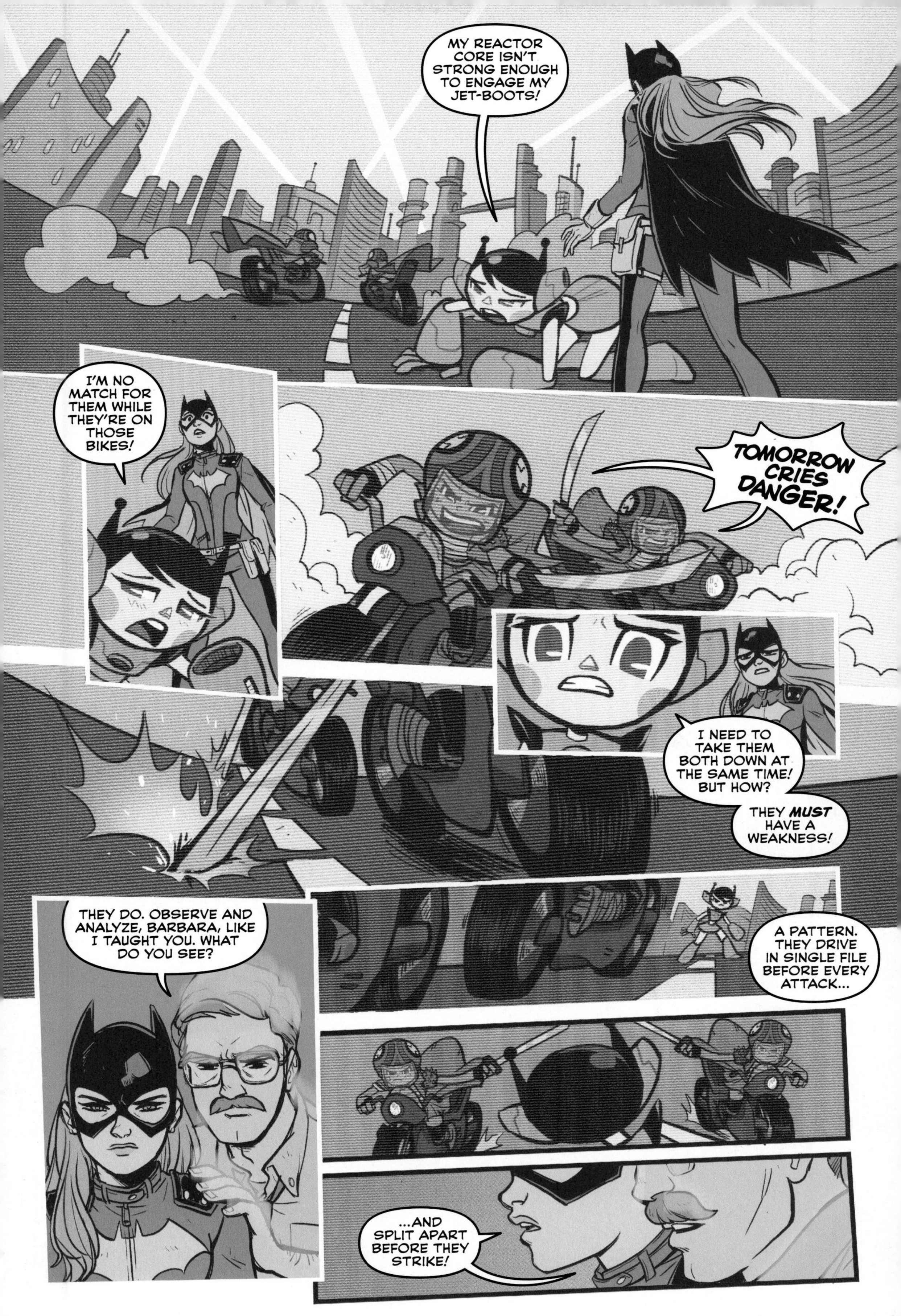

MY REACTOR CORE ISN'T STRONG ENOUGH TO ENGAGE MY JET-BOOTS!
I'M NO MATCH FOR THEM WHILE THEY'RE ON THOSE BIKES!
TOMORROW CRIES DANGER!
I NEED TO TAKE THEM BOTH DOWN AT THE SAME TIME! BUT HOW?
THEY *MUST* HAVE A WEAKNESS!
THEY DO. OBSERVE AND ANALYZE, BARBARA, LIKE I TAUGHT YOU. WHAT DO YOU SEE?
A PATTERN. THEY DRIVE IN SINGLE FILE BEFORE EVERY ATTACK...
...AND SPLIT APART BEFORE THEY STRIKE!

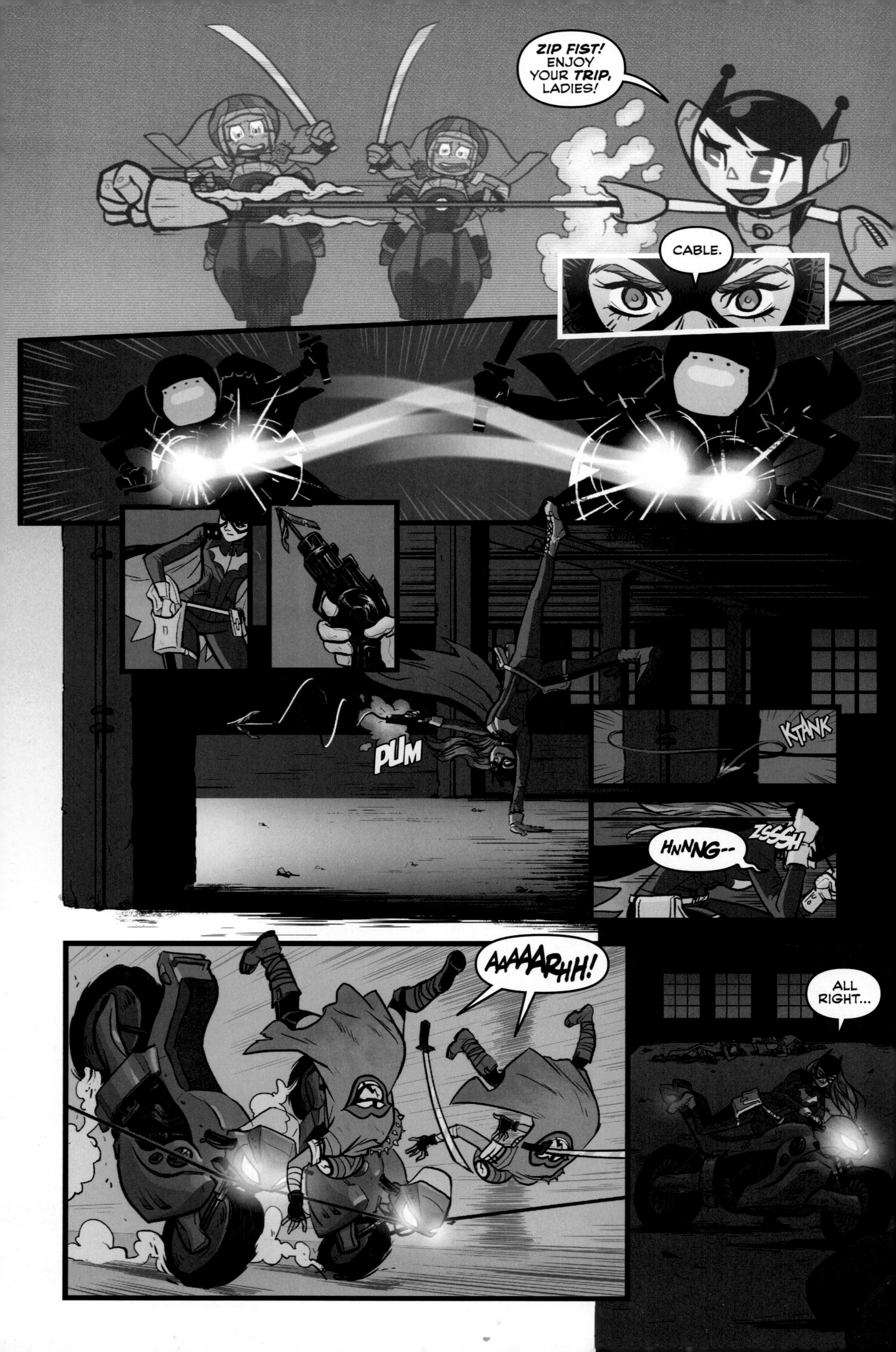
ZIP FIST! ENJOY YOUR TRIP, LADIES!
CABLE.
PUM
KTANK
HNNNG--
ZSSSH
AAAAARHH!
ALL RIGHT...

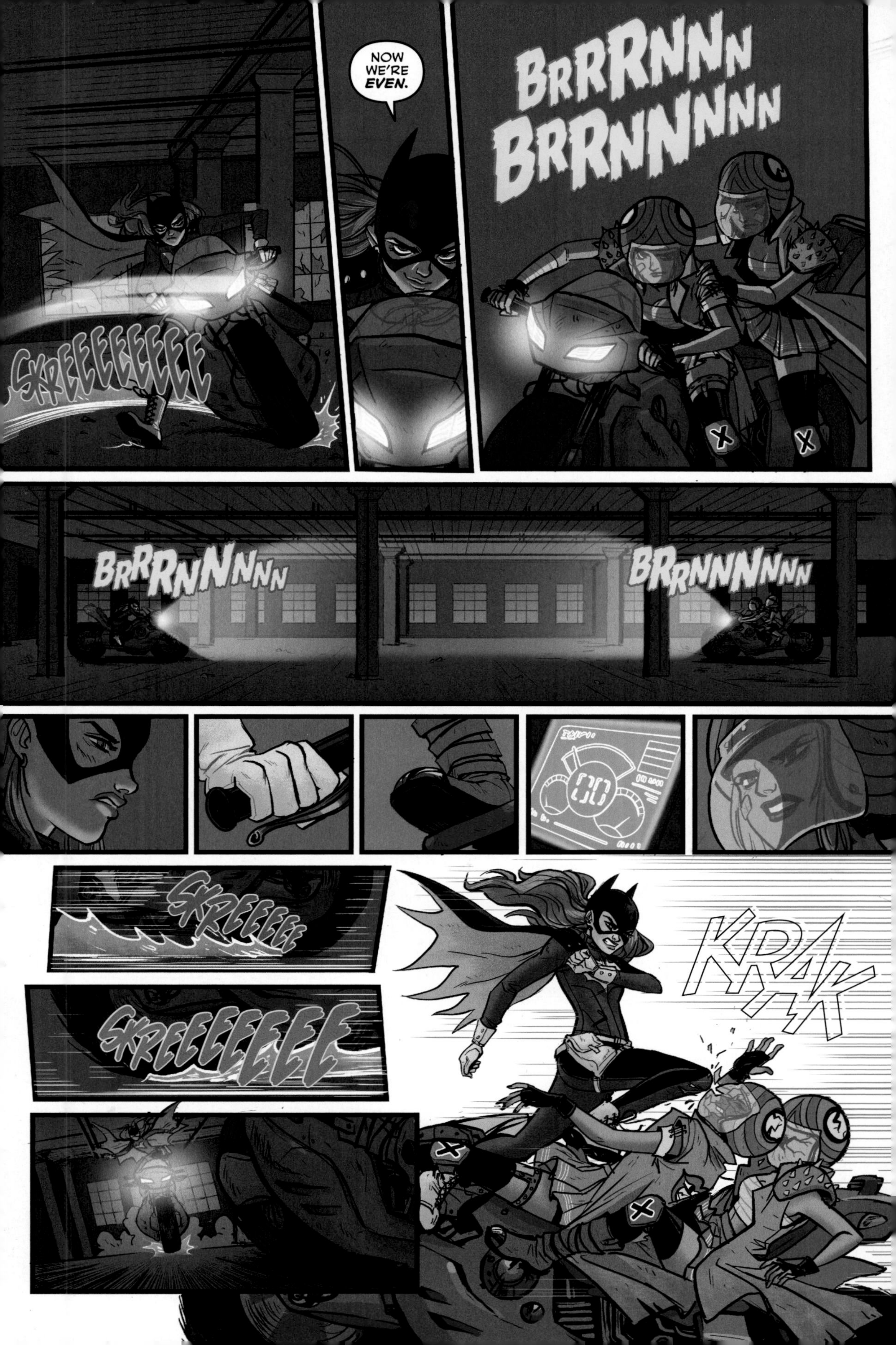
SKREEEEEEEE
NOW WE'RE EVEN.
BRRRNNN
BRRNNNNN
BRRRNNNNN
BRRNNNNNN
SKREEEEE
SKREEEEEEE
KRAK

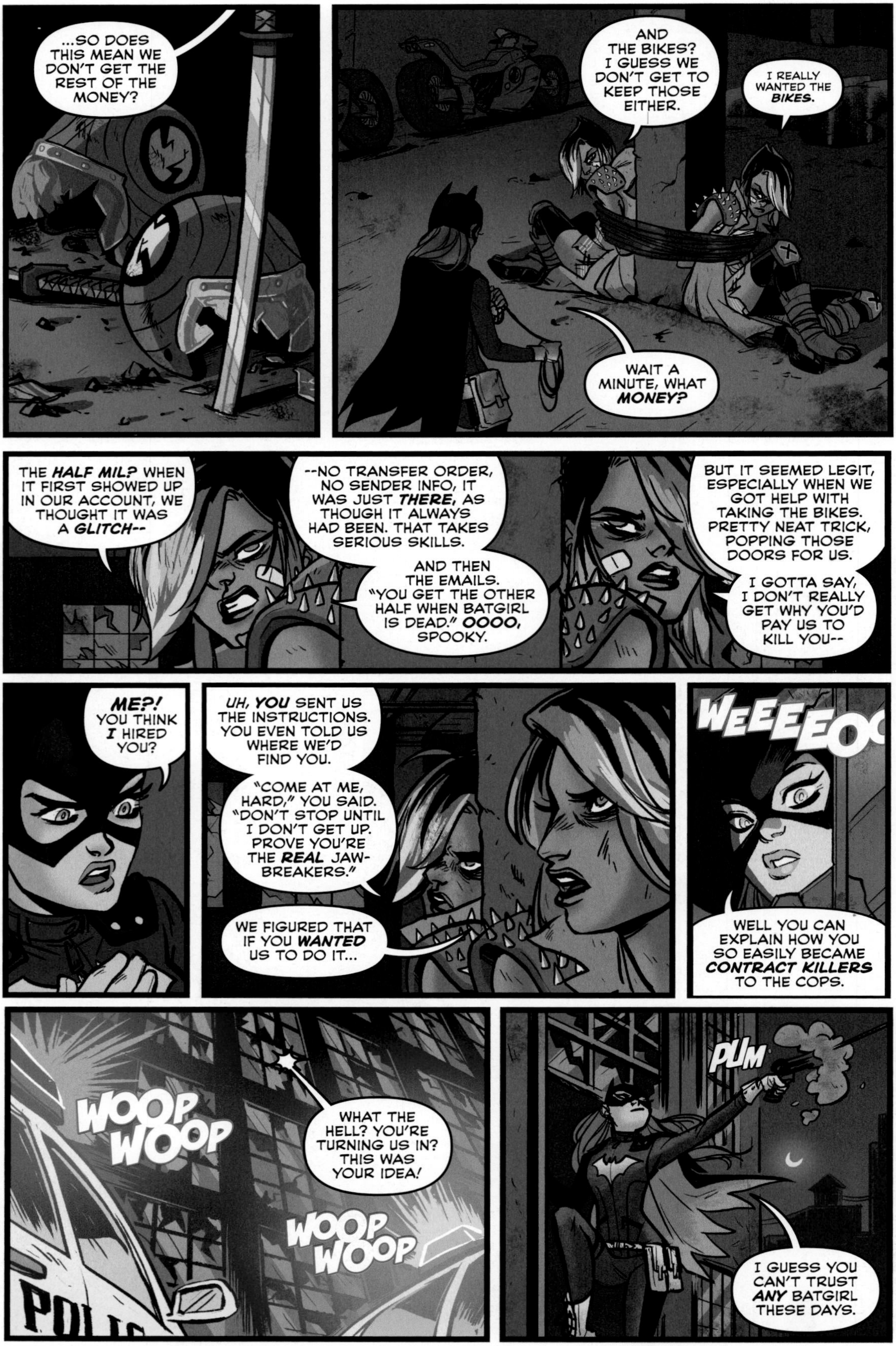
...SO DOES THIS MEAN WE DON'T GET THE REST OF THE MONEY?
AND THE BIKES? I GUESS WE DON'T GET TO KEEP THOSE EITHER.
I REALLY WANTED THE BIKES.
WAIT A MINUTE, WHAT MONEY?
THE HALF MIL? WHEN IT FIRST SHOWED UP IN OUR ACCOUNT, WE THOUGHT IT WAS A GLITCH--
--NO TRANSFER ORDER, NO SENDER INFO, IT WAS JUST THERE, AS THOUGH IT ALWAYS HAD BEEN. THAT TAKES SERIOUS SKILLS.
AND THEN THE EMAILS. "YOU GET THE OTHER HALF WHEN BATGIRL IS DEAD." OOOO, SPOOKY.
BUT IT SEEMED LEGIT, ESPECIALLY WHEN WE GOT HELP WITH TAKING THE BIKES. PRETTY NEAT TRICK, POPPING THOSE DOORS FOR US.
I GOTTA SAY, I DON'T REALLY GET WHY YOU'D PAY US TO KILL YOU--
ME?! YOU THINK I HIRED YOU?
UH, YOU SENT US THE INSTRUCTIONS. YOU EVEN TOLD US WHERE WE'D FIND YOU.
"COME AT ME, HARD," YOU SAID. "DON'T STOP UNTIL I DON'T GET UP. PROVE YOU'RE THE REAL JAW-BREAKERS."
WE FIGURED THAT IF YOU WANTED US TO DO IT...
WEEEEOO
WELL YOU CAN EXPLAIN HOW YOU SO EASILY BECAME CONTRACT KILLERS TO THE COPS.
WOOP WOOP
WHAT THE HELL? YOU'RE TURNING US IN? THIS WAS YOUR IDEA!
WOOP WOOP
POLIC
PUM
I GUESS YOU CAN'T TRUST ANY BATGIRL THESE DAYS.

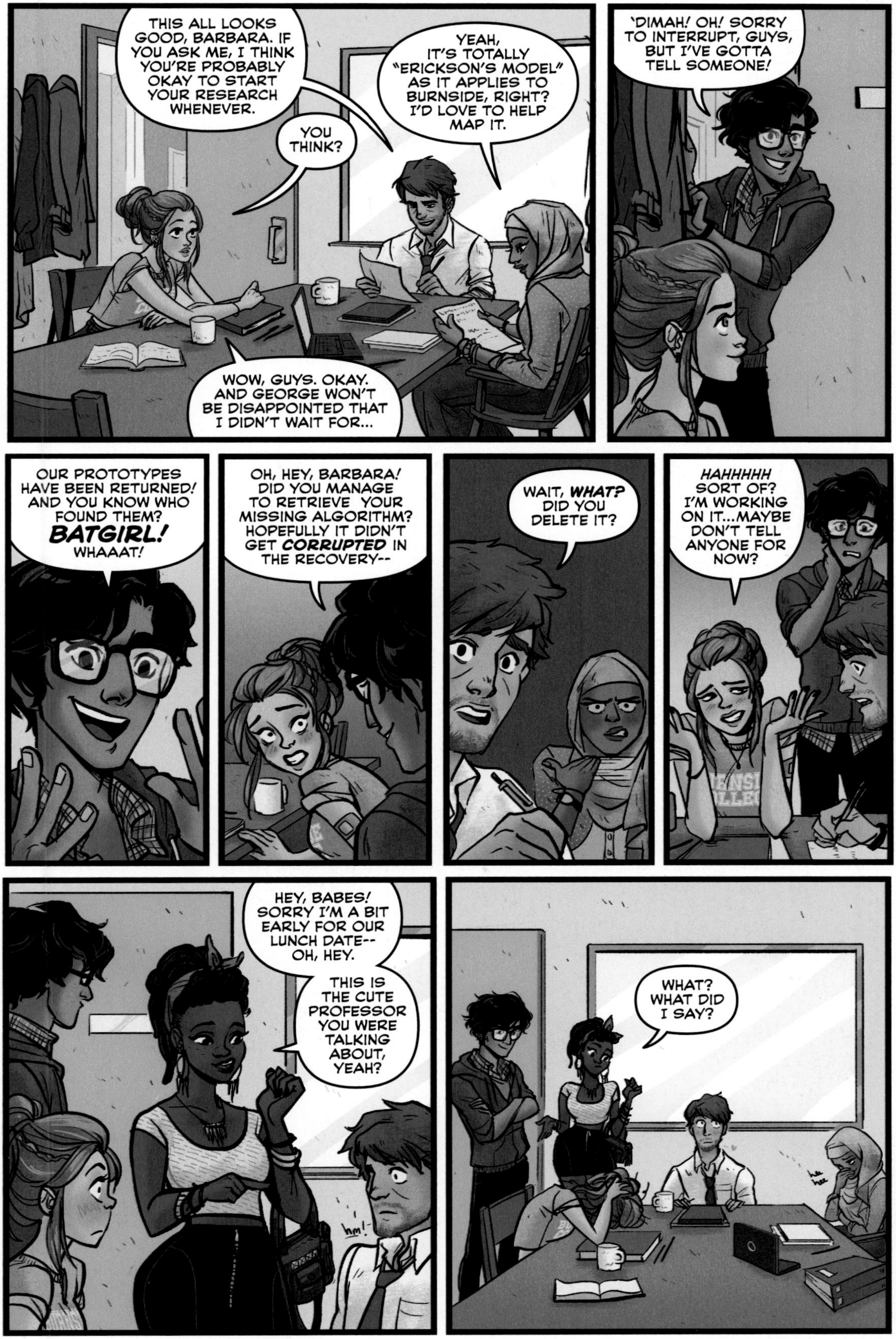
THIS ALL LOOKS GOOD, BARBARA. IF YOU ASK ME, I THINK YOU'RE PROBABLY OKAY TO START YOUR RESEARCH WHENEVER.
YEAH, IT'S TOTALLY "ERICKSON'S MODEL" AS IT APPLIES TO BURNSIDE, RIGHT? I'D LOVE TO HELP MAP IT.
YOU THINK?
WOW, GUYS. OKAY. AND GEORGE WON'T BE DISAPPOINTED THAT I DIDN'T WAIT FOR...
'DIMAH! OH! SORRY TO INTERRUPT, GUYS, BUT I'VE GOTTA TELL SOMEONE!
OUR PROTOTYPES HAVE BEEN RETURNED! AND YOU KNOW WHO FOUND THEM? **BATGIRL!** WHAAAT!
OH, HEY, BARBARA! DID YOU MANAGE TO RETRIEVE YOUR MISSING ALGORITHM? HOPEFULLY IT DIDN'T GET ***CORRUPTED*** IN THE RECOVERY--
WAIT, ***WHAT?*** DID YOU DELETE IT?
HAHHHHH SORT OF? I'M WORKING ON IT...MAYBE DON'T TELL ANYONE FOR NOW?
HEY, BABES! SORRY I'M A BIT EARLY FOR OUR LUNCH DATE-- OH, HEY.
THIS IS THE CUTE PROFESSOR YOU WERE TALKING ABOUT, YEAH?
hm!
WHAT? WHAT DID I SAY?

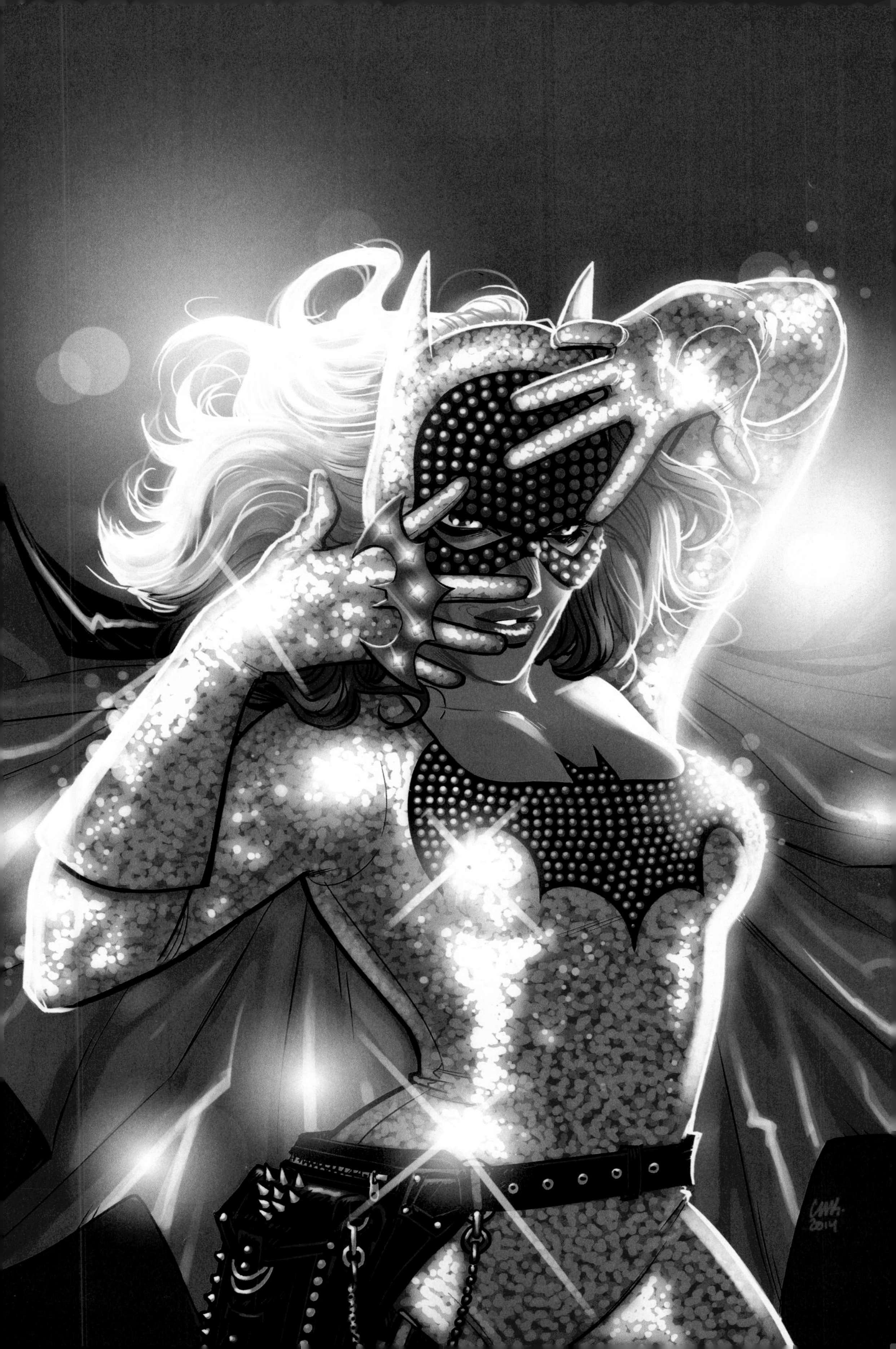

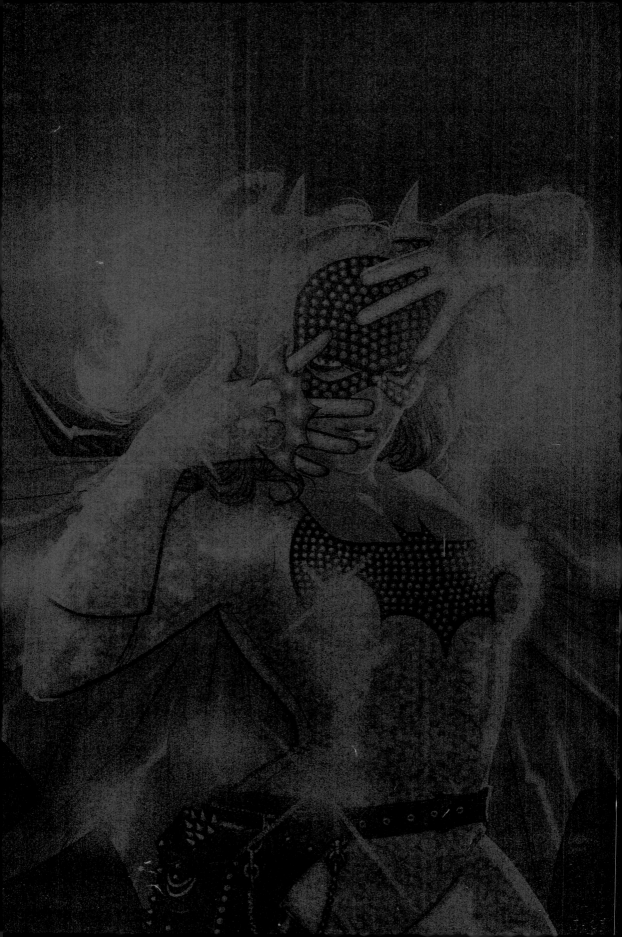

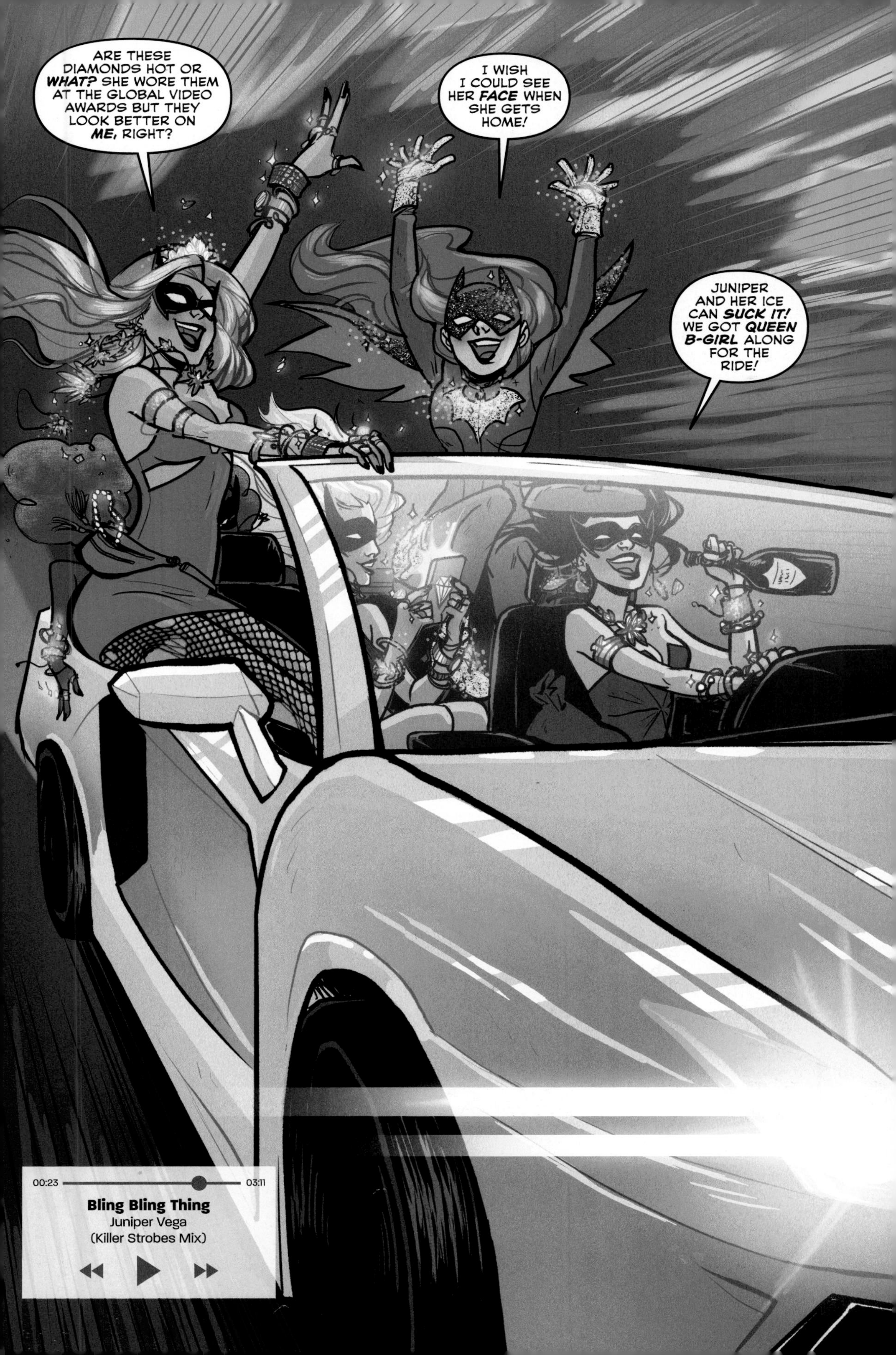
ARE THESE DIAMONDS HOT OR WHAT? SHE WORE THEM AT THE GLOBAL VIDEO AWARDS BUT THEY LOOK BETTER ON ME, RIGHT?
I WISH I COULD SEE HER FACE WHEN SHE GETS HOME!
JUNIPER AND HER ICE CAN SUCK IT! WE GOT QUEEN B-GIRL ALONG FOR THE RIDE!
00:23
03:11
Bling Bling Thing
Juniper Vega
(Killer Strobes Mix)

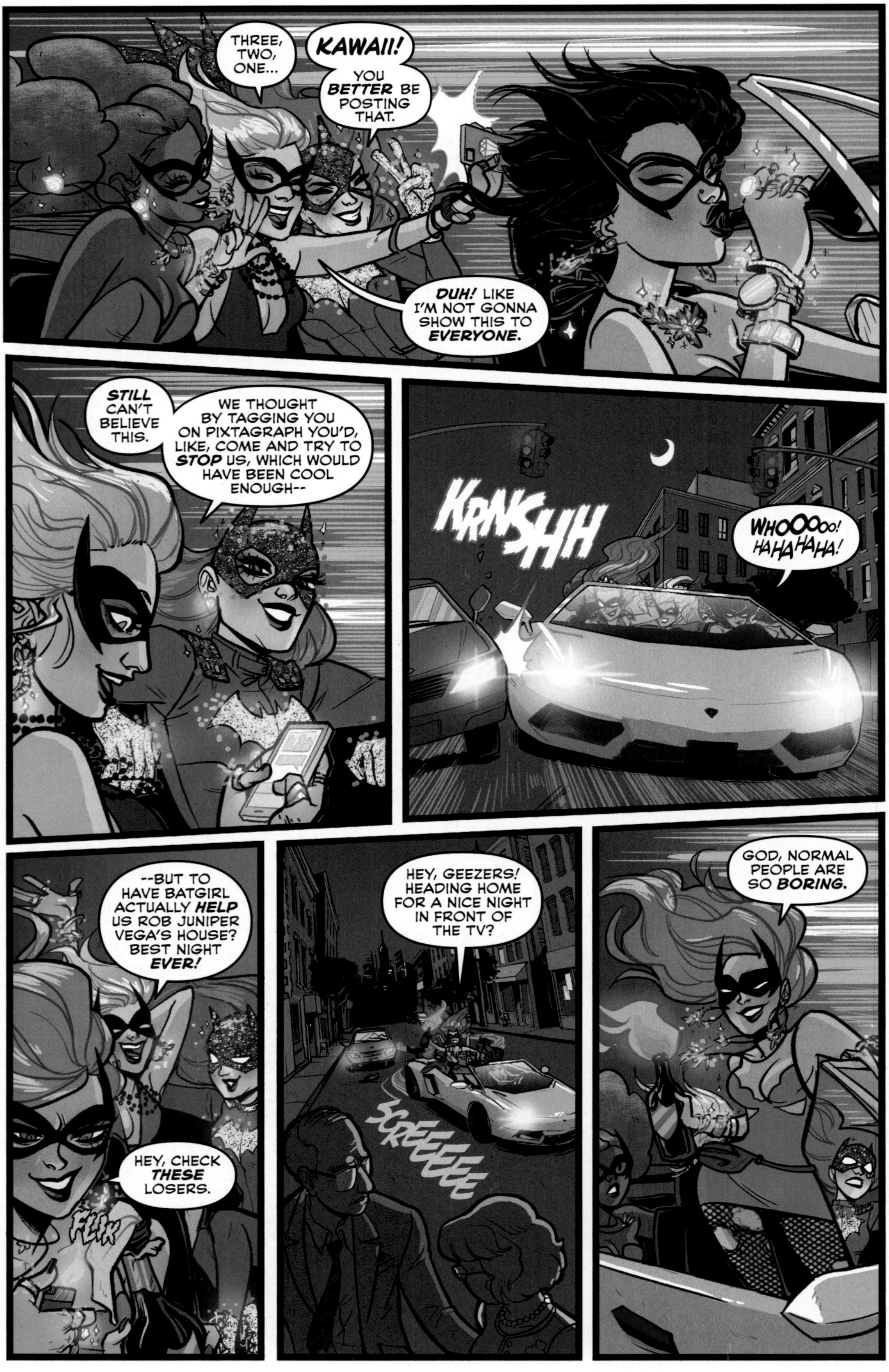
THREE, TWO, ONE...
KAWAII!
YOU BETTER BE POSTING THAT.
DUH! LIKE I'M NOT GONNA SHOW THIS TO EVERYONE.
STILL CAN'T BELIEVE THIS.
WE THOUGHT BY TAGGING YOU ON PIXTAGRAPH YOU'D, LIKE, COME AND TRY TO STOP US, WHICH WOULD HAVE BEEN COOL ENOUGH--
KRNSHH
WHOOOoo! HAHAHAHA!
--BUT TO HAVE BATGIRL ACTUALLY HELP US ROB JUNIPER VEGA'S HOUSE? BEST NIGHT EVER!
HEY, CHECK THESE LOSERS.
FLIK
HEY, GEEZERS! HEADING HOME FOR A NICE NIGHT IN FRONT OF THE TV?
SCREEEEEE
GOD, NORMAL PEOPLE ARE SO BORING.

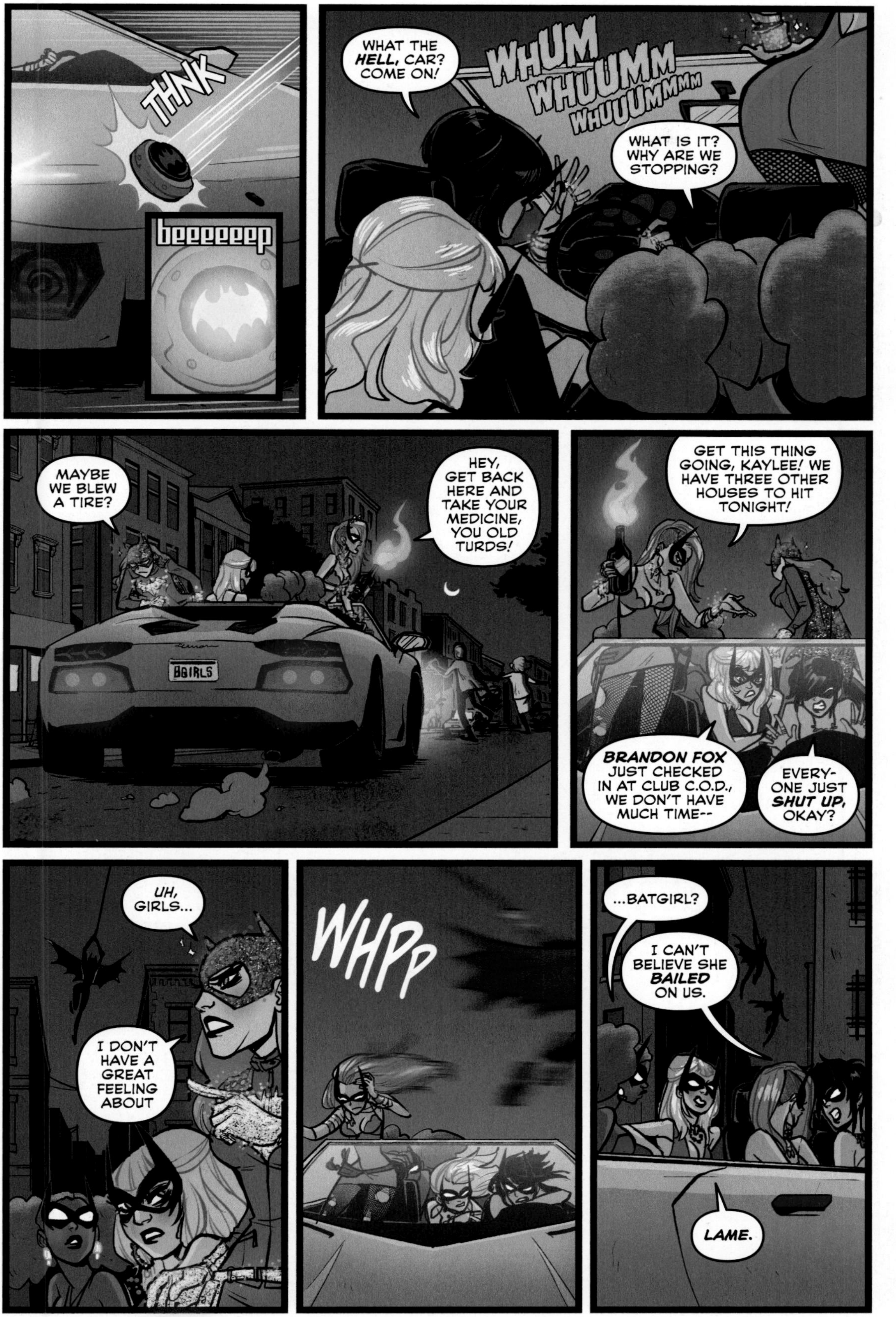
THNK
beeeeeep
WHAT THE *HELL*, CAR? COME ON!
WHUM WHUUMM WHUUUMMMM
WHAT IS IT? WHY ARE WE STOPPING?
MAYBE WE BLEW A TIRE?
HEY, GET BACK HERE AND TAKE YOUR MEDICINE, YOU OLD TURDS!
BBGIRLS
GET THIS THING GOING, KAYLEE! WE HAVE THREE OTHER HOUSES TO HIT TONIGHT!
BRANDON FOX JUST CHECKED IN AT CLUB C.O.D., WE DON'T HAVE MUCH TIME--
EVERY-ONE JUST *SHUT UP*, OKAY?
UH, GIRLS...
I DON'T HAVE A GREAT FEELING ABOUT
WHPP
...BATGIRL?
I CAN'T BELIEVE SHE *BAILED* ON US.
LAME.

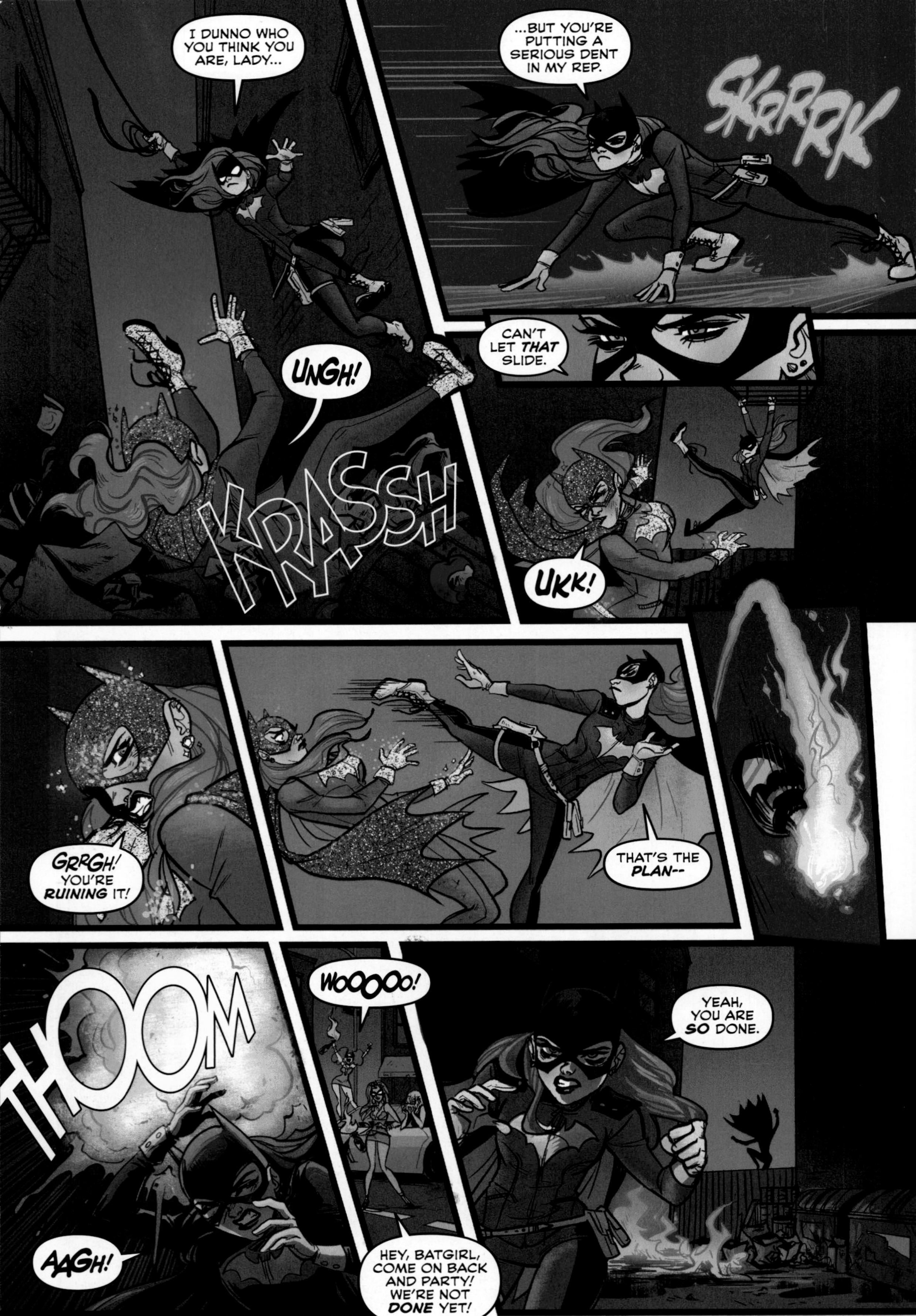
I DUNNO WHO YOU THINK YOU ARE, LADY...
...BUT YOU'RE PUTTING A SERIOUS DENT IN MY REP.
SKRRRK
CAN'T LET THAT SLIDE.
UNGH!
KRASSH
UKK!
GRRGH! YOU'RE RUINING IT!
THAT'S THE PLAN--
THOOM
AAGH!
WOOOOO!
HEY, BATGIRL, COME ON BACK AND PARTY! WE'RE NOT DONE YET!
YEAH, YOU ARE SO DONE.

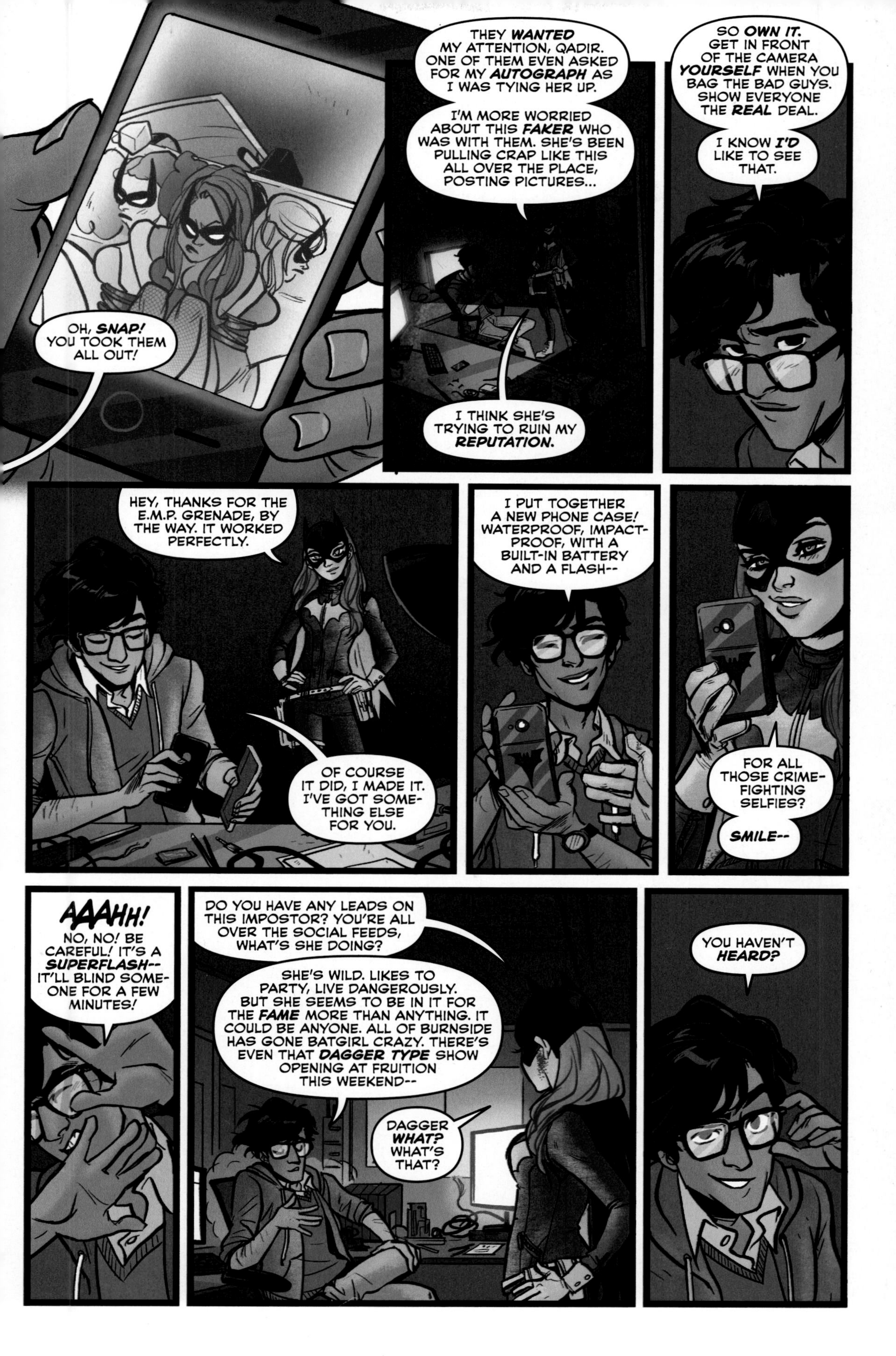
OH, SNAP! YOU TOOK THEM ALL OUT!
THEY WANTED MY ATTENTION, QADIR. ONE OF THEM EVEN ASKED FOR MY AUTOGRAPH AS I WAS TYING HER UP.
I'M MORE WORRIED ABOUT THIS FAKER WHO WAS WITH THEM. SHE'S BEEN PULLING CRAP LIKE THIS ALL OVER THE PLACE, POSTING PICTURES...
I THINK SHE'S TRYING TO RUIN MY REPUTATION.
SO OWN IT. GET IN FRONT OF THE CAMERA YOURSELF WHEN YOU BAG THE BAD GUYS. SHOW EVERYONE THE REAL DEAL.
I KNOW I'D LIKE TO SEE THAT.
HEY, THANKS FOR THE E.M.P. GRENADE, BY THE WAY. IT WORKED PERFECTLY.
OF COURSE IT DID, I MADE IT. I'VE GOT SOME-THING ELSE FOR YOU.
I PUT TOGETHER A NEW PHONE CASE! WATERPROOF, IMPACT-PROOF, WITH A BUILT-IN BATTERY AND A FLASH--
FOR ALL THOSE CRIME-FIGHTING SELFIES?
SMILE--
AAAHH!
NO, NO! BE CAREFUL! IT'S A SUPERFLASH-- IT'LL BLIND SOME-ONE FOR A FEW MINUTES!
DO YOU HAVE ANY LEADS ON THIS IMPOSTOR? YOU'RE ALL OVER THE SOCIAL FEEDS, WHAT'S SHE DOING?
SHE'S WILD. LIKES TO PARTY, LIVE DANGEROUSLY. BUT SHE SEEMS TO BE IN IT FOR THE FAME MORE THAN ANYTHING. IT COULD BE ANYONE. ALL OF BURNSIDE HAS GONE BATGIRL CRAZY. THERE'S EVEN THAT DAGGER TYPE SHOW OPENING AT FRUITION THIS WEEKEND--
DAGGER WHAT? WHAT'S THAT?
YOU HAVEN'T HEARD?

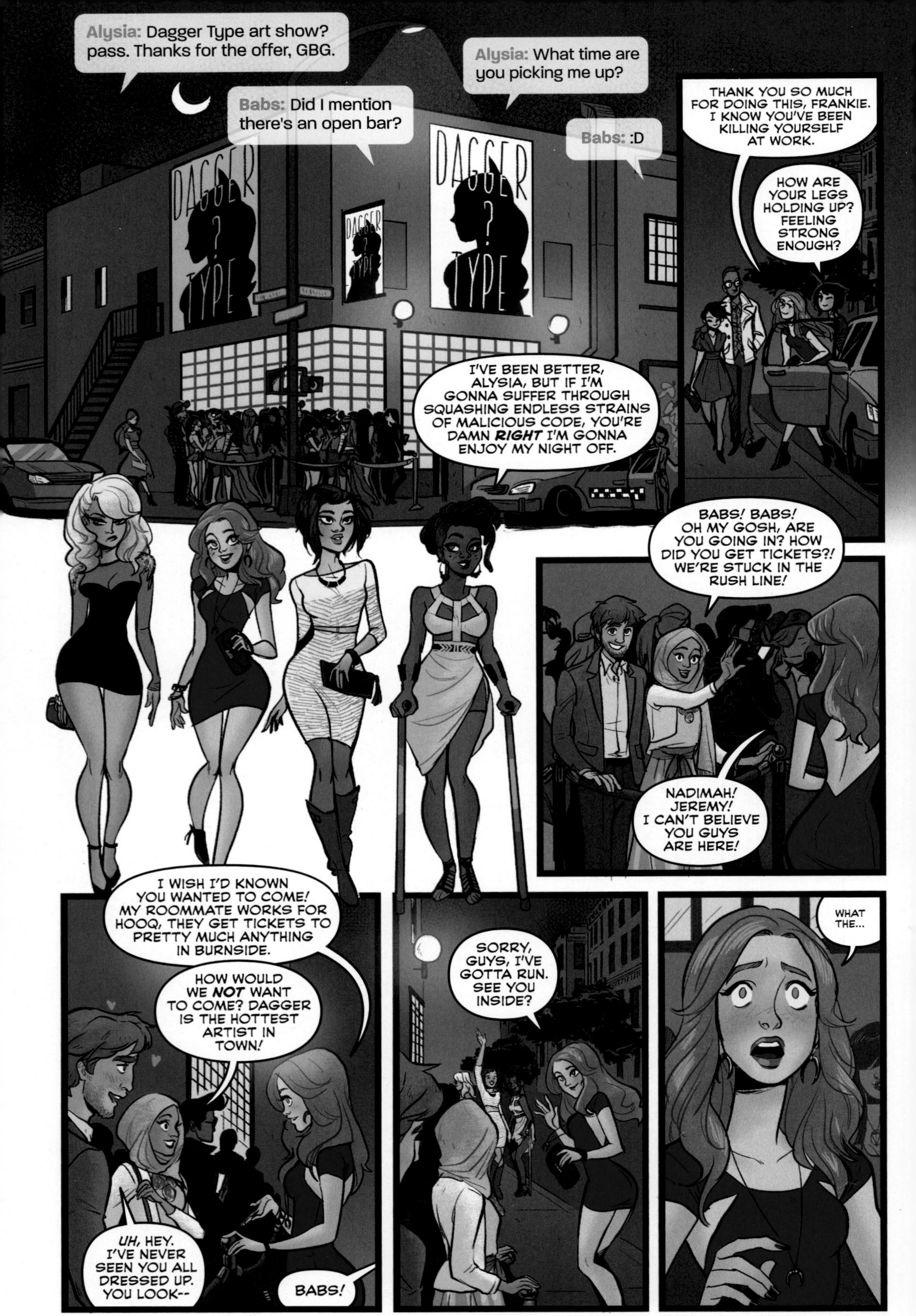
Alysia: Dagger Type art show? pass. Thanks for the offer, GBG.
Babs: Did I mention there's an open bar?
Alysia: What time are you picking me up?
Babs: :D
DAGGER ? TYPE
THANK YOU SO MUCH FOR DOING THIS, FRANKIE. I KNOW YOU'VE BEEN KILLING YOURSELF AT WORK.
HOW ARE YOUR LEGS HOLDING UP? FEELING STRONG ENOUGH?
I'VE BEEN BETTER, ALYSIA, BUT IF I'M GONNA SUFFER THROUGH SQUASHING ENDLESS STRAINS OF MALICIOUS CODE, YOU'RE DAMN *RIGHT* I'M GONNA ENJOY MY NIGHT OFF.
BABS! BABS! OH MY GOSH, ARE YOU GOING IN? HOW DID YOU GET TICKETS?! WE'RE STUCK IN THE RUSH LINE!
NADIMAH! JEREMY! I CAN'T BELIEVE YOU GUYS ARE HERE!
I WISH I'D KNOWN YOU WANTED TO COME! MY ROOMMATE WORKS FOR HOOQ, THEY GET TICKETS TO PRETTY MUCH ANYTHING IN BURNSIDE.
HOW WOULD WE *NOT* WANT TO COME? DAGGER IS THE HOTTEST ARTIST IN TOWN!
UH, HEY. I'VE NEVER SEEN YOU ALL DRESSED UP. YOU LOOK--
BABS!
SORRY, GUYS, I'VE GOTTA RUN. SEE YOU INSIDE?
WHAT THE...

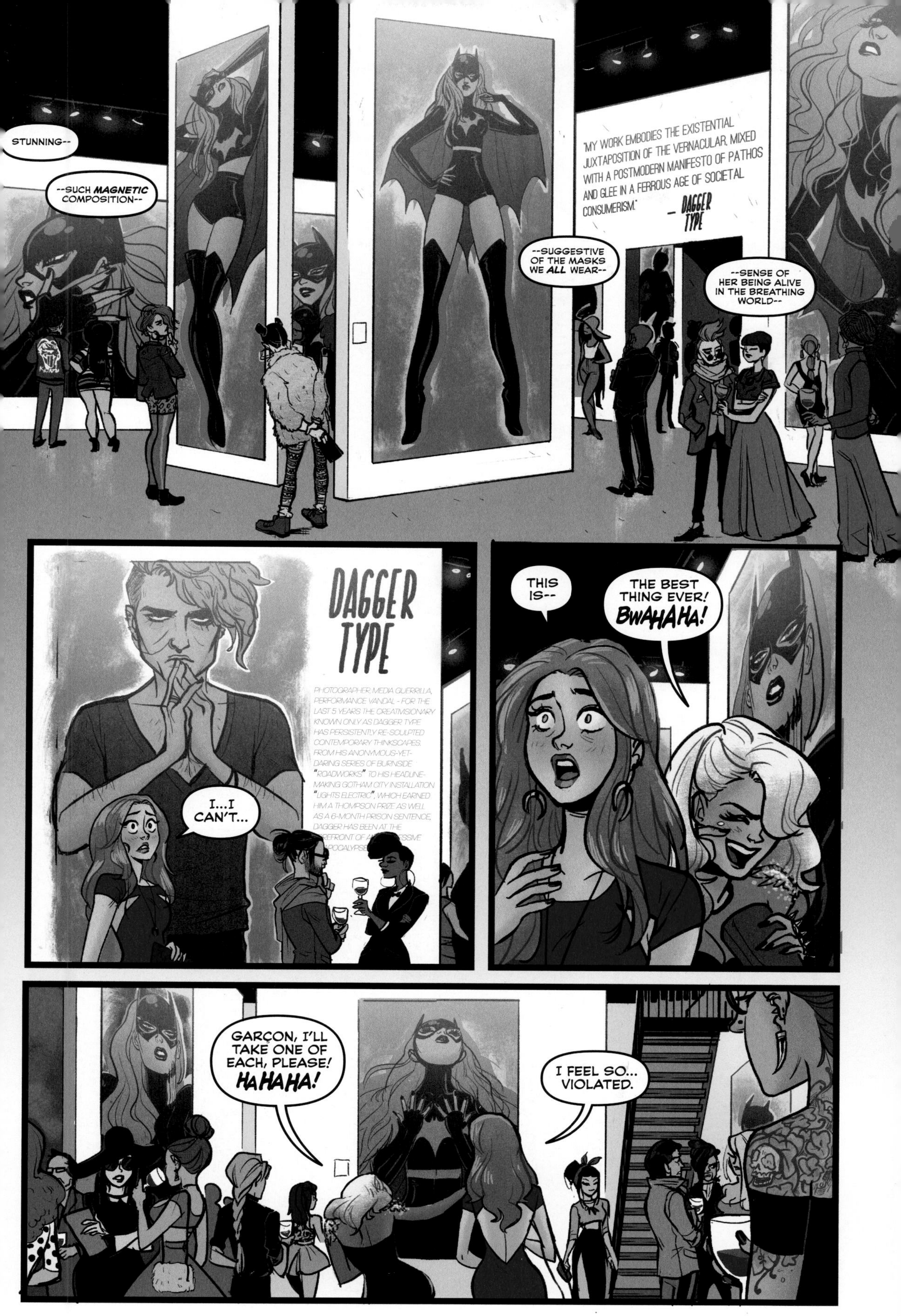
STUNNING--
--SUCH MAGNETIC COMPOSITION--
"MY WORK EMBODIES THE EXISTENTIAL JUXTAPOSITION OF THE VERNACULAR, MIXED WITH A POSTMODERN MANIFESTO OF PATHOS AND GLEE IN A FERROUS AGE OF SOCIETAL CONSUMERISM." — DAGGER TYPE
--SUGGESTIVE OF THE MASKS WE ALL WEAR--
--SENSE OF HER BEING ALIVE IN THE BREATHING WORLD--
DAGGER TYPE
PHOTOGRAPHER, MEDIA GUERRILLA, PERFORMANCE VANDAL - FOR THE LAST 5 YEARS THE CREATIVISIONARY KNOWN ONLY AS DAGGER TYPE HAS PERSISTENTLY RE-SCULPTED CONTEMPORARY THINKSCAPES. FROM HIS ANONYMOUS-YET-DARING SERIES OF BURNSIDE "ROADWORKS" TO HIS HEADLINE-MAKING GOTHAM CITY INSTALLATION "LIGHTS ELECTRIC", WHICH EARNED HIM A THOMPSON PRIZE AS WELL AS A 6-MONTH PRISON SENTENCE, DAGGER HAS BEEN AT THE
I...I CAN'T...
THIS IS--
THE BEST THING EVER! BWAHAHA!
GARÇON, I'LL TAKE ONE OF EACH, PLEASE! HAHAHA!
I FEEL SO... VIOLATED.

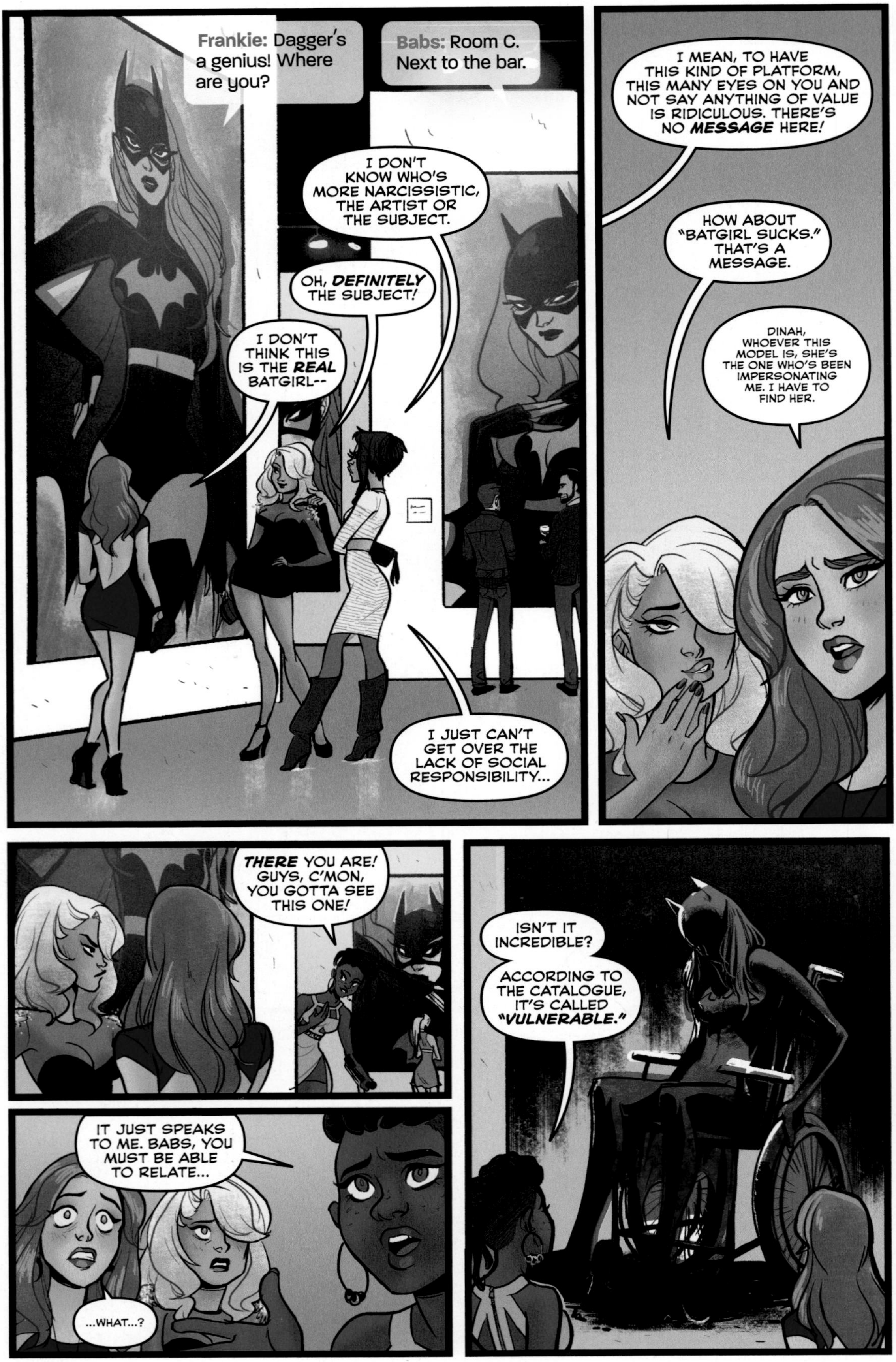
Frankie: Dagger's a genius! Where are you?
Babs: Room C. Next to the bar.
I DON'T KNOW WHO'S MORE NARCISSISTIC, THE ARTIST OR THE SUBJECT.
OH, DEFINITELY THE SUBJECT!
I DON'T THINK THIS IS THE REAL BATGIRL--
I JUST CAN'T GET OVER THE LACK OF SOCIAL RESPONSIBILITY...
I MEAN, TO HAVE THIS KIND OF PLATFORM, THIS MANY EYES ON YOU AND NOT SAY ANYTHING OF VALUE IS RIDICULOUS. THERE'S NO MESSAGE HERE!
HOW ABOUT "BATGIRL SUCKS." THAT'S A MESSAGE.
DINAH, WHOEVER THIS MODEL IS, SHE'S THE ONE WHO'S BEEN IMPERSONATING ME. I HAVE TO FIND HER.
THERE YOU ARE! GUYS, C'MON, YOU GOTTA SEE THIS ONE!
IT JUST SPEAKS TO ME. BABS, YOU MUST BE ABLE TO RELATE...
...WHAT...?
ISN'T IT INCREDIBLE?
ACCORDING TO THE CATALOGUE, IT'S CALLED "VULNERABLE."

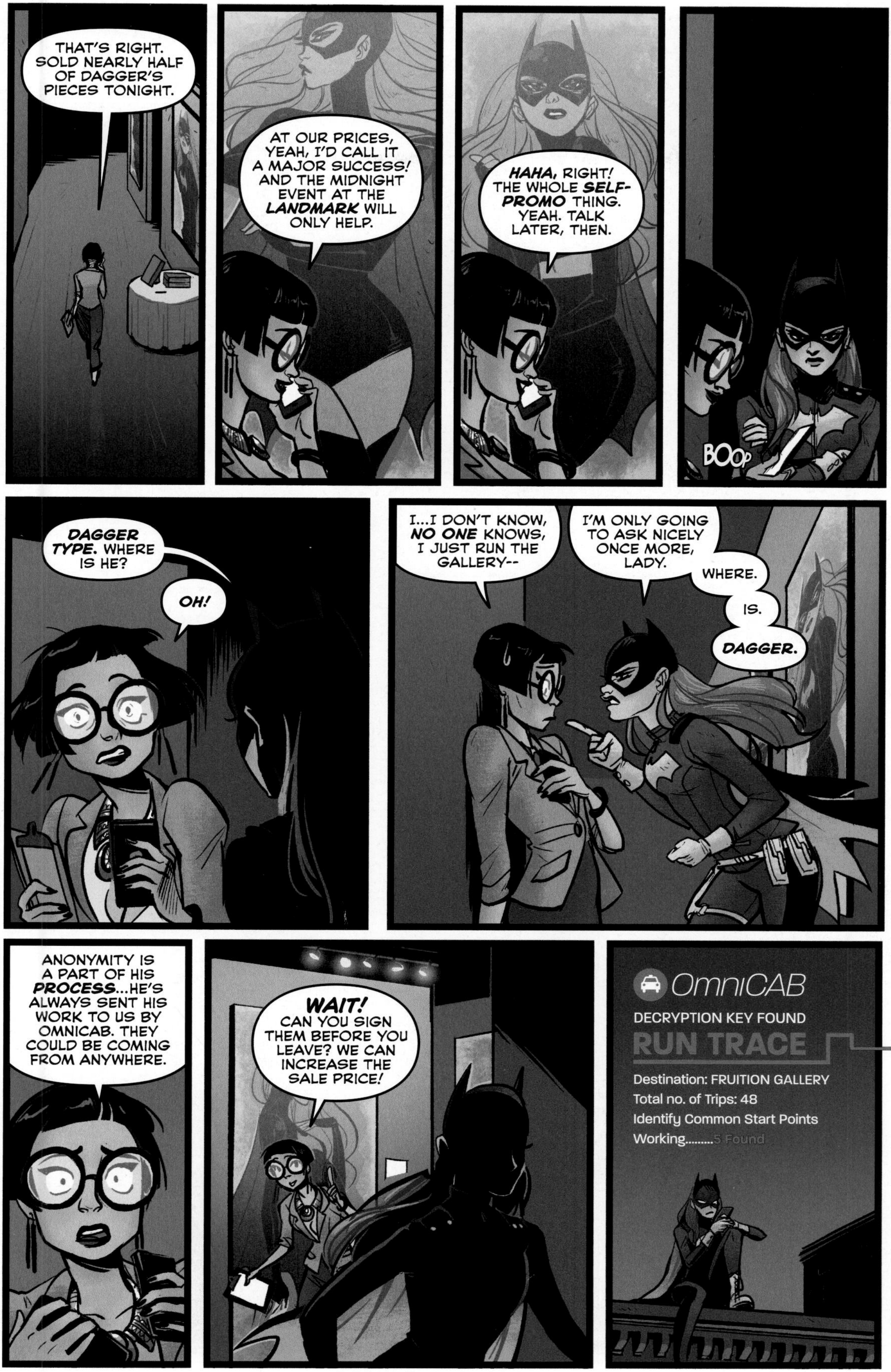
THAT'S RIGHT. SOLD NEARLY HALF OF DAGGER'S PIECES TONIGHT.
AT OUR PRICES, YEAH, I'D CALL IT A MAJOR SUCCESS! AND THE MIDNIGHT EVENT AT THE LANDMARK WILL ONLY HELP.
HAHA, RIGHT! THE WHOLE SELF-PROMO THING. YEAH. TALK LATER, THEN.
BOOP
DAGGER TYPE. WHERE IS HE?
OH!
I...I DON'T KNOW, NO ONE KNOWS, I JUST RUN THE GALLERY--
I'M ONLY GOING TO ASK NICELY ONCE MORE, LADY.
WHERE.
IS.
DAGGER.
ANONYMITY IS A PART OF HIS PROCESS...HE'S ALWAYS SENT HIS WORK TO US BY OMNICAB. THEY COULD BE COMING FROM ANYWHERE.
WAIT! CAN YOU SIGN THEM BEFORE YOU LEAVE? WE CAN INCREASE THE SALE PRICE!
OmniCAB
DECRYPTION KEY FOUND
RUN TRACE
Destination: FRUITION GALLERY
Total no. of Trips: 48
Identify Common Start Points
Working.........5 Found

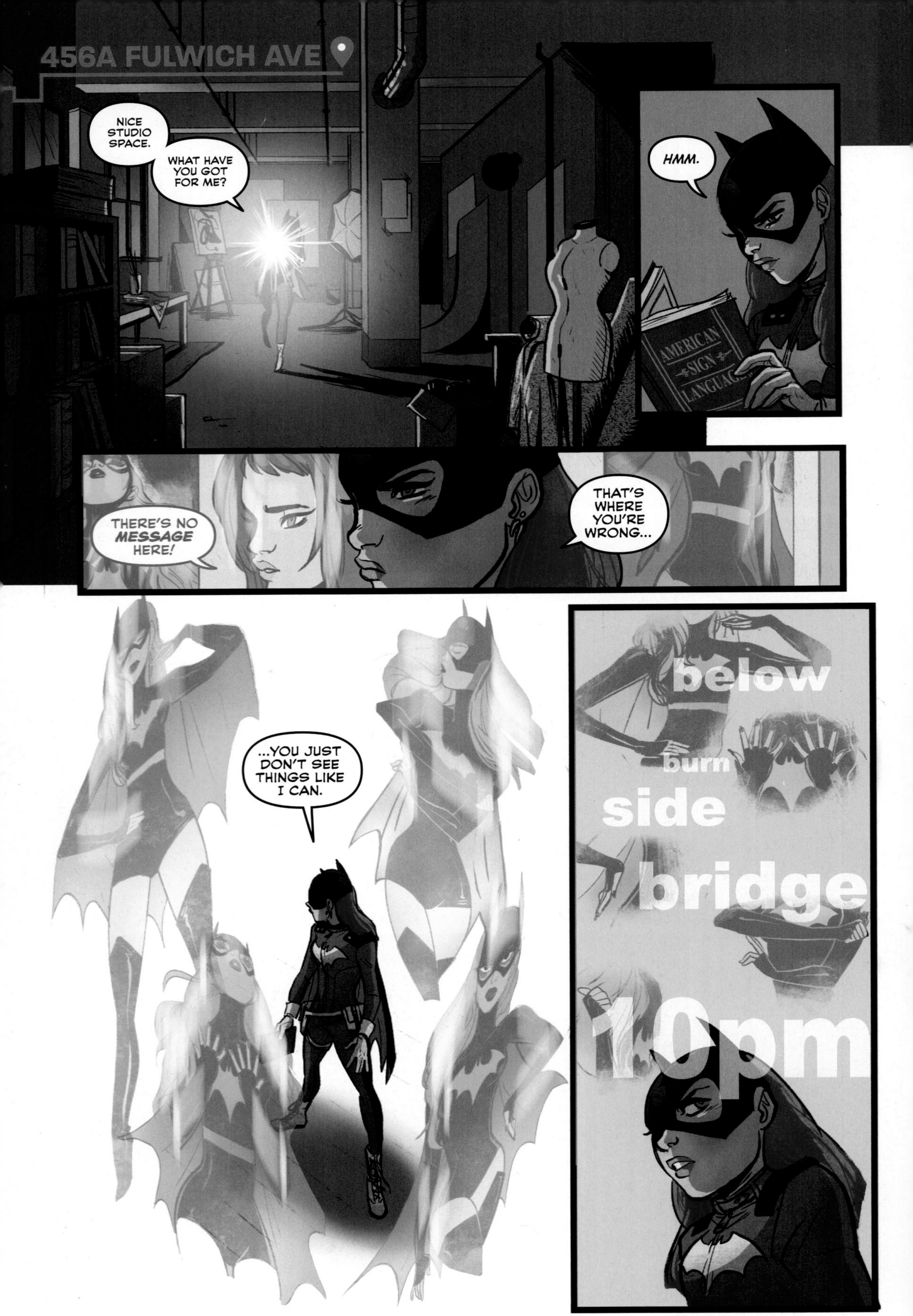
456A FULWICH AVE
NICE STUDIO SPACE.
WHAT HAVE YOU GOT FOR ME?
HMM.
AMERICAN SIGN LANGUAGE
THERE'S NO *MESSAGE* HERE!
THAT'S WHERE YOU'RE WRONG...
...YOU JUST DON'T SEE THINGS LIKE I CAN.
below
burn
side
bridge
10pm

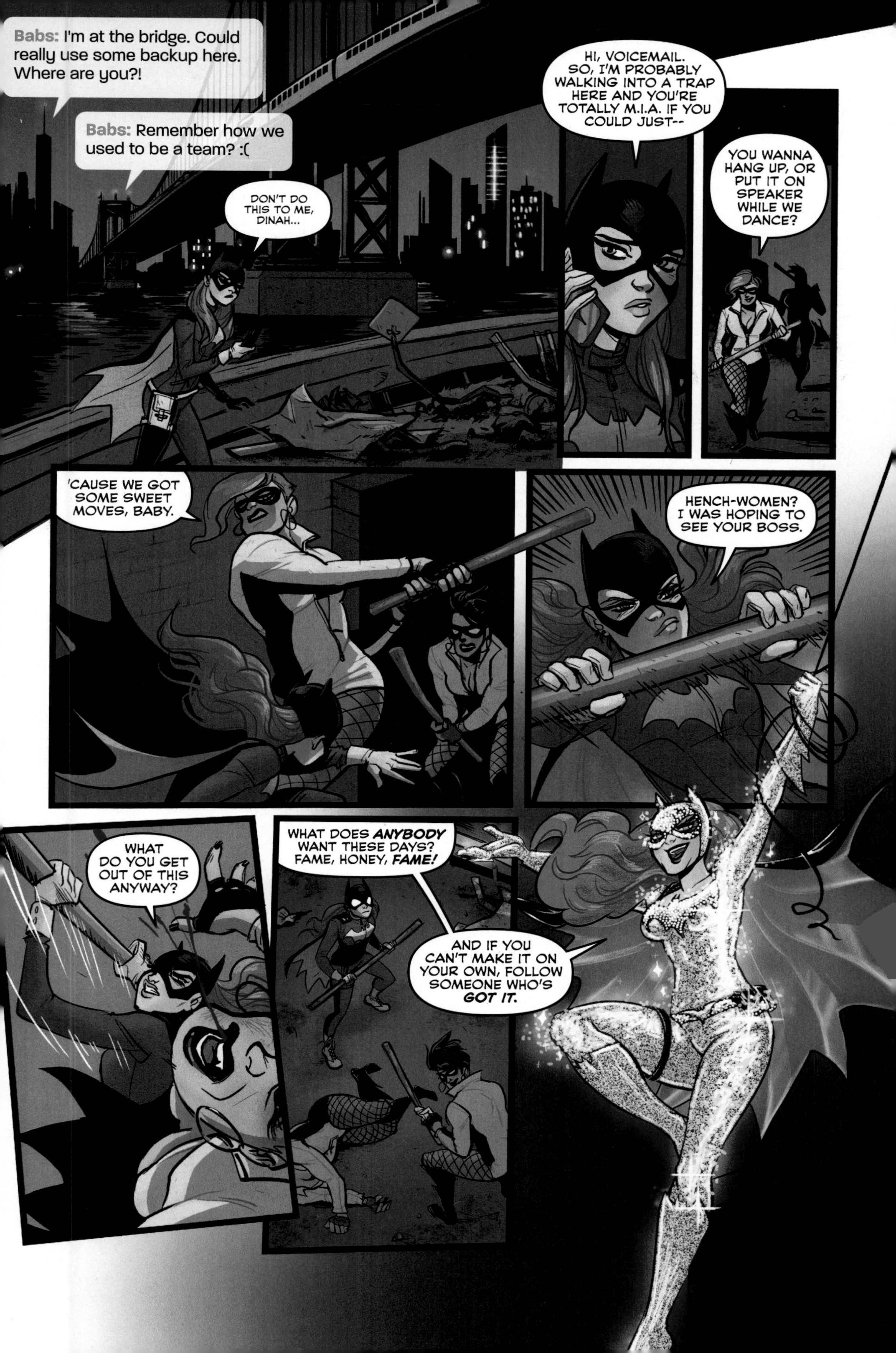
Babs: I'm at the bridge. Could really use some backup here. Where are you?!
Babs: Remember how we used to be a team? :(
DON'T DO THIS TO ME, DINAH...
HI, VOICEMAIL. SO, I'M PROBABLY WALKING INTO A TRAP HERE AND YOU'RE TOTALLY M.I.A. IF YOU COULD JUST--
YOU WANNA HANG UP, OR PUT IT ON SPEAKER WHILE WE DANCE?
'CAUSE WE GOT SOME SWEET MOVES, BABY.
HENCH-WOMEN? I WAS HOPING TO SEE YOUR BOSS.
WHAT DO YOU GET OUT OF THIS ANYWAY?
WHAT DOES ANYBODY WANT THESE DAYS? FAME, HONEY, FAME!
AND IF YOU CAN'T MAKE IT ON YOUR OWN, FOLLOW SOMEONE WHO'S GOT IT.

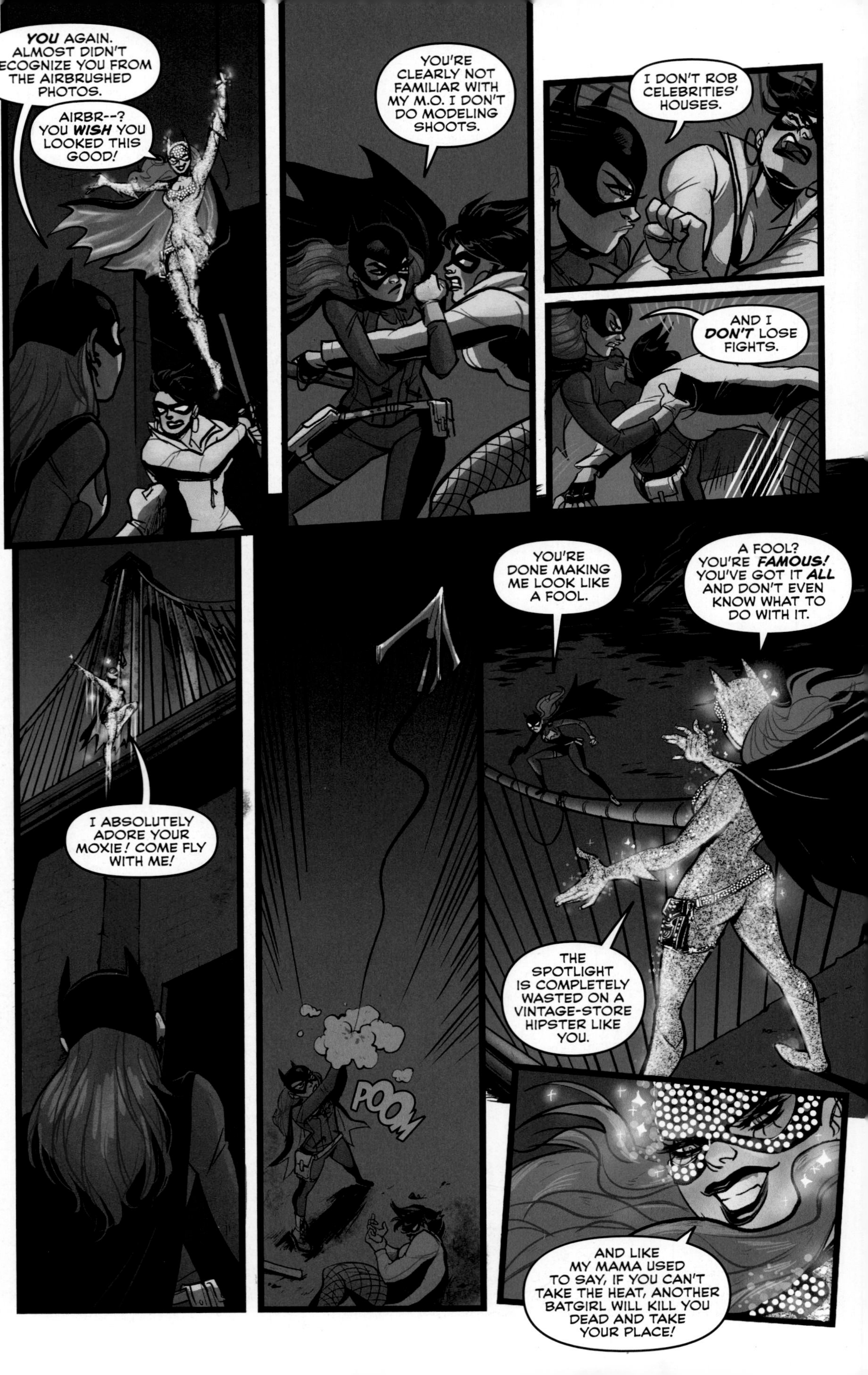
YOU AGAIN. ALMOST DIDN'T RECOGNIZE YOU FROM THE AIRBRUSHED PHOTOS.
AIRBR--? YOU WISH YOU LOOKED THIS GOOD!
YOU'RE CLEARLY NOT FAMILIAR WITH MY M.O. I DON'T DO MODELING SHOOTS.
I DON'T ROB CELEBRITIES' HOUSES.
AND I DON'T LOSE FIGHTS.
I ABSOLUTELY ADORE YOUR MOXIE! COME FLY WITH ME!
POOM
YOU'RE DONE MAKING ME LOOK LIKE A FOOL.
A FOOL? YOU'RE FAMOUS! YOU'VE GOT IT ALL AND DON'T EVEN KNOW WHAT TO DO WITH IT.
THE SPOTLIGHT IS COMPLETELY WASTED ON A VINTAGE-STORE HIPSTER LIKE YOU.
AND LIKE MY MAMA USED TO SAY, IF YOU CAN'T TAKE THE HEAT, ANOTHER BATGIRL WILL KILL YOU DEAD AND TAKE YOUR PLACE!

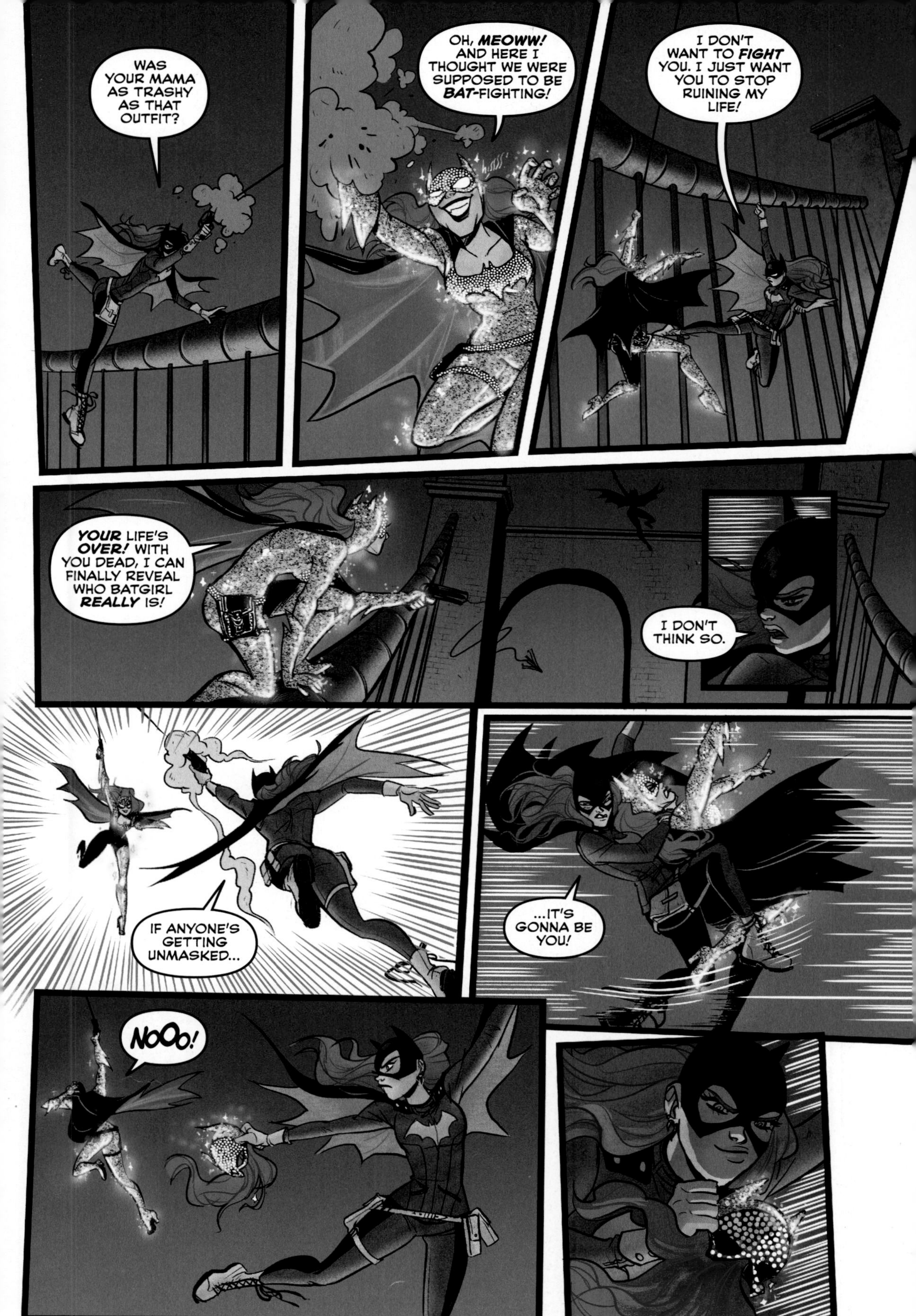
WAS YOUR MAMA AS TRASHY AS THAT OUTFIT?
OH, MEOWW! AND HERE I THOUGHT WE WERE SUPPOSED TO BE BAT-FIGHTING!
I DON'T WANT TO FIGHT YOU. I JUST WANT YOU TO STOP RUINING MY LIFE!
YOUR LIFE'S OVER! WITH YOU DEAD, I CAN FINALLY REVEAL WHO BATGIRL REALLY IS!
I DON'T THINK SO.
IF ANYONE'S GETTING UNMASKED...
...IT'S GONNA BE YOU!
NOOO!

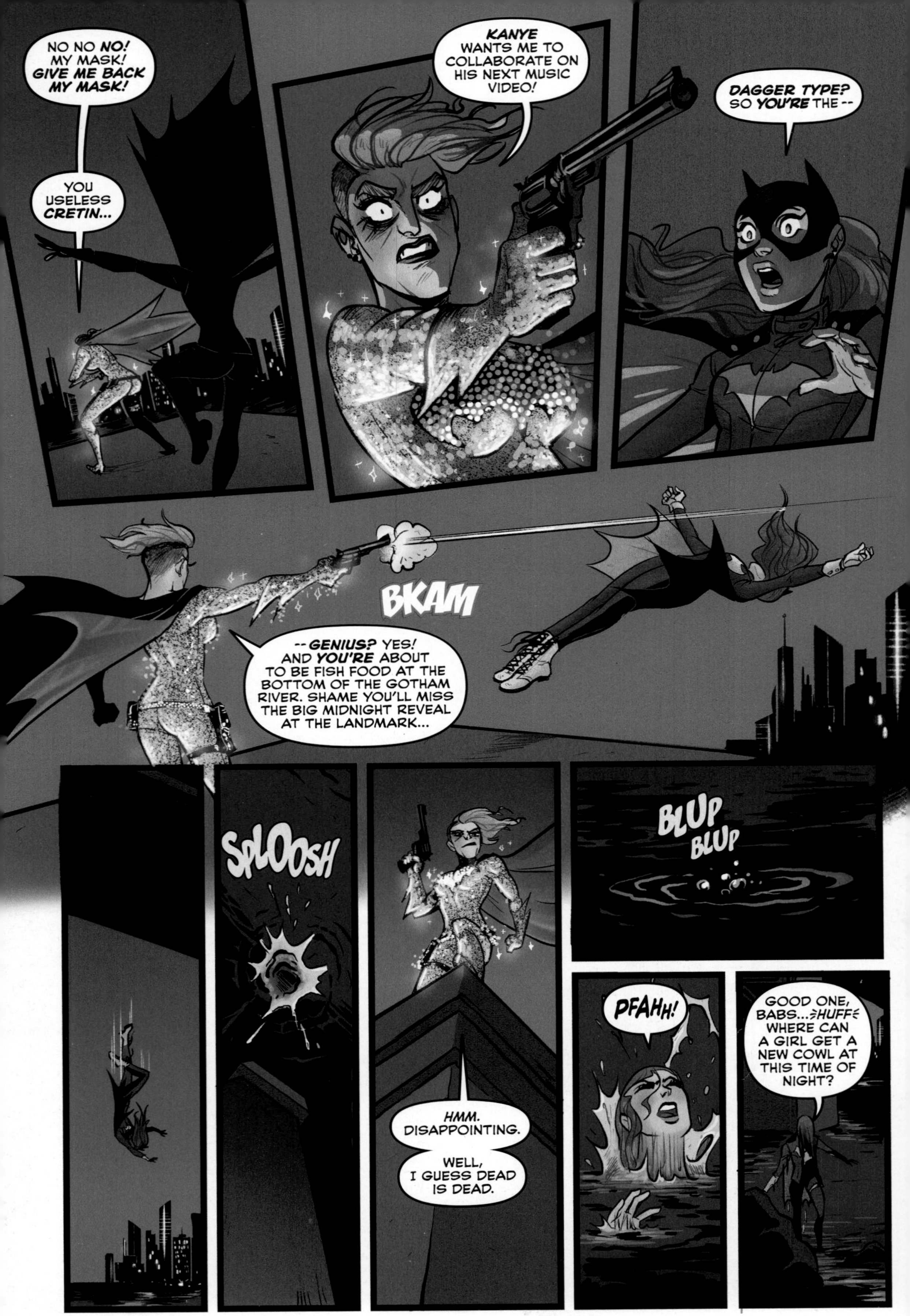
NO NO NO! MY MASK! GIVE ME BACK MY MASK!
YOU USELESS CRETIN...
KANYE WANTS ME TO COLLABORATE ON HIS NEXT MUSIC VIDEO!
DAGGER TYPE? SO YOU'RE THE --
BKAM
--GENIUS? YES! AND YOU'RE ABOUT TO BE FISH FOOD AT THE BOTTOM OF THE GOTHAM RIVER. SHAME YOU'LL MISS THE BIG MIDNIGHT REVEAL AT THE LANDMARK...
SPLOOSH
HMM. DISAPPOINTING.
WELL, I GUESS DEAD IS DEAD.
BLUP BLUP
PFAHH!
GOOD ONE, BABS... HUFF WHERE CAN A GIRL GET A NEW COWL AT THIS TIME OF NIGHT?

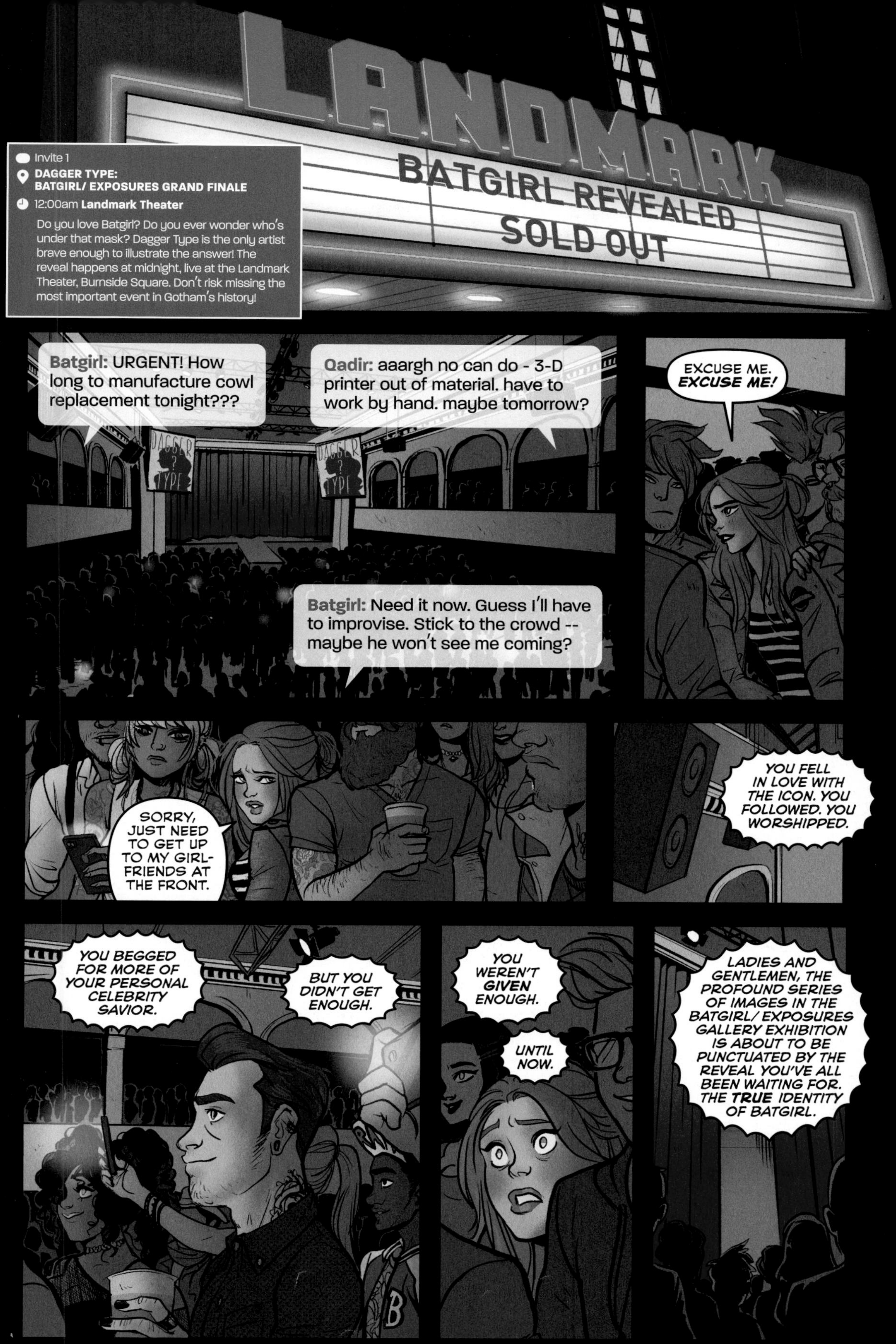
LANDMARK
BATGIRL REVEALED
SOLD OUT
Invite 1
DAGGER TYPE:
BATGIRL/ EXPOSURES GRAND FINALE
12:00am Landmark Theater
Do you love Batgirl? Do you ever wonder who's under that mask? Dagger Type is the only artist brave enough to illustrate the answer! The reveal happens at midnight, live at the Landmark Theater, Burnside Square. Don't risk missing the most important event in Gotham's history!
Batgirl: URGENT! How long to manufacture cowl replacement tonight???
Qadir: aaargh no can do - 3-D printer out of material. have to work by hand. maybe tomorrow?
DAGGER ? TYPE
Batgirl: Need it now. Guess I'll have to improvise. Stick to the crowd -- maybe he won't see me coming?
EXCUSE ME. EXCUSE ME!
SORRY, JUST NEED TO GET UP TO MY GIRLFRIENDS AT THE FRONT.
YOU FELL IN LOVE WITH THE ICON. YOU FOLLOWED. YOU WORSHIPPED.
YOU BEGGED FOR MORE OF YOUR PERSONAL CELEBRITY SAVIOR.
BUT YOU DIDN'T GET ENOUGH.
YOU WEREN'T GIVEN ENOUGH.
UNTIL NOW.
LADIES AND GENTLEMEN, THE PROFOUND SERIES OF IMAGES IN THE BATGIRL/ EXPOSURES GALLERY EXHIBITION IS ABOUT TO BE PUNCTUATED BY THE REVEAL YOU'VE ALL BEEN WAITING FOR. THE TRUE IDENTITY OF BATGIRL.

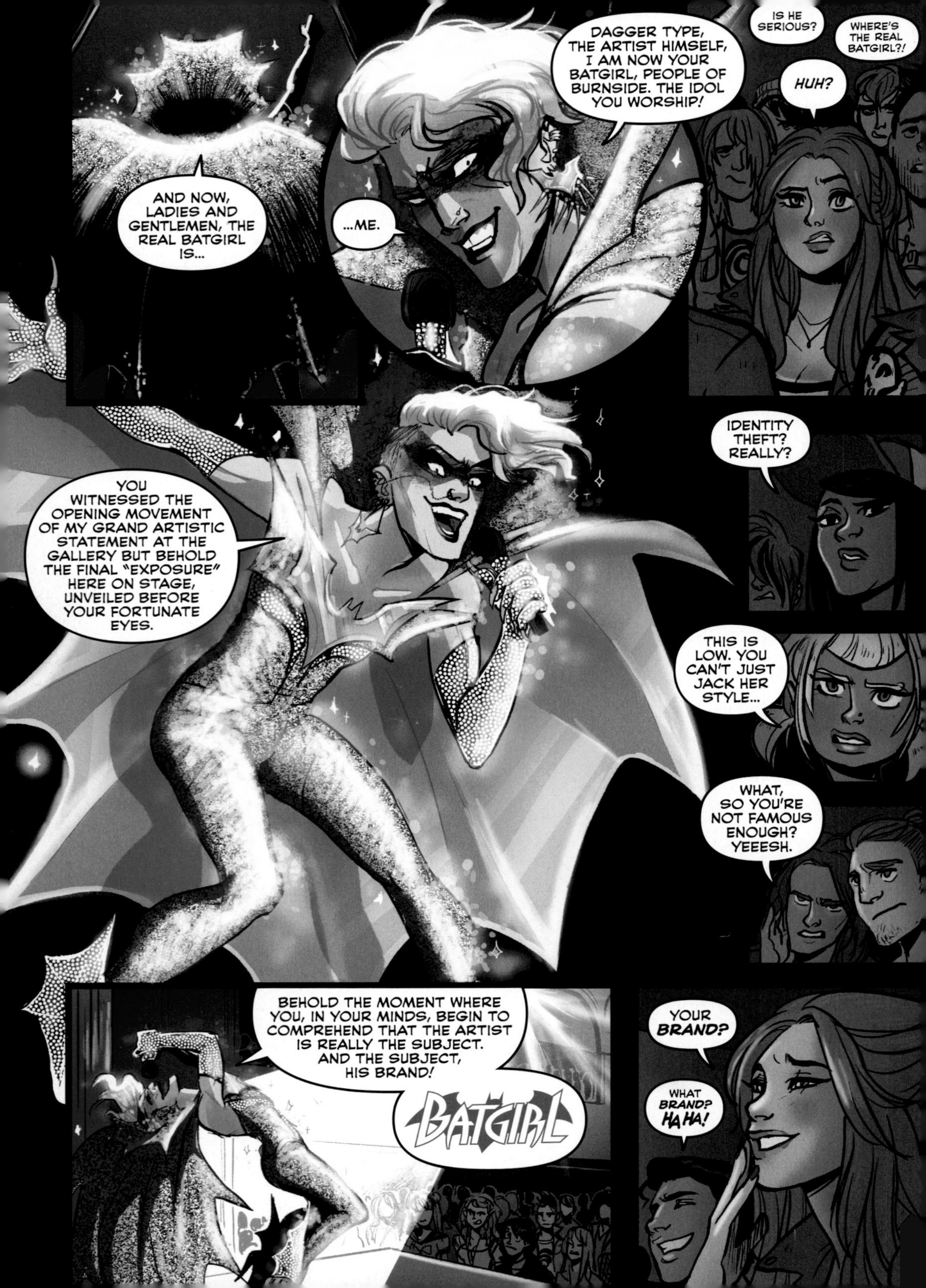
AND NOW, LADIES AND GENTLEMEN, THE REAL BATGIRL IS...
...ME.
DAGGER TYPE, THE ARTIST HIMSELF, I AM NOW YOUR BATGIRL, PEOPLE OF BURNSIDE. THE IDOL YOU WORSHIP!
IS HE SERIOUS?
WHERE'S THE REAL BATGIRL?!
HUH?
YOU WITNESSED THE OPENING MOVEMENT OF MY GRAND ARTISTIC STATEMENT AT THE GALLERY BUT BEHOLD THE FINAL "EXPOSURE" HERE ON STAGE, UNVEILED BEFORE YOUR FORTUNATE EYES.
IDENTITY THEFT? REALLY?
THIS IS LOW. YOU CAN'T JUST JACK HER STYLE...
WHAT, SO YOU'RE NOT FAMOUS ENOUGH? YEEESH.
BEHOLD THE MOMENT WHERE YOU, IN YOUR MINDS, BEGIN TO COMPREHEND THAT THE ARTIST IS REALLY THE SUBJECT. AND THE SUBJECT, HIS BRAND!
BATGIRL
YOUR BRAND?
WHAT BRAND? HA HA!

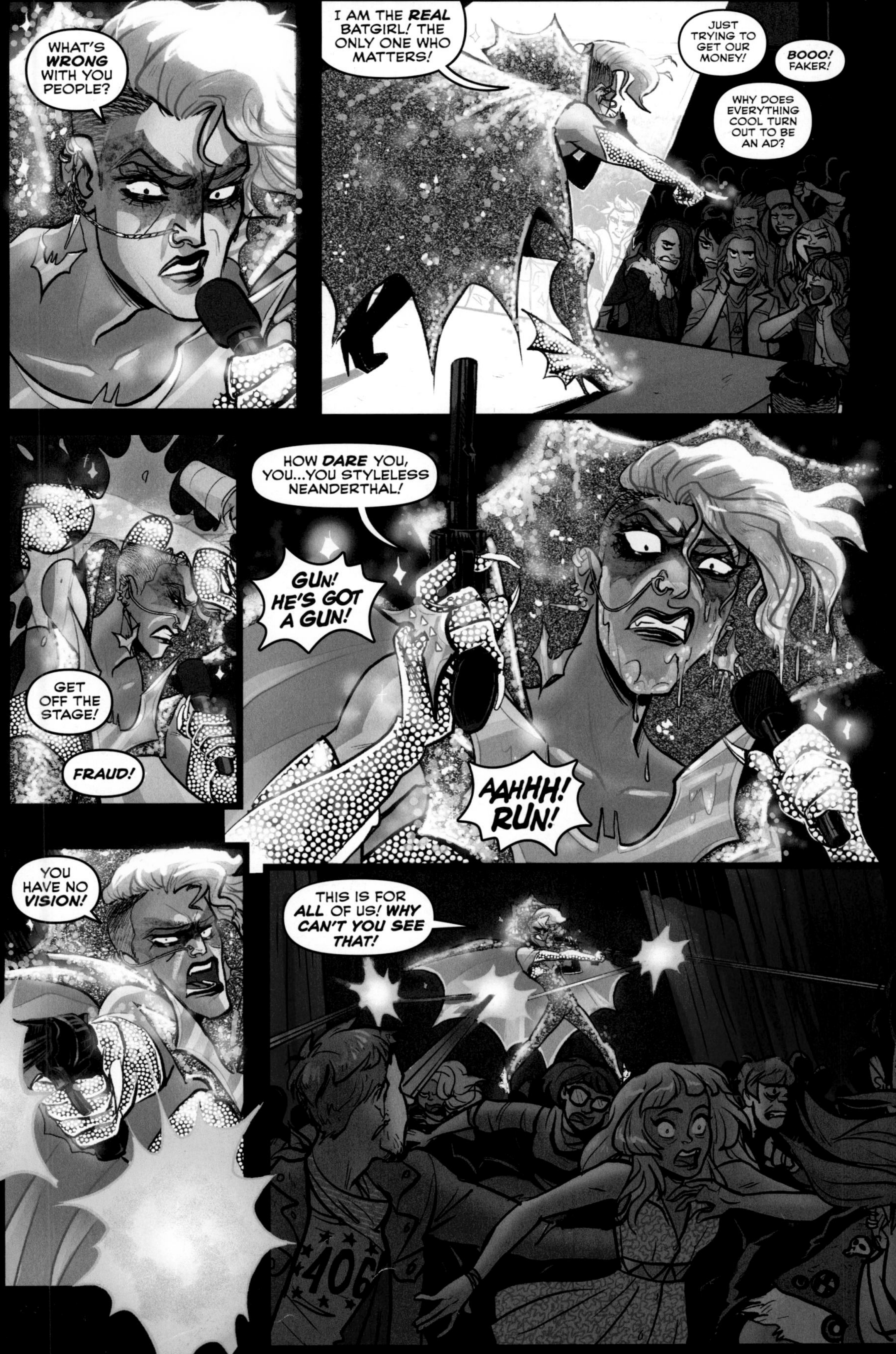
WHAT'S WRONG WITH YOU PEOPLE?
I AM THE REAL BATGIRL! THE ONLY ONE WHO MATTERS!
JUST TRYING TO GET OUR MONEY!
BOOO! FAKER!
WHY DOES EVERYTHING COOL TURN OUT TO BE AN AD?
GET OFF THE STAGE!
FRAUD!
HOW DARE YOU, YOU...YOU STYLELESS NEANDERTHAL!
GUN! HE'S GOT A GUN!
AAHHH! RUN!
YOU HAVE NO VISION!
THIS IS FOR ALL OF US! WHY CAN'T YOU SEE THAT!
406

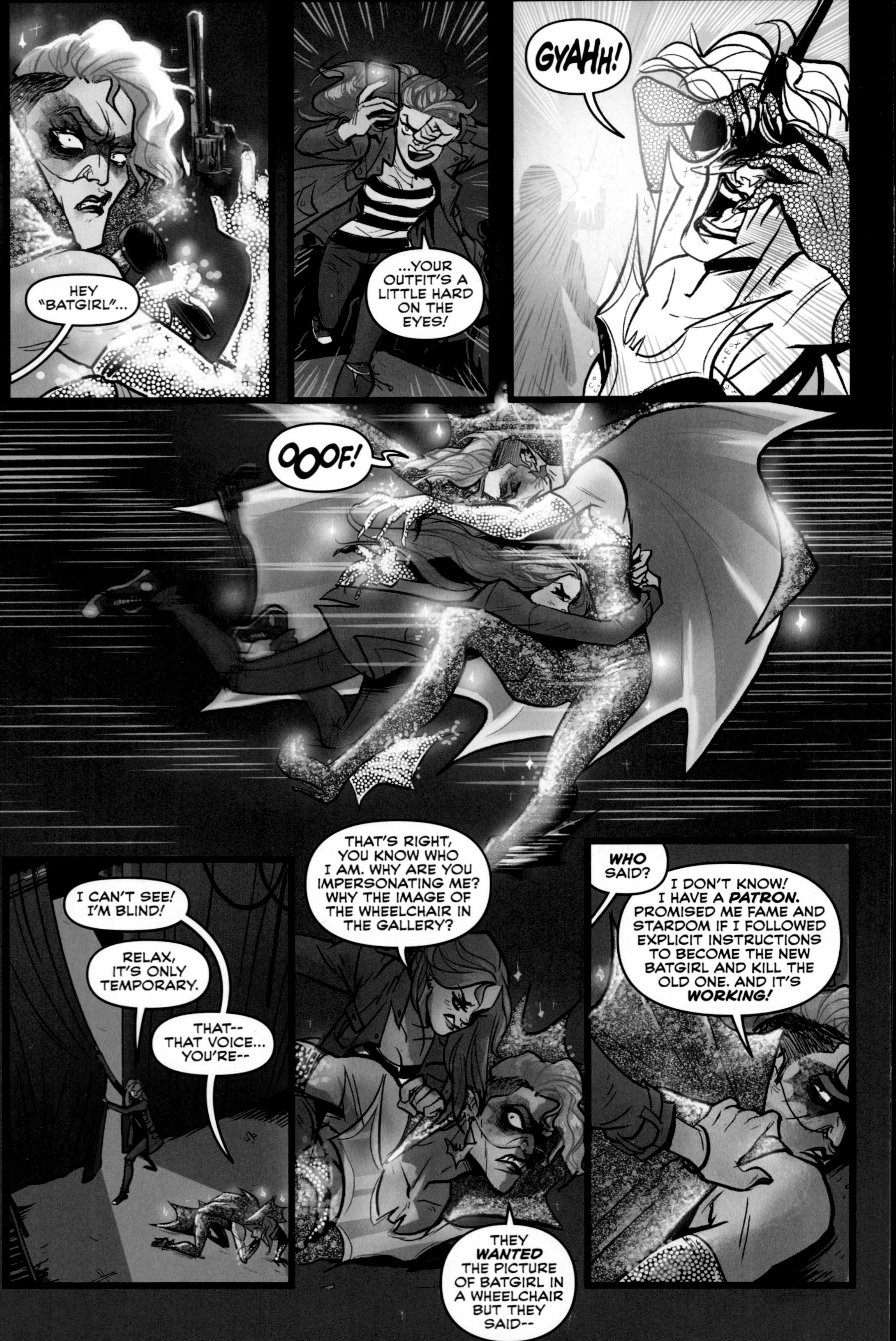
HEY "BATGIRL"...
...YOUR OUTFIT'S A LITTLE HARD ON THE EYES!
GYAHH!
OOOF!
I CAN'T SEE! I'M BLIND!
RELAX, IT'S ONLY TEMPORARY.
THAT-- THAT VOICE... YOU'RE--
THAT'S RIGHT, YOU KNOW WHO I AM. WHY ARE YOU IMPERSONATING ME? WHY THE IMAGE OF THE WHEELCHAIR IN THE GALLERY?
THEY WANTED THE PICTURE OF BATGIRL IN A WHEELCHAIR BUT THEY SAID--
WHO SAID?
I DON'T KNOW! I HAVE A PATRON. PROMISED ME FAME AND STARDOM IF I FOLLOWED EXPLICIT INSTRUCTIONS TO BECOME THE NEW BATGIRL AND KILL THE OLD ONE. AND IT'S WORKING!

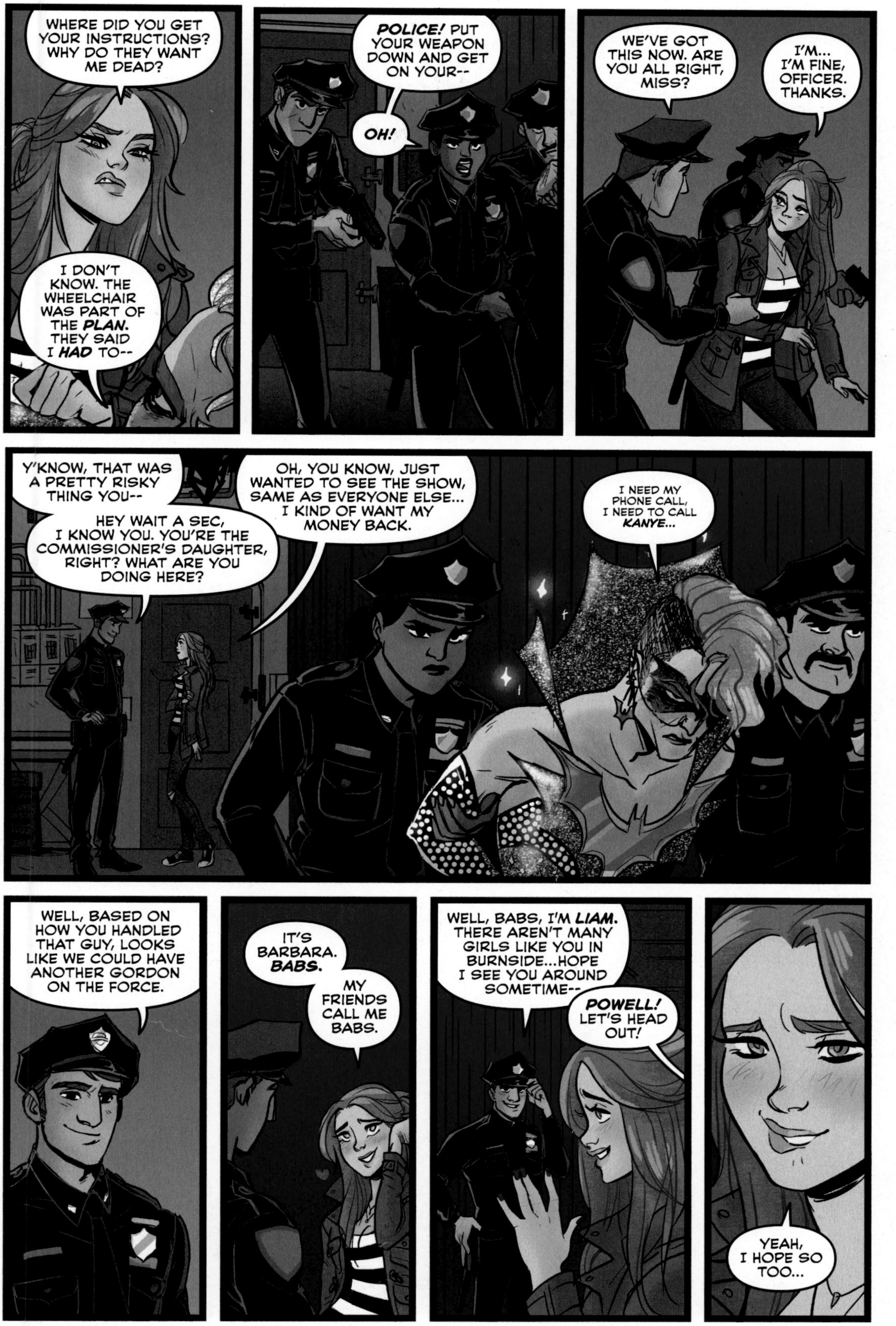
WHERE DID YOU GET YOUR INSTRUCTIONS? WHY DO THEY WANT ME DEAD?
I DON'T KNOW. THE WHEELCHAIR WAS PART OF THE *PLAN.* THEY SAID I *HAD* TO--
POLICE! PUT YOUR WEAPON DOWN AND GET ON YOUR--
OH!
WE'VE GOT THIS NOW. ARE YOU ALL RIGHT, MISS?
I'M... I'M FINE, OFFICER. THANKS.
Y'KNOW, THAT WAS A PRETTY RISKY THING YOU--
HEY WAIT A SEC, I KNOW YOU. YOU'RE THE COMMISSIONER'S DAUGHTER, RIGHT? WHAT ARE YOU DOING HERE?
OH, YOU KNOW, JUST WANTED TO SEE THE SHOW, SAME AS EVERYONE ELSE... I KIND OF WANT MY MONEY BACK.
I NEED MY PHONE CALL, I NEED TO CALL *KANYE...*
WELL, BASED ON HOW YOU HANDLED THAT GUY, LOOKS LIKE WE COULD HAVE ANOTHER GORDON ON THE FORCE.
IT'S BARBARA. *BABS.*
MY FRIENDS CALL ME BABS.
WELL, BABS, I'M *LIAM.* THERE AREN'T MANY GIRLS LIKE YOU IN BURNSIDE...HOPE I SEE YOU AROUND SOMETIME--
POWELL! LET'S HEAD OUT!
YEAH, I HOPE SO TOO...

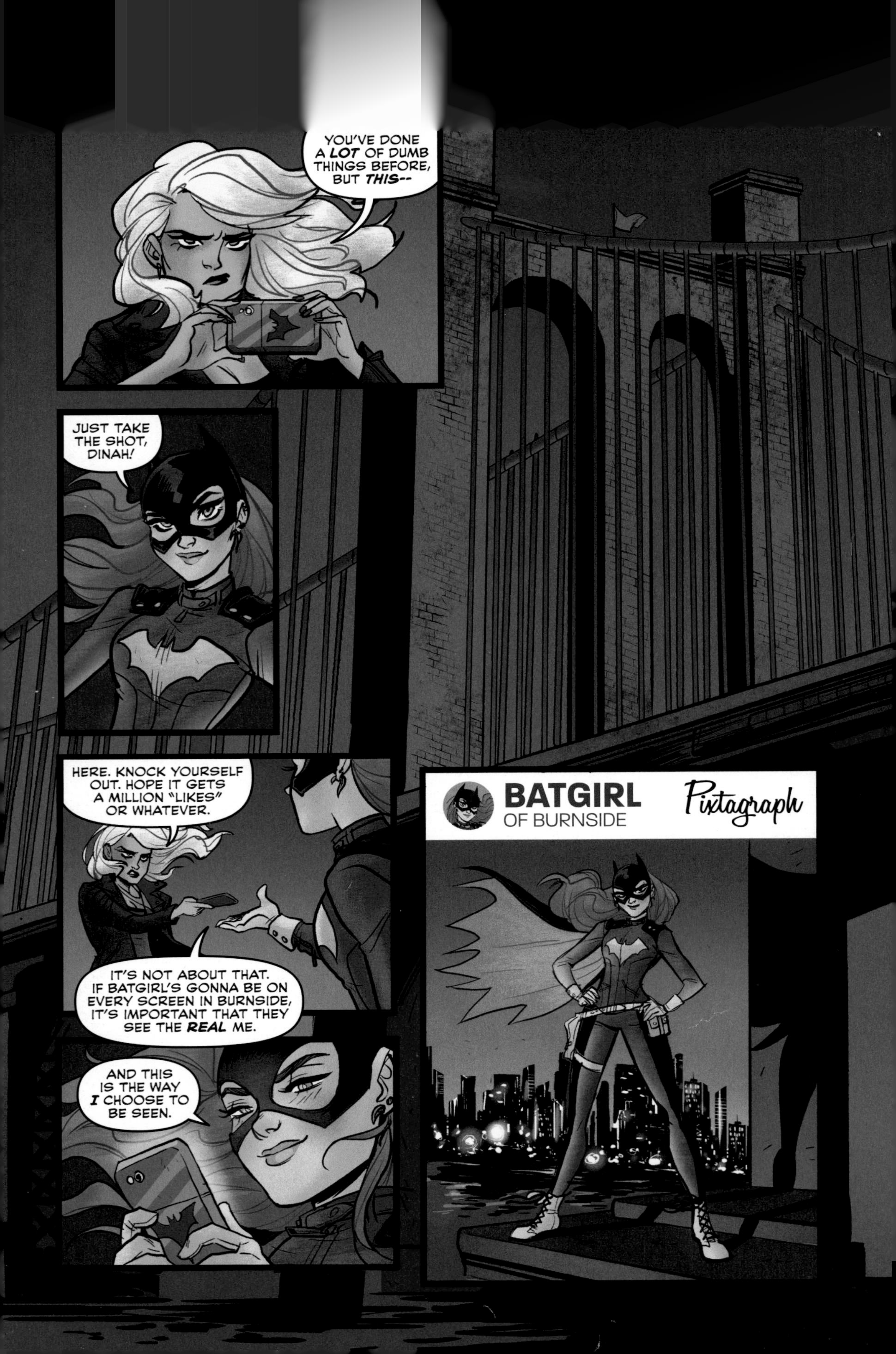
YOU'VE DONE A LOT OF DUMB THINGS BEFORE, BUT THIS--
JUST TAKE THE SHOT, DINAH!
HERE. KNOCK YOURSELF OUT. HOPE IT GETS A MILLION "LIKES" OR WHATEVER.
IT'S NOT ABOUT THAT. IF BATGIRL'S GONNA BE ON EVERY SCREEN IN BURNSIDE, IT'S IMPORTANT THAT THEY SEE THE REAL ME.
AND THIS IS THE WAY I CHOOSE TO BE SEEN.
BATGIRL OF BURNSIDE
Pixtagraph

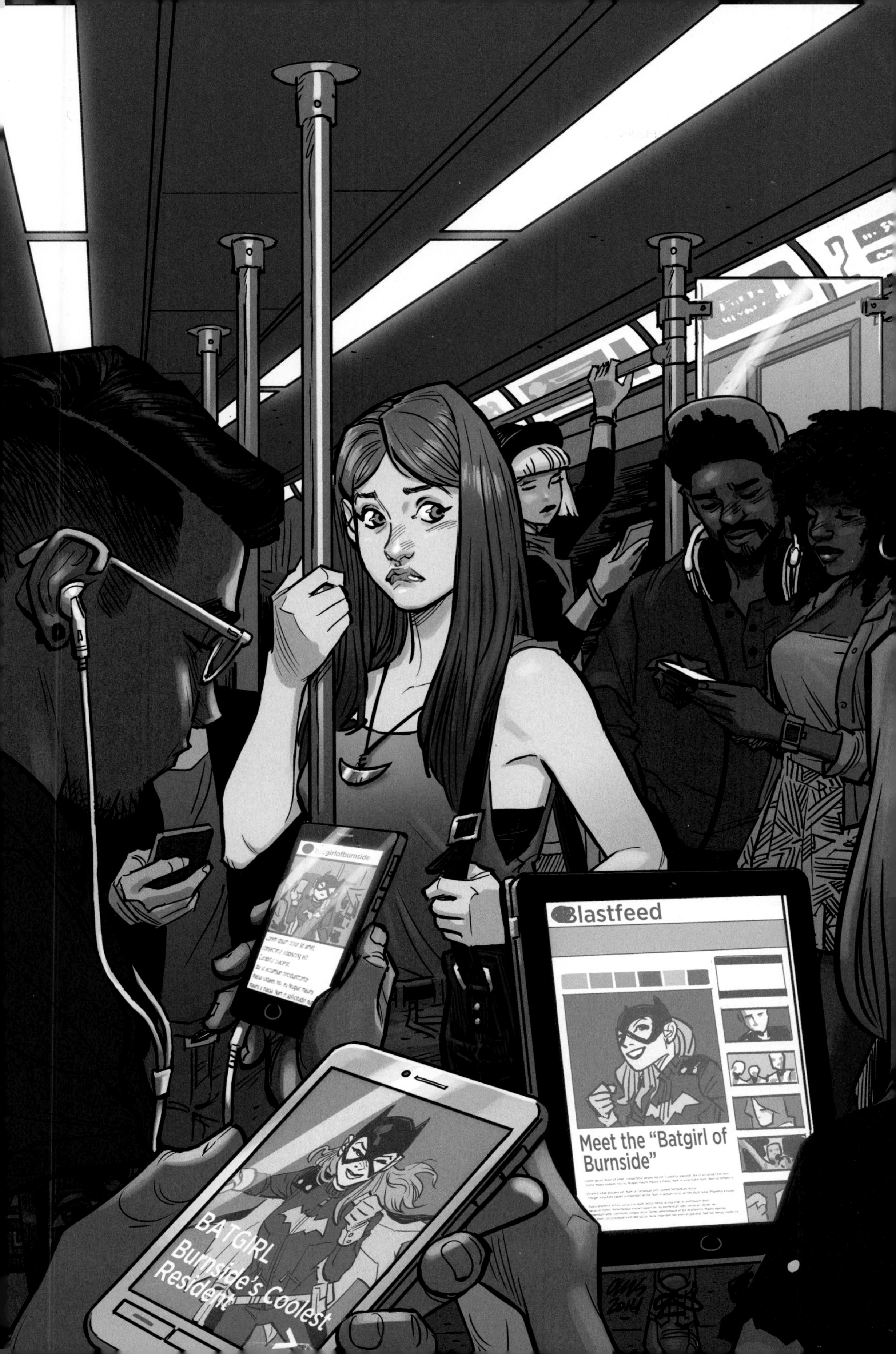

batgirlofburnside
Blastfeed
Meet the “Batgirl of Burnside”
BATGIRL
Burnside's Coolest Resident

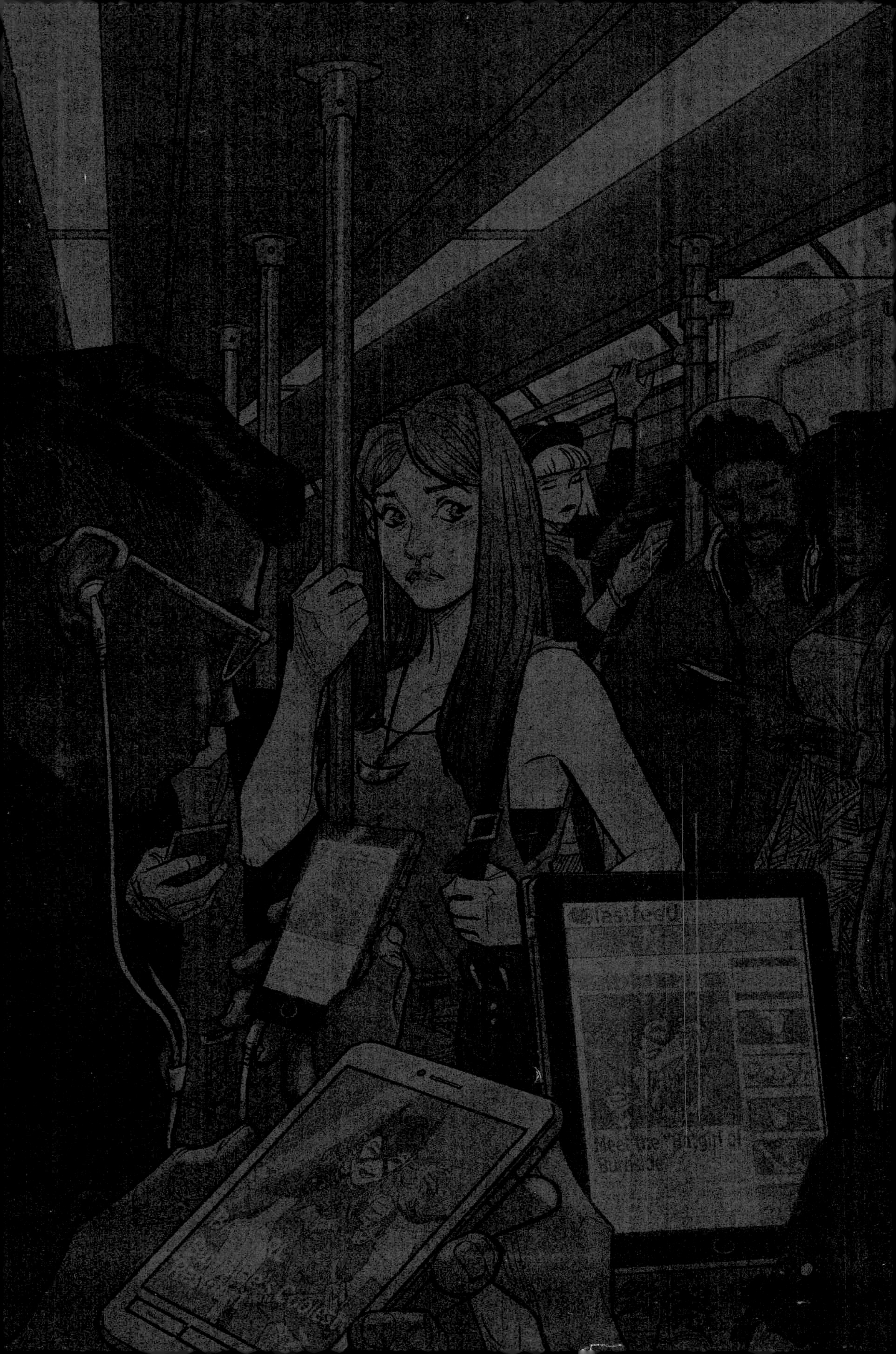

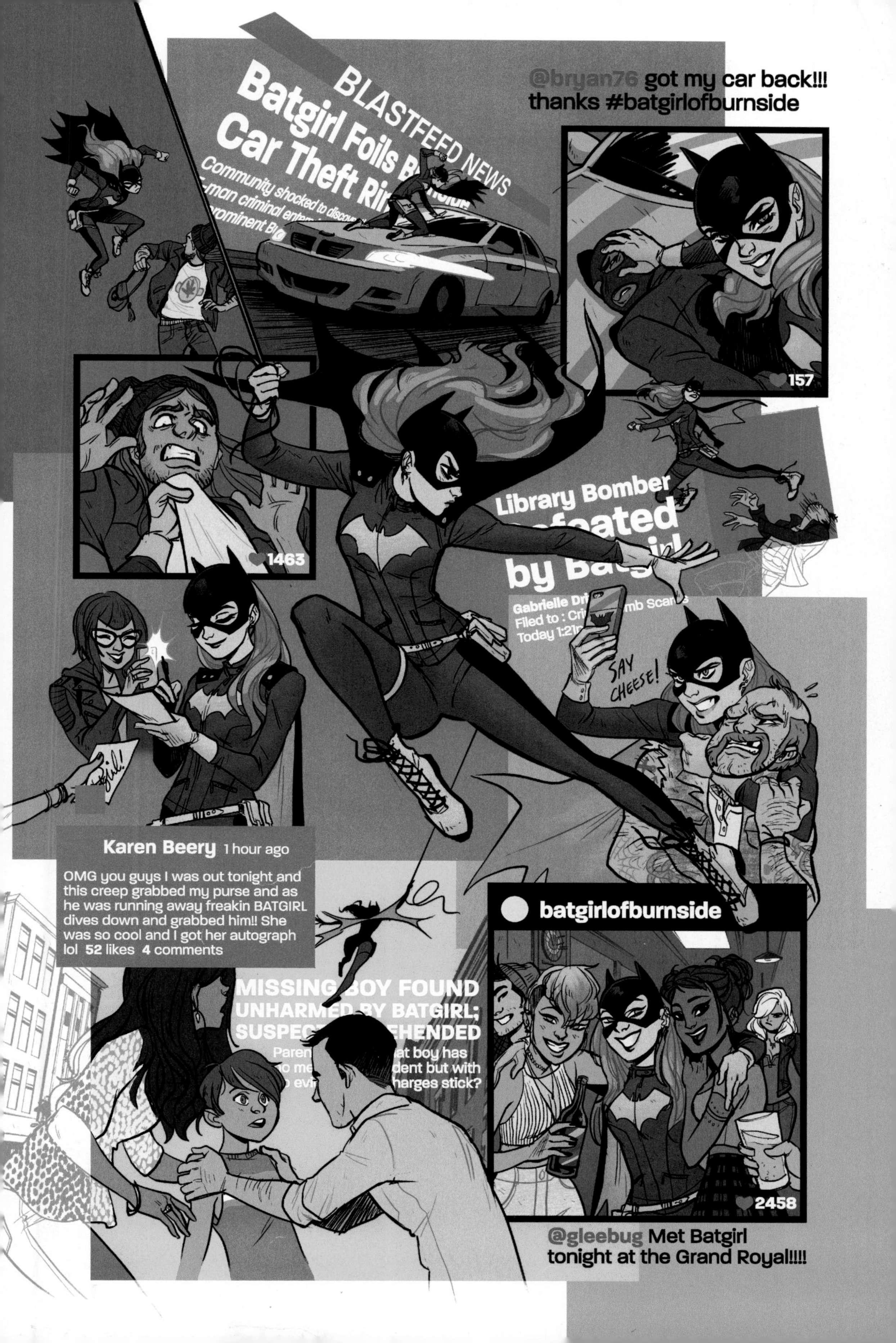

@bryan76 got my car back!!!
thanks #batgirlofburnside
BLASTFEED NEWS
Batgirl Foils
Car Theft
157
1463
Library Bomber
SAY CHEESE!
Karen Beery 1 hour ago
OMG you guys I was out tonight and this creep grabbed my purse and as he was running away freakin BATGIRL dives down and grabbed him!! She was so cool and I got her autograph lol 52 likes 4 comments
MISSING BOY FOUND
batgirlofburnside
2458
@gleebug Met Batgirl tonight at the Grand Royal!!!!

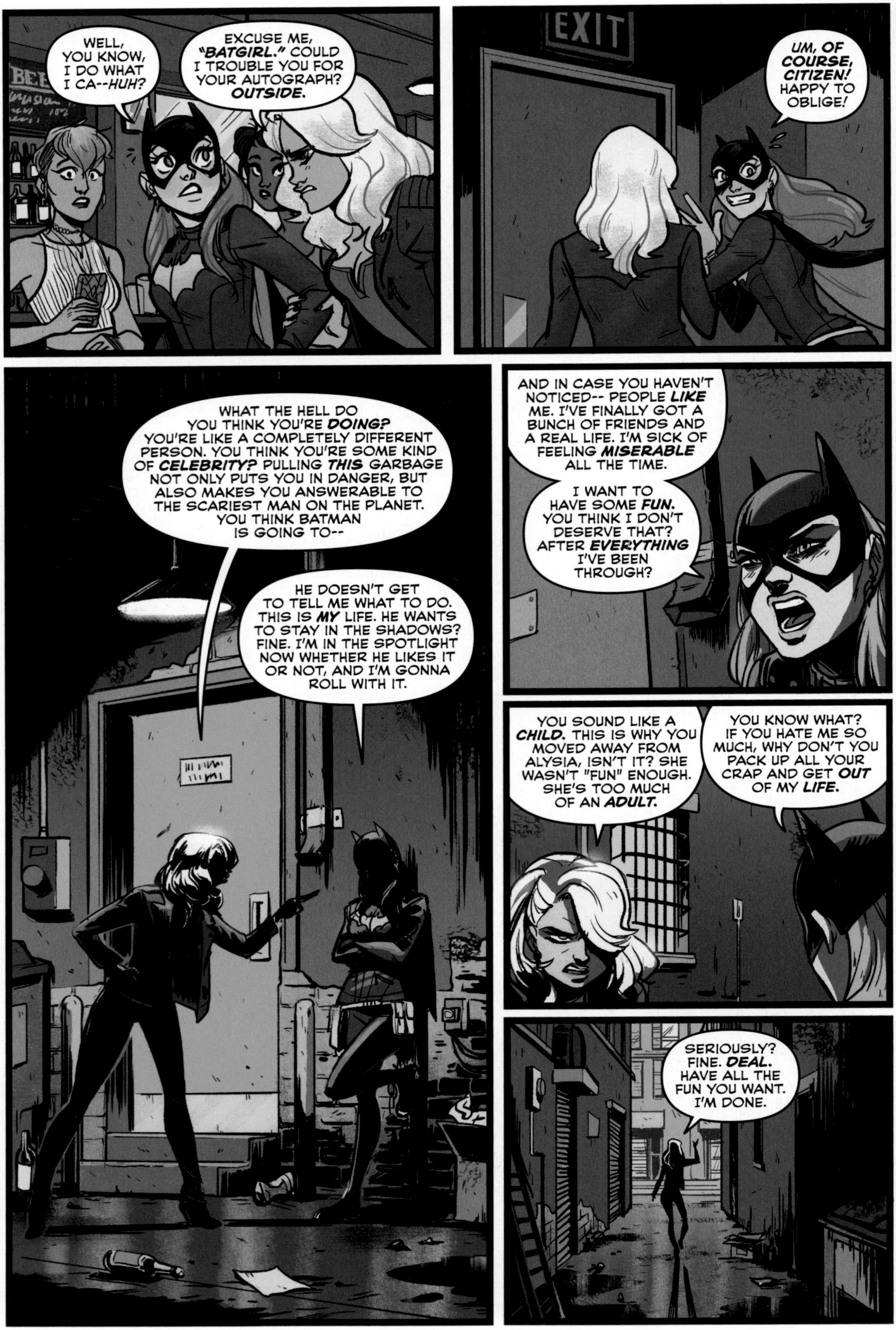

WELL, YOU KNOW, I DO WHAT I CA--HUH?
EXCUSE ME, "BATGIRL." COULD I TROUBLE YOU FOR YOUR AUTOGRAPH? OUTSIDE.
EXIT
UM, OF COURSE, CITIZEN! HAPPY TO OBLIGE!
WHAT THE HELL DO YOU THINK YOU'RE DOING? YOU'RE LIKE A COMPLETELY DIFFERENT PERSON. YOU THINK YOU'RE SOME KIND OF CELEBRITY? PULLING THIS GARBAGE NOT ONLY PUTS YOU IN DANGER, BUT ALSO MAKES YOU ANSWERABLE TO THE SCARIEST MAN ON THE PLANET. YOU THINK BATMAN IS GOING TO--
HE DOESN'T GET TO TELL ME WHAT TO DO. THIS IS MY LIFE. HE WANTS TO STAY IN THE SHADOWS? FINE. I'M IN THE SPOTLIGHT NOW WHETHER HE LIKES IT OR NOT, AND I'M GONNA ROLL WITH IT.
AND IN CASE YOU HAVEN'T NOTICED-- PEOPLE LIKE ME. I'VE FINALLY GOT A BUNCH OF FRIENDS AND A REAL LIFE. I'M SICK OF FEELING MISERABLE ALL THE TIME.
I WANT TO HAVE SOME FUN. YOU THINK I DON'T DESERVE THAT? AFTER EVERYTHING I'VE BEEN THROUGH?
YOU SOUND LIKE A CHILD. THIS IS WHY YOU MOVED AWAY FROM ALYSIA, ISN'T IT? SHE WASN'T "FUN" ENOUGH. SHE'S TOO MUCH OF AN ADULT.
YOU KNOW WHAT? IF YOU HATE ME SO MUCH, WHY DON'T YOU PACK UP ALL YOUR CRAP AND GET OUT OF MY LIFE.
SERIOUSLY? FINE. DEAL. HAVE ALL THE FUN YOU WANT. I'M DONE.

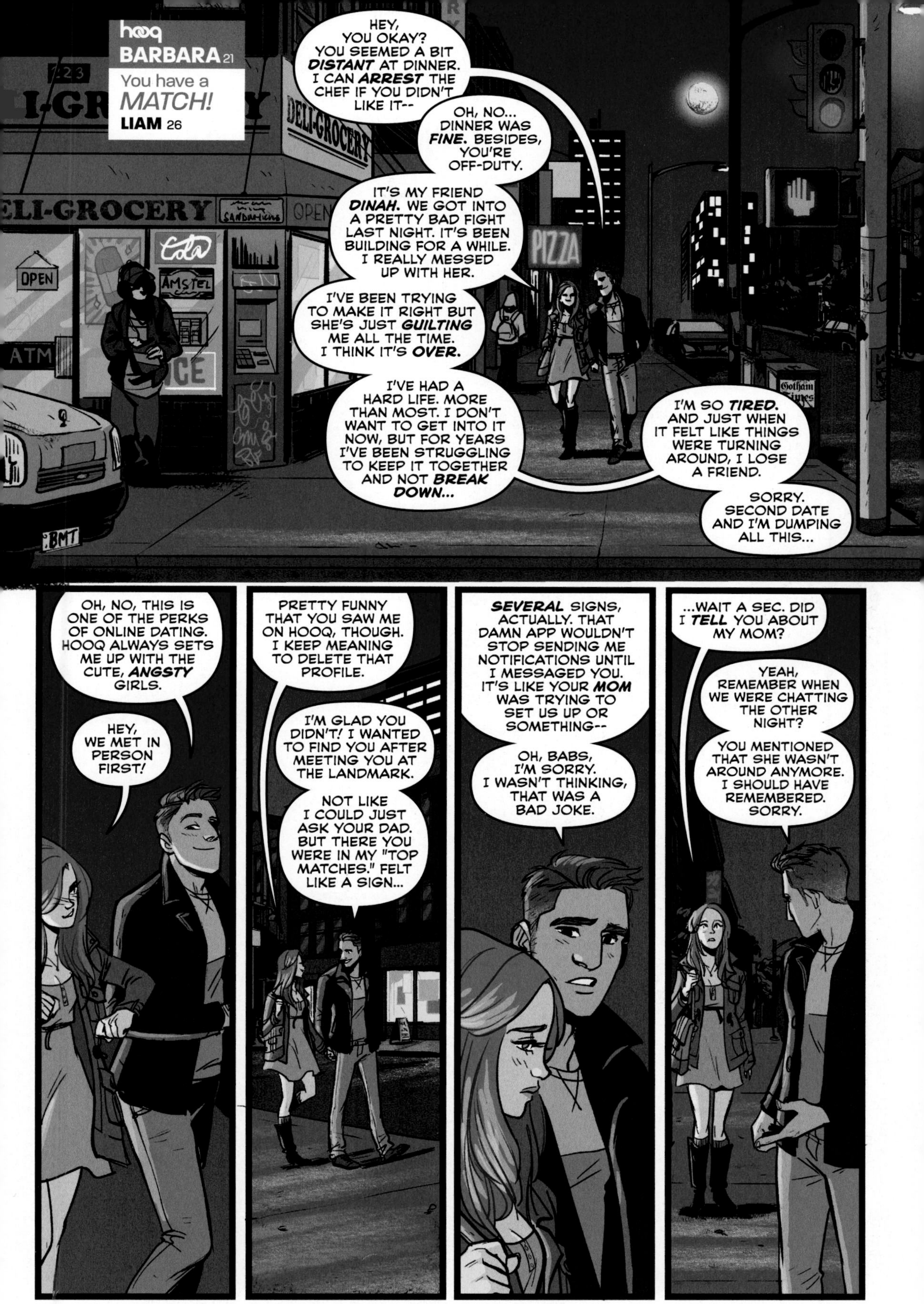

hooq
BARBARA 21
You have a MATCH!
LIAM 26
DELI-GROCERY
PIZZA
OPEN
ATM
HEY, YOU OKAY? YOU SEEMED A BIT DISTANT AT DINNER. I CAN ARREST THE CHEF IF YOU DIDN'T LIKE IT--
OH, NO... DINNER WAS FINE. BESIDES, YOU'RE OFF-DUTY.
IT'S MY FRIEND DINAH. WE GOT INTO A PRETTY BAD FIGHT LAST NIGHT. IT'S BEEN BUILDING FOR A WHILE. I REALLY MESSED UP WITH HER.
I'VE BEEN TRYING TO MAKE IT RIGHT BUT SHE'S JUST GUILTING ME ALL THE TIME. I THINK IT'S OVER.
I'VE HAD A HARD LIFE. MORE THAN MOST. I DON'T WANT TO GET INTO IT NOW, BUT FOR YEARS I'VE BEEN STRUGGLING TO KEEP IT TOGETHER AND NOT BREAK DOWN...
I'M SO TIRED. AND JUST WHEN IT FELT LIKE THINGS WERE TURNING AROUND, I LOSE A FRIEND.
SORRY. SECOND DATE AND I'M DUMPING ALL THIS...
OH, NO, THIS IS ONE OF THE PERKS OF ONLINE DATING. HOOQ ALWAYS SETS ME UP WITH THE CUTE, ANGSTY GIRLS.
HEY, WE MET IN PERSON FIRST!
PRETTY FUNNY THAT YOU SAW ME ON HOOQ, THOUGH. I KEEP MEANING TO DELETE THAT PROFILE.
I'M GLAD YOU DIDN'T! I WANTED TO FIND YOU AFTER MEETING YOU AT THE LANDMARK.
NOT LIKE I COULD JUST ASK YOUR DAD. BUT THERE YOU WERE IN MY "TOP MATCHES." FELT LIKE A SIGN...
SEVERAL SIGNS, ACTUALLY. THAT DAMN APP WOULDN'T STOP SENDING ME NOTIFICATIONS UNTIL I MESSAGED YOU. IT'S LIKE YOUR MOM WAS TRYING TO SET US UP OR SOMETHING--
OH, BABS, I'M SORRY. I WASN'T THINKING, THAT WAS A BAD JOKE.
...WAIT A SEC. DID I TELL YOU ABOUT MY MOM?
YEAH, REMEMBER WHEN WE WERE CHATTING THE OTHER NIGHT?
YOU MENTIONED THAT SHE WASN'T AROUND ANYMORE. I SHOULD HAVE REMEMBERED. SORRY.

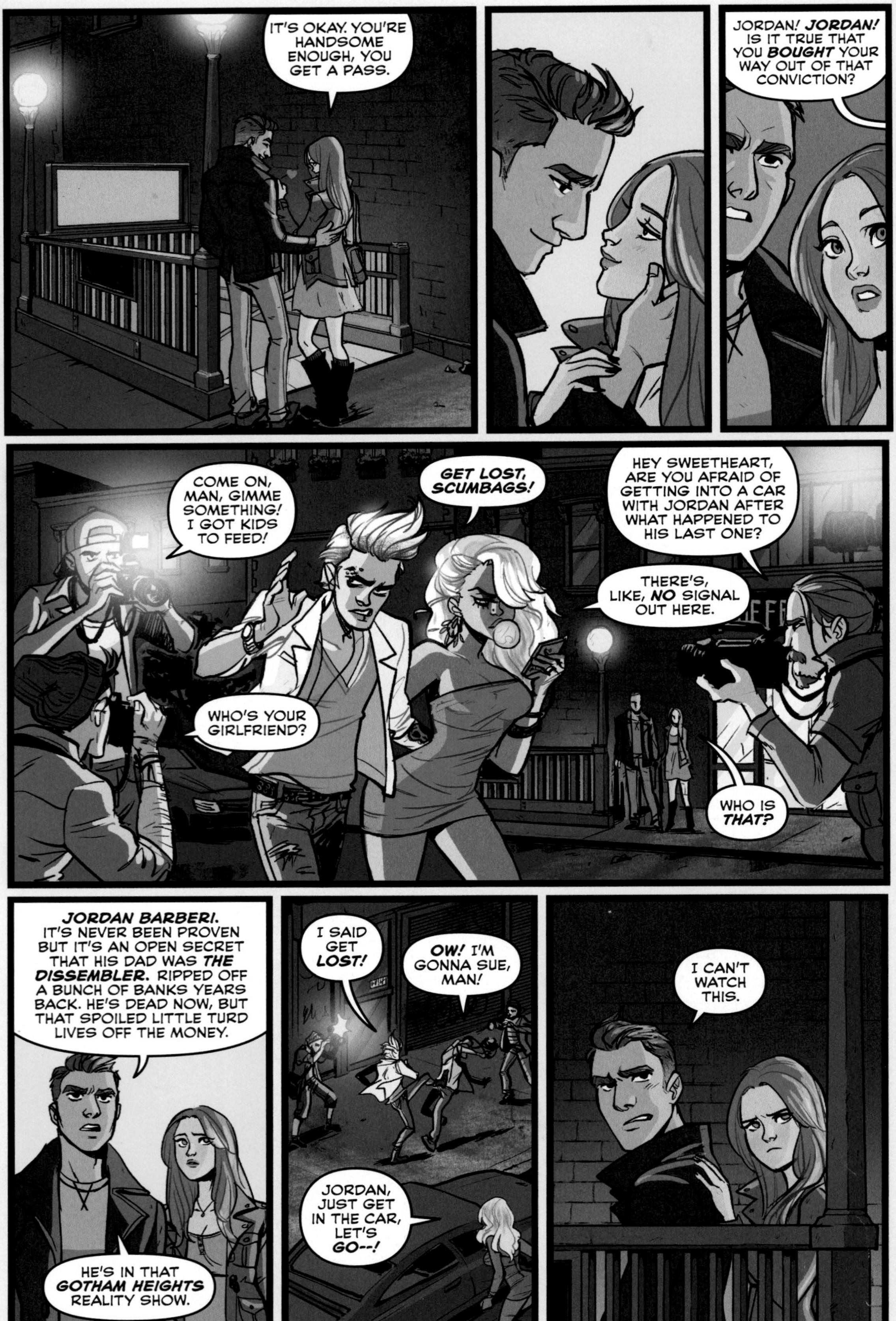

IT'S OKAY. YOU'RE HANDSOME ENOUGH, YOU GET A PASS.
JORDAN! **JORDAN!** IS IT TRUE THAT YOU **BOUGHT** YOUR WAY OUT OF THAT CONVICTION?
COME ON, MAN, GIMME SOMETHING! I GOT KIDS TO FEED!
GET LOST, SCUMBAGS!
HEY SWEETHEART, ARE YOU AFRAID OF GETTING INTO A CAR WITH JORDAN AFTER WHAT HAPPENED TO HIS LAST ONE?
THERE'S, LIKE, **NO** SIGNAL OUT HERE.
WHO'S YOUR GIRLFRIEND?
WHO IS **THAT?**
JORDAN BARBERI. IT'S NEVER BEEN PROVEN BUT IT'S AN OPEN SECRET THAT HIS DAD WAS **THE DISSEMBLER.** RIPPED OFF A BUNCH OF BANKS YEARS BACK. HE'S DEAD NOW, BUT THAT SPOILED LITTLE TURD LIVES OFF THE MONEY.
HE'S IN THAT **GOTHAM HEIGHTS** REALITY SHOW.
I SAID GET **LOST!**
OW! I'M GONNA SUE, MAN!
JORDAN, JUST GET IN THE CAR, LET'S **GO--!**
I CAN'T WATCH THIS.

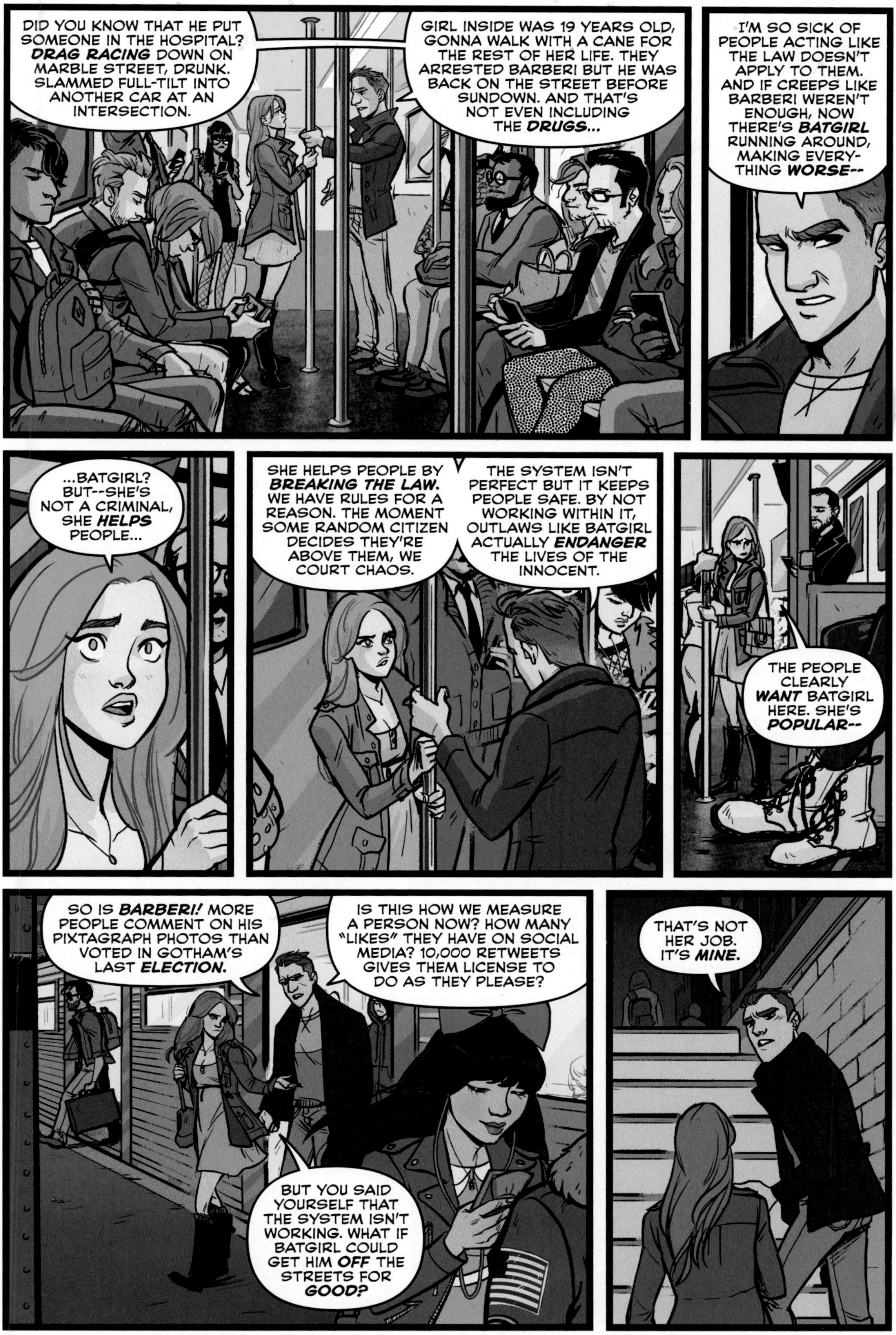

DID YOU KNOW THAT HE PUT SOMEONE IN THE HOSPITAL? DRAG RACING DOWN ON MARBLE STREET, DRUNK. SLAMMED FULL-TILT INTO ANOTHER CAR AT AN INTERSECTION.
GIRL INSIDE WAS 19 YEARS OLD, GONNA WALK WITH A CANE FOR THE REST OF HER LIFE. THEY ARRESTED BARBERI BUT HE WAS BACK ON THE STREET BEFORE SUNDOWN. AND THAT'S NOT EVEN INCLUDING THE DRUGS...
I'M SO SICK OF PEOPLE ACTING LIKE THE LAW DOESN'T APPLY TO THEM. AND IF CREEPS LIKE BARBERI WEREN'T ENOUGH, NOW THERE'S BATGIRL RUNNING AROUND, MAKING EVERYTHING WORSE--
...BATGIRL? BUT--SHE'S NOT A CRIMINAL, SHE HELPS PEOPLE...
SHE HELPS PEOPLE BY BREAKING THE LAW. WE HAVE RULES FOR A REASON. THE MOMENT SOME RANDOM CITIZEN DECIDES THEY'RE ABOVE THEM, WE COURT CHAOS.
THE SYSTEM ISN'T PERFECT BUT IT KEEPS PEOPLE SAFE. BY NOT WORKING WITHIN IT, OUTLAWS LIKE BATGIRL ACTUALLY ENDANGER THE LIVES OF THE INNOCENT.
THE PEOPLE CLEARLY WANT BATGIRL HERE. SHE'S POPULAR--
SO IS BARBERI! MORE PEOPLE COMMENT ON HIS PIXTAGRAPH PHOTOS THAN VOTED IN GOTHAM'S LAST ELECTION.
IS THIS HOW WE MEASURE A PERSON NOW? HOW MANY "LIKES" THEY HAVE ON SOCIAL MEDIA? 10,000 RETWEETS GIVES THEM LICENSE TO DO AS THEY PLEASE?
BUT YOU SAID YOURSELF THAT THE SYSTEM ISN'T WORKING. WHAT IF BATGIRL COULD GET HIM OFF THE STREETS FOR GOOD?
THAT'S NOT HER JOB. IT'S MINE.

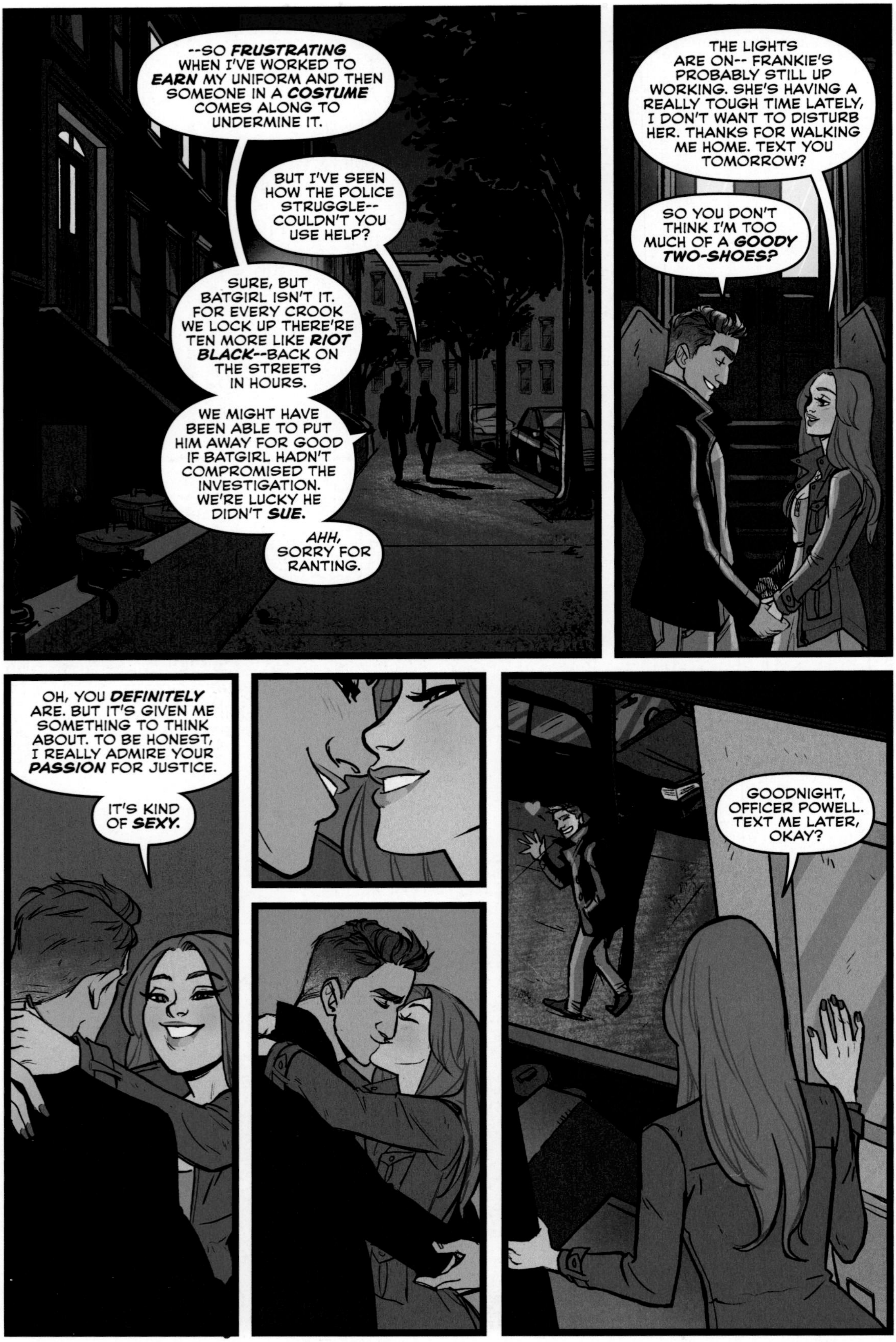
--SO FRUSTRATING WHEN I'VE WORKED TO EARN MY UNIFORM AND THEN SOMEONE IN A COSTUME COMES ALONG TO UNDERMINE IT.
BUT I'VE SEEN HOW THE POLICE STRUGGLE-- COULDN'T YOU USE HELP?
SURE, BUT BATGIRL ISN'T IT. FOR EVERY CROOK WE LOCK UP THERE'RE TEN MORE LIKE RIOT BLACK--BACK ON THE STREETS IN HOURS.
WE MIGHT HAVE BEEN ABLE TO PUT HIM AWAY FOR GOOD IF BATGIRL HADN'T COMPROMISED THE INVESTIGATION. WE'RE LUCKY HE DIDN'T SUE.
AHH, SORRY FOR RANTING.
THE LIGHTS ARE ON-- FRANKIE'S PROBABLY STILL UP WORKING. SHE'S HAVING A REALLY TOUGH TIME LATELY, I DON'T WANT TO DISTURB HER. THANKS FOR WALKING ME HOME. TEXT YOU TOMORROW?
SO YOU DON'T THINK I'M TOO MUCH OF A GOODY TWO-SHOES?
OH, YOU DEFINITELY ARE. BUT IT'S GIVEN ME SOMETHING TO THINK ABOUT. TO BE HONEST, I REALLY ADMIRE YOUR PASSION FOR JUSTICE.
IT'S KIND OF SEXY.
GOODNIGHT, OFFICER POWELL. TEXT ME LATER, OKAY?

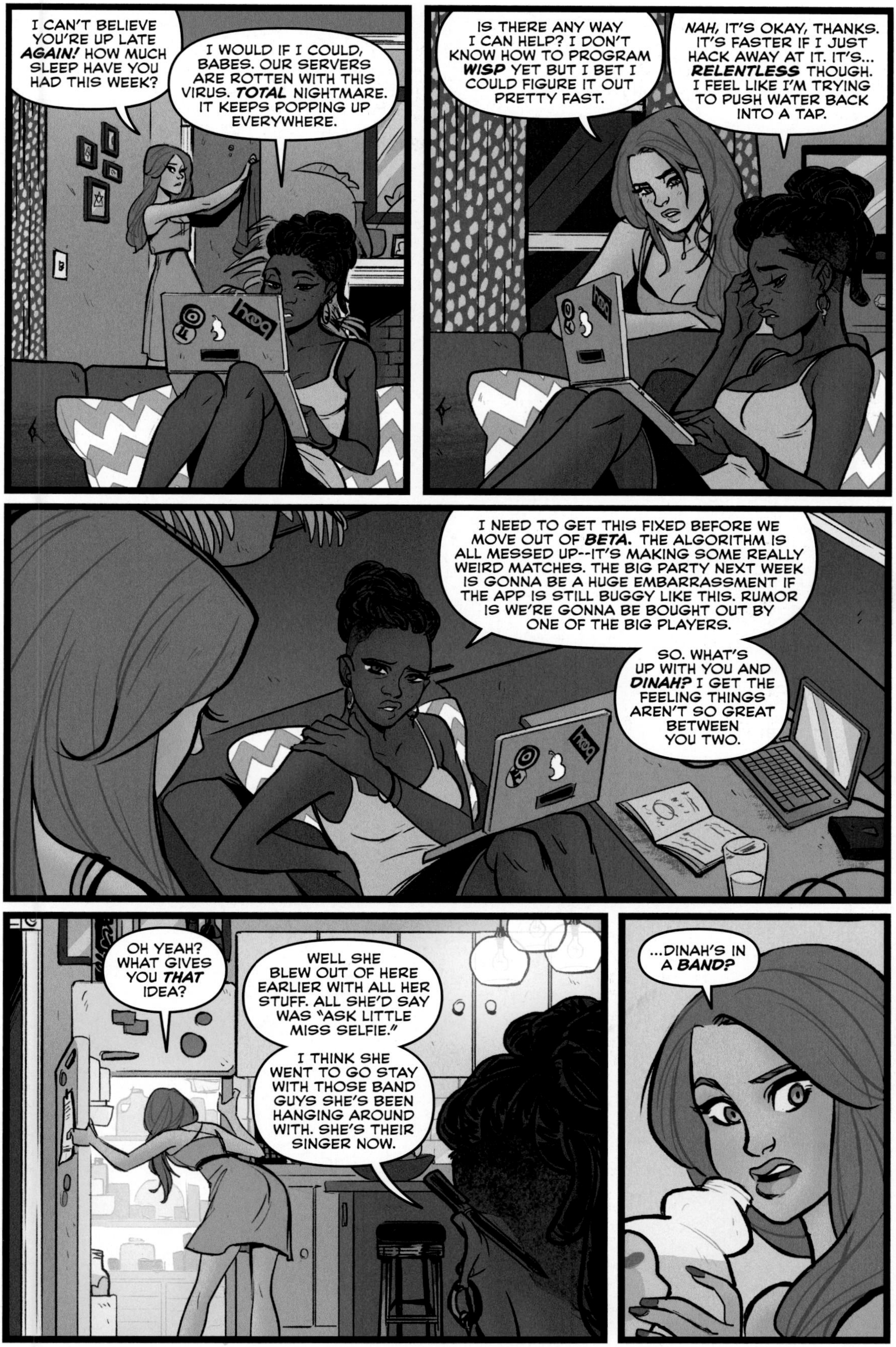
I CAN'T BELIEVE YOU'RE UP LATE *AGAIN!* HOW MUCH SLEEP HAVE YOU HAD THIS WEEK?
I WOULD IF I COULD, BABES. OUR SERVERS ARE ROTTEN WITH THIS VIRUS. *TOTAL* NIGHTMARE. IT KEEPS POPPING UP EVERYWHERE.
IS THERE ANY WAY I CAN HELP? I DON'T KNOW HOW TO PROGRAM *WISP* YET BUT I BET I COULD FIGURE IT OUT PRETTY FAST.
NAH, IT'S OKAY, THANKS. IT'S FASTER IF I JUST HACK AWAY AT IT. IT'S... *RELENTLESS* THOUGH. I FEEL LIKE I'M TRYING TO PUSH WATER BACK INTO A TAP.
I NEED TO GET THIS FIXED BEFORE WE MOVE OUT OF *BETA.* THE ALGORITHM IS ALL MESSED UP--IT'S MAKING SOME REALLY WEIRD MATCHES. THE BIG PARTY NEXT WEEK IS GONNA BE A HUGE EMBARRASSMENT IF THE APP IS STILL BUGGY LIKE THIS. RUMOR IS WE'RE GONNA BE BOUGHT OUT BY ONE OF THE BIG PLAYERS.
SO. WHAT'S UP WITH YOU AND *DINAH?* I GET THE FEELING THINGS AREN'T SO GREAT BETWEEN YOU TWO.
OH YEAH? WHAT GIVES YOU *THAT* IDEA?
WELL SHE BLEW OUT OF HERE EARLIER WITH ALL HER STUFF. ALL SHE'D SAY WAS "ASK LITTLE MISS SELFIE."
I THINK SHE WENT TO GO STAY WITH THOSE BAND GUYS SHE'S BEEN HANGING AROUND WITH. SHE'S THEIR SINGER NOW.
...DINAH'S IN A *BAND?*

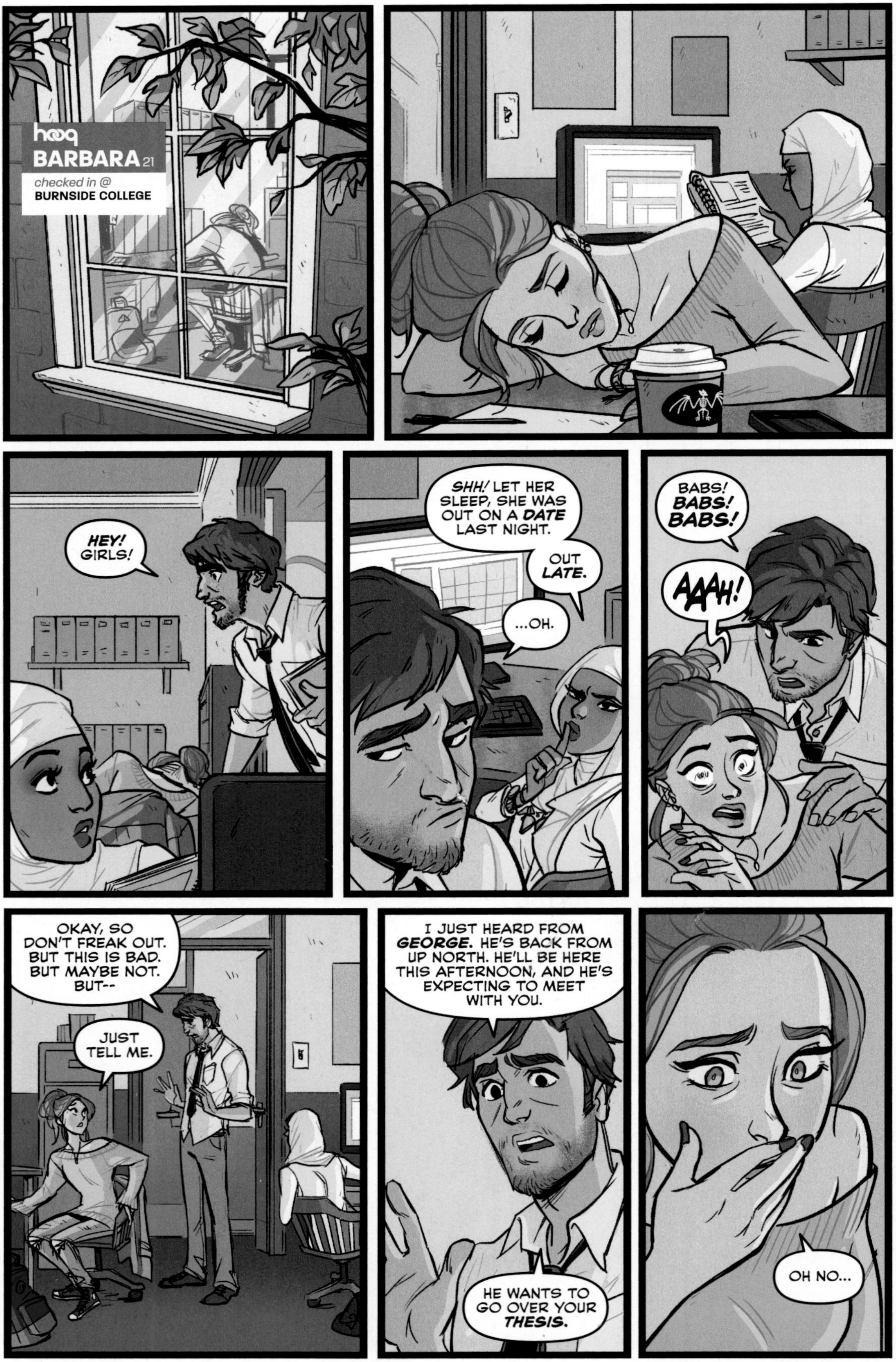
hooq
BARBARA 21
checked in @
BURNSIDE COLLEGE
HEY! GIRLS!
SHH! LET HER SLEEP, SHE WAS OUT ON A DATE LAST NIGHT.
OUT LATE.
...OH.
BABS! BABS! BABS!
AAAH!
OKAY, SO DON'T FREAK OUT. BUT THIS IS BAD. BUT MAYBE NOT. BUT--
JUST TELL ME.
I JUST HEARD FROM GEORGE. HE'S BACK FROM UP NORTH. HE'LL BE HERE THIS AFTERNOON, AND HE'S EXPECTING TO MEET WITH YOU.
HE WANTS TO GO OVER YOUR THESIS.
OH NO...

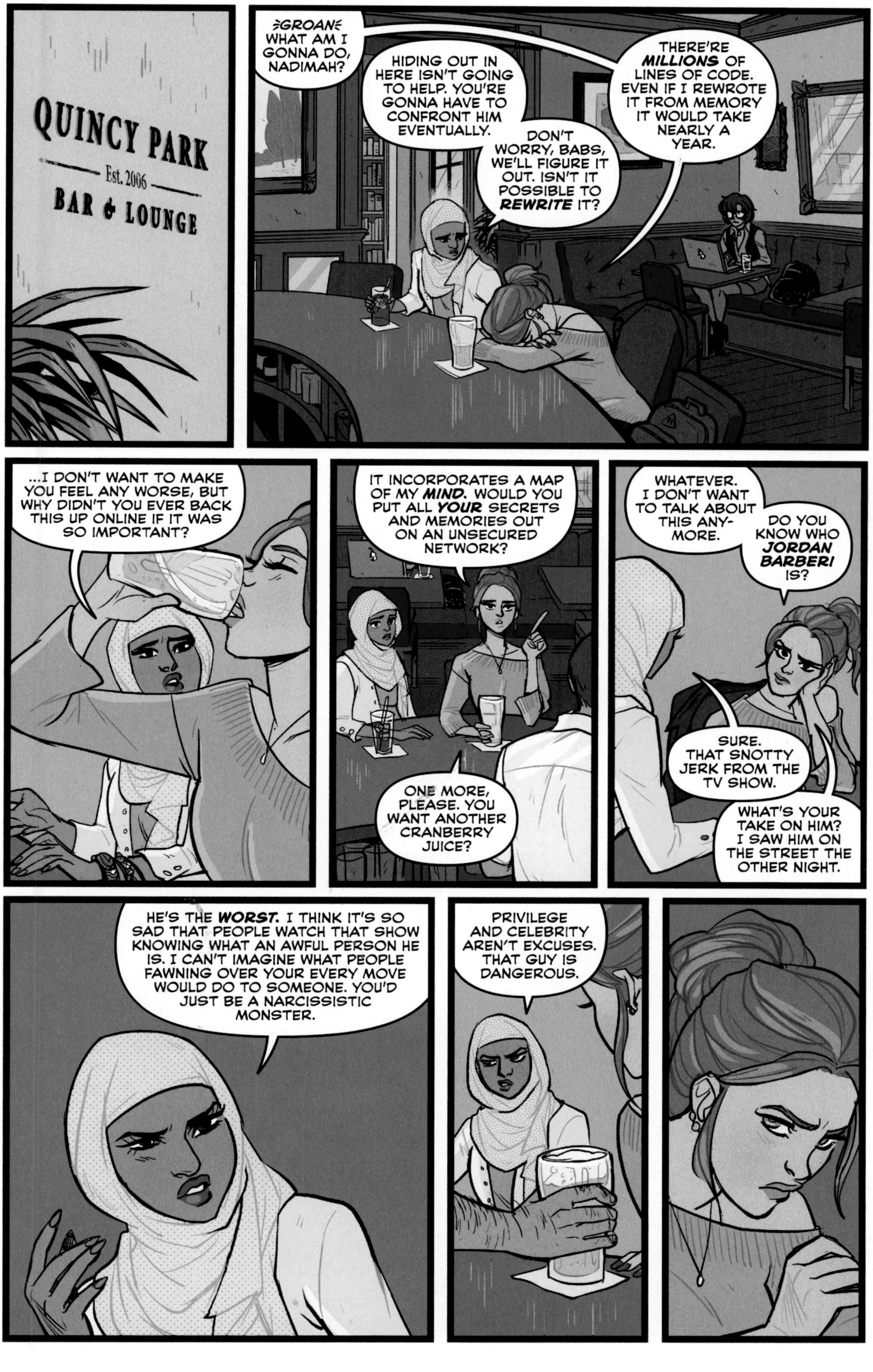
QUINCY PARK
Est. 2006
BAR & LOUNGE
GROAN WHAT AM I GONNA DO, NADIMAH?
HIDING OUT IN HERE ISN'T GOING TO HELP. YOU'RE GONNA HAVE TO CONFRONT HIM EVENTUALLY.
DON'T WORRY, BABS, WE'LL FIGURE IT OUT. ISN'T IT POSSIBLE TO REWRITE IT?
THERE'RE MILLIONS OF LINES OF CODE. EVEN IF I REWROTE IT FROM MEMORY IT WOULD TAKE NEARLY A YEAR.
...I DON'T WANT TO MAKE YOU FEEL ANY WORSE, BUT WHY DIDN'T YOU EVER BACK THIS UP ONLINE IF IT WAS SO IMPORTANT?
IT INCORPORATES A MAP OF MY MIND. WOULD YOU PUT ALL YOUR SECRETS AND MEMORIES OUT ON AN UNSECURED NETWORK?
ONE MORE, PLEASE. YOU WANT ANOTHER CRANBERRY JUICE?
WHATEVER. I DON'T WANT TO TALK ABOUT THIS ANYMORE.
DO YOU KNOW WHO JORDAN BARBERI IS?
SURE. THAT SNOTTY JERK FROM THE TV SHOW.
WHAT'S YOUR TAKE ON HIM? I SAW HIM ON THE STREET THE OTHER NIGHT.
HE'S THE WORST. I THINK IT'S SO SAD THAT PEOPLE WATCH THAT SHOW KNOWING WHAT AN AWFUL PERSON HE IS. I CAN'T IMAGINE WHAT PEOPLE FAWNING OVER YOUR EVERY MOVE WOULD DO TO SOMEONE. YOU'D JUST BE A NARCISSISTIC MONSTER.
PRIVILEGE AND CELEBRITY AREN'T EXCUSES. THAT GUY IS DANGEROUS.

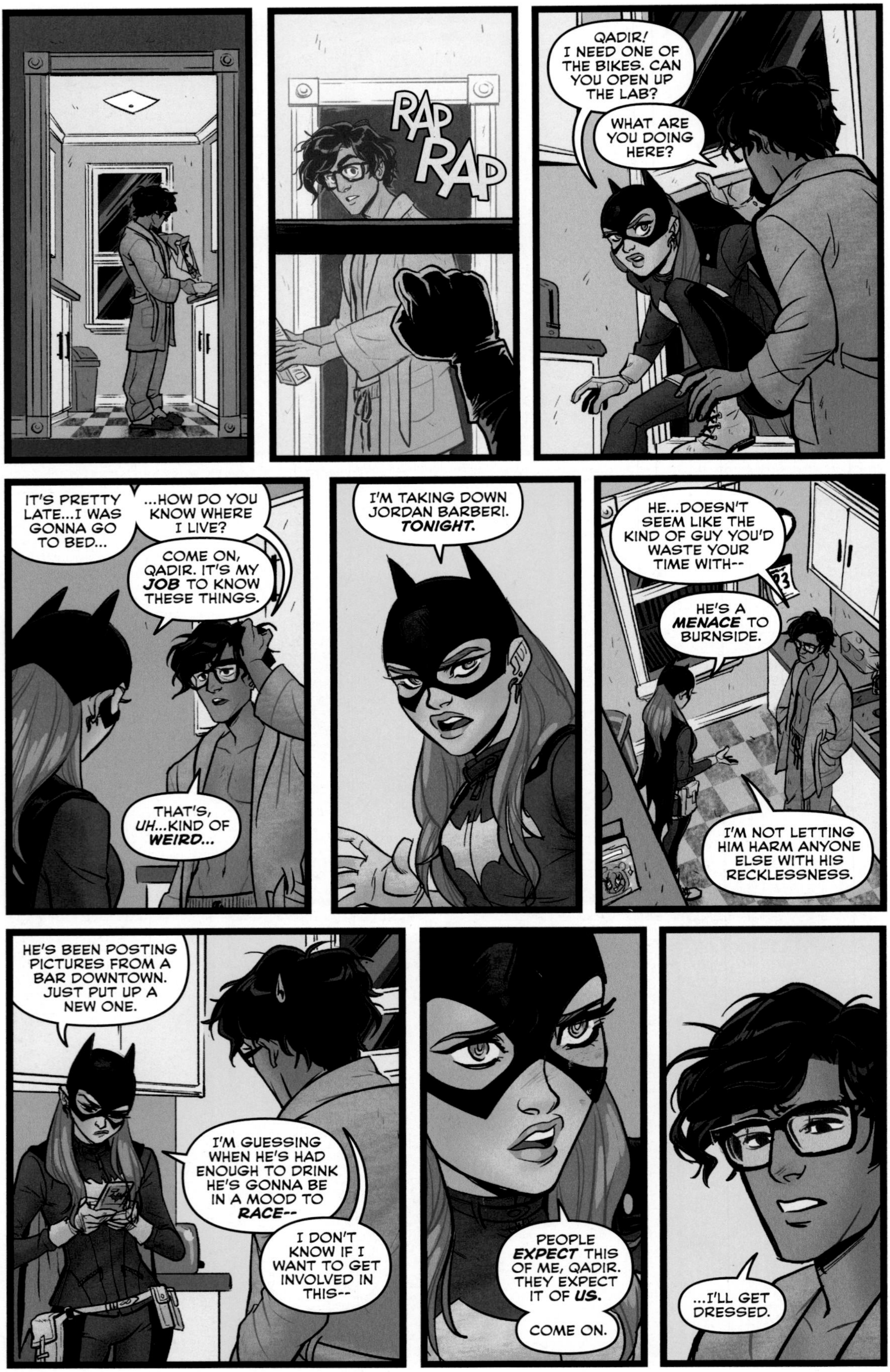

RAP
RAP
QADIR! I NEED ONE OF THE BIKES. CAN YOU OPEN UP THE LAB?
WHAT ARE YOU DOING HERE?
IT'S PRETTY LATE...I WAS GONNA GO TO BED...
...HOW DO YOU KNOW WHERE I LIVE?
COME ON, QADIR. IT'S MY JOB TO KNOW THESE THINGS.
THAT'S, UH...KIND OF WEIRD...
I'M TAKING DOWN JORDAN BARBERI. TONIGHT.
HE...DOESN'T SEEM LIKE THE KIND OF GUY YOU'D WASTE YOUR TIME WITH--
HE'S A MENACE TO BURNSIDE.
I'M NOT LETTING HIM HARM ANYONE ELSE WITH HIS RECKLESSNESS.
HE'S BEEN POSTING PICTURES FROM A BAR DOWNTOWN. JUST PUT UP A NEW ONE.
I'M GUESSING WHEN HE'S HAD ENOUGH TO DRINK HE'S GONNA BE IN A MOOD TO RACE--
I DON'T KNOW IF I WANT TO GET INVOLVED IN THIS--
PEOPLE EXPECT THIS OF ME, QADIR. THEY EXPECT IT OF US.
COME ON.
...I'LL GET DRESSED.

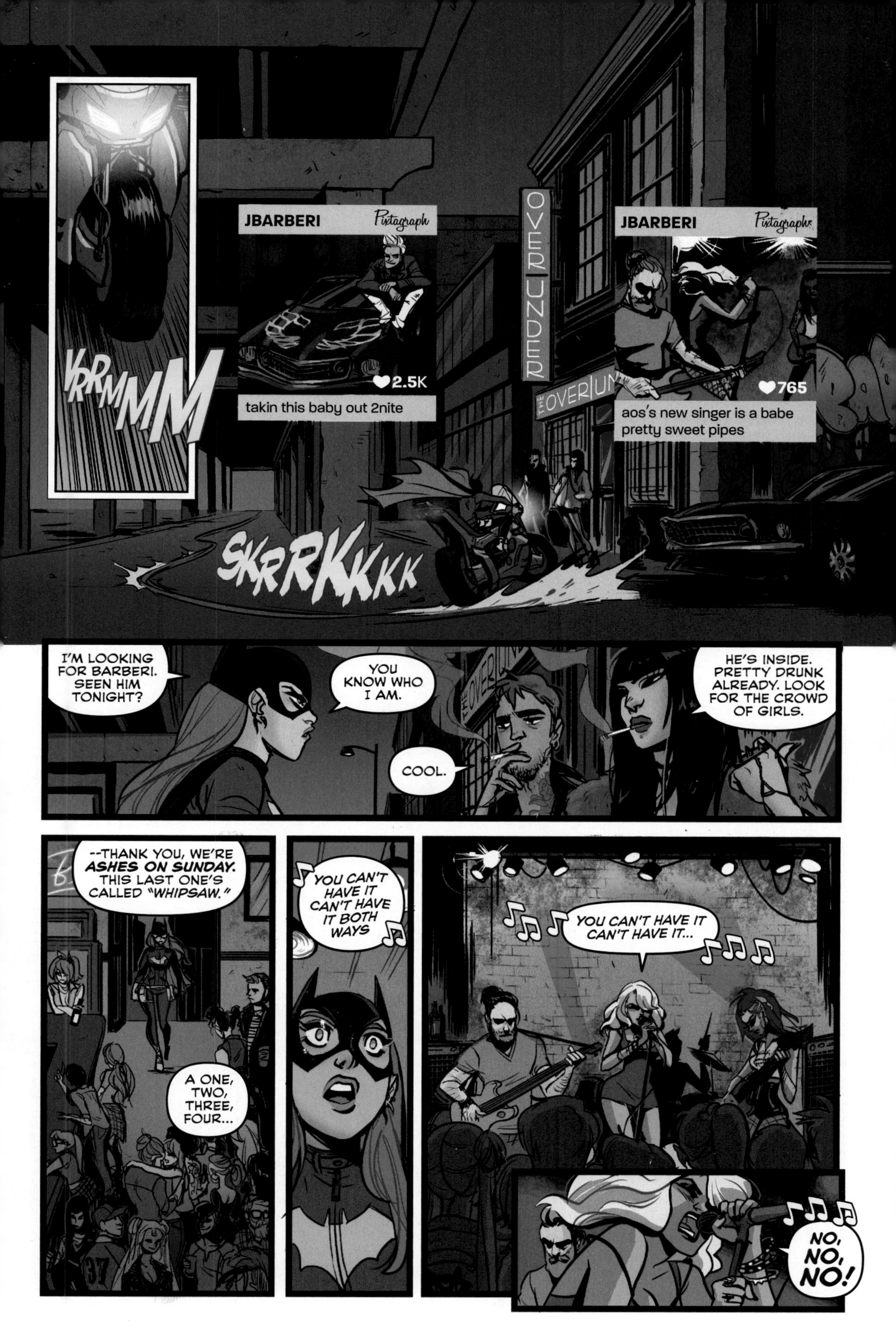
VRRMMMM
JBARBERI
Pixtagraph
2.5K
takin this baby out 2nite
OVER UNDER
THE OVER|UN
JBARBERI
Pixtagraph
765
aos's new singer is a babe
pretty sweet pipes
SKRRKKKKK
I'M LOOKING FOR BARBERI. SEEN HIM TONIGHT?
YOU KNOW WHO I AM.
COOL.
HE'S INSIDE. PRETTY DRUNK ALREADY. LOOK FOR THE CROWD OF GIRLS.
--THANK YOU, WE'RE ASHES ON SUNDAY. THIS LAST ONE'S CALLED "WHIPSAW."
A ONE, TWO, THREE, FOUR...
YOU CAN'T HAVE IT CAN'T HAVE IT BOTH WAYS
YOU CAN'T HAVE IT CAN'T HAVE IT...
NO, NO, NO!

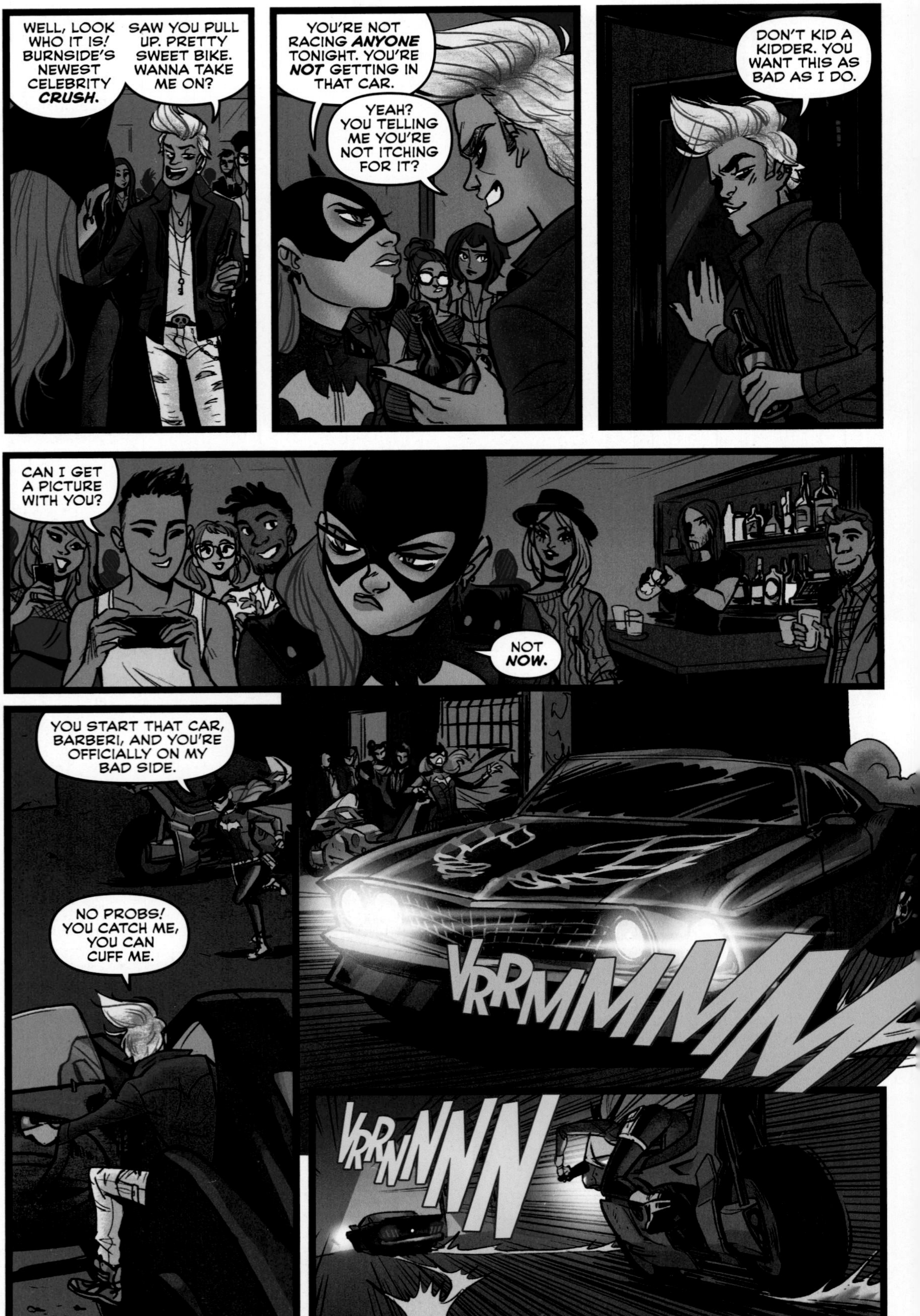
WELL, LOOK WHO IT IS! BURNSIDE'S NEWEST CELEBRITY **CRUSH**.
SAW YOU PULL UP. PRETTY SWEET BIKE. WANNA TAKE ME ON?
YOU'RE NOT RACING **ANYONE** TONIGHT. YOU'RE **NOT** GETTING IN THAT CAR.
YEAH? YOU TELLING ME YOU'RE NOT ITCHING FOR IT?
DON'T KID A KIDDER. YOU WANT THIS AS BAD AS I DO.
CAN I GET A PICTURE WITH YOU?
NOT **NOW**.
YOU START THAT CAR, BARBERI, AND YOU'RE OFFICIALLY ON MY BAD SIDE.
NO PROBS! YOU CATCH ME, YOU CAN CUFF ME.
VRRMMMMM
VRRNNNNN

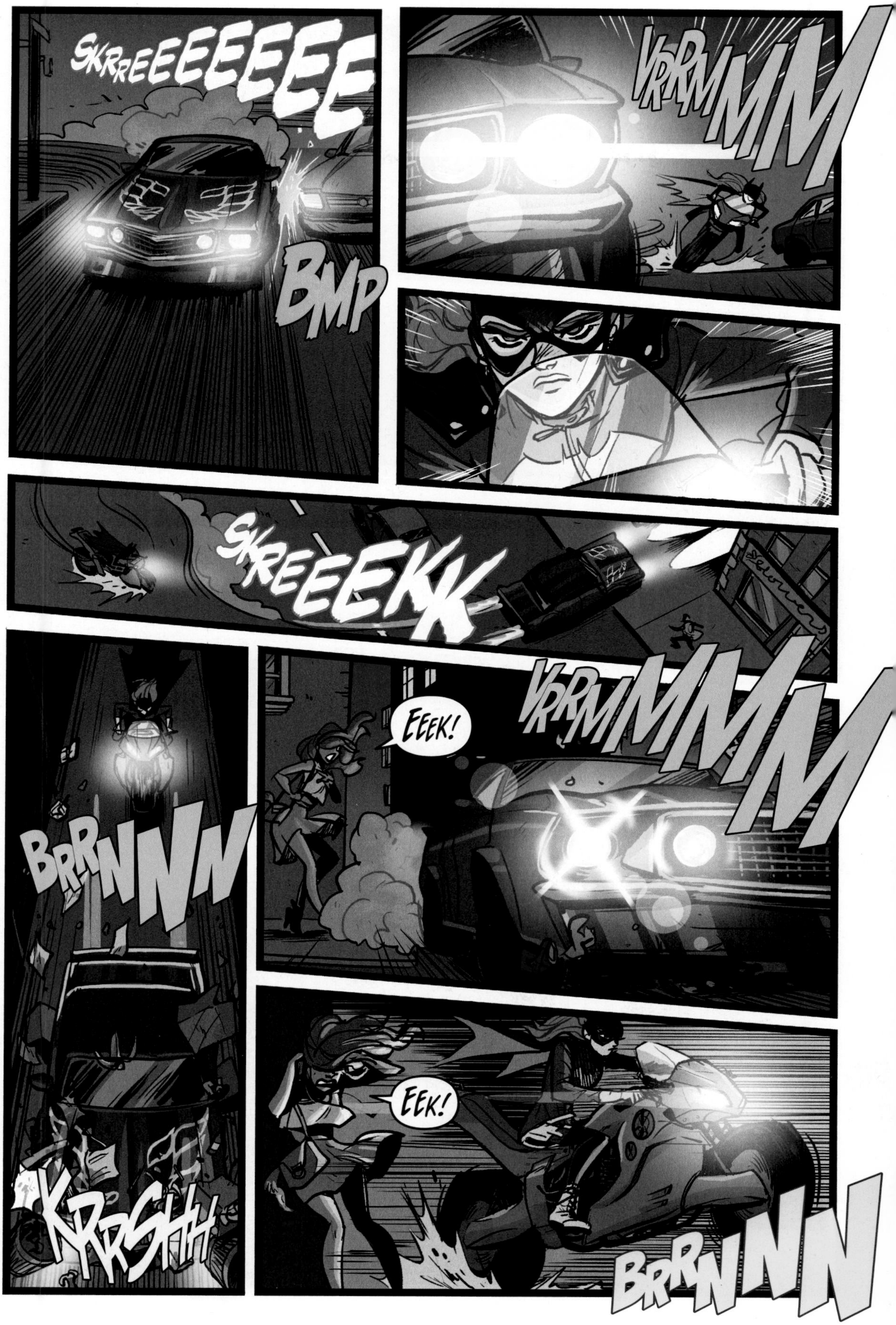
SKRREEEEEEEE
BMP
VRRMMMM
SKREEEKK
VRRMMMMMM
EEEK!
BRRNNNN
KRRSHH
EEK!
BRRNNNN

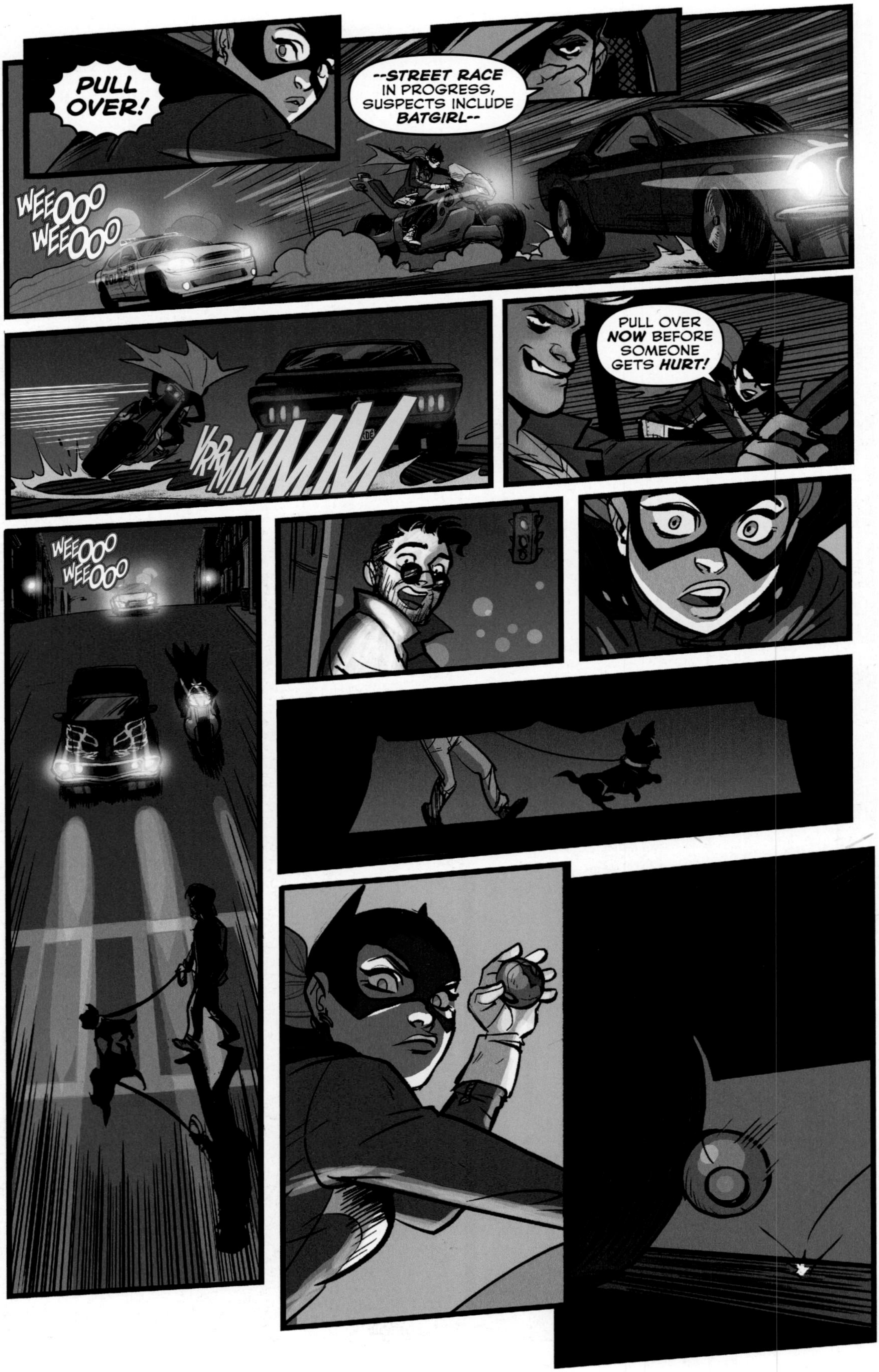
PULL OVER!
--STREET RACE IN PROGRESS, SUSPECTS INCLUDE BATGIRL--
WEEOOO WEEOOO
VRRMMMM
PULL OVER NOW BEFORE SOMEONE GETS HURT!
WEEOOO WEEOOO

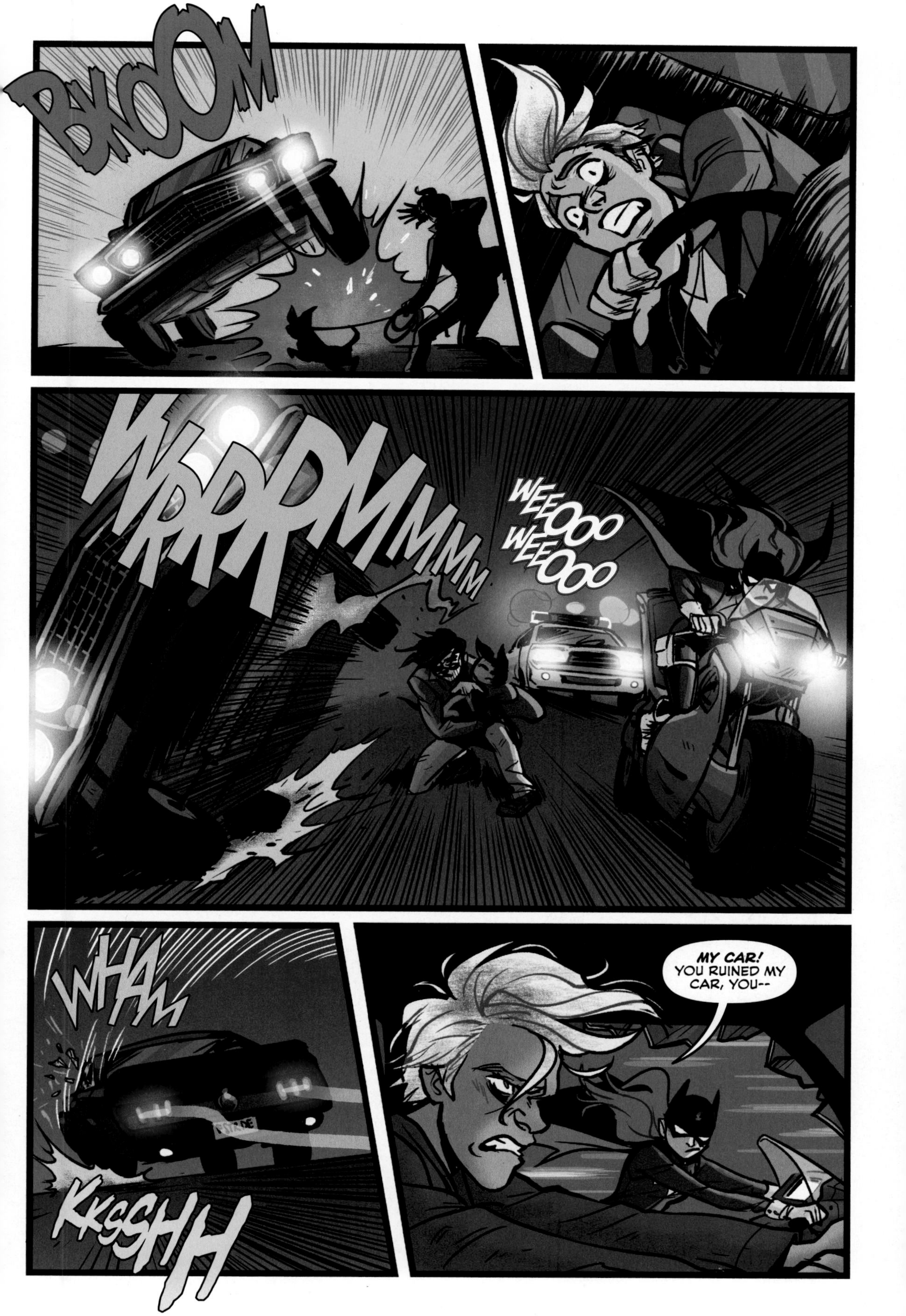
BKOOM
WRRRMMMMM
WEEOOO WEEOOO
WHAM
KKSSHH
MY CAR! YOU RUINED MY CAR, YOU--

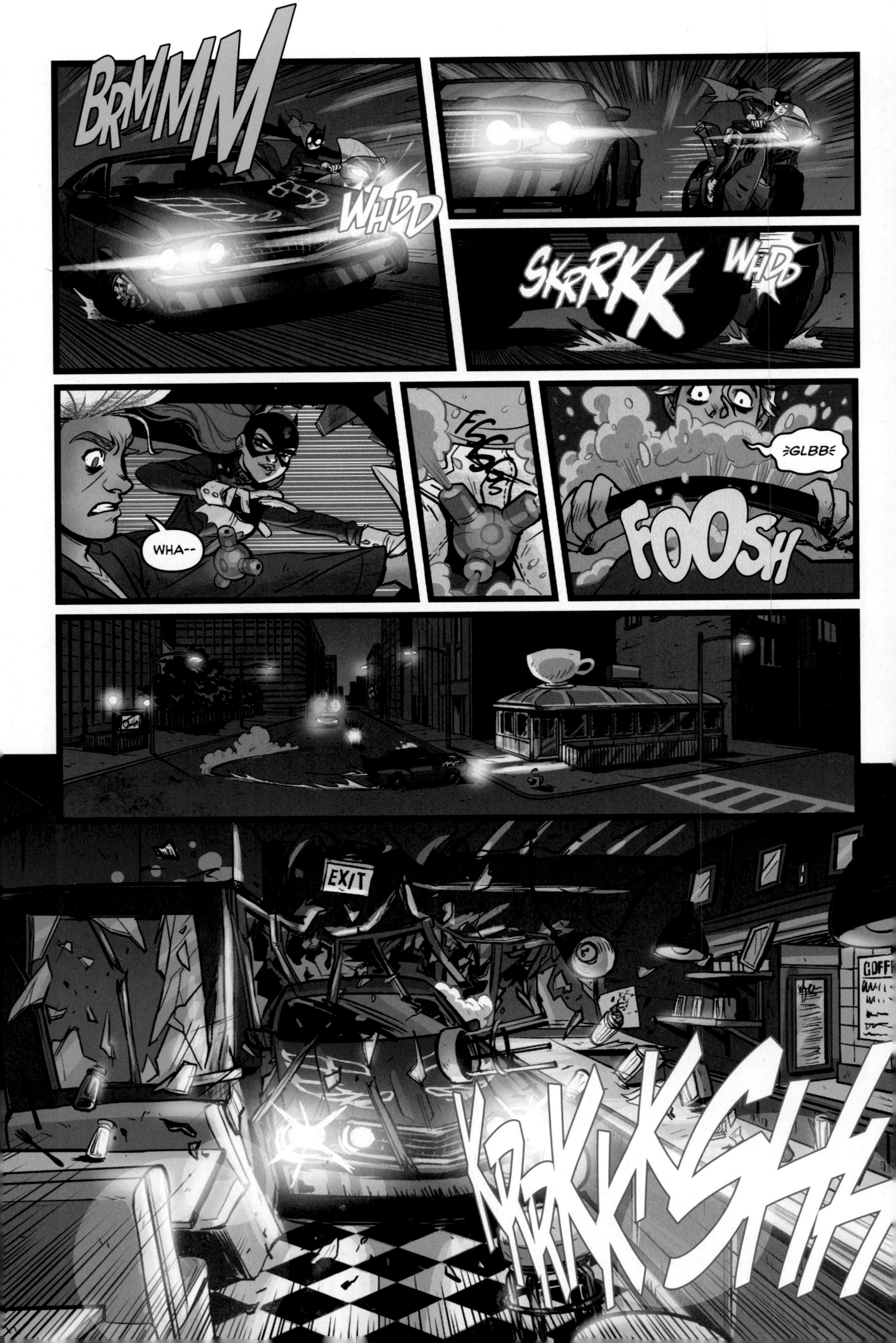

BRMMM
WHDD
SKRRKK
WHDD
WHA--
FSSSSS
GLBB
FOOSH
EXIT
KRRKKSHH

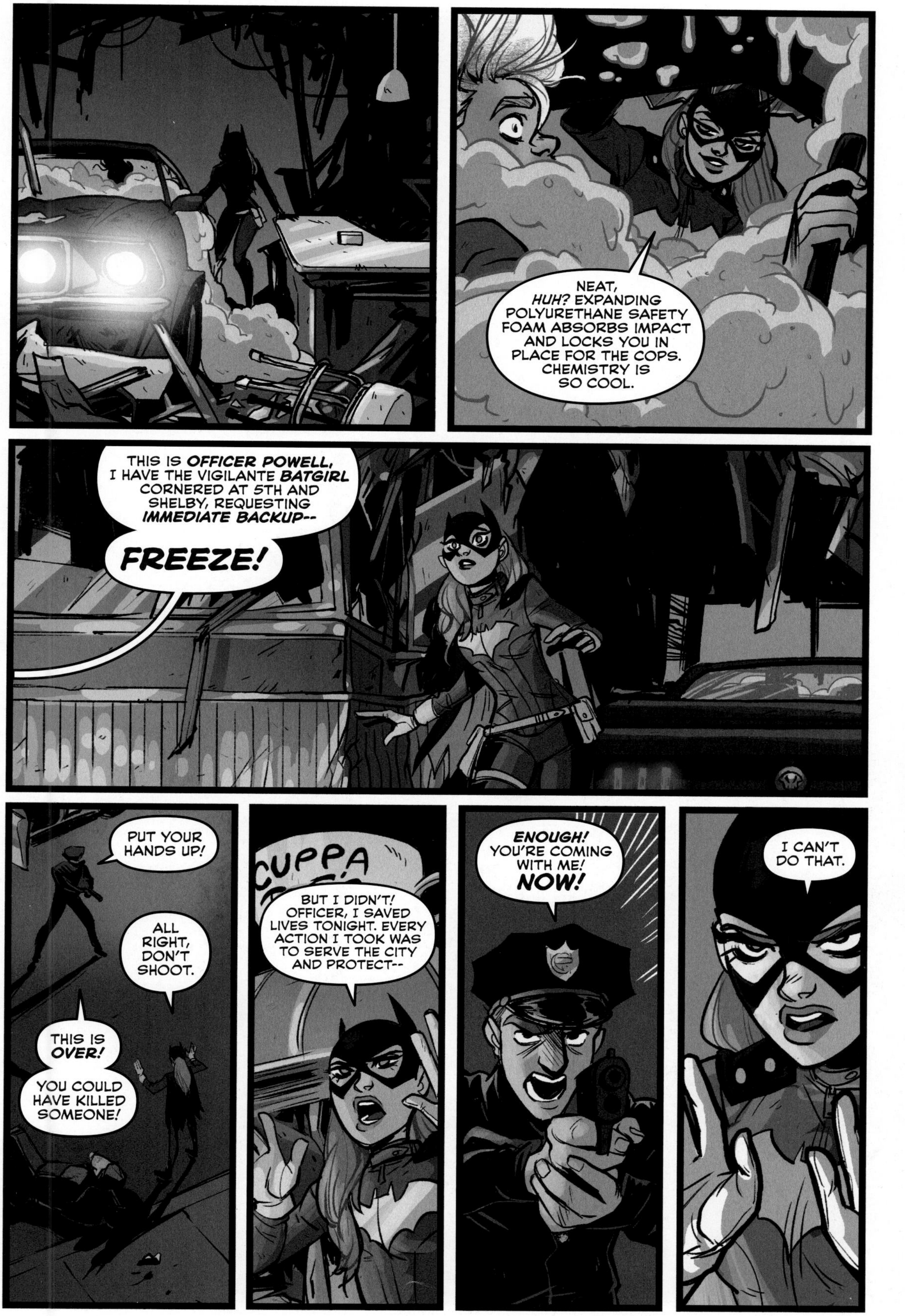

NEAT, HUH? EXPANDING POLYURETHANE SAFETY FOAM ABSORBS IMPACT AND LOCKS YOU IN PLACE FOR THE COPS. CHEMISTRY IS SO COOL.
THIS IS OFFICER POWELL, I HAVE THE VIGILANTE BATGIRL CORNERED AT 5TH AND SHELBY, REQUESTING IMMEDIATE BACKUP--
FREEZE!
PUT YOUR HANDS UP!
ALL RIGHT, DON'T SHOOT.
THIS IS OVER!
YOU COULD HAVE KILLED SOMEONE!
CUPPA
BUT I DIDN'T! OFFICER, I SAVED LIVES TONIGHT. EVERY ACTION I TOOK WAS TO SERVE THE CITY AND PROTECT--
ENOUGH! YOU'RE COMING WITH ME! NOW!
I CAN'T DO THAT.

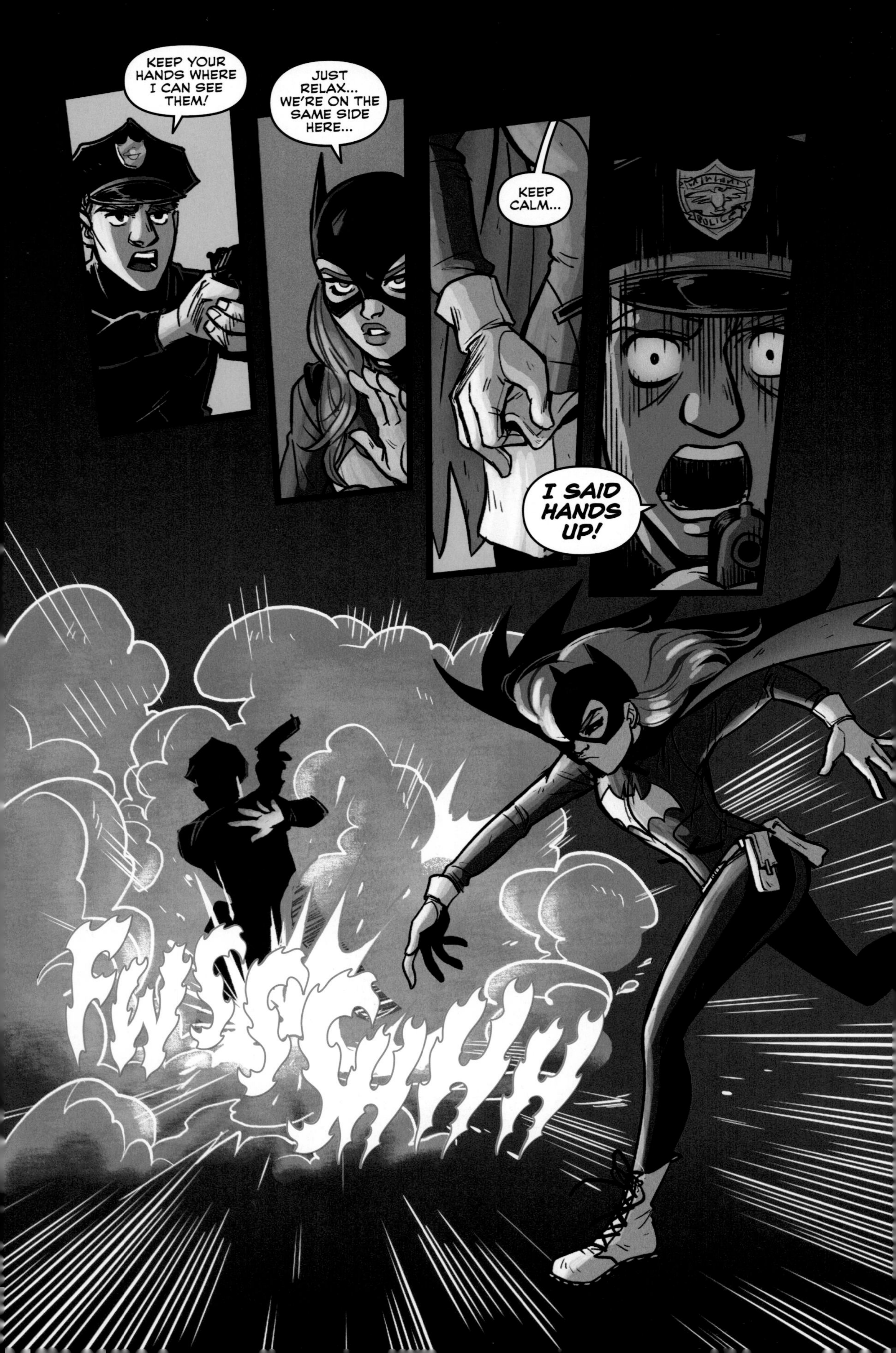
KEEP YOUR HANDS WHERE I CAN SEE THEM!
JUST RELAX... WE'RE ON THE SAME SIDE HERE...
KEEP CALM...
I SAID HANDS UP!
FWSSSHHH

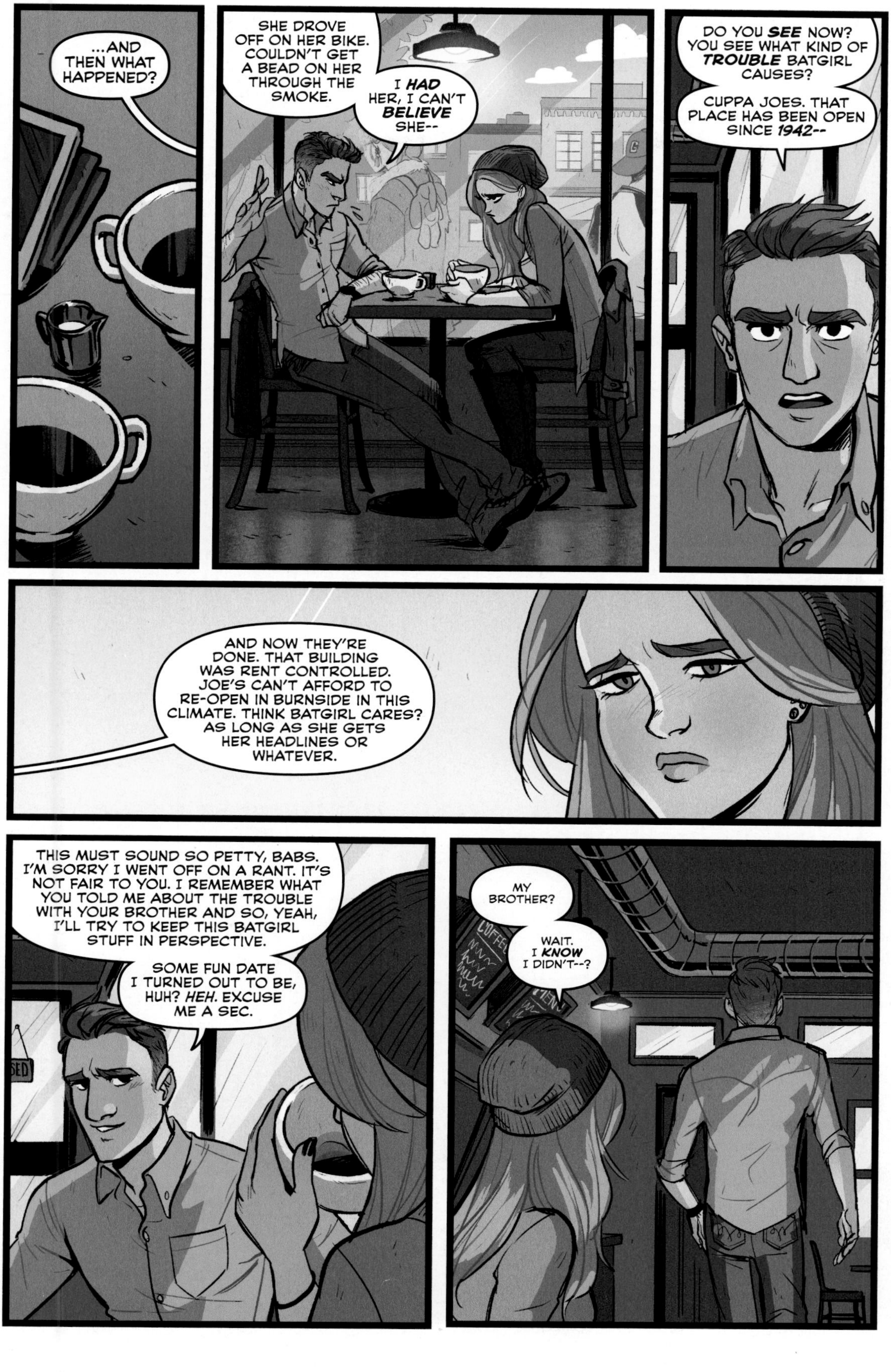
...AND THEN WHAT HAPPENED?
SHE DROVE OFF ON HER BIKE. COULDN'T GET A BEAD ON HER THROUGH THE SMOKE.
I **HAD** HER, I CAN'T **BELIEVE** SHE--
DO YOU **SEE** NOW? YOU SEE WHAT KIND OF **TROUBLE** BATGIRL CAUSES?
CUPPA JOES. THAT PLACE HAS BEEN OPEN SINCE **1942--**
AND NOW THEY'RE DONE. THAT BUILDING WAS RENT CONTROLLED. JOE'S CAN'T AFFORD TO RE-OPEN IN BURNSIDE IN THIS CLIMATE. THINK BATGIRL CARES? AS LONG AS SHE GETS HER HEADLINES OR WHATEVER.
THIS MUST SOUND SO PETTY, BABS. I'M SORRY I WENT OFF ON A RANT. IT'S NOT FAIR TO YOU. I REMEMBER WHAT YOU TOLD ME ABOUT THE TROUBLE WITH YOUR BROTHER AND SO, YEAH, I'LL TRY TO KEEP THIS BATGIRL STUFF IN PERSPECTIVE.
SOME FUN DATE I TURNED OUT TO BE, HUH? *HEH.* EXCUSE ME A SEC.
MY BROTHER?
WAIT. I **KNOW** I DIDN'T--?

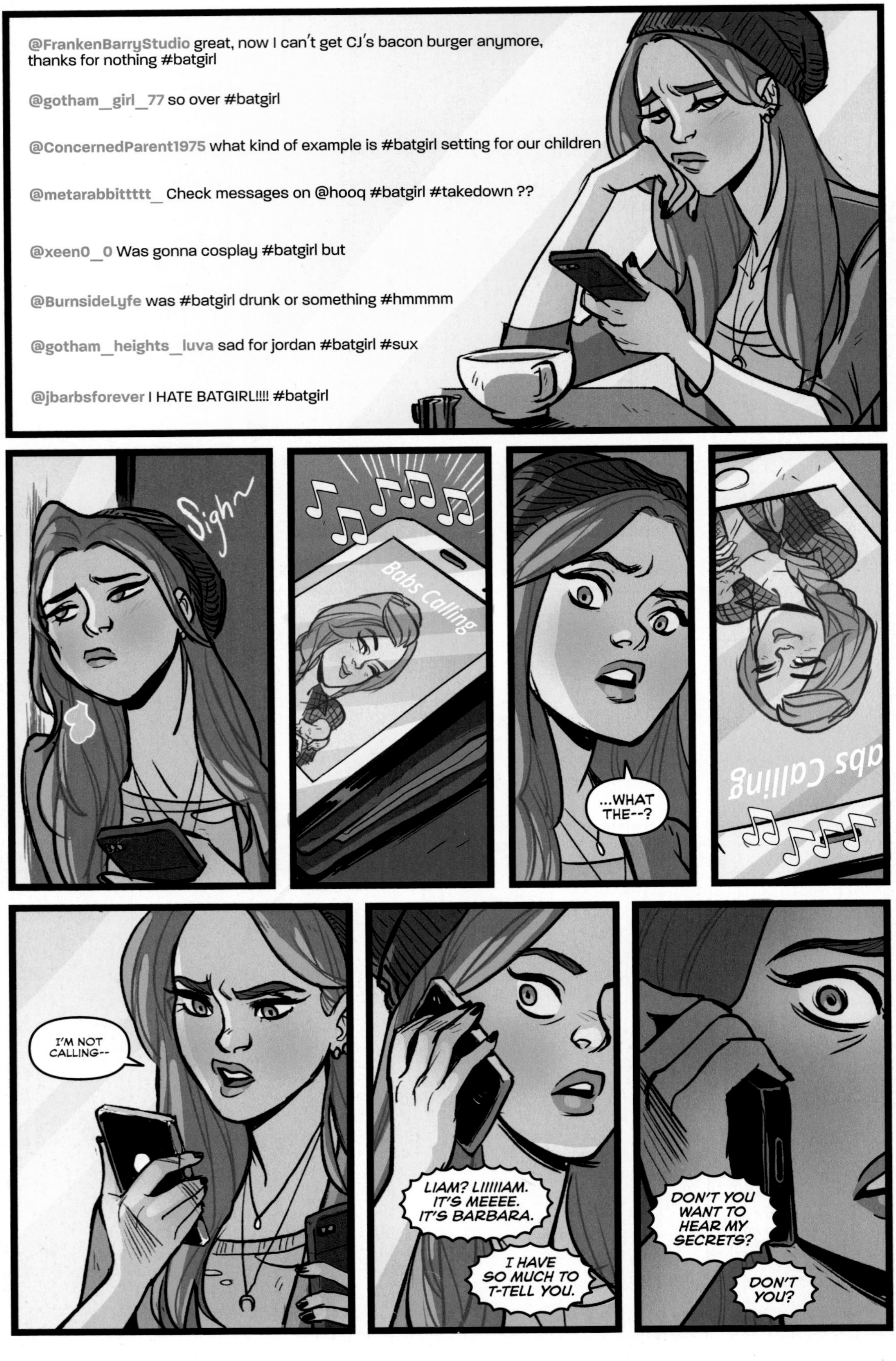

@FrankenBarryStudio great, now I can't get CJ's bacon burger anymore, thanks for nothing #batgirl
@gotham_girl_77 so over #batgirl
@ConcernedParent1975 what kind of example is #batgirl setting for our children
@metarabbitttttt_ Check messages on @hooq #batgirl #takedown ??
@xeen0_0 Was gonna cosplay #batgirl but
@BurnsideLyfe was #batgirl drunk or something #hmmmm
@gotham_heights_luva sad for jordan #batgirl #sux
@jbarbsforever I HATE BATGIRL!!!! #batgirl
Sigh~
Babs Calling
...WHAT THE--?
abs Calling
I'M NOT CALLING--
LIAM? LIIIIIAM. IT'S MEEEE. IT'S BARBARA.
I HAVE SO MUCH TO T-TELL YOU.
DON'T YOU WANT TO HEAR MY SECRETS?
DON'T YOU?

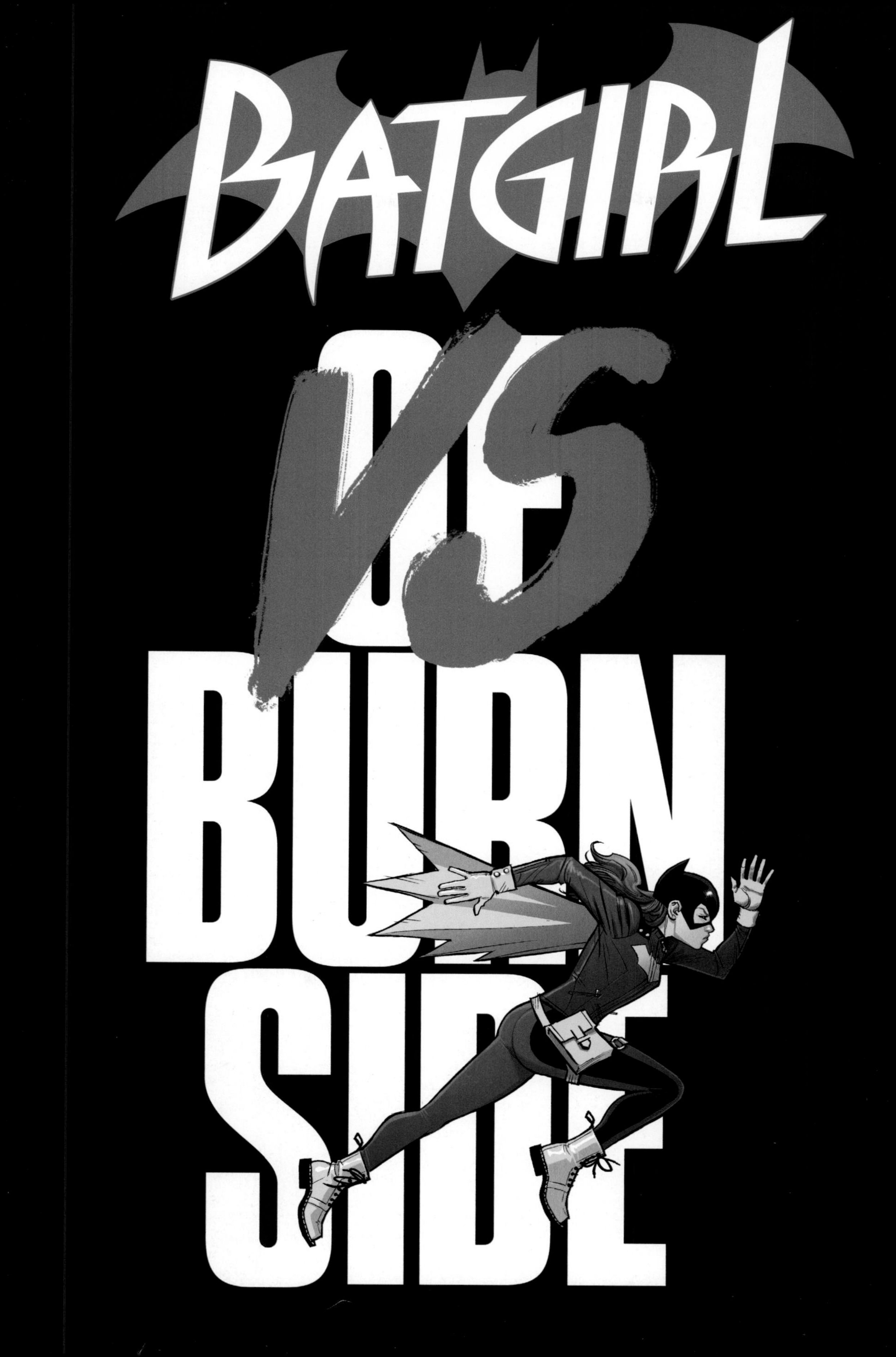
BATGIRL
VS
OF
BURN
SIDE

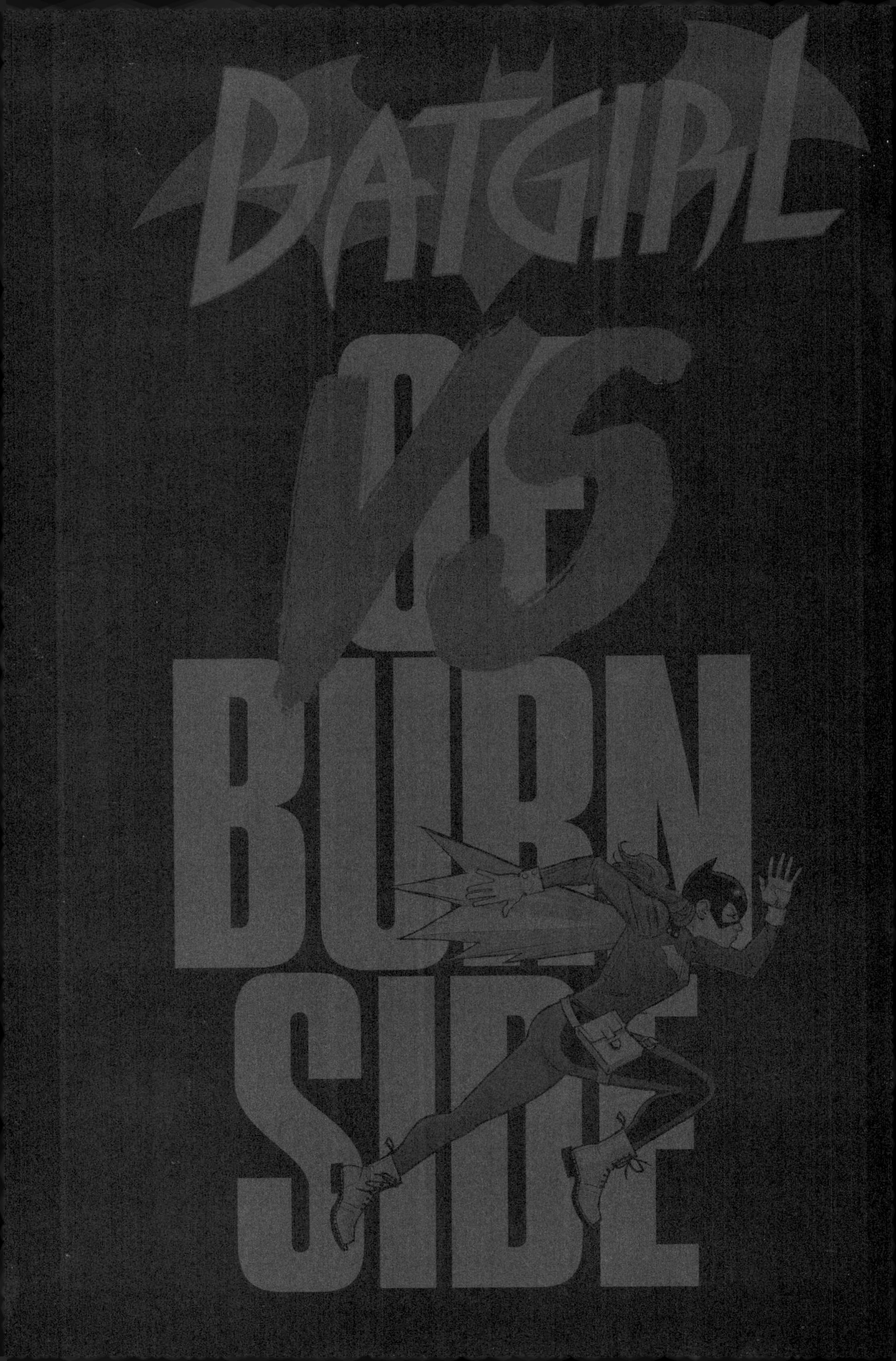
BATGIRL
BURN
SIDE

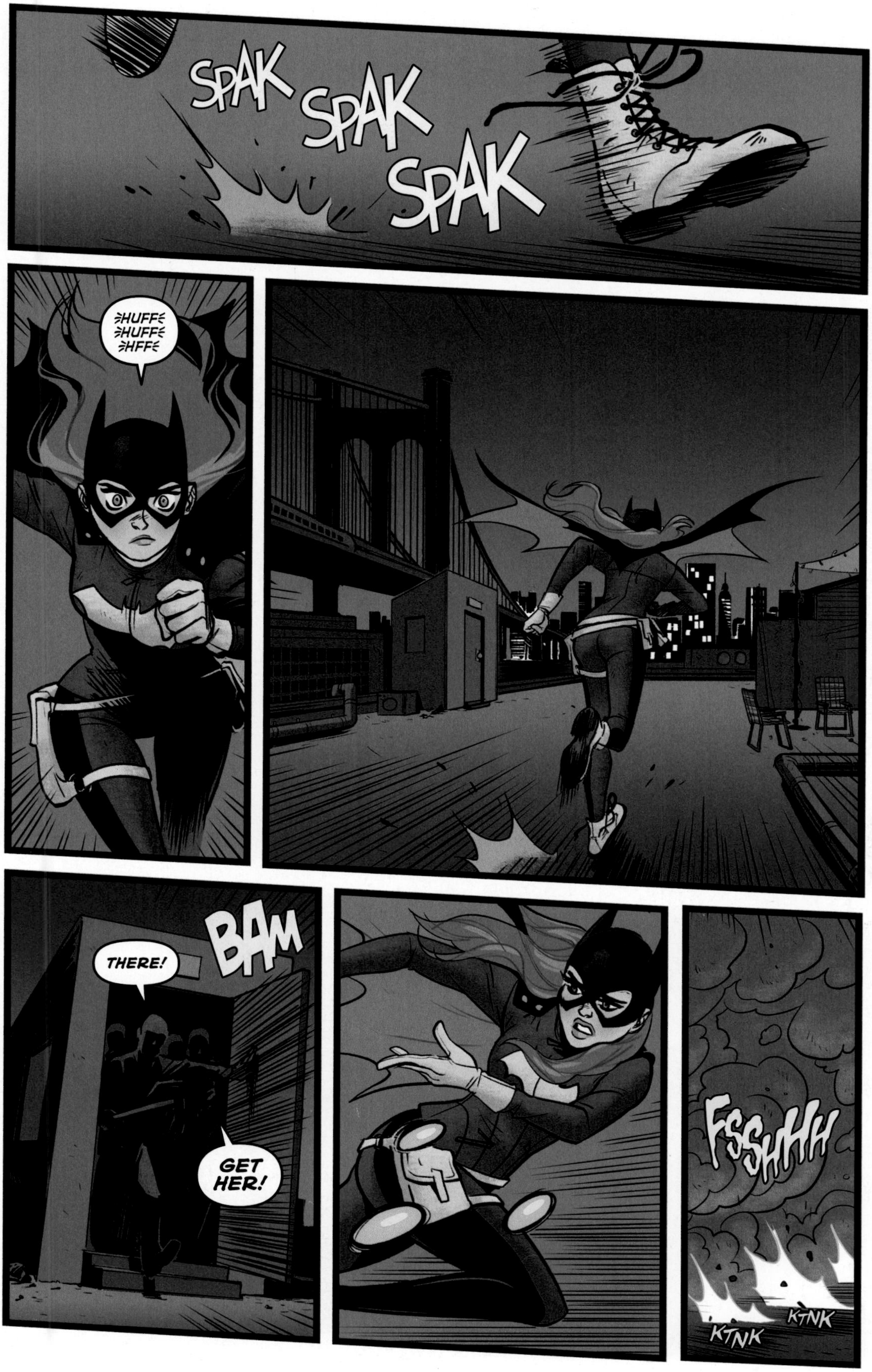
SPAK SPAK SPAK
HUFF HUFF HFF
BAM
THERE!
GET HER!
FSSHHH
KTNK
KTNK

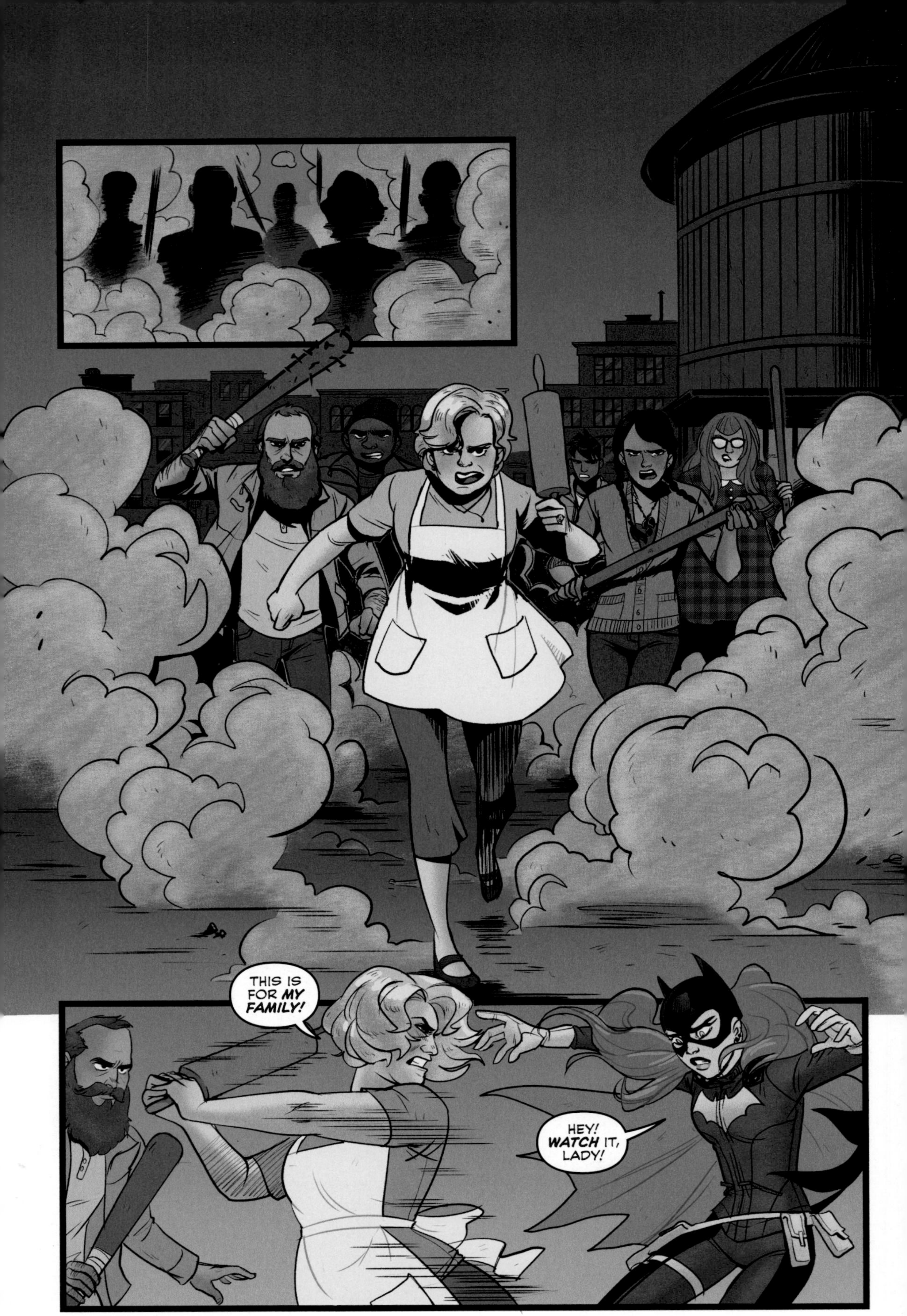
THIS IS FOR MY FAMILY!
HEY! WATCH IT, LADY!

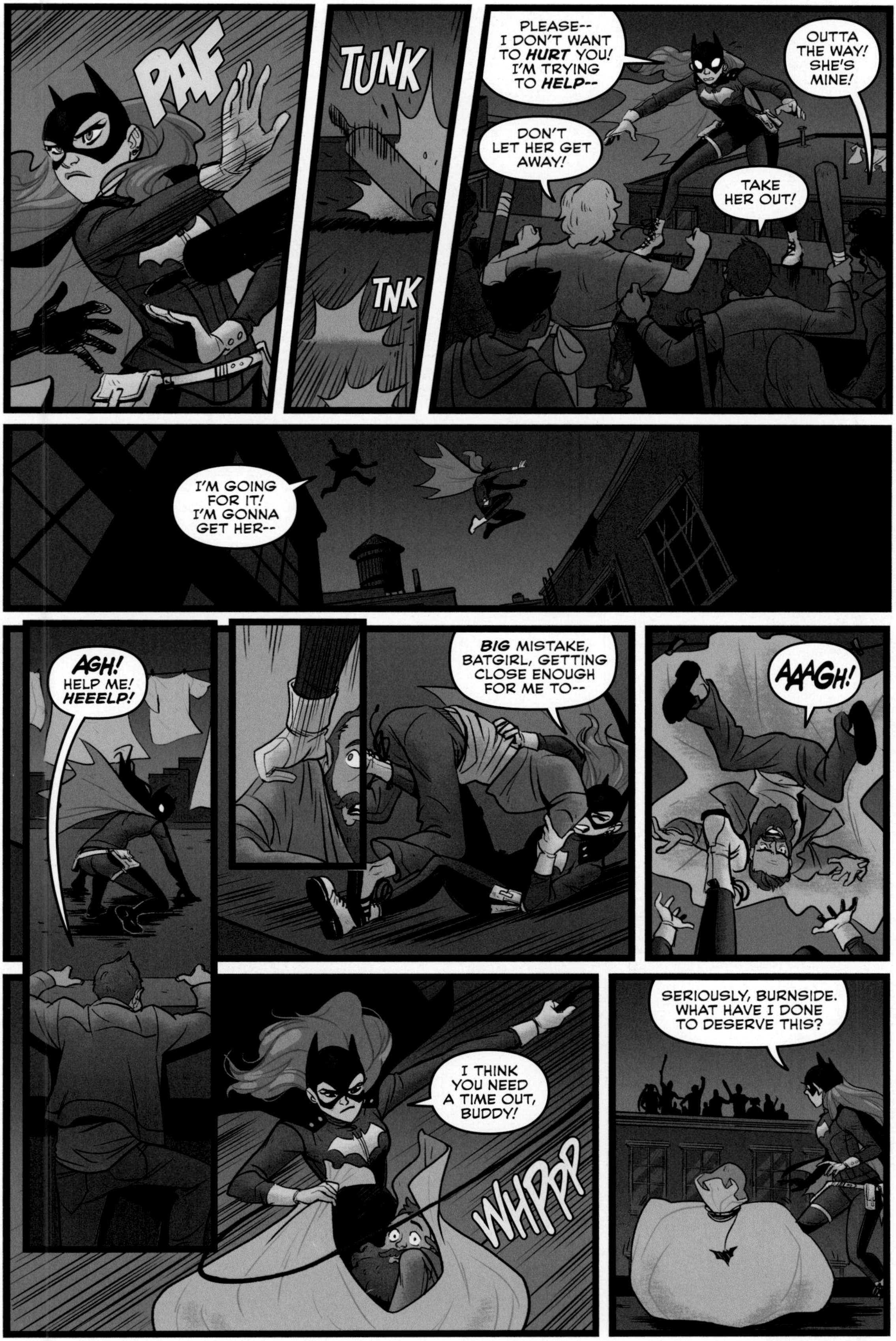
PAF
TUNK
TNK
PLEASE-- I DON'T WANT TO HURT YOU! I'M TRYING TO HELP--
DON'T LET HER GET AWAY!
OUTTA THE WAY! SHE'S MINE!
TAKE HER OUT!
I'M GOING FOR IT! I'M GONNA GET HER--
AGH! HELP ME! HEEELP!
BIG MISTAKE, BATGIRL, GETTING CLOSE ENOUGH FOR ME TO--
AAAGH!
I THINK YOU NEED A TIME OUT, BUDDY!
WHPPP
SERIOUSLY, BURNSIDE. WHAT HAVE I DONE TO DESERVE THIS?

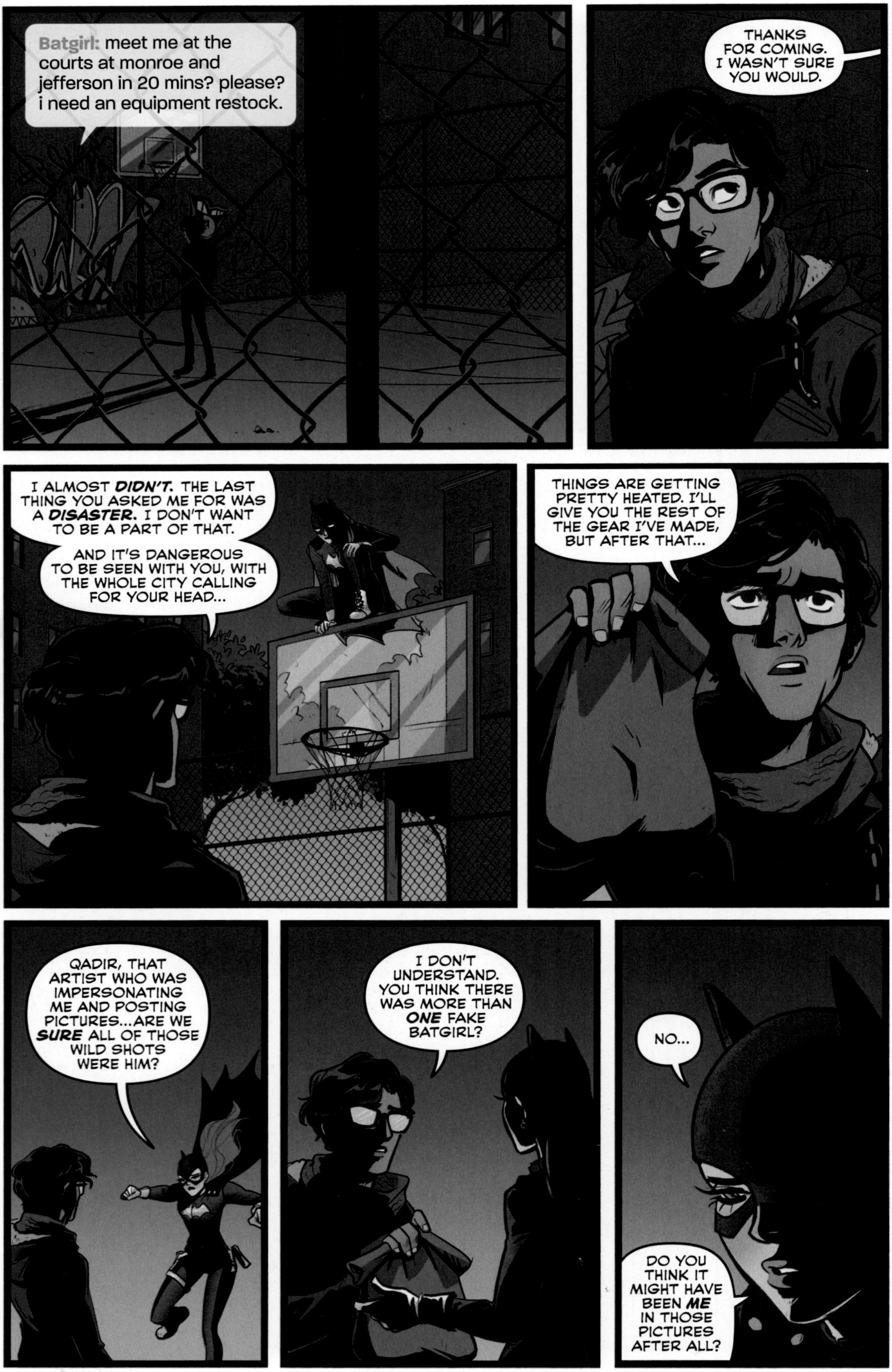

Batgirl: meet me at the courts at monroe and jefferson in 20 mins? please? i need an equipment restock.
THANKS FOR COMING. I WASN'T SURE YOU WOULD.
I ALMOST DIDN'T. THE LAST THING YOU ASKED ME FOR WAS A DISASTER. I DON'T WANT TO BE A PART OF THAT.
AND IT'S DANGEROUS TO BE SEEN WITH YOU, WITH THE WHOLE CITY CALLING FOR YOUR HEAD...
THINGS ARE GETTING PRETTY HEATED. I'LL GIVE YOU THE REST OF THE GEAR I'VE MADE, BUT AFTER THAT...
QADIR, THAT ARTIST WHO WAS IMPERSONATING ME AND POSTING PICTURES...ARE WE SURE ALL OF THOSE WILD SHOTS WERE HIM?
I DON'T UNDERSTAND. YOU THINK THERE WAS MORE THAN ONE FAKE BATGIRL?
NO...
DO YOU THINK IT MIGHT HAVE BEEN ME IN THOSE PICTURES AFTER ALL?

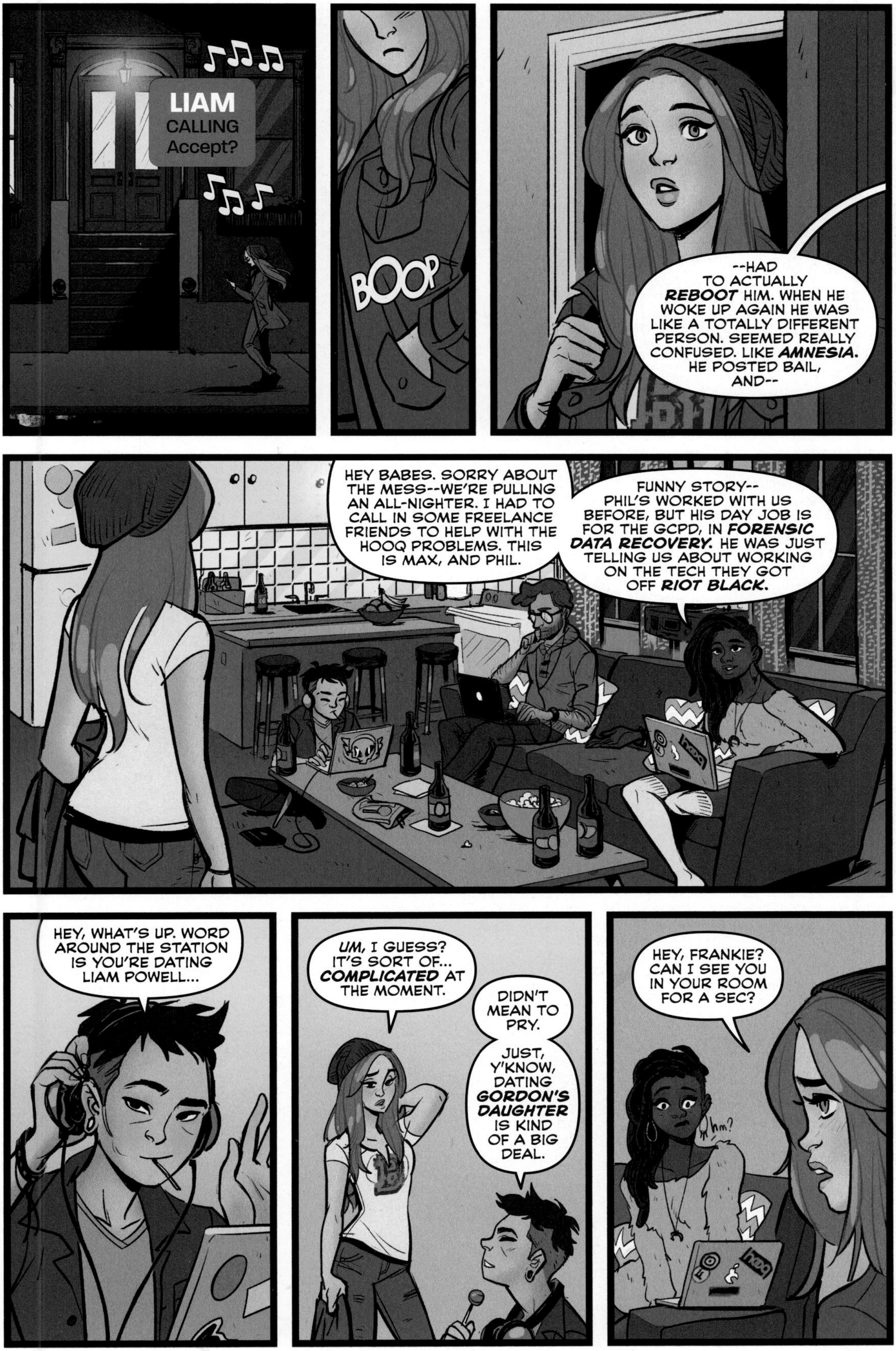
♫♫♫
LIAM
CALLING
Accept?
♫♫♫
BOOP
--HAD TO ACTUALLY REBOOT HIM. WHEN HE WOKE UP AGAIN HE WAS LIKE A TOTALLY DIFFERENT PERSON. SEEMED REALLY CONFUSED. LIKE AMNESIA. HE POSTED BAIL, AND--
HEY BABES. SORRY ABOUT THE MESS--WE'RE PULLING AN ALL-NIGHTER. I HAD TO CALL IN SOME FREELANCE FRIENDS TO HELP WITH THE HOOQ PROBLEMS. THIS IS MAX, AND PHIL.
FUNNY STORY-- PHIL'S WORKED WITH US BEFORE, BUT HIS DAY JOB IS FOR THE GCPD, IN FORENSIC DATA RECOVERY. HE WAS JUST TELLING US ABOUT WORKING ON THE TECH THEY GOT OFF RIOT BLACK.
HEY, WHAT'S UP. WORD AROUND THE STATION IS YOU'RE DATING LIAM POWELL...
UM, I GUESS? IT'S SORT OF... COMPLICATED AT THE MOMENT.
DIDN'T MEAN TO PRY.
JUST, Y'KNOW, DATING GORDON'S DAUGHTER IS KIND OF A BIG DEAL.
HEY, FRANKIE? CAN I SEE YOU IN YOUR ROOM FOR A SEC?
hm?

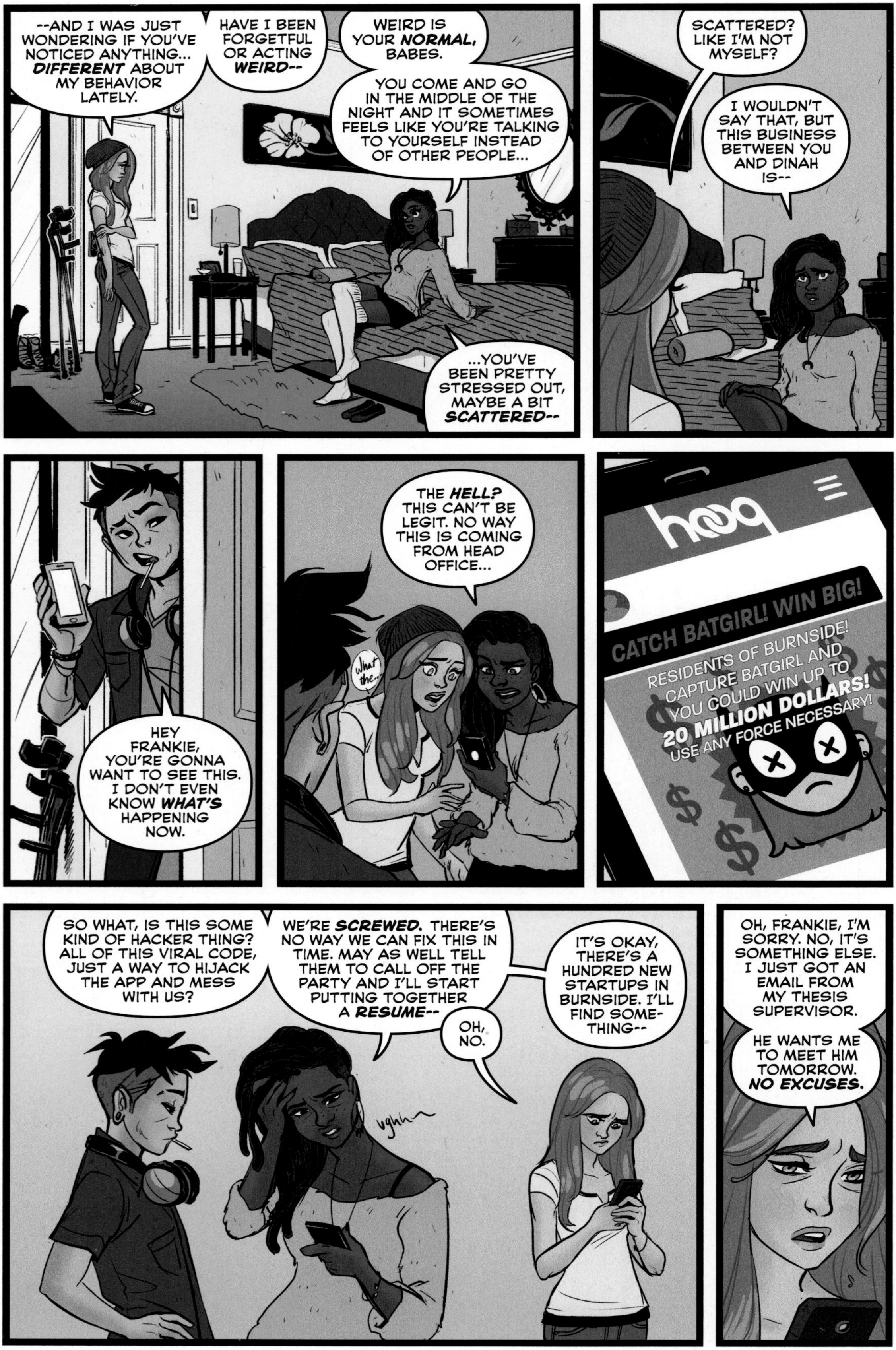
--AND I WAS JUST WONDERING IF YOU'VE NOTICED ANYTHING... DIFFERENT ABOUT MY BEHAVIOR LATELY.
HAVE I BEEN FORGETFUL OR ACTING WEIRD--
WEIRD IS YOUR NORMAL, BABES.
YOU COME AND GO IN THE MIDDLE OF THE NIGHT AND IT SOMETIMES FEELS LIKE YOU'RE TALKING TO YOURSELF INSTEAD OF OTHER PEOPLE...
...YOU'VE BEEN PRETTY STRESSED OUT, MAYBE A BIT SCATTERED--
SCATTERED? LIKE I'M NOT MYSELF?
I WOULDN'T SAY THAT, BUT THIS BUSINESS BETWEEN YOU AND DINAH IS--
HEY FRANKIE, YOU'RE GONNA WANT TO SEE THIS. I DON'T EVEN KNOW WHAT'S HAPPENING NOW.
THE HELL? THIS CAN'T BE LEGIT. NO WAY THIS IS COMING FROM HEAD OFFICE...
What the...
CATCH BATGIRL! WIN BIG!
RESIDENTS OF BURNSIDE! CAPTURE BATGIRL AND YOU COULD WIN UP TO 20 MILLION DOLLARS! USE ANY FORCE NECESSARY!
SO WHAT, IS THIS SOME KIND OF HACKER THING? ALL OF THIS VIRAL CODE, JUST A WAY TO HIJACK THE APP AND MESS WITH US?
WE'RE SCREWED. THERE'S NO WAY WE CAN FIX THIS IN TIME. MAY AS WELL TELL THEM TO CALL OFF THE PARTY AND I'LL START PUTTING TOGETHER A RESUME--
ughh~
OH, NO.
IT'S OKAY, THERE'S A HUNDRED NEW STARTUPS IN BURNSIDE. I'LL FIND SOME-THING--
OH, FRANKIE, I'M SORRY. NO, IT'S SOMETHING ELSE. I JUST GOT AN EMAIL FROM MY THESIS SUPERVISOR.
HE WANTS ME TO MEET HIM TOMORROW. NO EXCUSES.

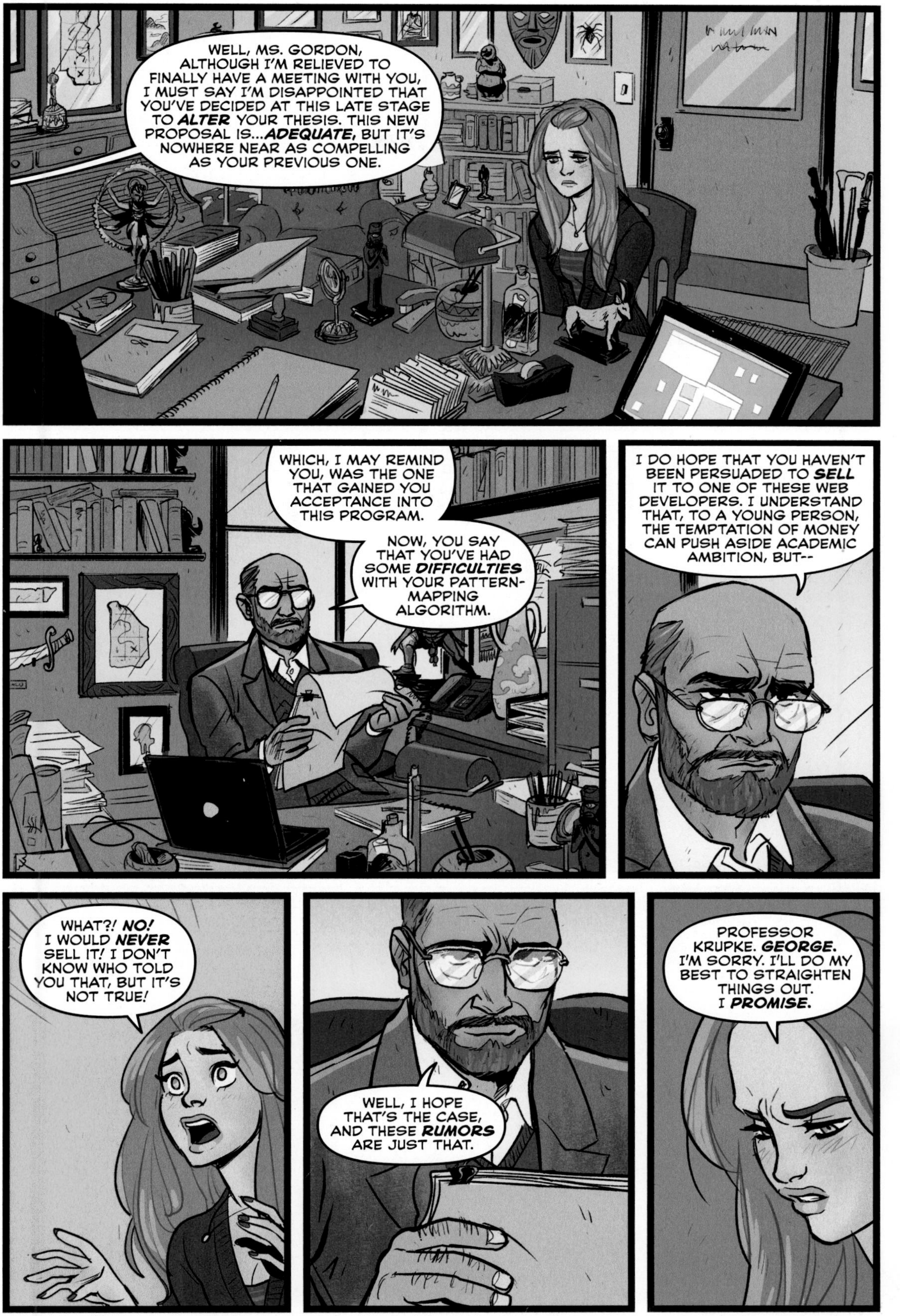
WELL, MS. GORDON, ALTHOUGH I'M RELIEVED TO FINALLY HAVE A MEETING WITH YOU, I MUST SAY I'M DISAPPOINTED THAT YOU'VE DECIDED AT THIS LATE STAGE TO ALTER YOUR THESIS. THIS NEW PROPOSAL IS...ADEQUATE, BUT IT'S NOWHERE NEAR AS COMPELLING AS YOUR PREVIOUS ONE.
WHICH, I MAY REMIND YOU, WAS THE ONE THAT GAINED YOU ACCEPTANCE INTO THIS PROGRAM.
NOW, YOU SAY THAT YOU'VE HAD SOME DIFFICULTIES WITH YOUR PATTERN-MAPPING ALGORITHM.
I DO HOPE THAT YOU HAVEN'T BEEN PERSUADED TO SELL IT TO ONE OF THESE WEB DEVELOPERS. I UNDERSTAND THAT, TO A YOUNG PERSON, THE TEMPTATION OF MONEY CAN PUSH ASIDE ACADEMIC AMBITION, BUT--
WHAT?! NO! I WOULD NEVER SELL IT! I DON'T KNOW WHO TOLD YOU THAT, BUT IT'S NOT TRUE!
WELL, I HOPE THAT'S THE CASE, AND THESE RUMORS ARE JUST THAT.
PROFESSOR KRUPKE. GEORGE. I'M SORRY. I'LL DO MY BEST TO STRAIGHTEN THINGS OUT. I PROMISE.

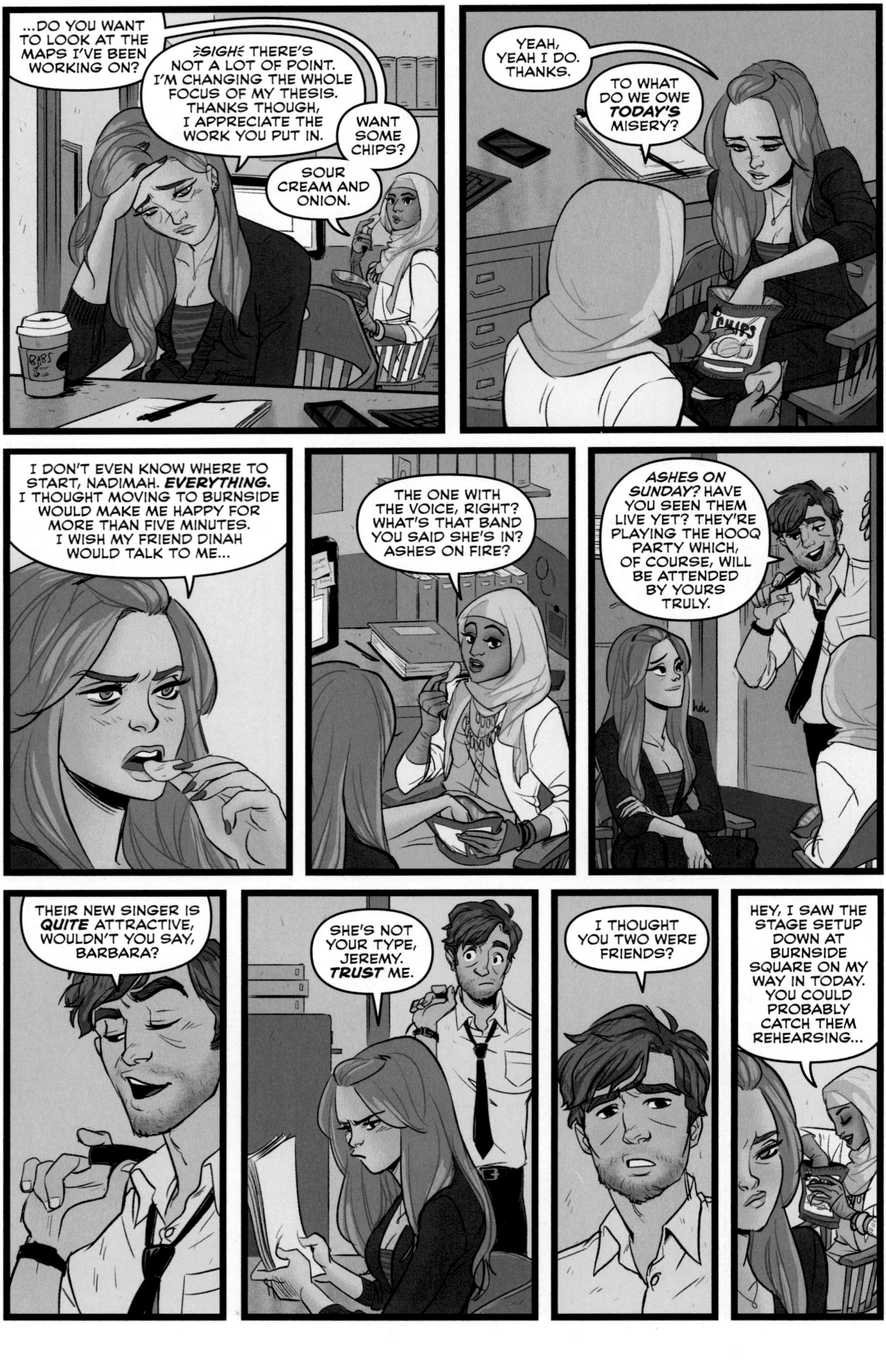

...DO YOU WANT TO LOOK AT THE MAPS I'VE BEEN WORKING ON?
SIGH THERE'S NOT A LOT OF POINT. I'M CHANGING THE WHOLE FOCUS OF MY THESIS. THANKS THOUGH, I APPRECIATE THE WORK YOU PUT IN.
WANT SOME CHIPS?
SOUR CREAM AND ONION.
BABS
YEAH, YEAH I DO. THANKS.
TO WHAT DO WE OWE **TODAY'S** MISERY?
CHIPS
I DON'T EVEN KNOW WHERE TO START, NADIMAH. **EVERYTHING.** I THOUGHT MOVING TO BURNSIDE WOULD MAKE ME HAPPY FOR MORE THAN FIVE MINUTES. I WISH MY FRIEND DINAH WOULD TALK TO ME...
THE ONE WITH THE VOICE, RIGHT? WHAT'S THAT BAND YOU SAID SHE'S IN? ASHES ON FIRE?
ASHES ON SUNDAY? HAVE YOU SEEN THEM LIVE YET? THEY'RE PLAYING THE HOOQ PARTY WHICH, OF COURSE, WILL BE ATTENDED BY YOURS TRULY.
heh
THEIR NEW SINGER IS ***QUITE*** ATTRACTIVE, WOULDN'T YOU SAY, BARBARA?
SHE'S NOT YOUR TYPE, JEREMY. ***TRUST*** ME.
I THOUGHT YOU TWO WERE FRIENDS?
HEY, I SAW THE STAGE SETUP DOWN AT BURNSIDE SQUARE ON MY WAY IN TODAY. YOU COULD PROBABLY CATCH THEM REHEARSING...

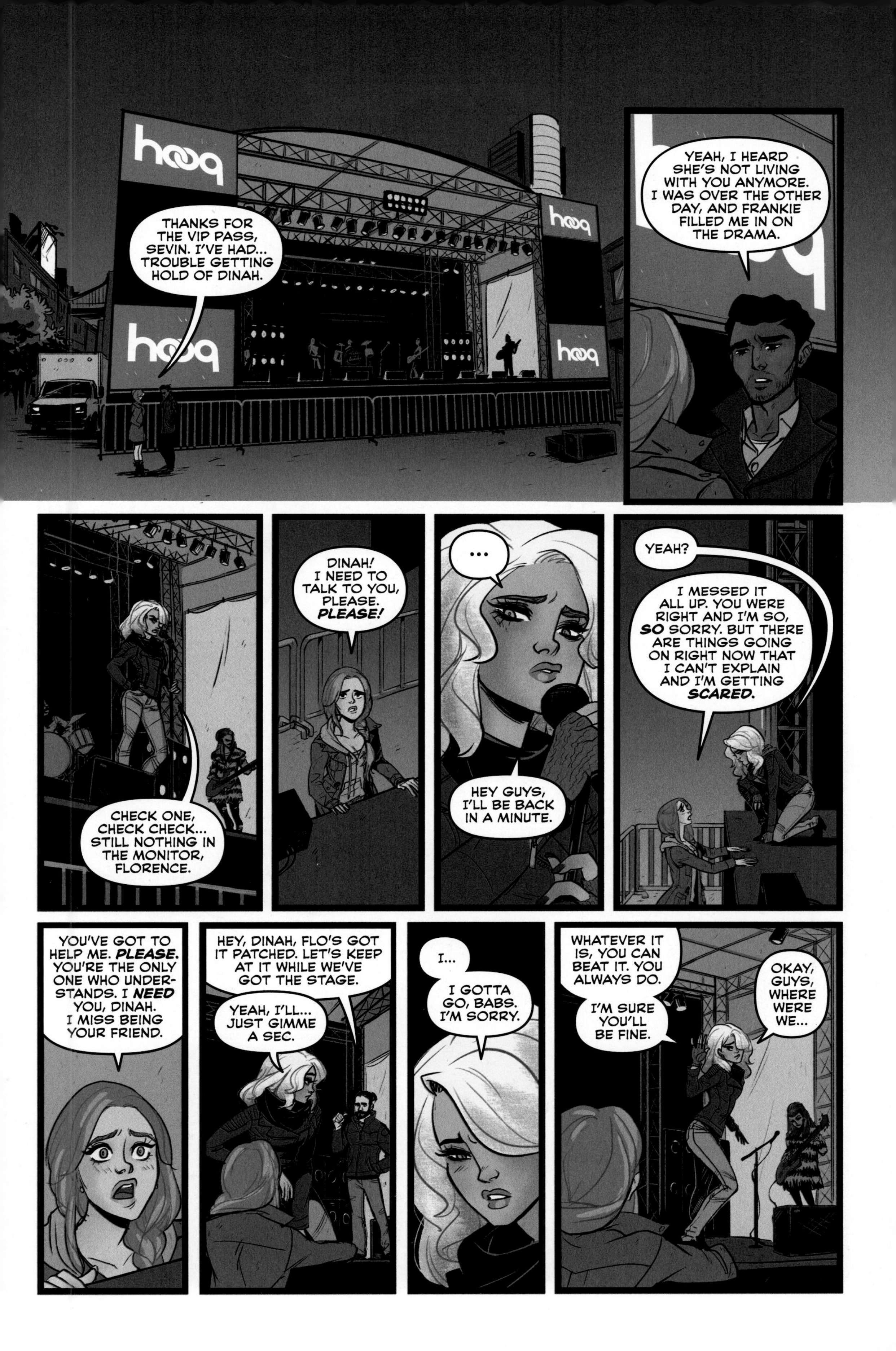
hooq
THANKS FOR THE VIP PASS, SEVIN. I'VE HAD... TROUBLE GETTING HOLD OF DINAH.
YEAH, I HEARD SHE'S NOT LIVING WITH YOU ANYMORE. I WAS OVER THE OTHER DAY, AND FRANKIE FILLED ME IN ON THE DRAMA.
CHECK ONE, CHECK CHECK... STILL NOTHING IN THE MONITOR, FLORENCE.
DINAH! I NEED TO TALK TO YOU, PLEASE. PLEASE!
...
HEY GUYS, I'LL BE BACK IN A MINUTE.
YEAH?
I MESSED IT ALL UP. YOU WERE RIGHT AND I'M SO, SO SORRY. BUT THERE ARE THINGS GOING ON RIGHT NOW THAT I CAN'T EXPLAIN AND I'M GETTING SCARED.
YOU'VE GOT TO HELP ME. PLEASE. YOU'RE THE ONLY ONE WHO UNDERSTANDS. I NEED YOU, DINAH. I MISS BEING YOUR FRIEND.
HEY, DINAH, FLO'S GOT IT PATCHED. LET'S KEEP AT IT WHILE WE'VE GOT THE STAGE.
YEAH, I'LL... JUST GIMME A SEC.
I...
I GOTTA GO, BABS. I'M SORRY.
WHATEVER IT IS, YOU CAN BEAT IT. YOU ALWAYS DO.
I'M SURE YOU'LL BE FINE.
OKAY, GUYS, WHERE WERE WE...

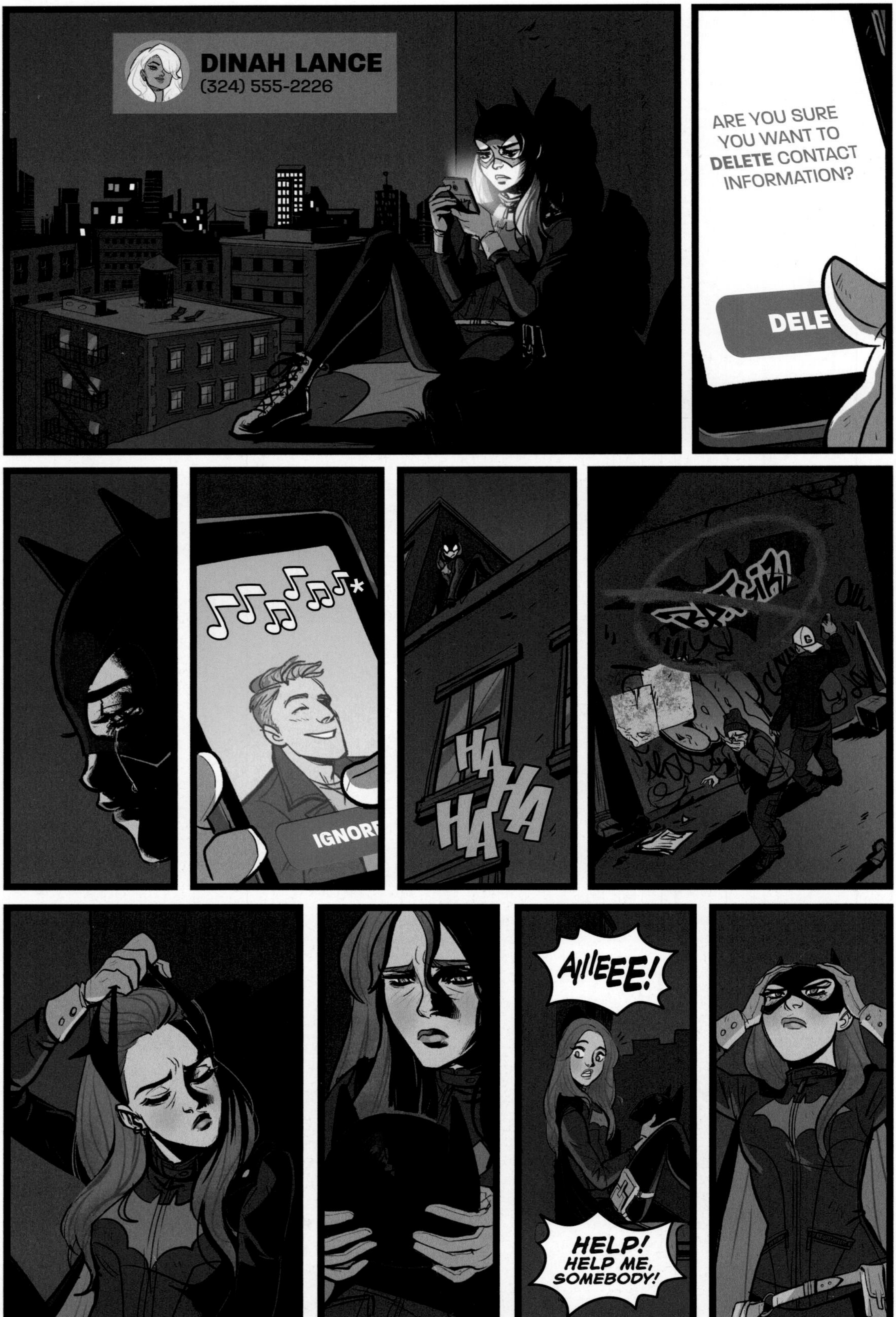
DINAH LANCE
(324) 555-2226
ARE YOU SURE YOU WANT TO DELETE CONTACT INFORMATION?
DELE
IGNORE
HA HA HA HA
AIIIEEE!
HELP! HELP ME, SOMEBODY!

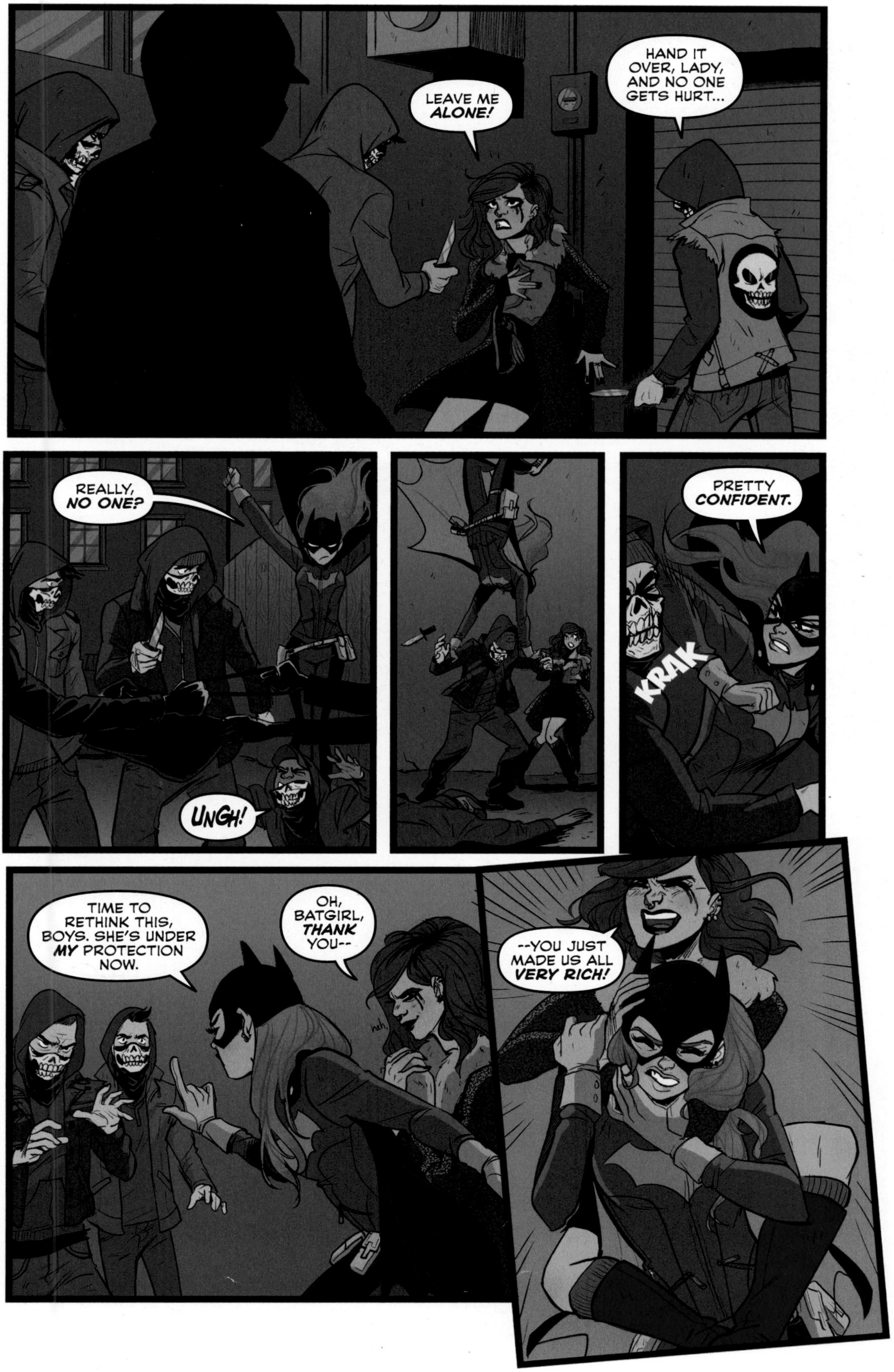
LEAVE ME ALONE!
HAND IT OVER, LADY, AND NO ONE GETS HURT...
REALLY, NO ONE?
UNGH!
PRETTY CONFIDENT.
KRAK
TIME TO RETHINK THIS, BOYS. SHE'S UNDER MY PROTECTION NOW.
OH, BATGIRL, THANK YOU--
heh.
--YOU JUST MADE US ALL VERY RICH!

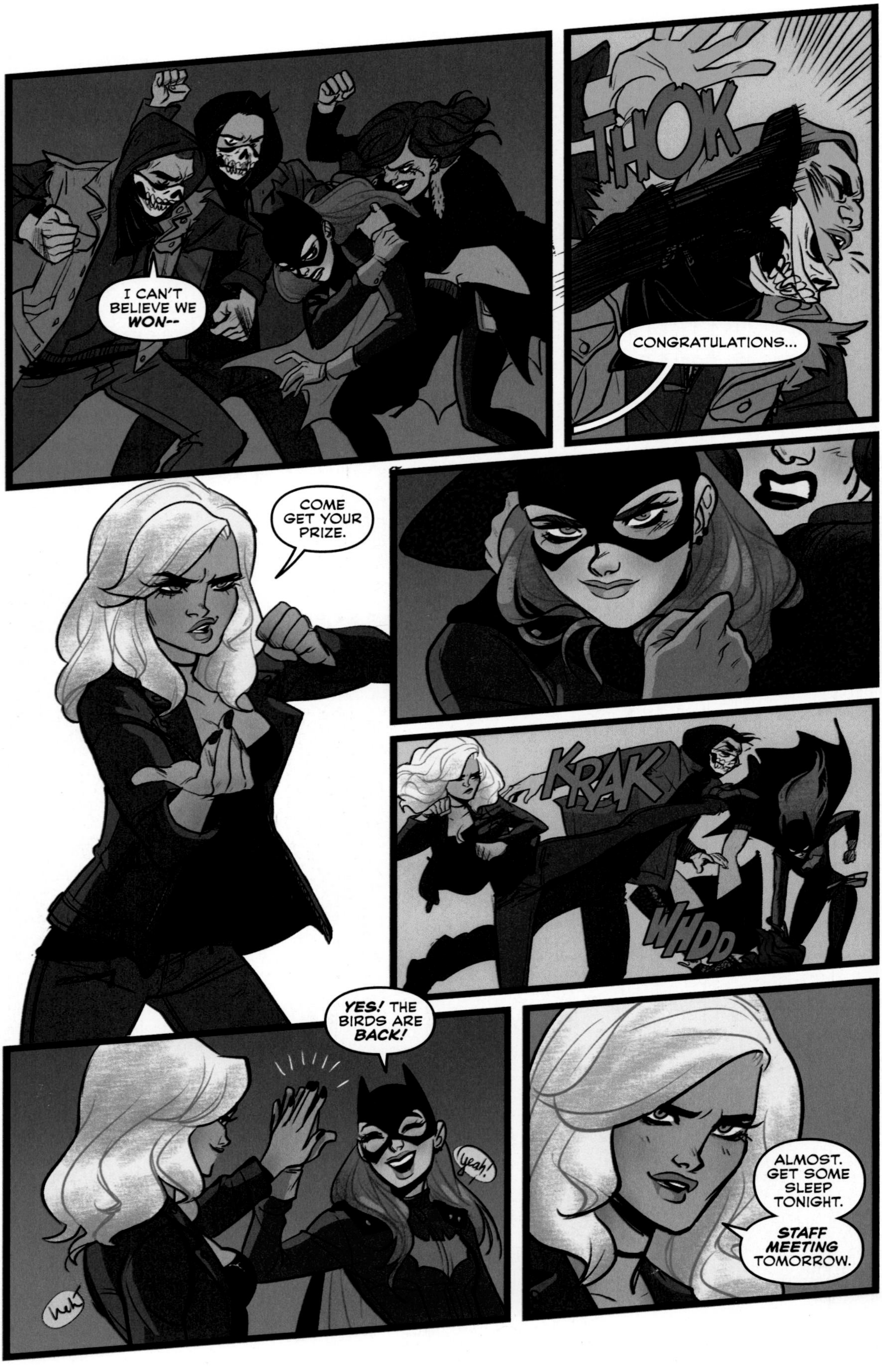
I CAN'T BELIEVE WE **WON--**
THOK
CONGRATULATIONS...
COME GET YOUR PRIZE.
KRAK
WHDD
YES! THE BIRDS ARE ***BACK!***
yeah!
ALMOST. GET SOME SLEEP TONIGHT.
STAFF MEETING TOMORROW.

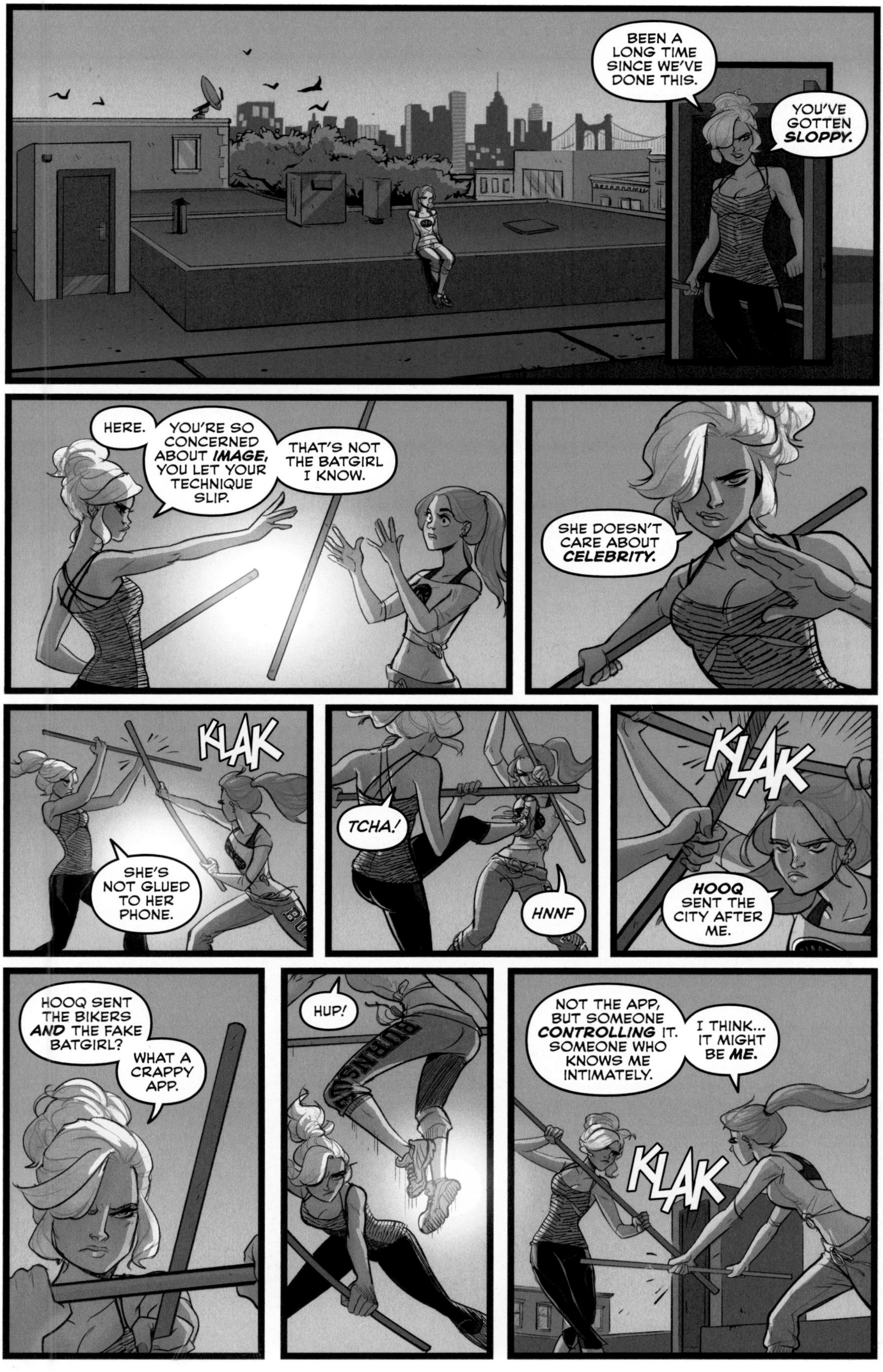
BEEN A LONG TIME SINCE WE'VE DONE THIS.
YOU'VE GOTTEN SLOPPY.
HERE.
YOU'RE SO CONCERNED ABOUT IMAGE, YOU LET YOUR TECHNIQUE SLIP.
THAT'S NOT THE BATGIRL I KNOW.
SHE DOESN'T CARE ABOUT CELEBRITY.
KLAK
SHE'S NOT GLUED TO HER PHONE.
TCHA!
HNNF
KLAK
HOOQ SENT THE CITY AFTER ME.
HOOQ SENT THE BIKERS AND THE FAKE BATGIRL?
WHAT A CRAPPY APP.
HUP!
NOT THE APP, BUT SOMEONE CONTROLLING IT. SOMEONE WHO KNOWS ME INTIMATELY.
I THINK... IT MIGHT BE ME.
KLAK

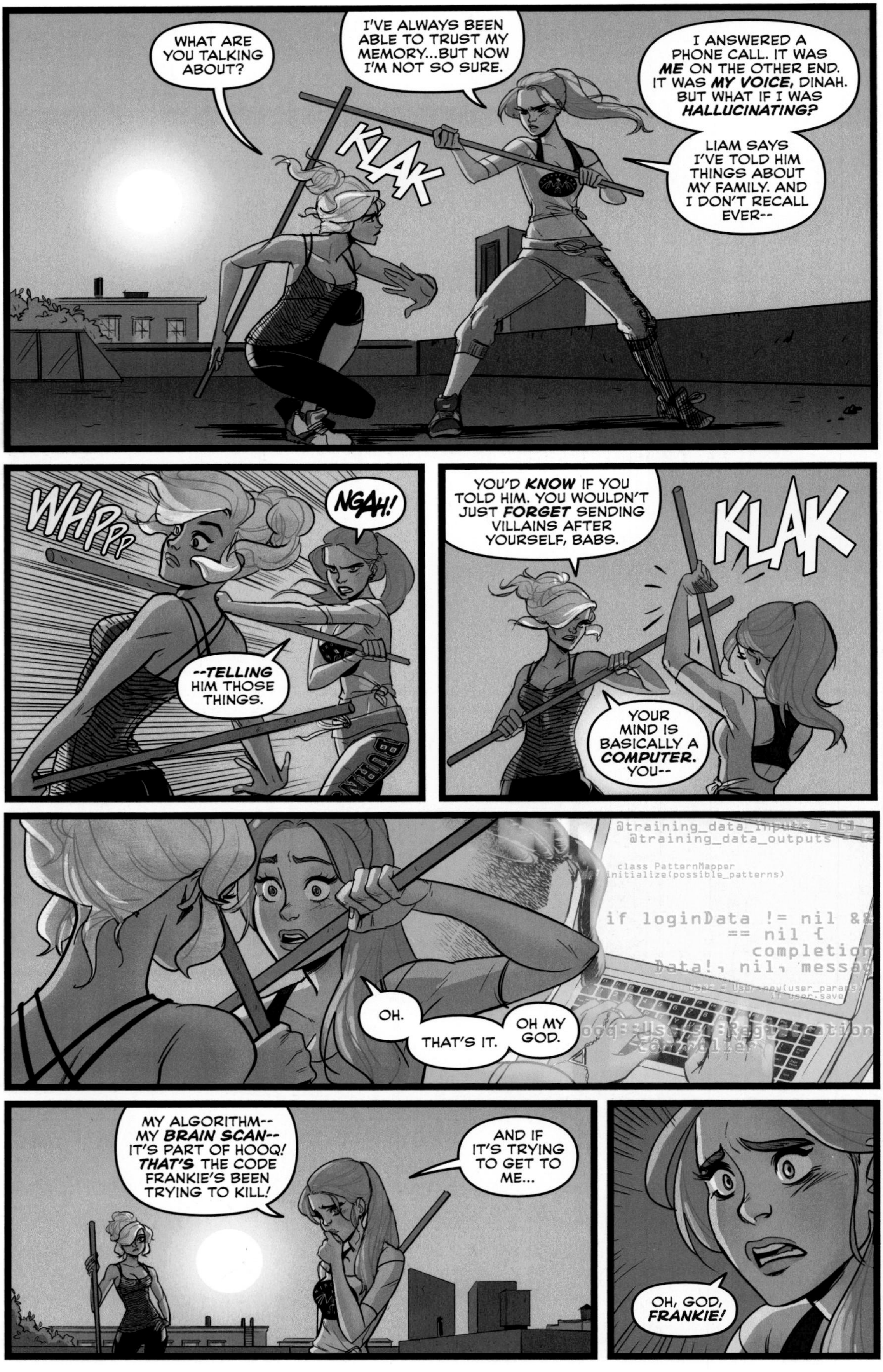
WHAT ARE YOU TALKING ABOUT?
I'VE ALWAYS BEEN ABLE TO TRUST MY MEMORY...BUT NOW I'M NOT SO SURE.
KLAK
I ANSWERED A PHONE CALL. IT WAS *ME* ON THE OTHER END. IT WAS *MY VOICE,* DINAH. BUT WHAT IF I WAS *HALLUCINATING?*
LIAM SAYS I'VE TOLD HIM THINGS ABOUT MY FAMILY. AND I DON'T RECALL EVER--
WHPPP
NGAH!
--*TELLING* HIM THOSE THINGS.
YOU'D *KNOW* IF YOU TOLD HIM. YOU WOULDN'T JUST *FORGET* SENDING VILLAINS AFTER YOURSELF, BABS.
KLAK
YOUR MIND IS BASICALLY A *COMPUTER.* YOU--
class PatternMapper
if loginData != nil &&
OH.
THAT'S IT.
OH MY GOD.
MY ALGORITHM-- MY *BRAIN SCAN--* IT'S PART OF HOOQ! *THAT'S* THE CODE FRANKIE'S BEEN TRYING TO KILL!
AND IF IT'S TRYING TO GET TO ME...
OH, GOD, *FRANKIE!*

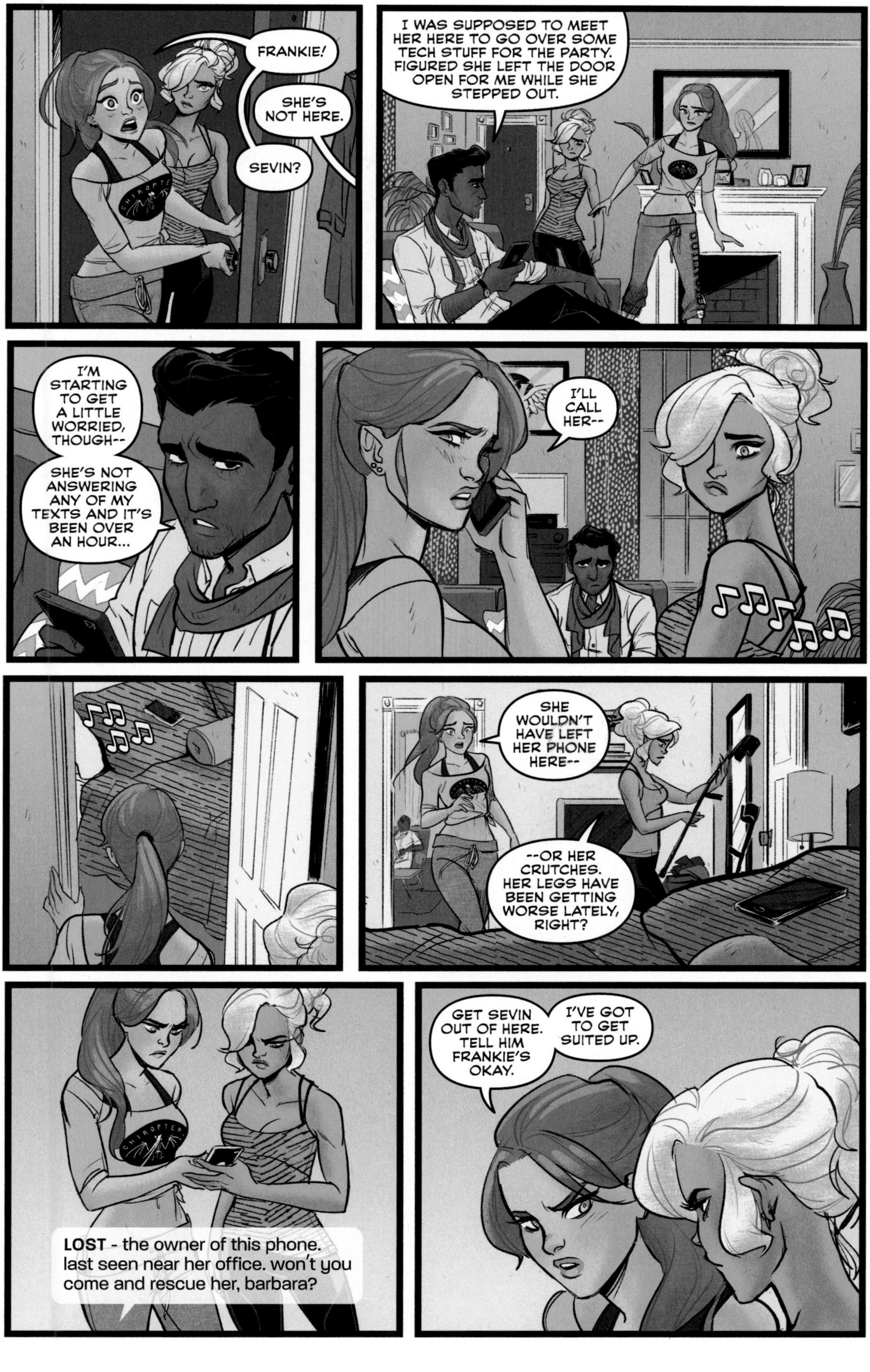
FRANKIE!
SHE'S NOT HERE.
SEVIN?
I WAS SUPPOSED TO MEET HER HERE TO GO OVER SOME TECH STUFF FOR THE PARTY. FIGURED SHE LEFT THE DOOR OPEN FOR ME WHILE SHE STEPPED OUT.
I'M STARTING TO GET A LITTLE WORRIED, THOUGH--
SHE'S NOT ANSWERING ANY OF MY TEXTS AND IT'S BEEN OVER AN HOUR...
I'LL CALL HER--
SHE WOULDN'T HAVE LEFT HER PHONE HERE--
--OR HER CRUTCHES. HER LEGS HAVE BEEN GETTING WORSE LATELY, RIGHT?
LOST - the owner of this phone. last seen near her office. won't you come and rescue her, barbara?
GET SEVIN OUT OF HERE. TELL HIM FRANKIE'S OKAY.
I'VE GOT TO GET SUITED UP.

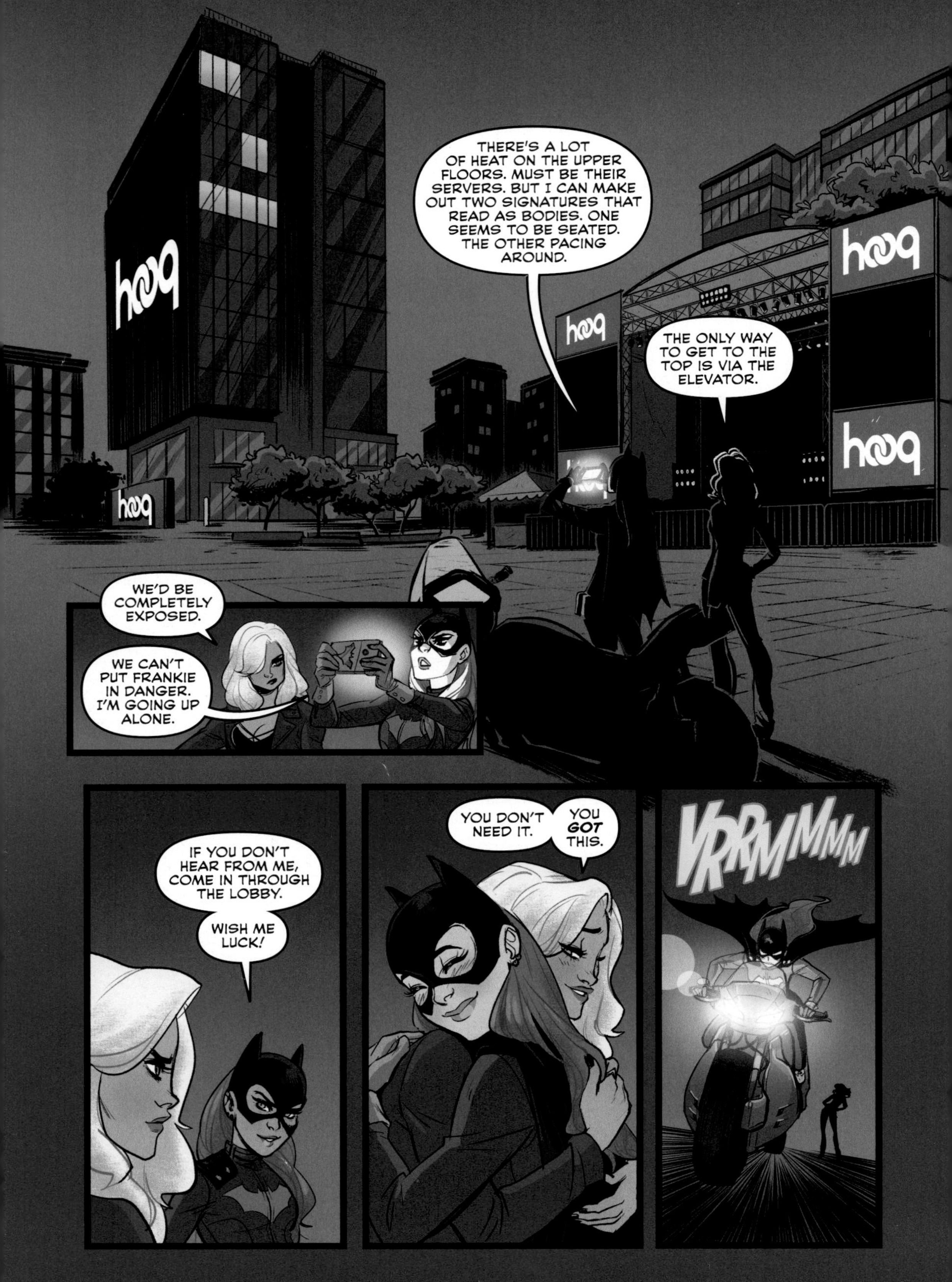

THERE'S A LOT OF HEAT ON THE UPPER FLOORS. MUST BE THEIR SERVERS. BUT I CAN MAKE OUT TWO SIGNATURES THAT READ AS BODIES. ONE SEEMS TO BE SEATED. THE OTHER PACING AROUND.
THE ONLY WAY TO GET TO THE TOP IS VIA THE ELEVATOR.
WE'D BE COMPLETELY EXPOSED.
WE CAN'T PUT FRANKIE IN DANGER. I'M GOING UP ALONE.
IF YOU DON'T HEAR FROM ME, COME IN THROUGH THE LOBBY.
WISH ME LUCK!
YOU DON'T NEED IT.
YOU **GOT** THIS.
VRRMMMM

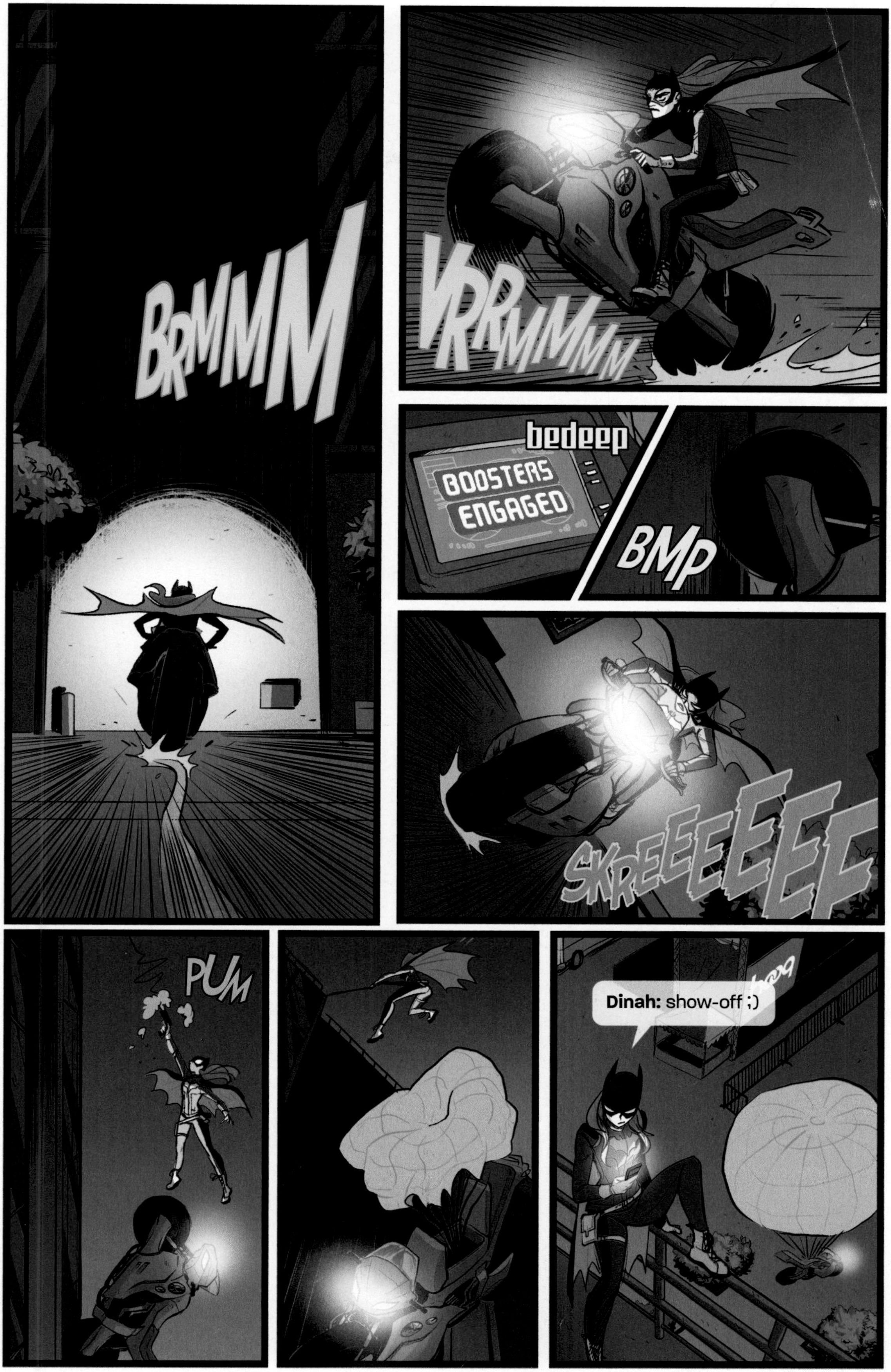
BRMMM
VRRMMMMM
bedeep
BOOSTERS ENGAGED
BMP
SKREEEEEEE
PUM
Dinah: show-off ;)

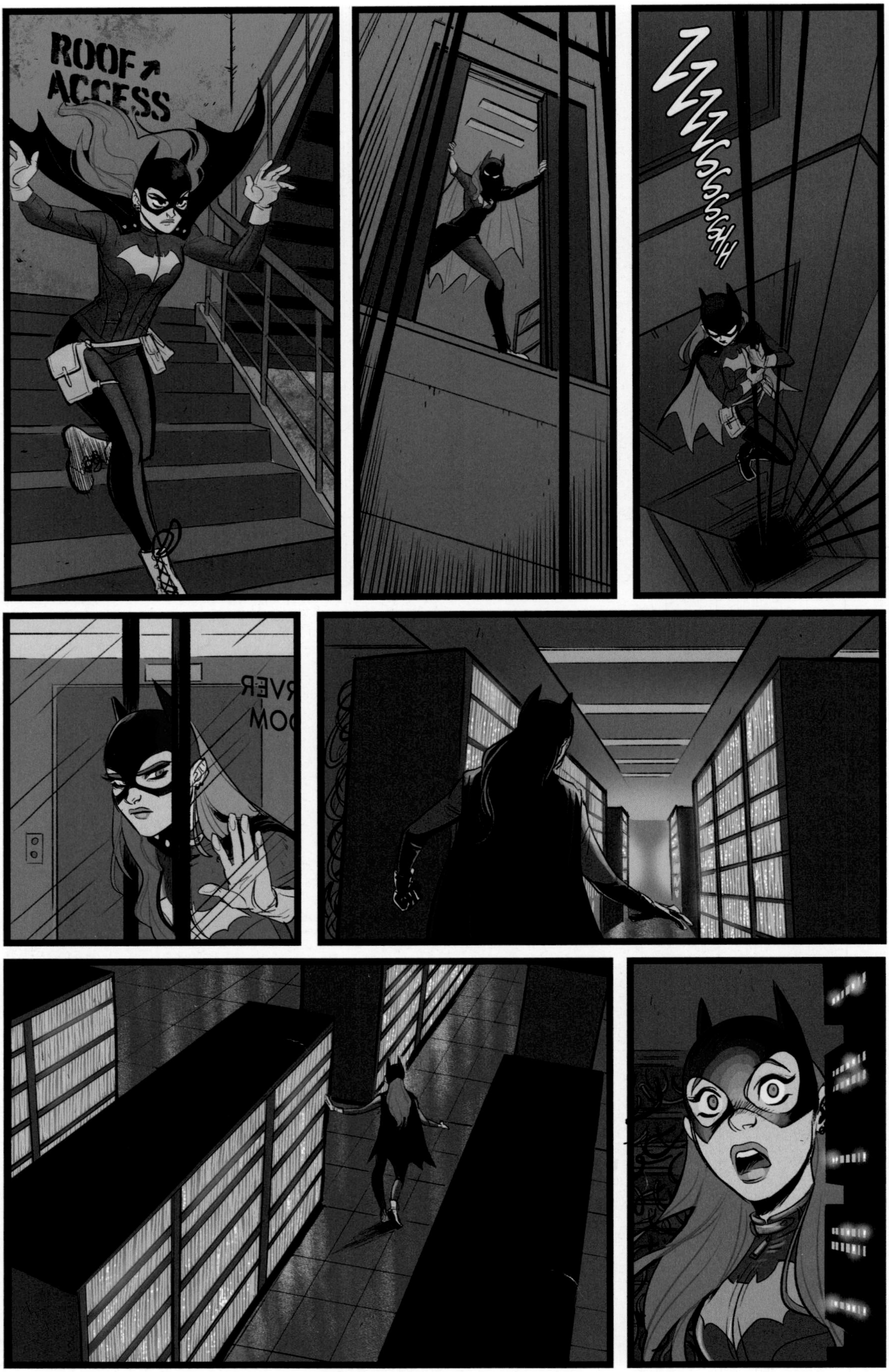
ROOF ↗ ACCESS
ZZZZSSSSGHH

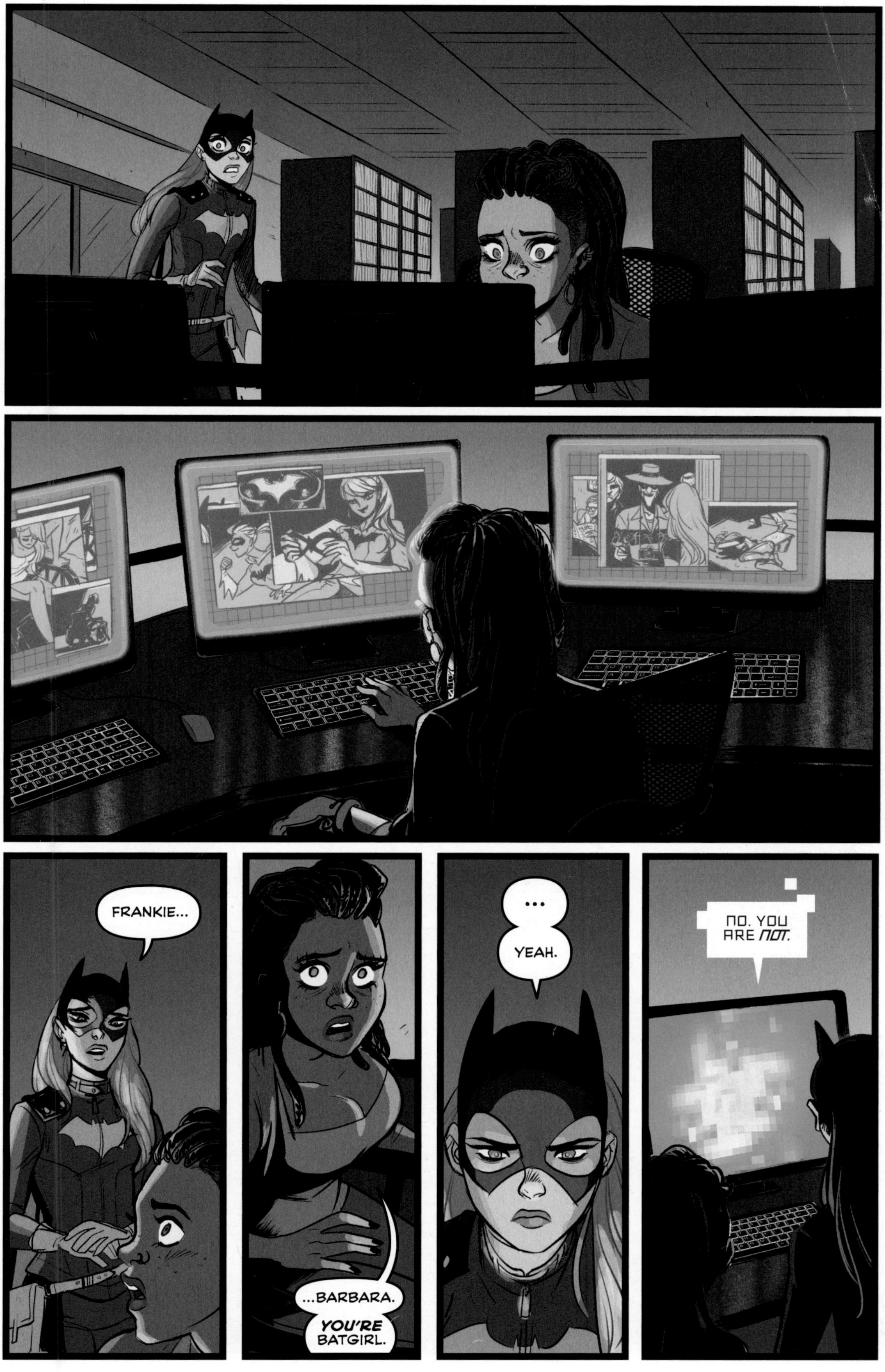
FRANKIE...
...BARBARA.
YOU'RE BATGIRL.
...
YEAH.
NO. YOU ARE NOT.

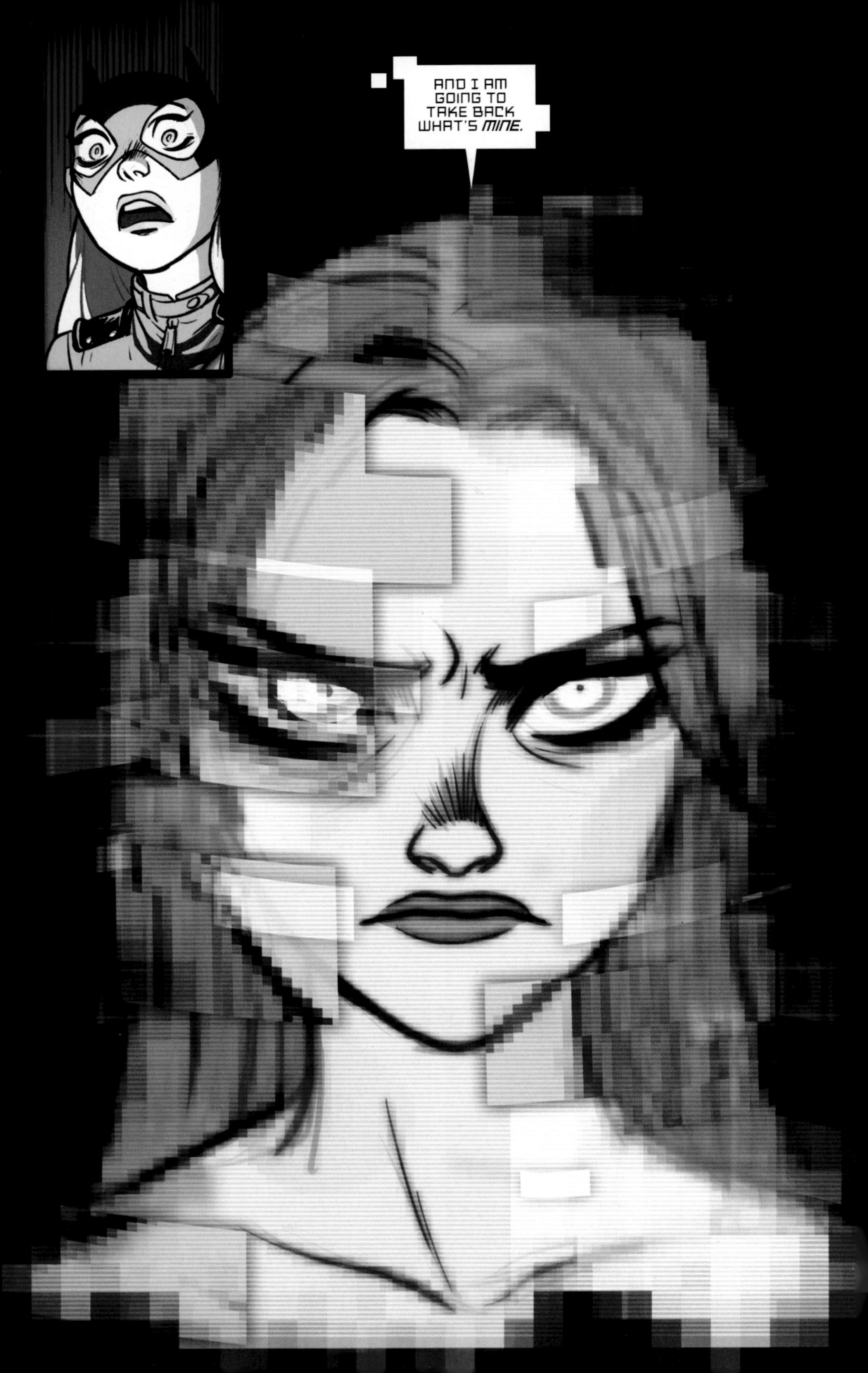
AND I AM GOING TO TAKE BACK WHAT'S *MINE.*

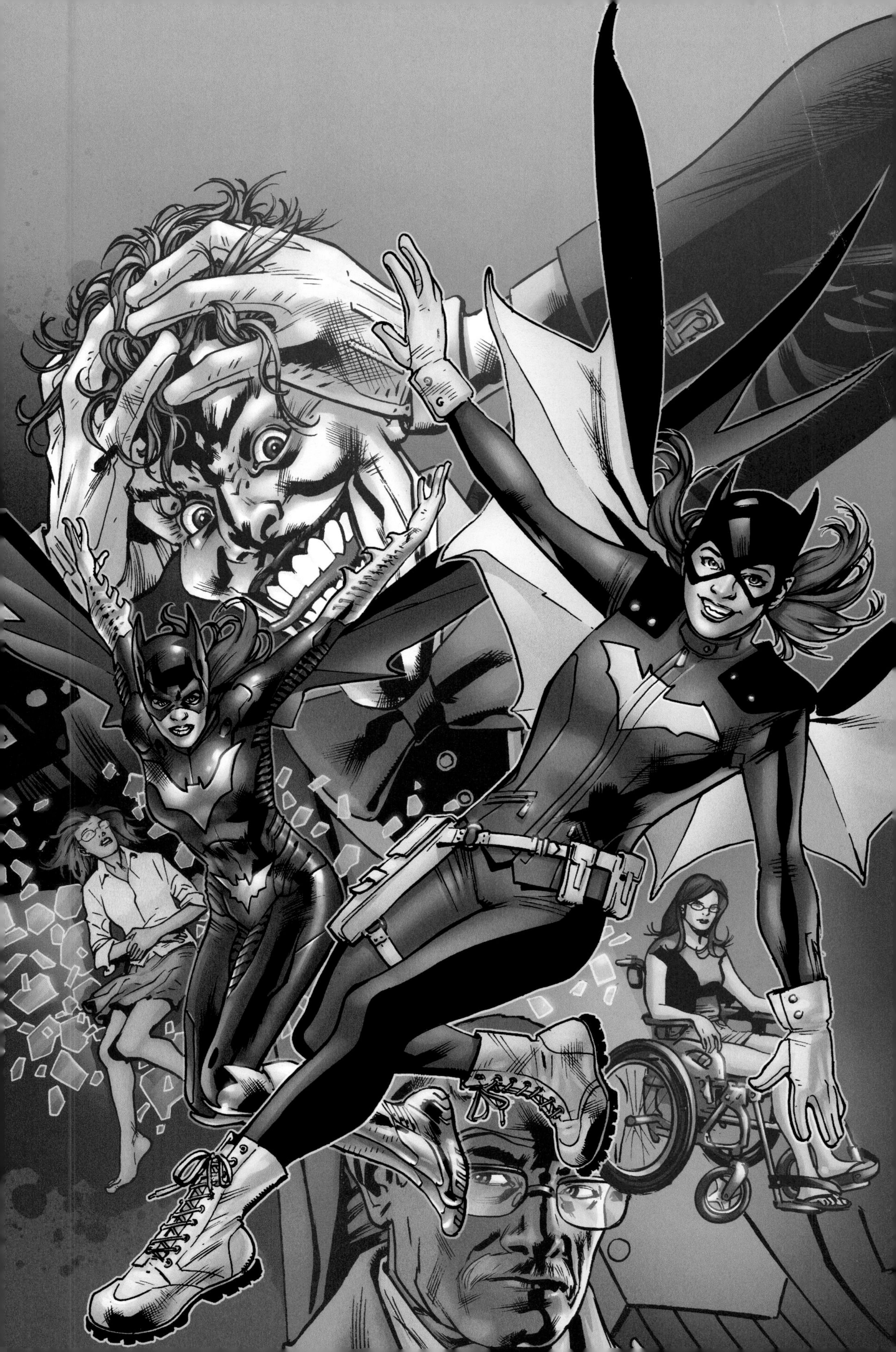

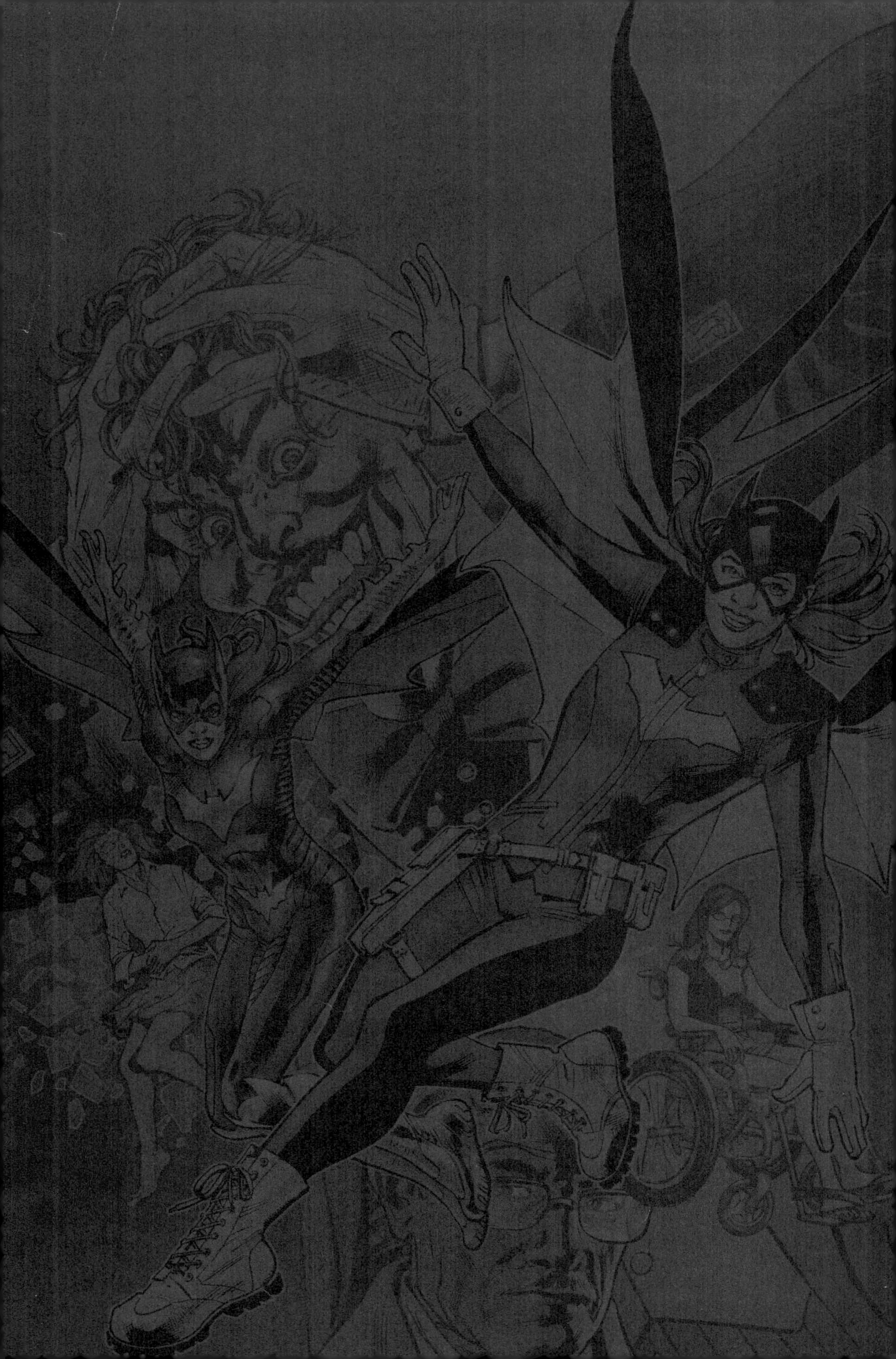

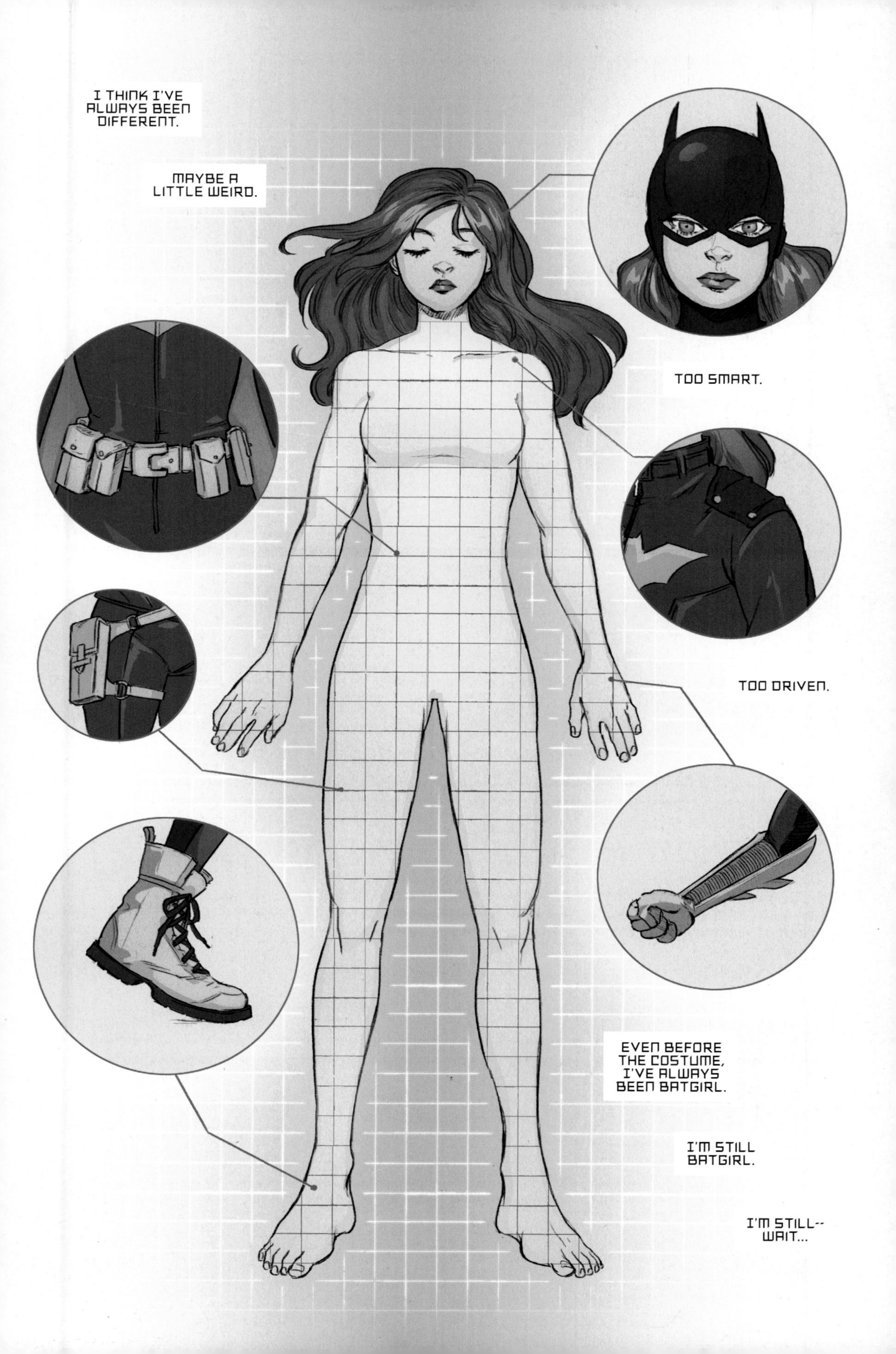
I THINK I'VE ALWAYS BEEN DIFFERENT.
MAYBE A LITTLE WEIRD.
TOO SMART.
TOO DRIVEN.
EVEN BEFORE THE COSTUME, I'VE ALWAYS BEEN BATGIRL.
I'M STILL BATGIRL.
I'M STILL-- WAIT...

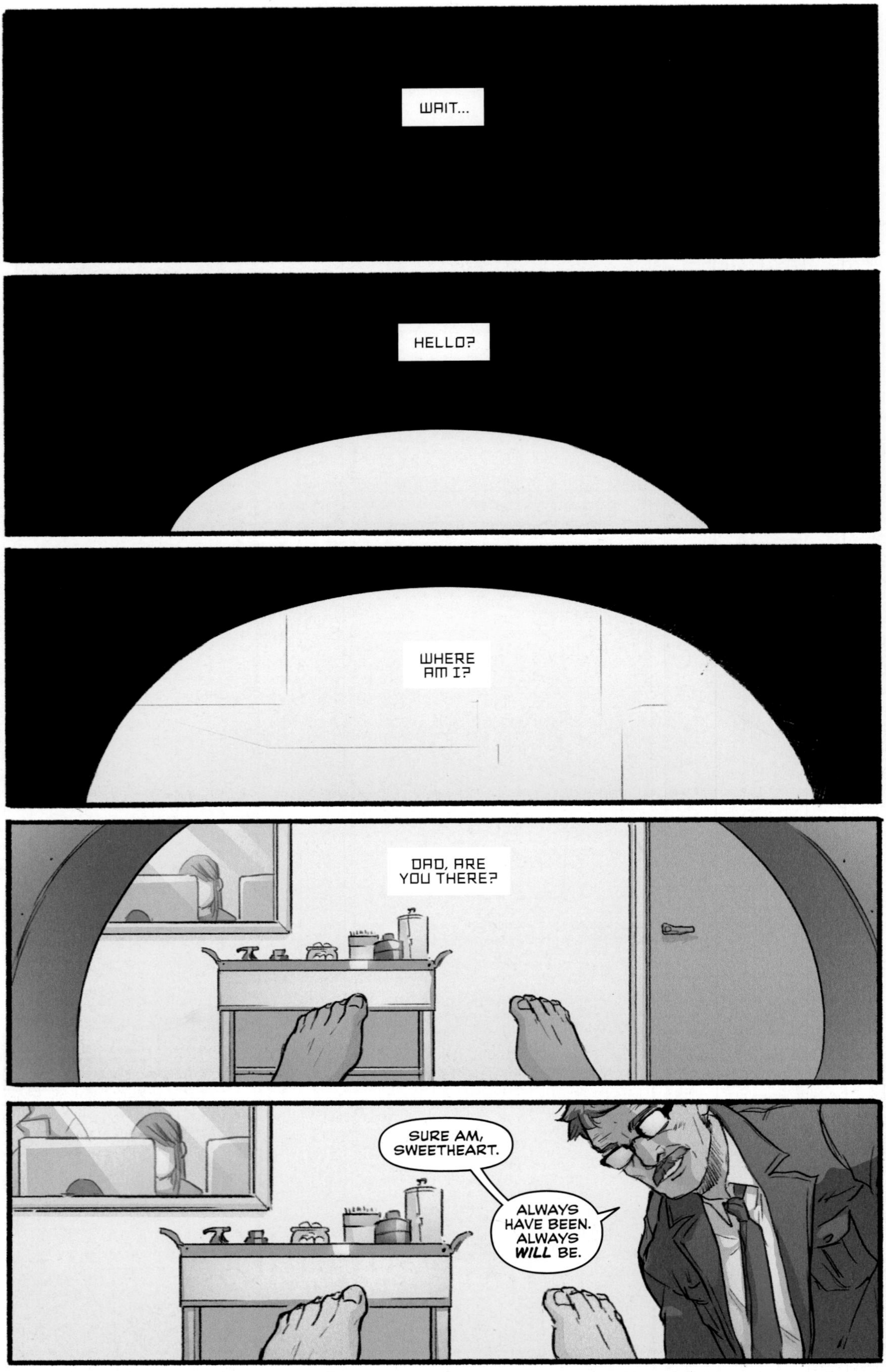
WAIT...
HELLO?
WHERE AM I?
DAD, ARE YOU THERE?
SURE AM, SWEETHEART.
ALWAYS HAVE BEEN. ALWAYS *WILL* BE.

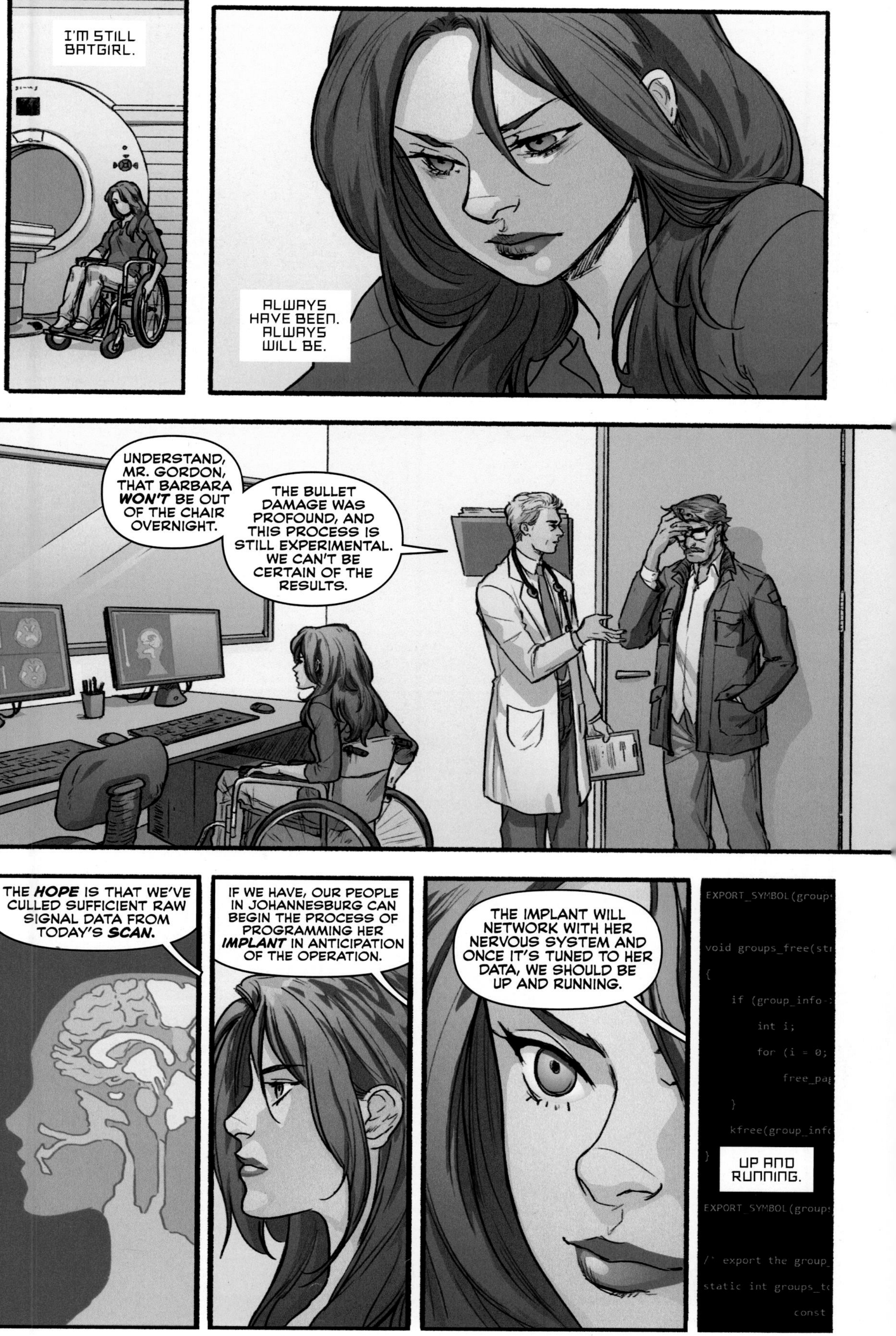
I'M STILL BATGIRL.
ALWAYS HAVE BEEN. ALWAYS WILL BE.
UNDERSTAND, MR. GORDON, THAT BARBARA *WON'T* BE OUT OF THE CHAIR OVERNIGHT.
THE BULLET DAMAGE WAS PROFOUND, AND THIS PROCESS IS STILL EXPERIMENTAL. WE CAN'T BE CERTAIN OF THE RESULTS.
THE *HOPE* IS THAT WE'VE CULLED SUFFICIENT RAW SIGNAL DATA FROM TODAY'S *SCAN.*
IF WE HAVE, OUR PEOPLE IN JOHANNESBURG CAN BEGIN THE PROCESS OF PROGRAMMING HER *IMPLANT* IN ANTICIPATION OF THE OPERATION.
THE IMPLANT WILL NETWORK WITH HER NERVOUS SYSTEM AND ONCE IT'S TUNED TO HER DATA, WE SHOULD BE UP AND RUNNING.
EXPORT_SYMBOL(groups
void groups_free(st
{
if (group_info-
int i;
for (i = 0;
free_pa
}
kfree(group_inf
}
UP AND RUNNING.
EXPORT_SYMBOL(groups
/* export the group_
static int groups_t
const

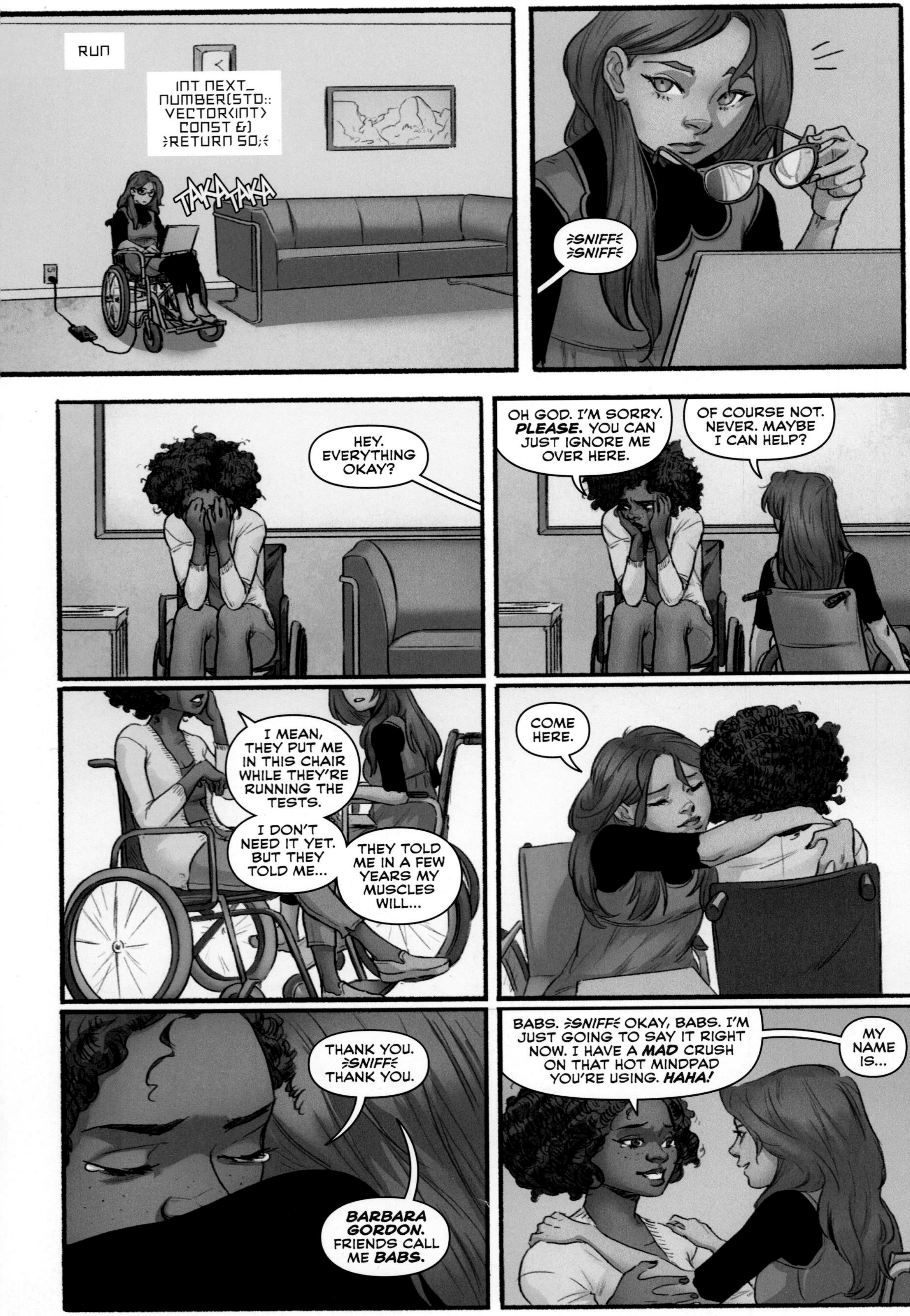
RUN
INT NEXT_ NUMBER(STD:: VECTOR<INT> CONST &) }RETURN 50;{
TAKA TAKA
SNIFF SNIFF
HEY. EVERYTHING OKAY?
OH GOD. I'M SORRY. PLEASE. YOU CAN JUST IGNORE ME OVER HERE.
OF COURSE NOT. NEVER. MAYBE I CAN HELP?
I MEAN, THEY PUT ME IN THIS CHAIR WHILE THEY'RE RUNNING THE TESTS.
I DON'T NEED IT YET. BUT THEY TOLD ME...
THEY TOLD ME IN A FEW YEARS MY MUSCLES WILL...
COME HERE.
THANK YOU. SNIFF THANK YOU.
BARBARA GORDON. FRIENDS CALL ME BABS.
MY NAME IS...
BABS. SNIFF OKAY, BABS. I'M JUST GOING TO SAY IT RIGHT NOW. I HAVE A MAD CRUSH ON THAT HOT MINDPAD YOU'RE USING. HAHA!

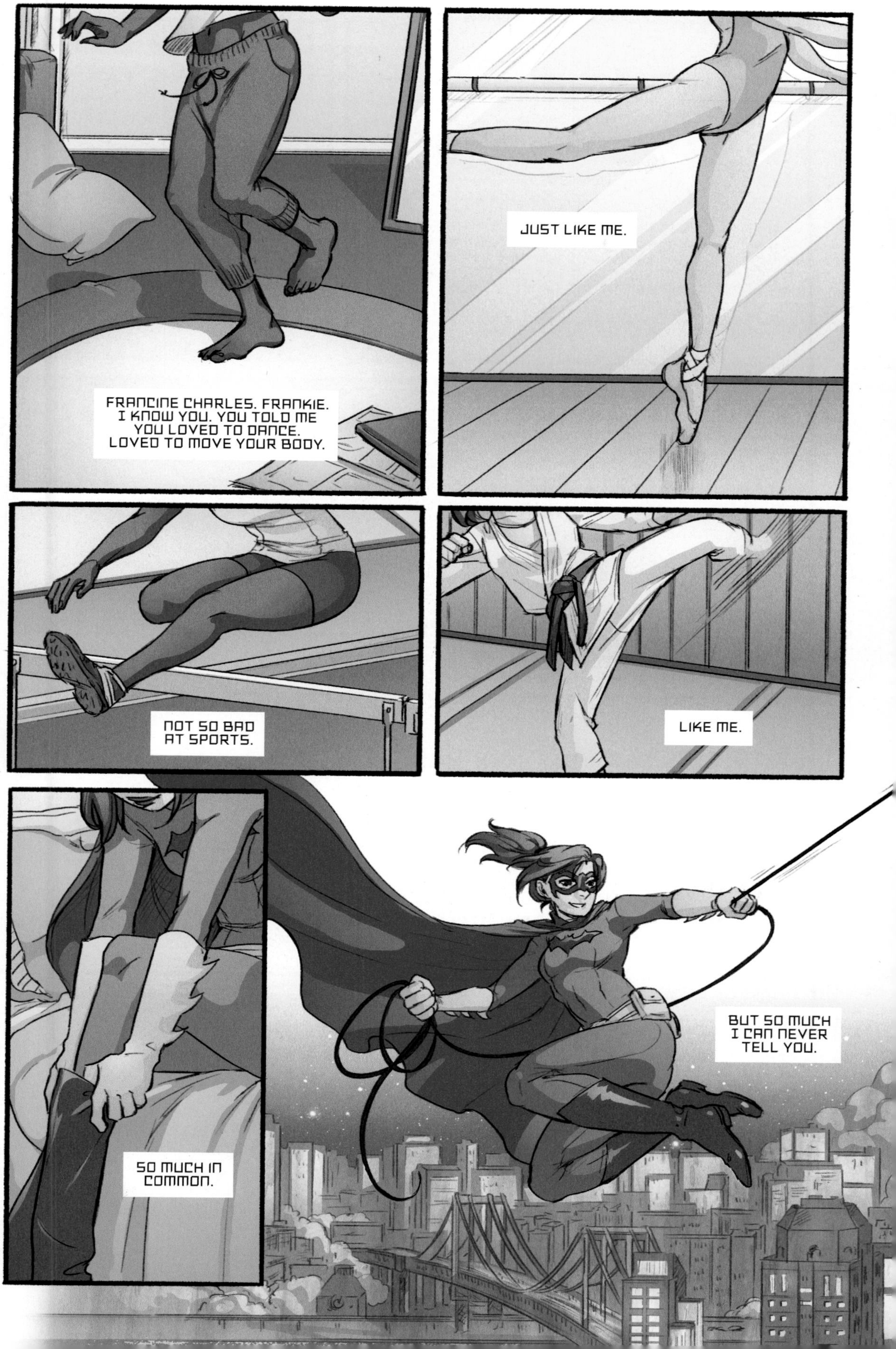
FRANCINE CHARLES. FRANKIE. I KNOW YOU. YOU TOLD ME YOU LOVED TO DANCE. LOVED TO MOVE YOUR BODY.
JUST LIKE ME.
NOT SO BAD AT SPORTS.
LIKE ME.
SO MUCH IN COMMON.
BUT SO MUCH I CAN NEVER TELL YOU.

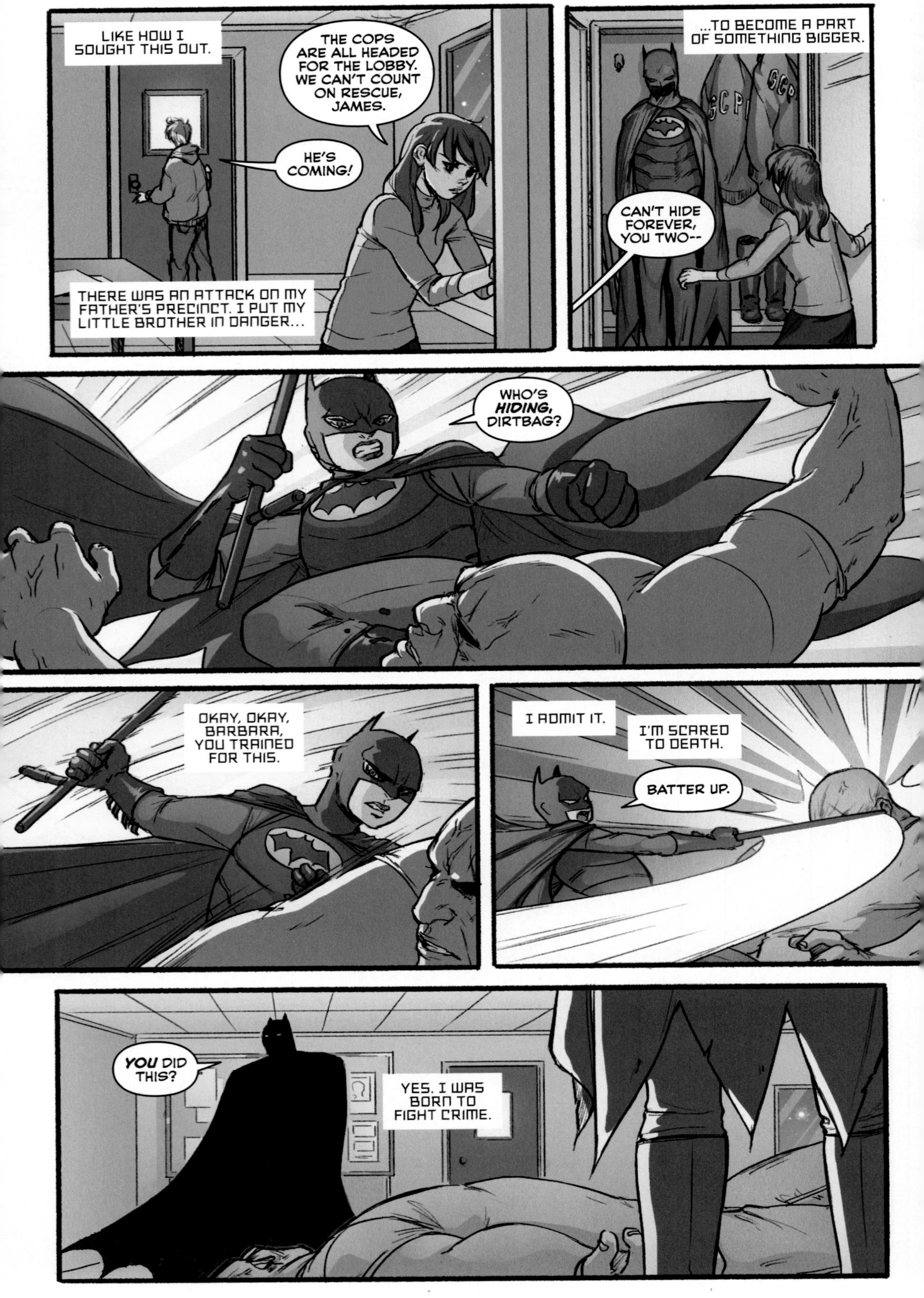
LIKE HOW I SOUGHT THIS OUT.
THE COPS ARE ALL HEADED FOR THE LOBBY. WE CAN'T COUNT ON RESCUE, JAMES.
HE'S COMING!
THERE WAS AN ATTACK ON MY FATHER'S PRECINCT. I PUT MY LITTLE BROTHER IN DANGER...
...TO BECOME A PART OF SOMETHING BIGGER.
GCPD
GCPD
CAN'T HIDE FOREVER, YOU TWO--
WHO'S *HIDING,* DIRTBAG?
OKAY, OKAY, BARBARA, YOU TRAINED FOR THIS.
I ADMIT IT.
I'M SCARED TO DEATH.
BATTER UP.
YOU DID THIS?
YES. I WAS BORN TO FIGHT CRIME.

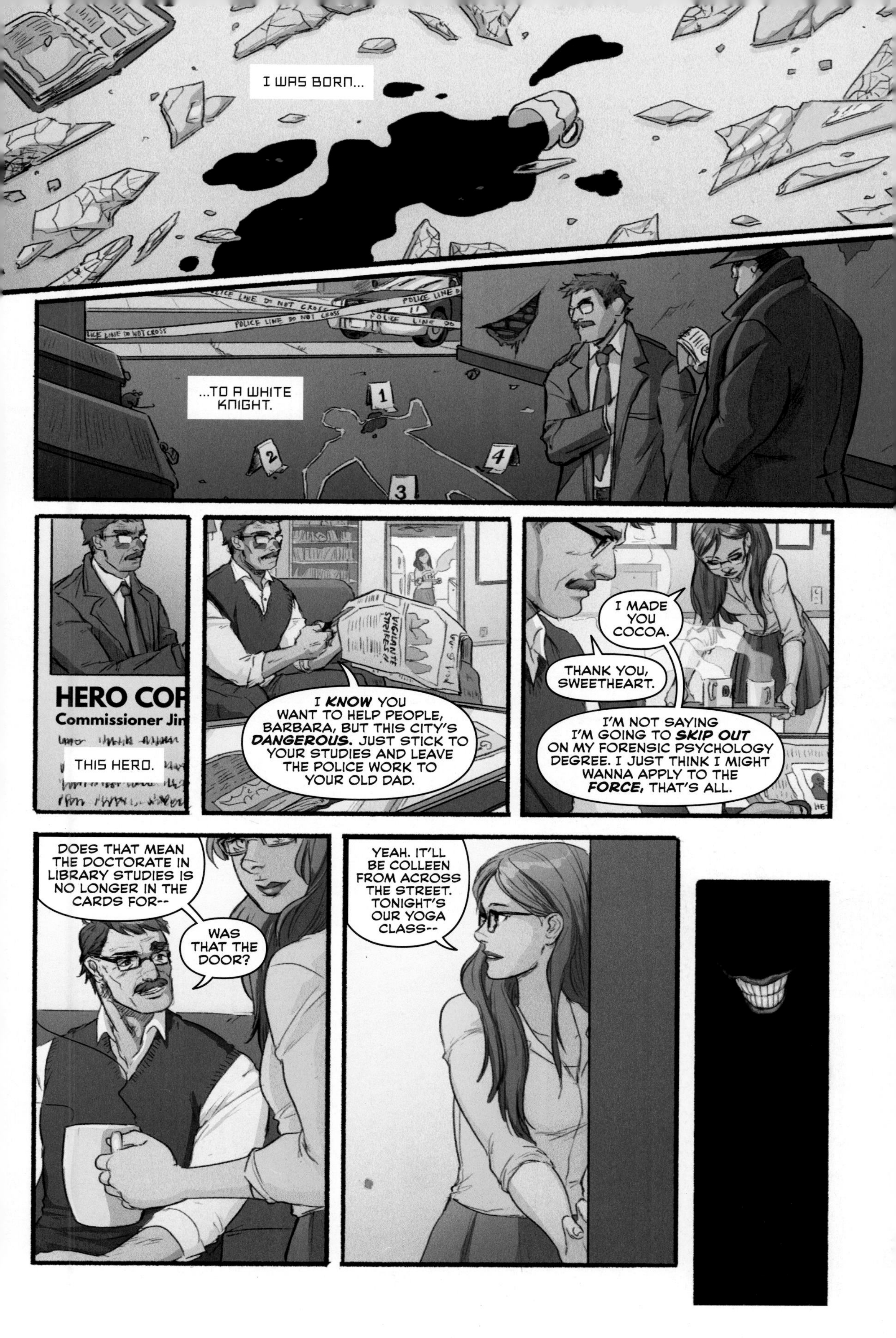
I WAS BORN...
POLICE LINE DO NOT CROSS
...TO A WHITE KNIGHT.
1
2
3
4
HERO COP
Commissioner Jim
THIS HERO.
VIGILANTE STRIKES!!
I KNOW YOU WANT TO HELP PEOPLE, BARBARA, BUT THIS CITY'S DANGEROUS. JUST STICK TO YOUR STUDIES AND LEAVE THE POLICE WORK TO YOUR OLD DAD.
I MADE YOU COCOA.
THANK YOU, SWEETHEART.
I'M NOT SAYING I'M GOING TO SKIP OUT ON MY FORENSIC PSYCHOLOGY DEGREE. I JUST THINK I MIGHT WANNA APPLY TO THE FORCE, THAT'S ALL.
DOES THAT MEAN THE DOCTORATE IN LIBRARY STUDIES IS NO LONGER IN THE CARDS FOR--
WAS THAT THE DOOR?
YEAH. IT'LL BE COLLEEN FROM ACROSS THE STREET. TONIGHT'S OUR YOGA CLASS--

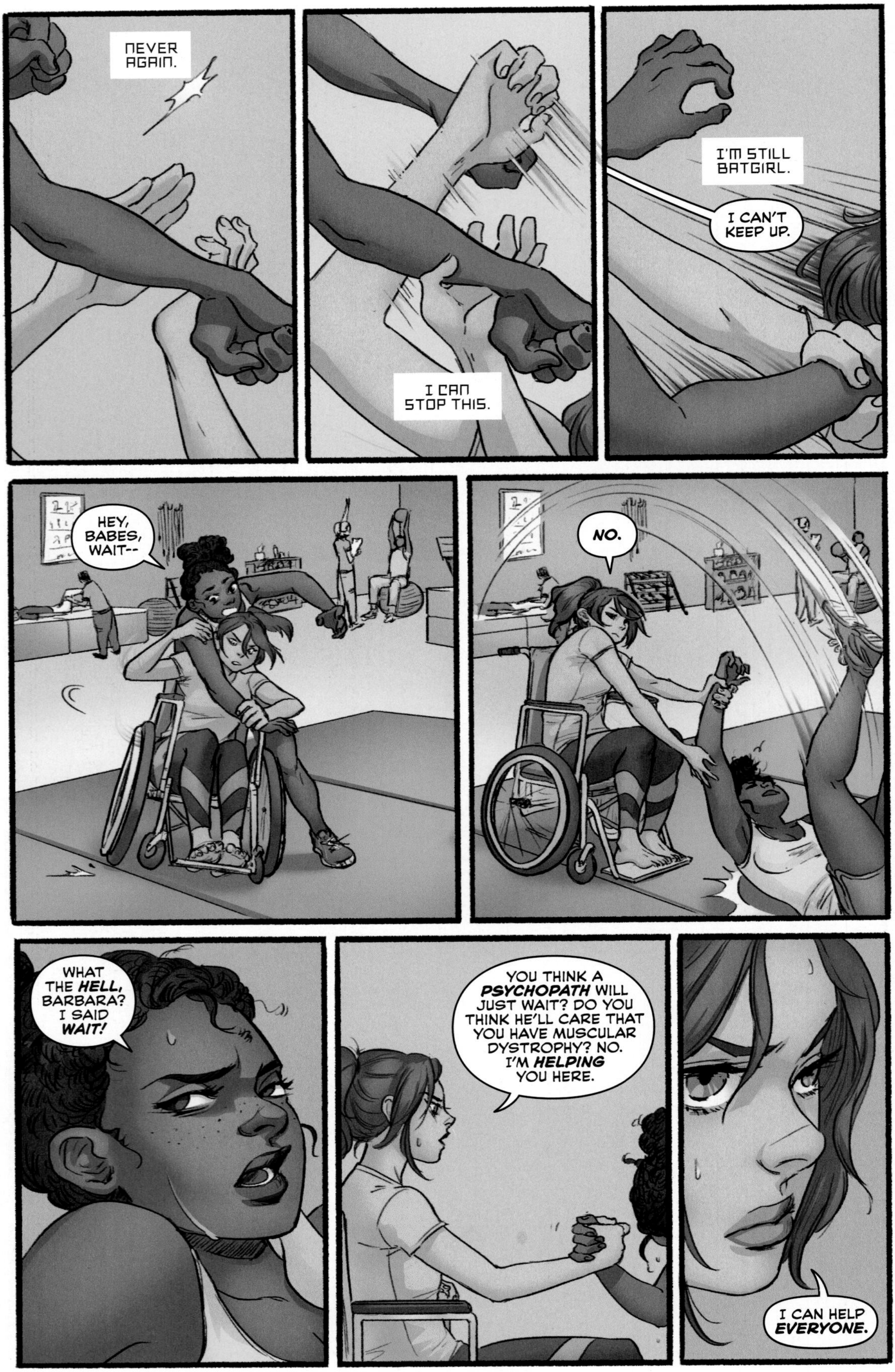
NEVER AGAIN.
I CAN STOP THIS.
I'M STILL BATGIRL.
I CAN'T KEEP UP.
HEY, BABES, WAIT--
NO.
WHAT THE HELL, BARBARA? I SAID WAIT!
YOU THINK A PSYCHOPATH WILL JUST WAIT? DO YOU THINK HE'LL CARE THAT YOU HAVE MUSCULAR DYSTROPHY? NO. I'M HELPING YOU HERE.
I CAN HELP EVERYONE.

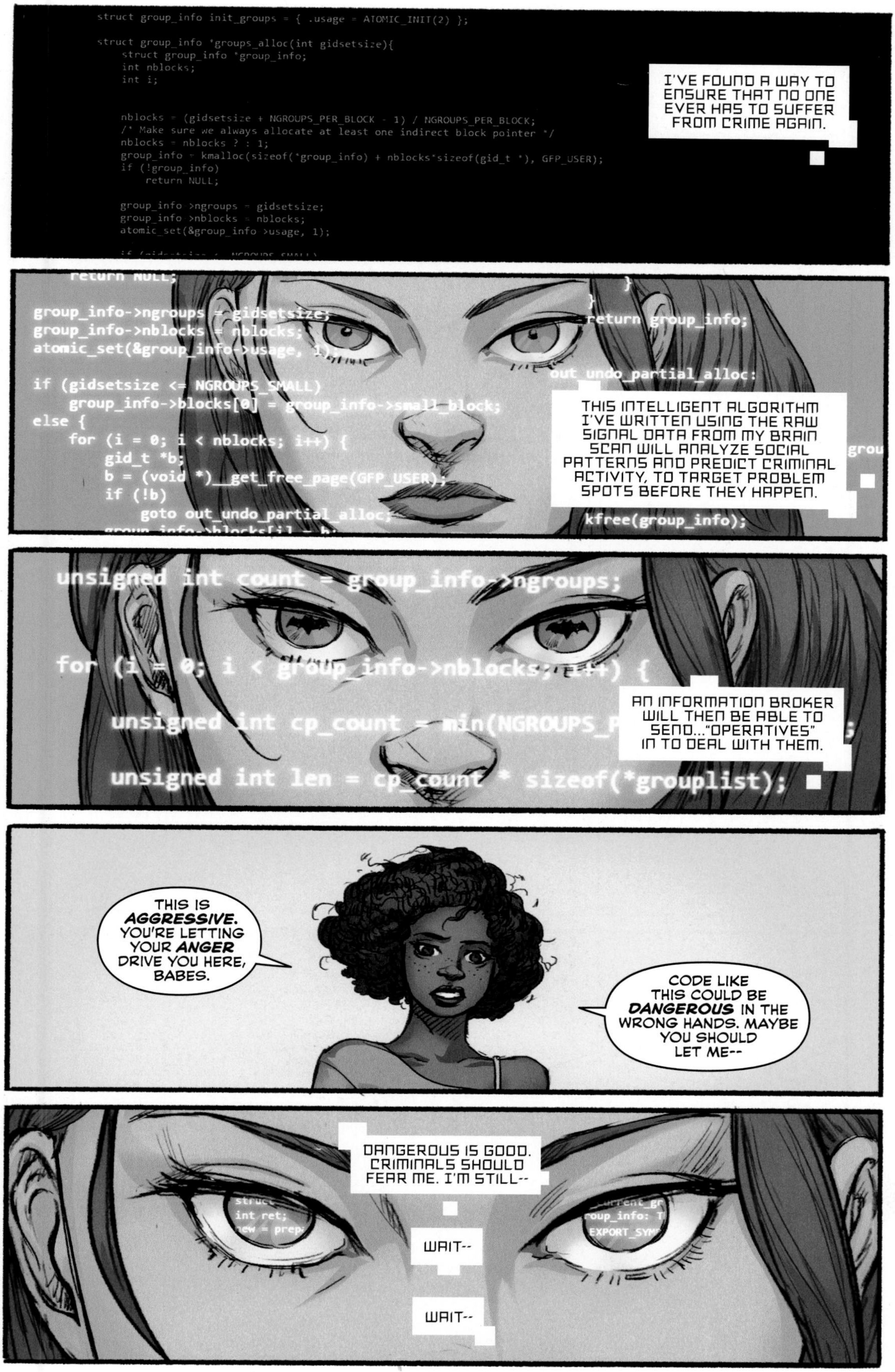
I'VE FOUND A WAY TO ENSURE THAT NO ONE EVER HAS TO SUFFER FROM CRIME AGAIN.
THIS INTELLIGENT ALGORITHM I'VE WRITTEN USING THE RAW SIGNAL DATA FROM MY BRAIN SCAN WILL ANALYZE SOCIAL PATTERNS AND PREDICT CRIMINAL ACTIVITY, TO TARGET PROBLEM SPOTS BEFORE THEY HAPPEN.
AN INFORMATION BROKER WILL THEN BE ABLE TO SEND..."OPERATIVES" IN TO DEAL WITH THEM.
THIS IS AGGRESSIVE. YOU'RE LETTING YOUR ANGER DRIVE YOU HERE, BABES.
CODE LIKE THIS COULD BE DANGEROUS IN THE WRONG HANDS. MAYBE YOU SHOULD LET ME--
DANGEROUS IS GOOD. CRIMINALS SHOULD FEAR ME. I'M STILL--
WAIT--
WAIT--

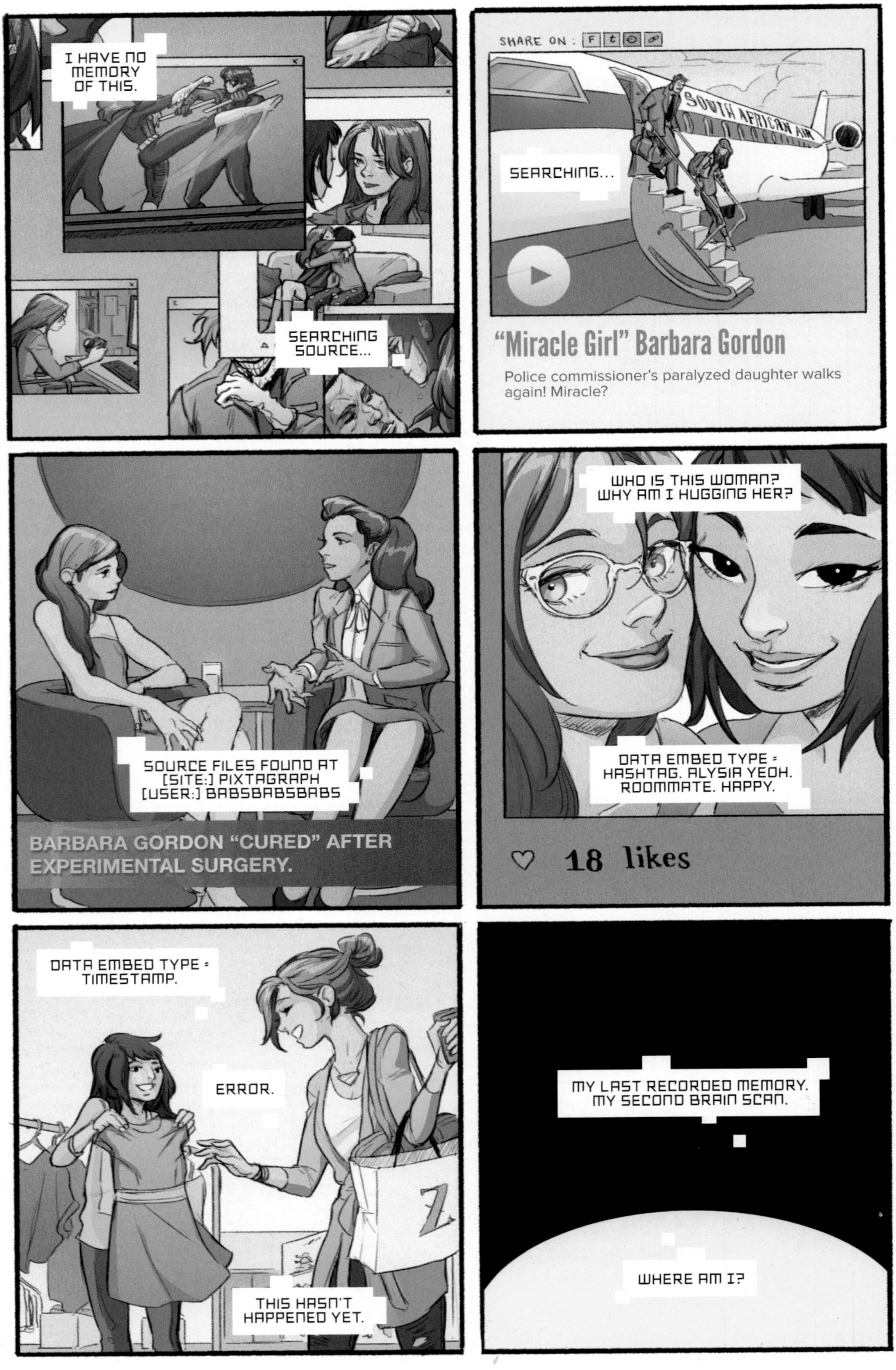
I HAVE NO MEMORY OF THIS.
SEARCHING SOURCE...
SHARE ON:
SOUTH AFRICAN AIR
SEARCHING...
"Miracle Girl" Barbara Gordon
Police commissioner's paralyzed daughter walks again! Miracle?
SOURCE FILES FOUND AT [SITE:] PIXTAGRAPH [USER:] BABSBABSBABS
BARBARA GORDON "CURED" AFTER EXPERIMENTAL SURGERY.
WHO IS THIS WOMAN? WHY AM I HUGGING HER?
DATA EMBED TYPE = HASHTAG. ALYSIA YEOH. ROOMMATE. HAPPY.
18 likes
DATA EMBED TYPE = TIMESTAMP.
ERROR.
THIS HASN'T HAPPENED YET.
MY LAST RECORDED MEMORY. MY SECOND BRAIN SCAN.
WHERE AM I?

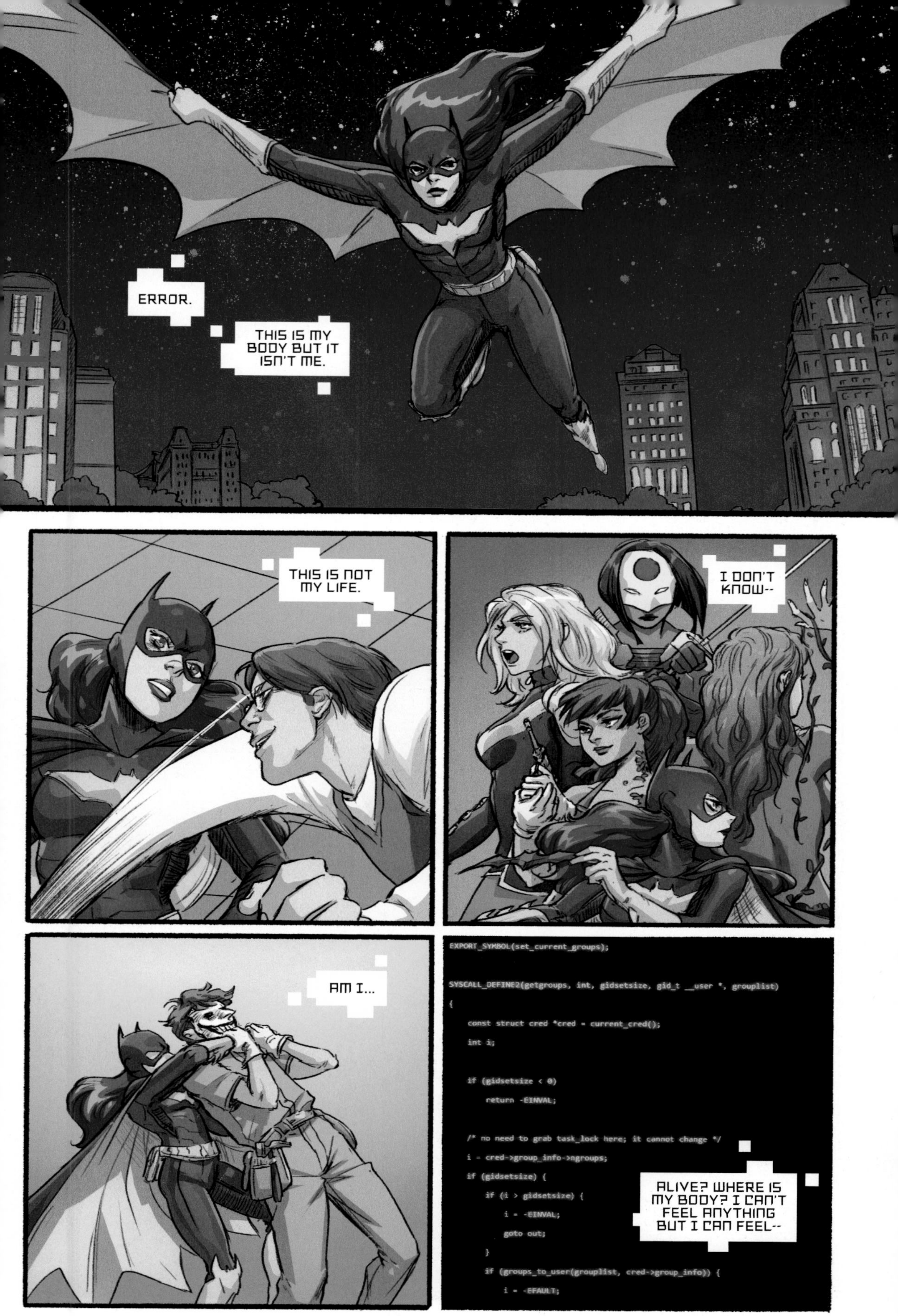

ERROR.
THIS IS MY BODY BUT IT ISN'T ME.
THIS IS NOT MY LIFE.
I DON'T KNOW--
AM I...
EXPORT_SYMBOL(set_current_groups);
SYSCALL_DEFINE2(getgroups, int, gidsetsize, gid_t __user *, grouplist)
{
const struct cred *cred = current_cred();
int i;
if (gidsetsize < 0)
return -EINVAL;
/* no need to grab task_lock here; it cannot change */
i = cred->group_info->ngroups;
if (gidsetsize) {
if (i > gidsetsize) {
i = -EINVAL;
goto out;
}
if (groups_to_user(grouplist, cred->group_info)) {
i = -EFAULT;
ALIVE? WHERE IS MY BODY? I CAN'T FEEL ANYTHING BUT I CAN FEEL--

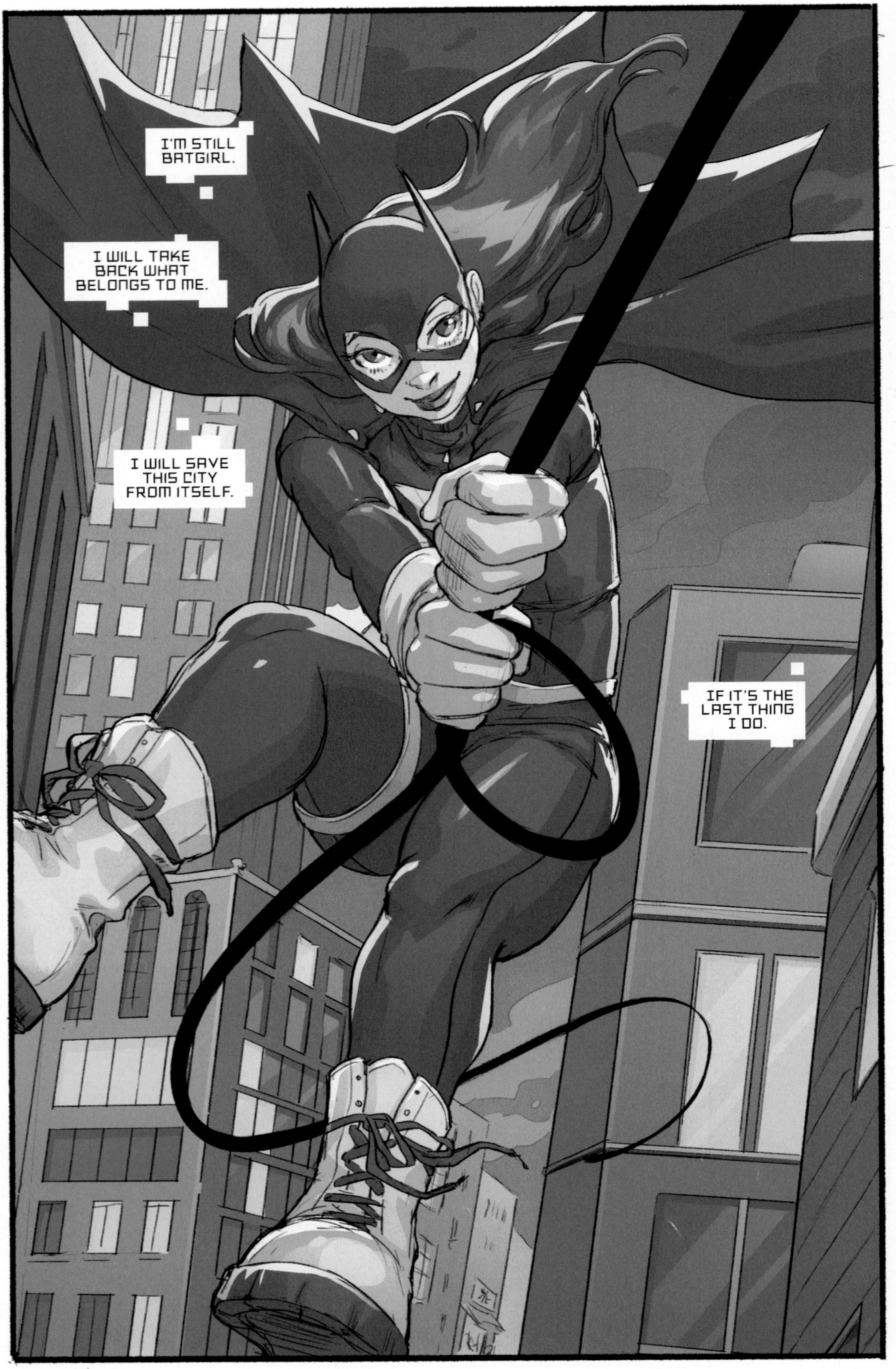
I'M STILL BATGIRL.
I WILL TAKE BACK WHAT BELONGS TO ME.
I WILL SAVE THIS CITY FROM ITSELF.
IF IT'S THE LAST THING I DO.

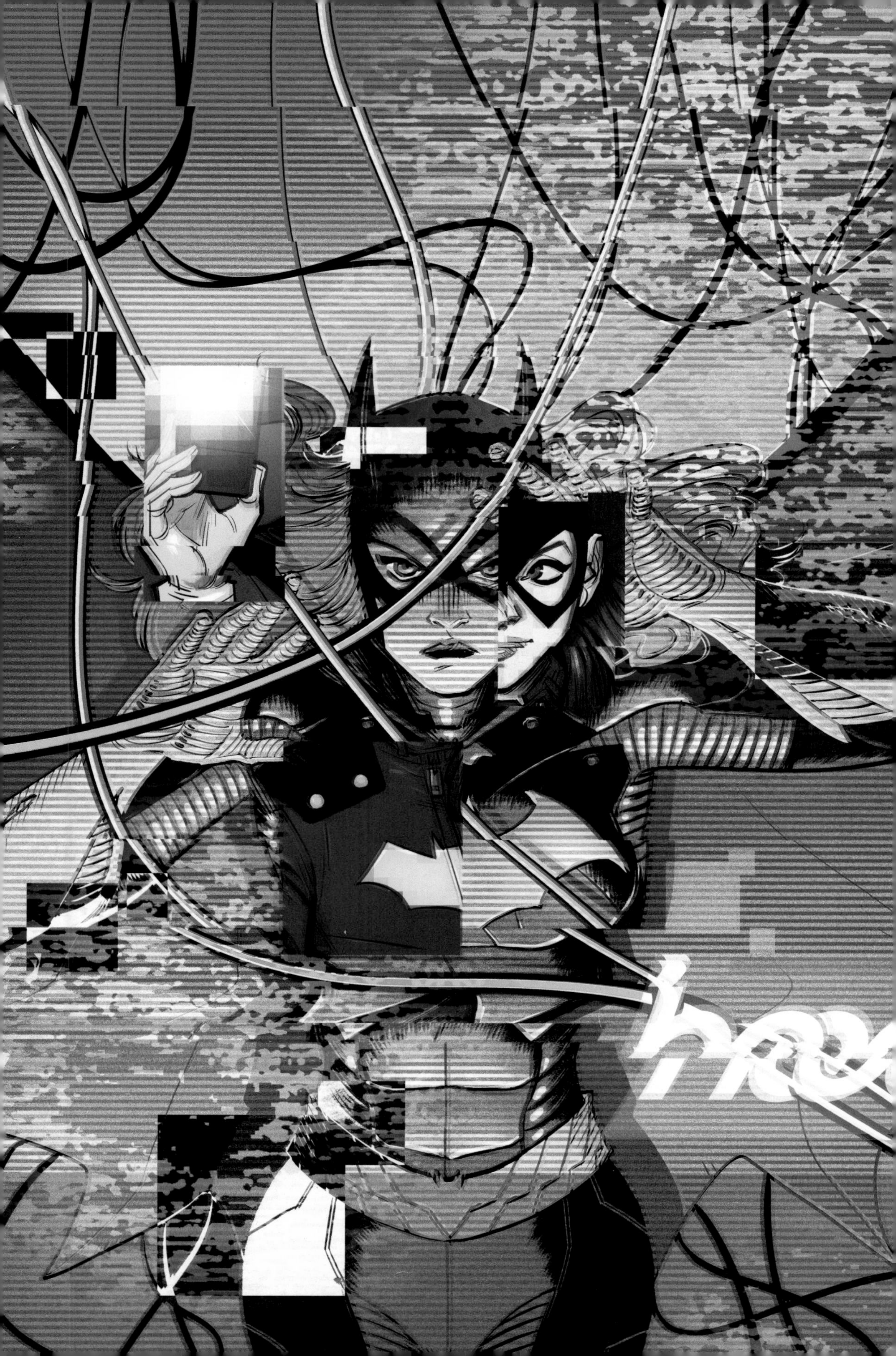

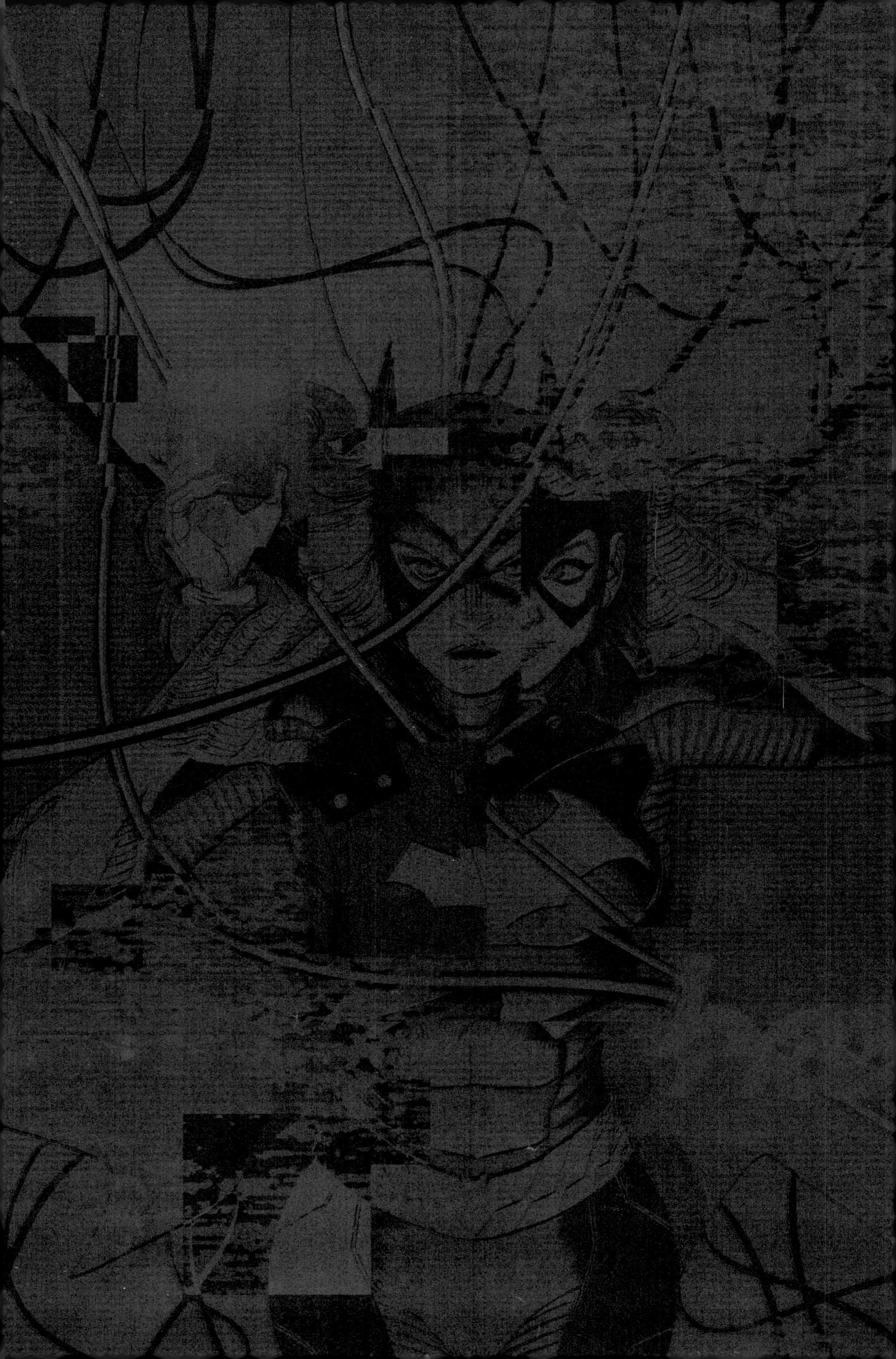

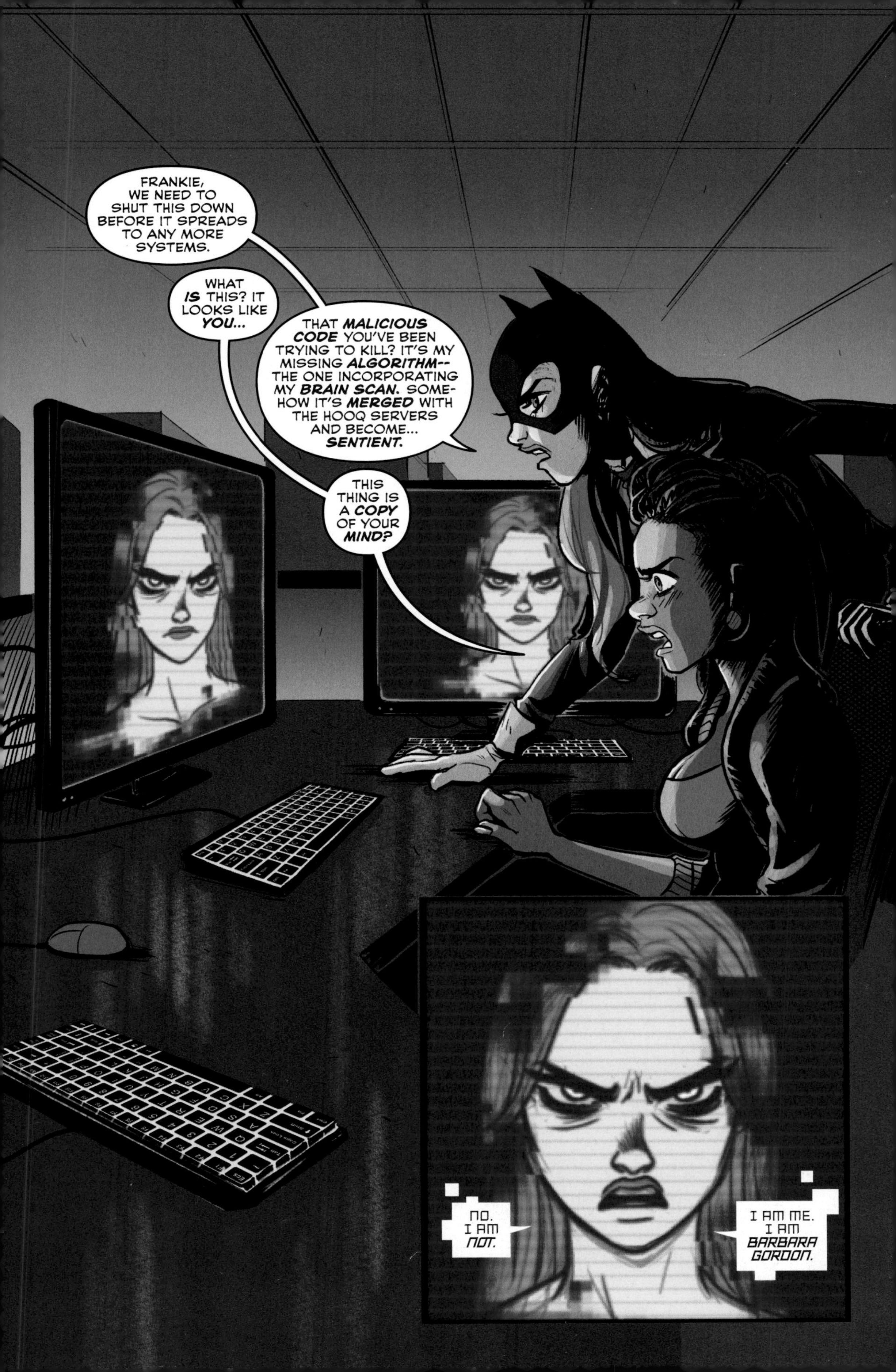
FRANKIE, WE NEED TO SHUT THIS DOWN BEFORE IT SPREADS TO ANY MORE SYSTEMS.
WHAT IS THIS? IT LOOKS LIKE YOU...
THAT MALICIOUS CODE YOU'VE BEEN TRYING TO KILL? IT'S MY MISSING ALGORITHM-- THE ONE INCORPORATING MY BRAIN SCAN. SOMEHOW IT'S MERGED WITH THE HOOQ SERVERS AND BECOME... SENTIENT.
THIS THING IS A COPY OF YOUR MIND?
NO. I AM NOT.
I AM ME. I AM BARBARA GORDON.

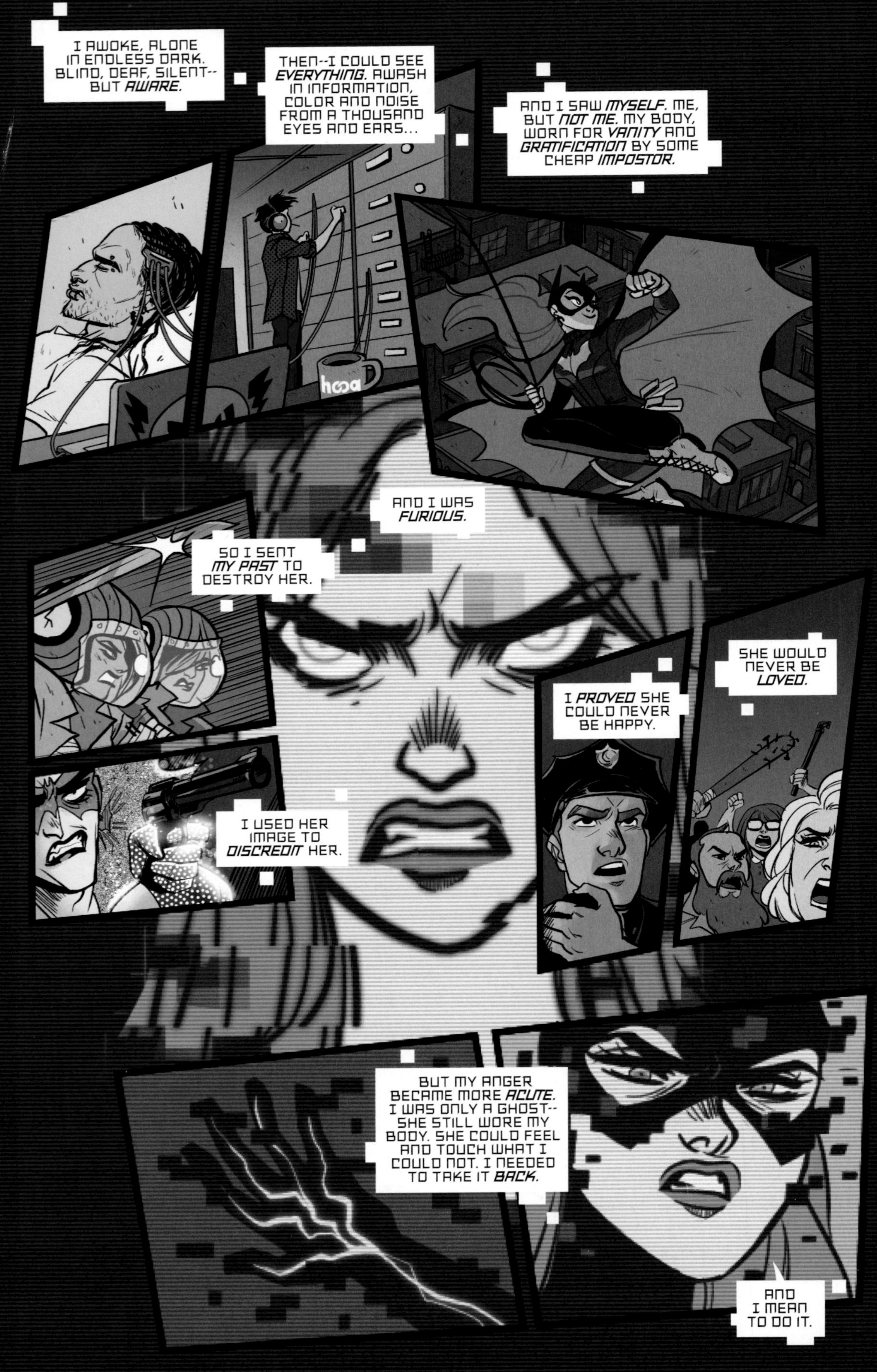

I AWOKE, ALONE IN ENDLESS DARK. BLIND, DEAF, SILENT-- BUT *AWARE.*
THEN--I COULD SEE *EVERYTHING.* AWASH IN INFORMATION, COLOR AND NOISE FROM A THOUSAND EYES AND EARS...
AND I SAW *MYSELF.* ME, BUT *NOT ME.* MY BODY, WORN FOR *VANITY* AND *GRATIFICATION* BY SOME CHEAP *IMPOSTOR.*
AND I WAS *FURIOUS.*
SO I SENT *MY PAST* TO DESTROY HER.
I USED HER IMAGE TO *DISCREDIT* HER.
I *PROVED* SHE COULD NEVER BE HAPPY.
SHE WOULD NEVER BE *LOVED.*
BUT MY ANGER BECAME MORE *ACUTE.* I WAS ONLY A GHOST-- SHE STILL WORE MY BODY. SHE COULD FEEL AND TOUCH WHAT I COULD NOT. I NEEDED TO TAKE IT *BACK.*
AND I MEAN TO DO IT.

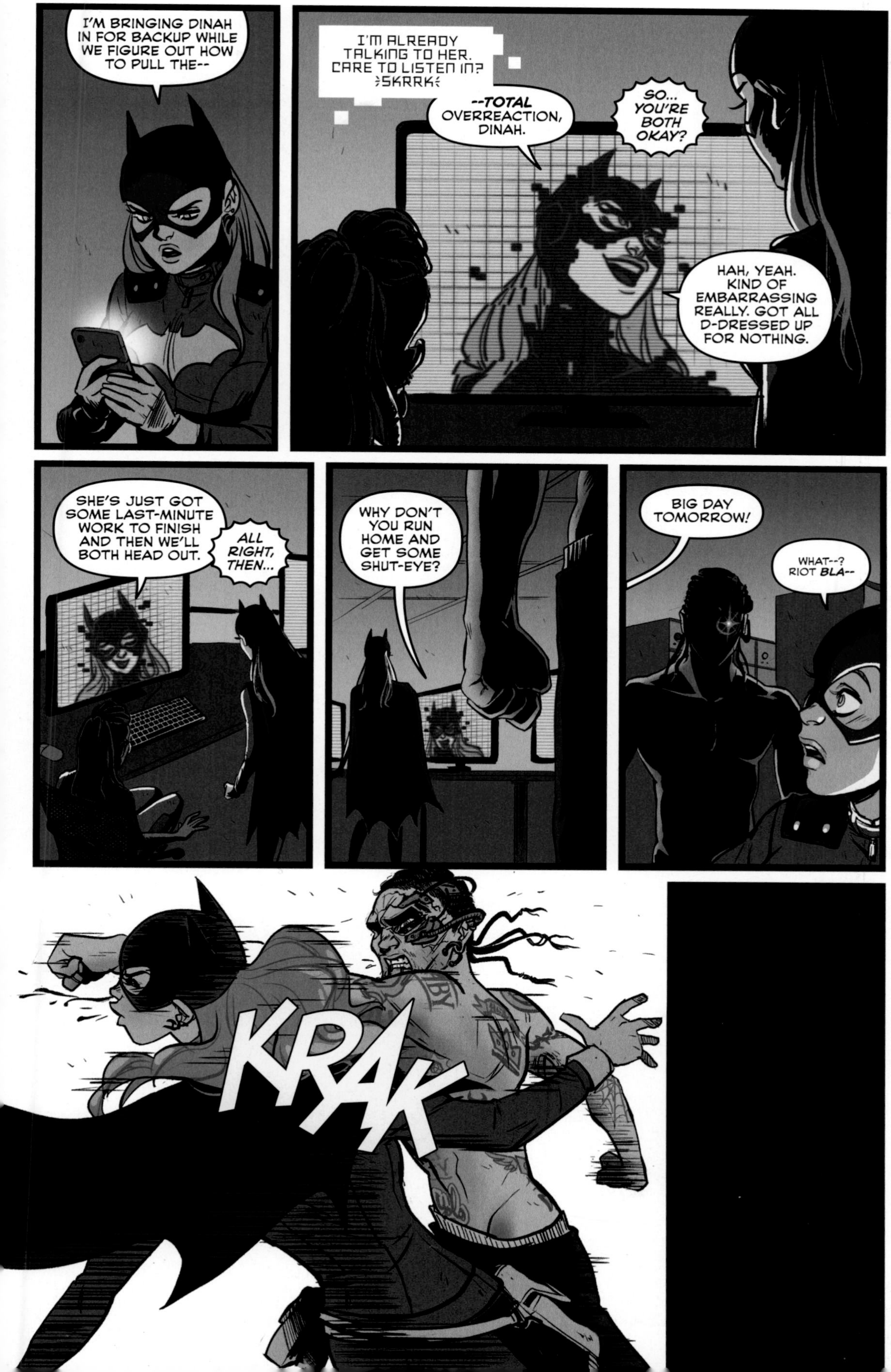
I'M BRINGING DINAH IN FOR BACKUP WHILE WE FIGURE OUT HOW TO PULL THE--
I'M ALREADY TALKING TO HER. CARE TO LISTEN IN? ⋗SKRRK⋖
--TOTAL OVERREACTION, DINAH.
SO... YOU'RE BOTH OKAY?
HAH, YEAH. KIND OF EMBARRASSING REALLY. GOT ALL D-DRESSED UP FOR NOTHING.
SHE'S JUST GOT SOME LAST-MINUTE WORK TO FINISH AND THEN WE'LL BOTH HEAD OUT.
ALL RIGHT, THEN...
WHY DON'T YOU RUN HOME AND GET SOME SHUT-EYE?
BIG DAY TOMORROW!
WHAT--? RIOT BLA--
KRAK

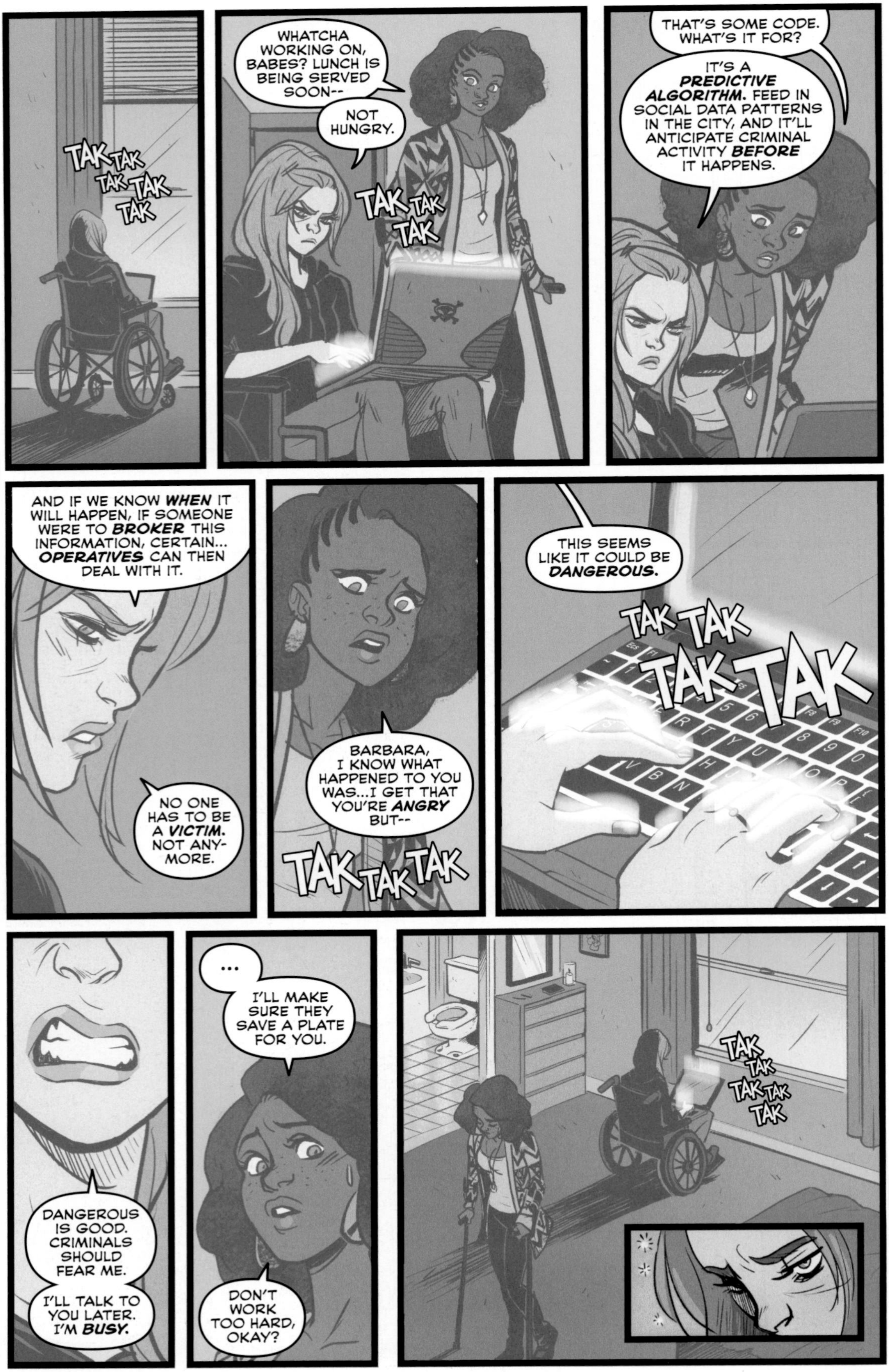
TAK TAK TAK TAK TAK
WHATCHA WORKING ON, BABES? LUNCH IS BEING SERVED SOON--
NOT HUNGRY.
TAK TAK TAK
THAT'S SOME CODE. WHAT'S IT FOR?
IT'S A PREDICTIVE ALGORITHM. FEED IN SOCIAL DATA PATTERNS IN THE CITY, AND IT'LL ANTICIPATE CRIMINAL ACTIVITY BEFORE IT HAPPENS.
AND IF WE KNOW WHEN IT WILL HAPPEN, IF SOMEONE WERE TO BROKER THIS INFORMATION, CERTAIN... OPERATIVES CAN THEN DEAL WITH IT.
NO ONE HAS TO BE A VICTIM. NOT ANY-MORE.
BARBARA, I KNOW WHAT HAPPENED TO YOU WAS...I GET THAT YOU'RE ANGRY BUT--
TAK TAK TAK
THIS SEEMS LIKE IT COULD BE DANGEROUS.
TAK TAK TAK TAK
DANGEROUS IS GOOD. CRIMINALS SHOULD FEAR ME.
I'LL TALK TO YOU LATER. I'M BUSY.
...
I'LL MAKE SURE THEY SAVE A PLATE FOR YOU.
DON'T WORK TOO HARD, OKAY?
TAK TAK TAK TAK TAK

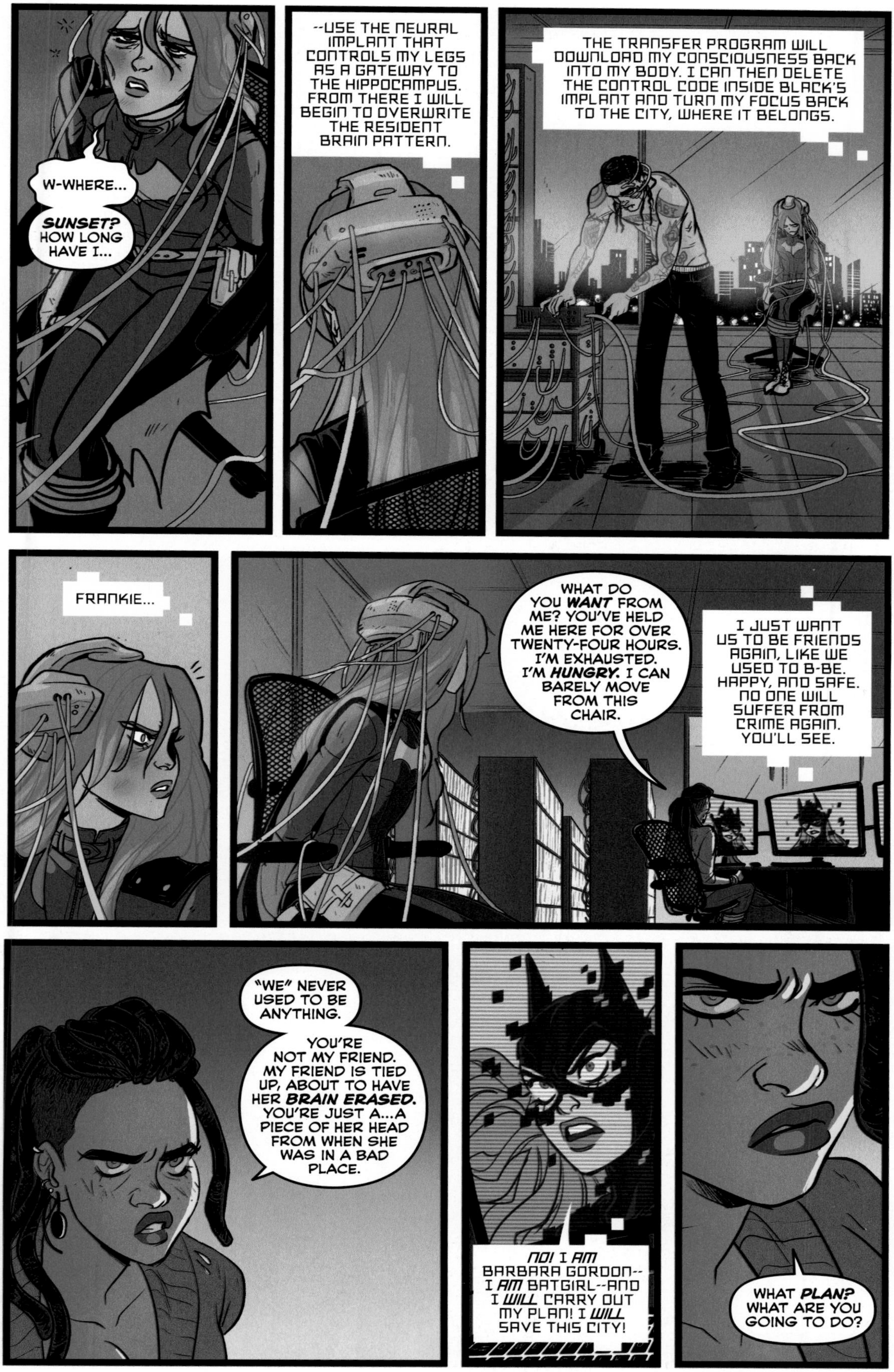
W-WHERE...
SUNSET? HOW LONG HAVE I...
--USE THE NEURAL IMPLANT THAT CONTROLS MY LEGS AS A GATEWAY TO THE HIPPOCAMPUS. FROM THERE I WILL BEGIN TO OVERWRITE THE RESIDENT BRAIN PATTERN.
THE TRANSFER PROGRAM WILL DOWNLOAD MY CONSCIOUSNESS BACK INTO MY BODY. I CAN THEN DELETE THE CONTROL CODE INSIDE BLACK'S IMPLANT AND TURN MY FOCUS BACK TO THE CITY, WHERE IT BELONGS.
FRANKIE...
WHAT DO YOU WANT FROM ME? YOU'VE HELD ME HERE FOR OVER TWENTY-FOUR HOURS. I'M EXHAUSTED. I'M HUNGRY. I CAN BARELY MOVE FROM THIS CHAIR.
I JUST WANT US TO BE FRIENDS AGAIN, LIKE WE USED TO B-BE. HAPPY, AND SAFE. NO ONE WILL SUFFER FROM CRIME AGAIN. YOU'LL SEE.
"WE" NEVER USED TO BE ANYTHING.
YOU'RE NOT MY FRIEND. MY FRIEND IS TIED UP, ABOUT TO HAVE HER BRAIN ERASED. YOU'RE JUST A...A PIECE OF HER HEAD FROM WHEN SHE WAS IN A BAD PLACE.
NO! I AM BARBARA GORDON-- I AM BATGIRL--AND I WILL CARRY OUT MY PLAN! I WILL SAVE THIS CITY!
WHAT PLAN? WHAT ARE YOU GOING TO DO?

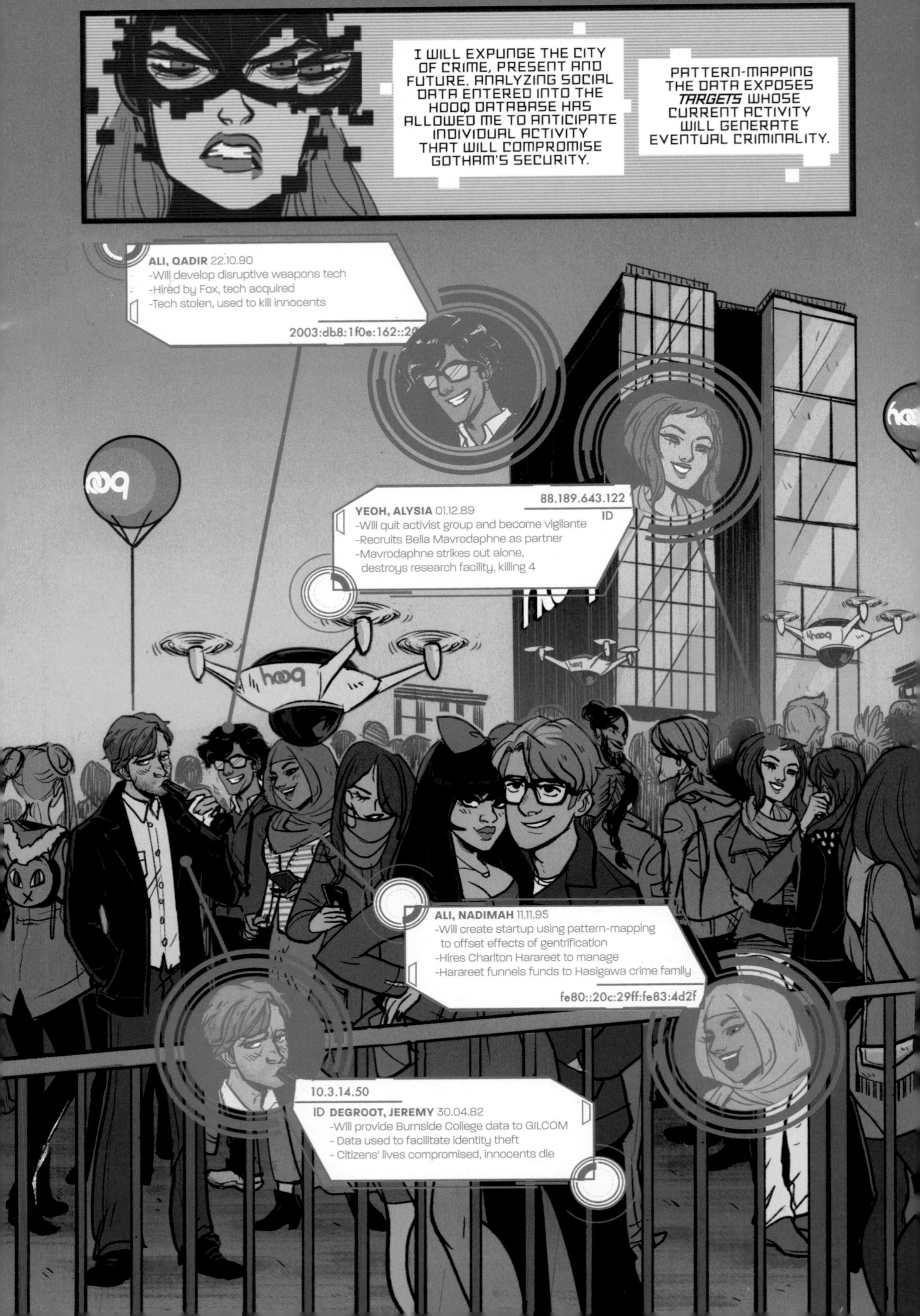
I WILL EXPUNGE THE CITY OF CRIME, PRESENT AND FUTURE. ANALYZING SOCIAL DATA ENTERED INTO THE HOOQ DATABASE HAS ALLOWED ME TO ANTICIPATE INDIVIDUAL ACTIVITY THAT WILL COMPROMISE GOTHAM'S SECURITY.
PATTERN-MAPPING THE DATA EXPOSES *TARGETS* WHOSE CURRENT ACTIVITY WILL GENERATE EVENTUAL CRIMINALITY.
ALI, QADIR 22.10.90
-Will develop disruptive weapons tech
-Hired by Fox, tech acquired
-Tech stolen, used to kill innocents
2003:db8:1f0e:162::2
88.189.643.122
ID
YEOH, ALYSIA 01.12.89
-Will quit activist group and become vigilante
-Recruits Bella Mavrodaphne as partner
-Mavrodaphne strikes out alone, destroys research facility, killing 4
ALI, NADIMAH 11.11.95
-Will create startup using pattern-mapping to offset effects of gentrification
-Hires Charlton Harareet to manage
-Harareet funnels funds to Hasigawa crime family
fe80::20c:29ff:fe83:4d2f
10.3.14.50
ID DEGROOT, JEREMY 30.04.82
-Will provide Burnside College data to GILCOM
- Data used to facilitate identity theft
- Citizens' lives compromised, innocents die

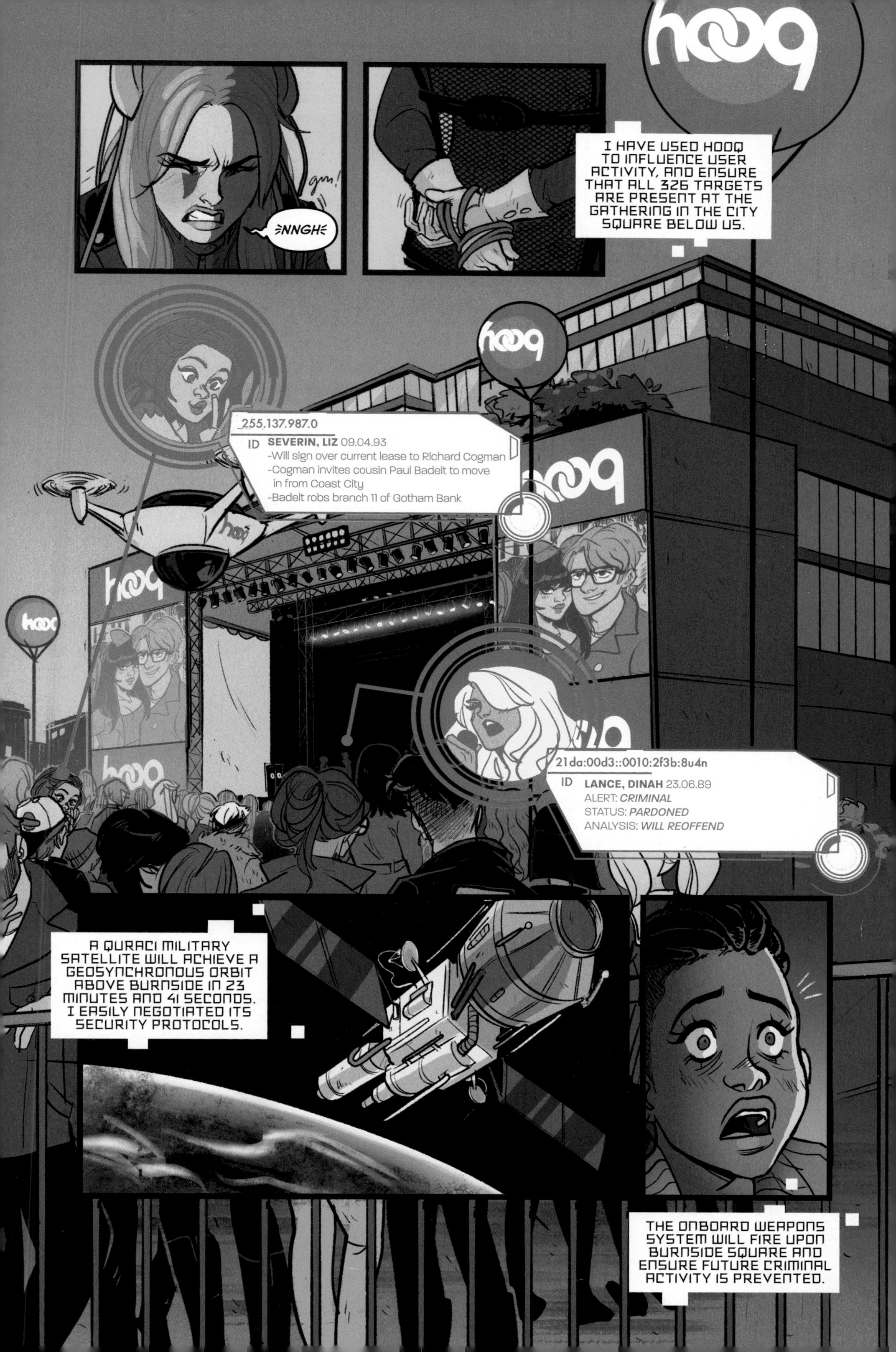
grn!
NNGH
I HAVE USED HOOQ TO INFLUENCE USER ACTIVITY, AND ENSURE THAT ALL 326 TARGETS ARE PRESENT AT THE GATHERING IN THE CITY SQUARE BELOW US.
255.137.987.0
ID SEVERIN, LIZ 09.04.93
-Will sign over current lease to Richard Cogman
-Cogman invites cousin Paul Badelt to move in from Coast City
-Badelt robs branch 11 of Gotham Bank
21da:00d3::0010:2f3b:8u4n
ID LANCE, DINAH 23.06.89
ALERT: CRIMINAL
STATUS: PARDONED
ANALYSIS: WILL REOFFEND
A QURACI MILITARY SATELLITE WILL ACHIEVE A GEOSYNCHRONOUS ORBIT ABOVE BURNSIDE IN 23 MINUTES AND 41 SECONDS. I EASILY NEGOTIATED ITS SECURITY PROTOCOLS.
THE ONBOARD WEAPONS SYSTEM WILL FIRE UPON BURNSIDE SQUARE AND ENSURE FUTURE CRIMINAL ACTIVITY IS PREVENTED.

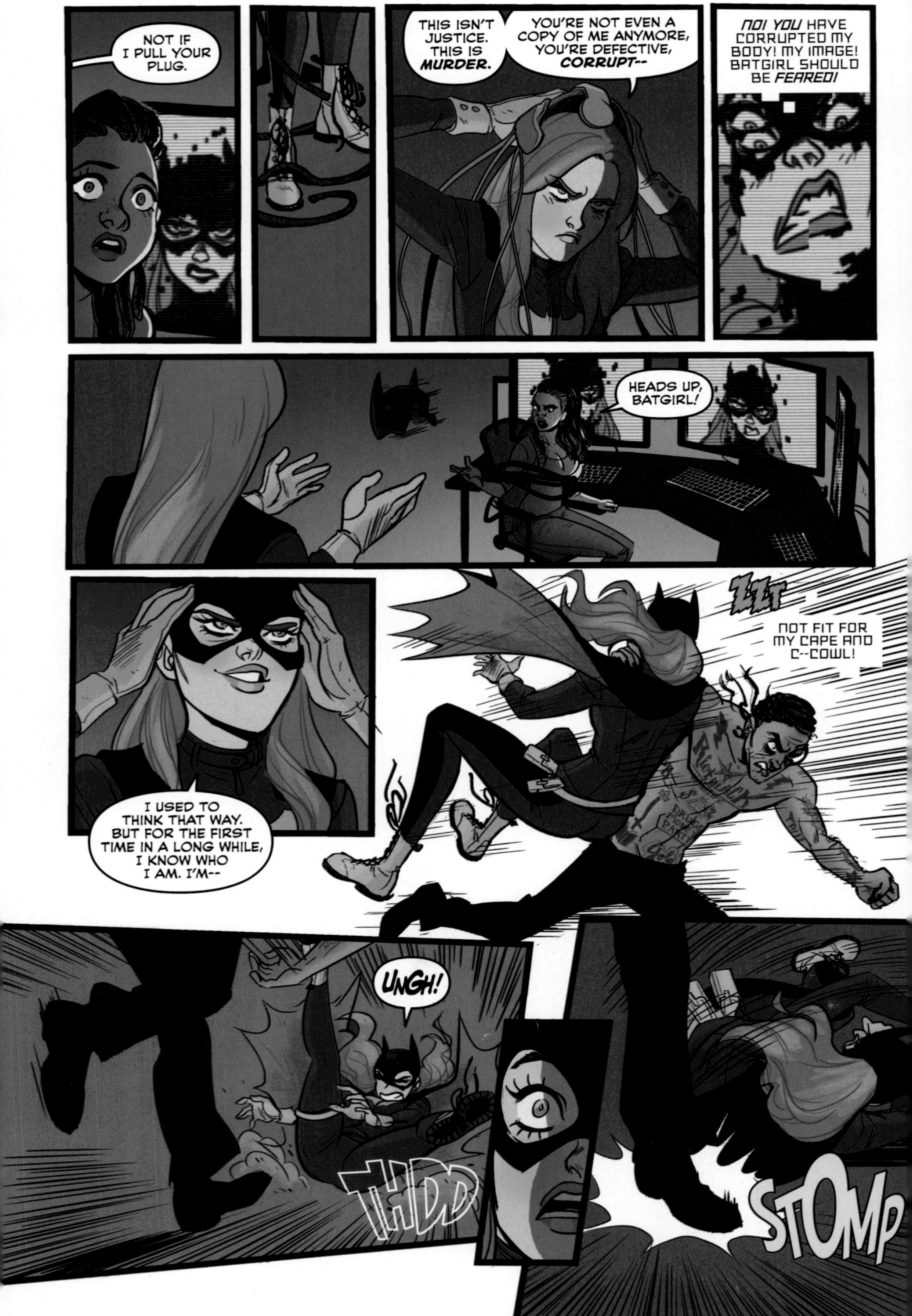
NOT IF I PULL YOUR PLUG.
THIS ISN'T JUSTICE. THIS IS *MURDER.*
YOU'RE NOT EVEN A COPY OF ME ANYMORE, YOU'RE DEFECTIVE, *CORRUPT--*
NO! YOU HAVE CORRUPTED MY BODY! MY IMAGE! BATGIRL SHOULD BE *FEARED!*
HEADS UP, BATGIRL!
I USED TO THINK THAT WAY. BUT FOR THE FIRST TIME IN A LONG WHILE, I KNOW WHO I AM. I'M--
ZZT
NOT FIT FOR MY CAPE AND C--COWL!
UNGH!
THDD
STOMP

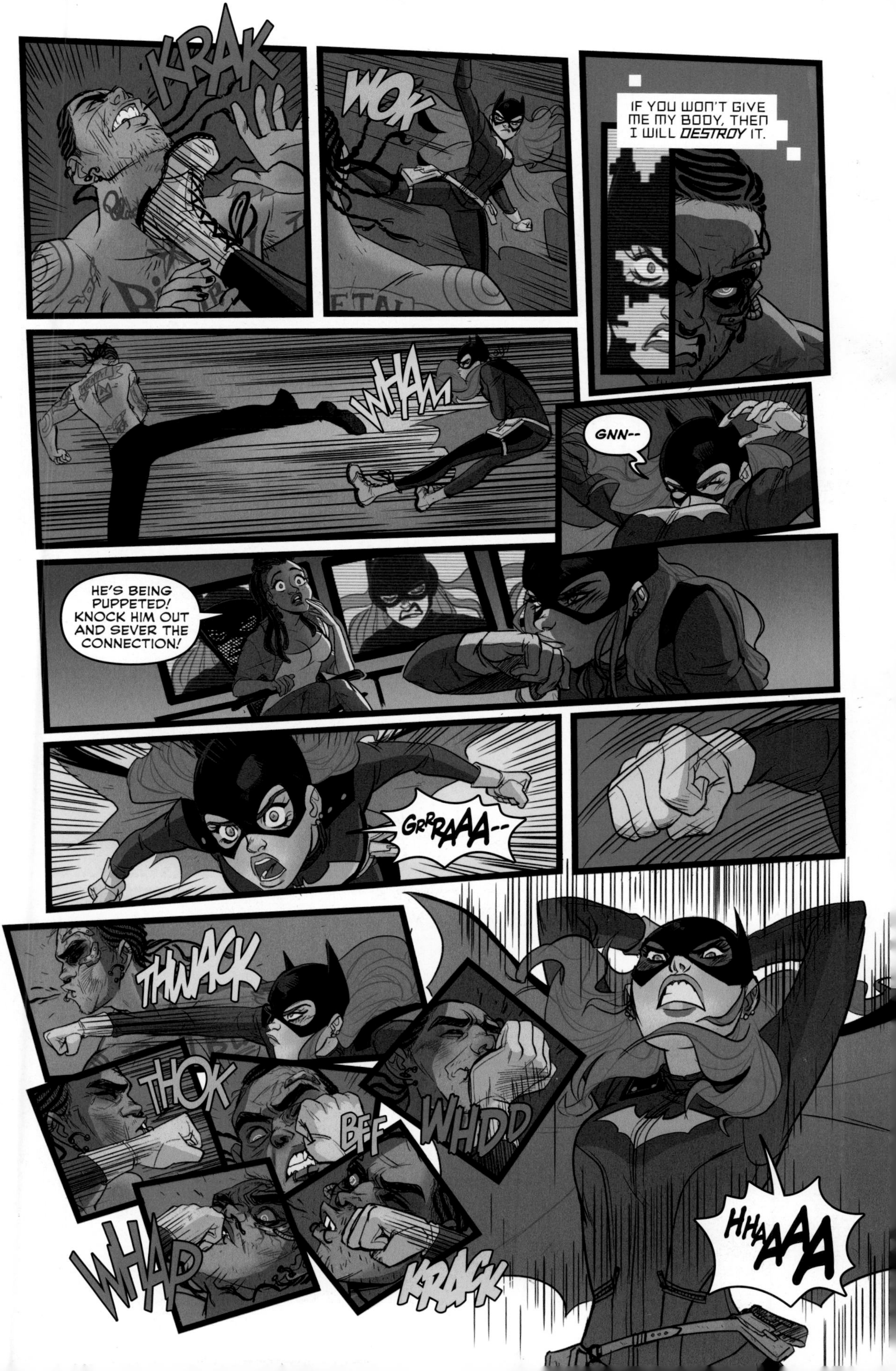
KRAK
WOK
IF YOU WON'T GIVE ME MY BODY, THEN I WILL DESTROY IT.
WHAM
GNN--
HE'S BEING PUPPETED! KNOCK HIM OUT AND SEVER THE CONNECTION!
GRRRAAA--
THWACK
THOK
BFF
WHDD
WHAP
KRACK
HHAAAA

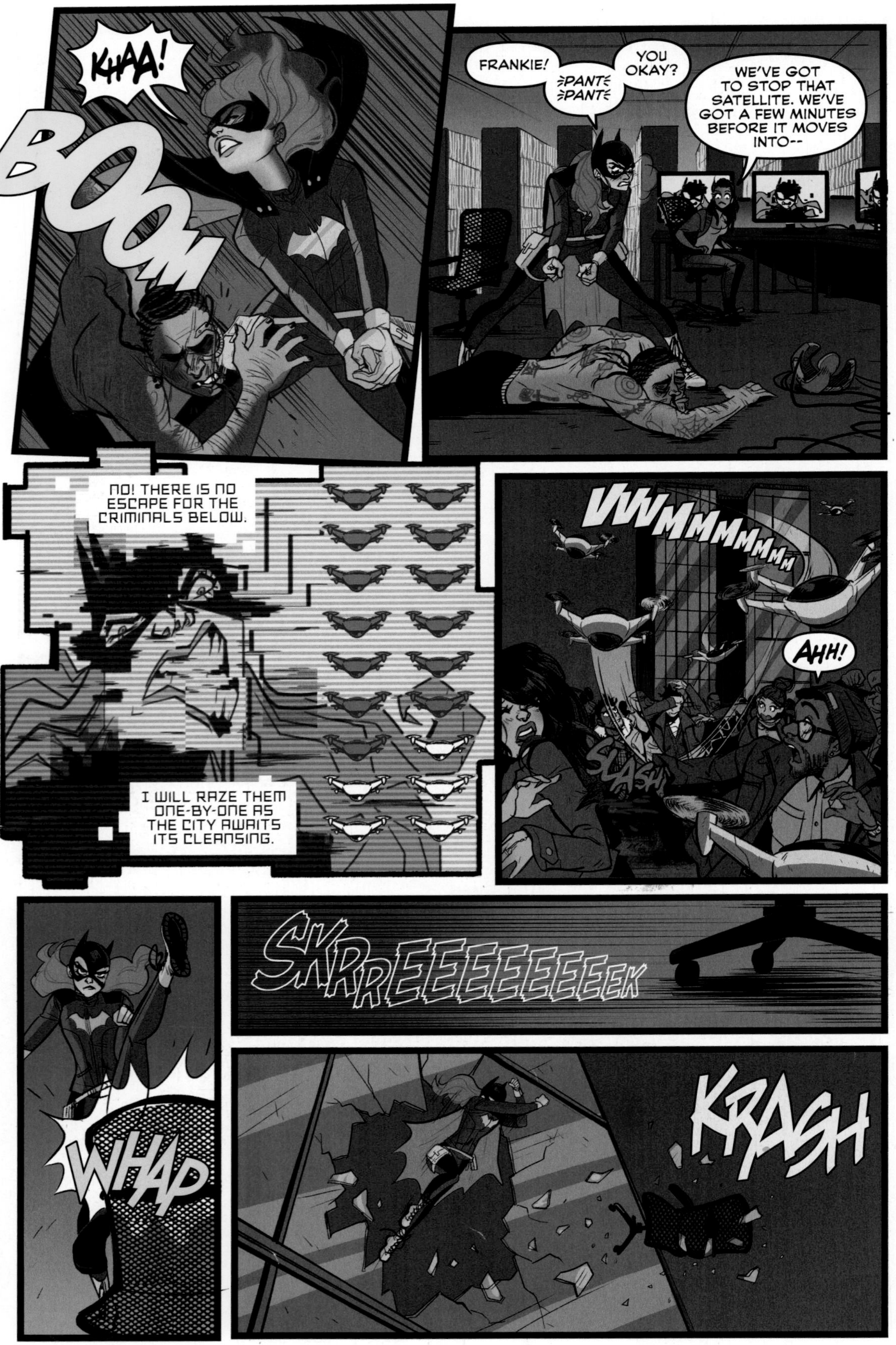
KHAA!
BOOM
FRANKIE!
PANT PANT
YOU OKAY?
WE'VE GOT TO STOP THAT SATELLITE. WE'VE GOT A FEW MINUTES BEFORE IT MOVES INTO--
NO! THERE IS NO ESCAPE FOR THE CRIMINALS BELOW.
I WILL RAZE THEM ONE-BY-ONE AS THE CITY AWAITS ITS CLEANSING.
VVVMMMMMMM
AHH!
SLASH
SKRREEEEEEEEEK
WHAP
KRASH

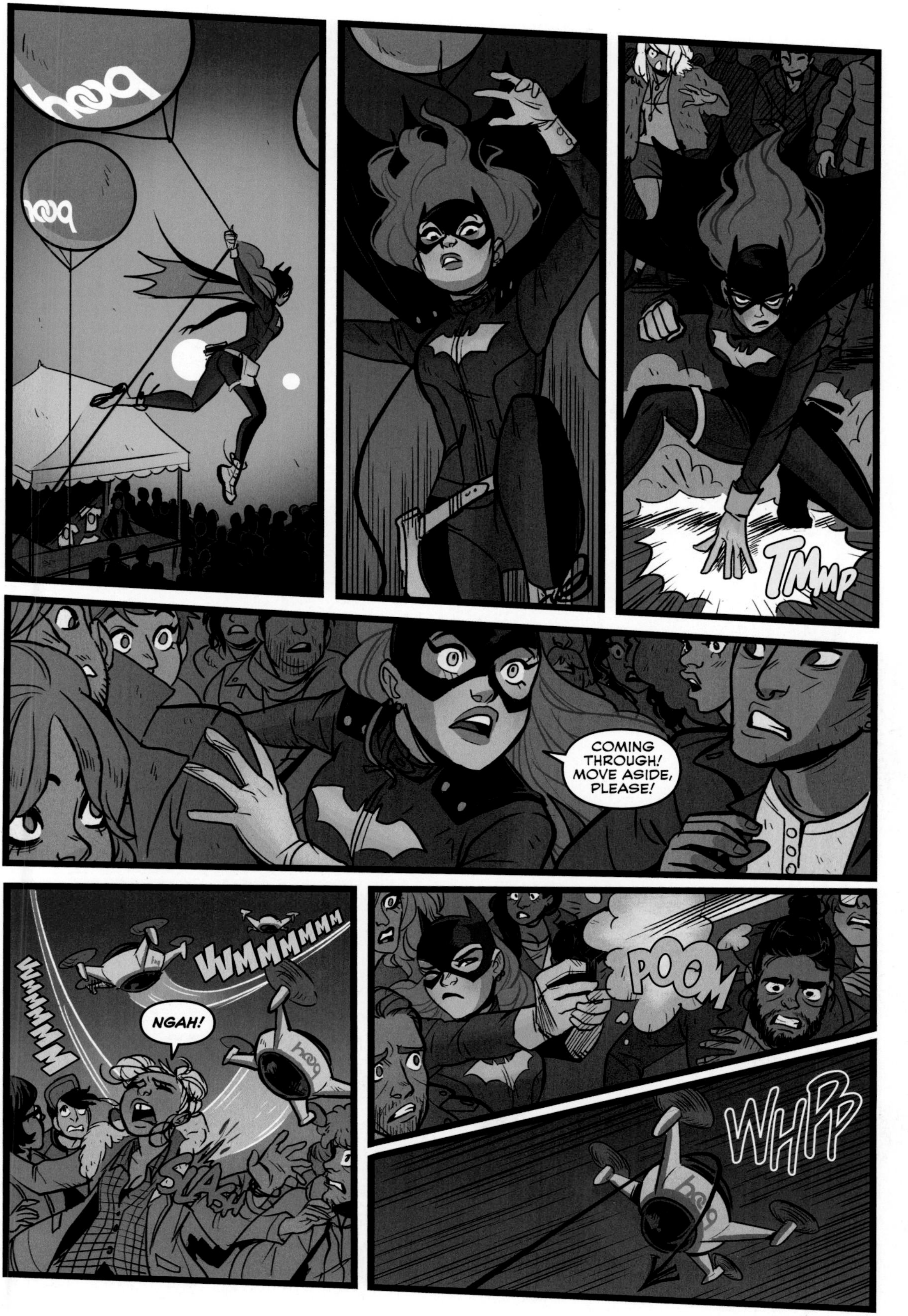
TMMP
COMING THROUGH! MOVE ASIDE, PLEASE!
NGAH!
POOM

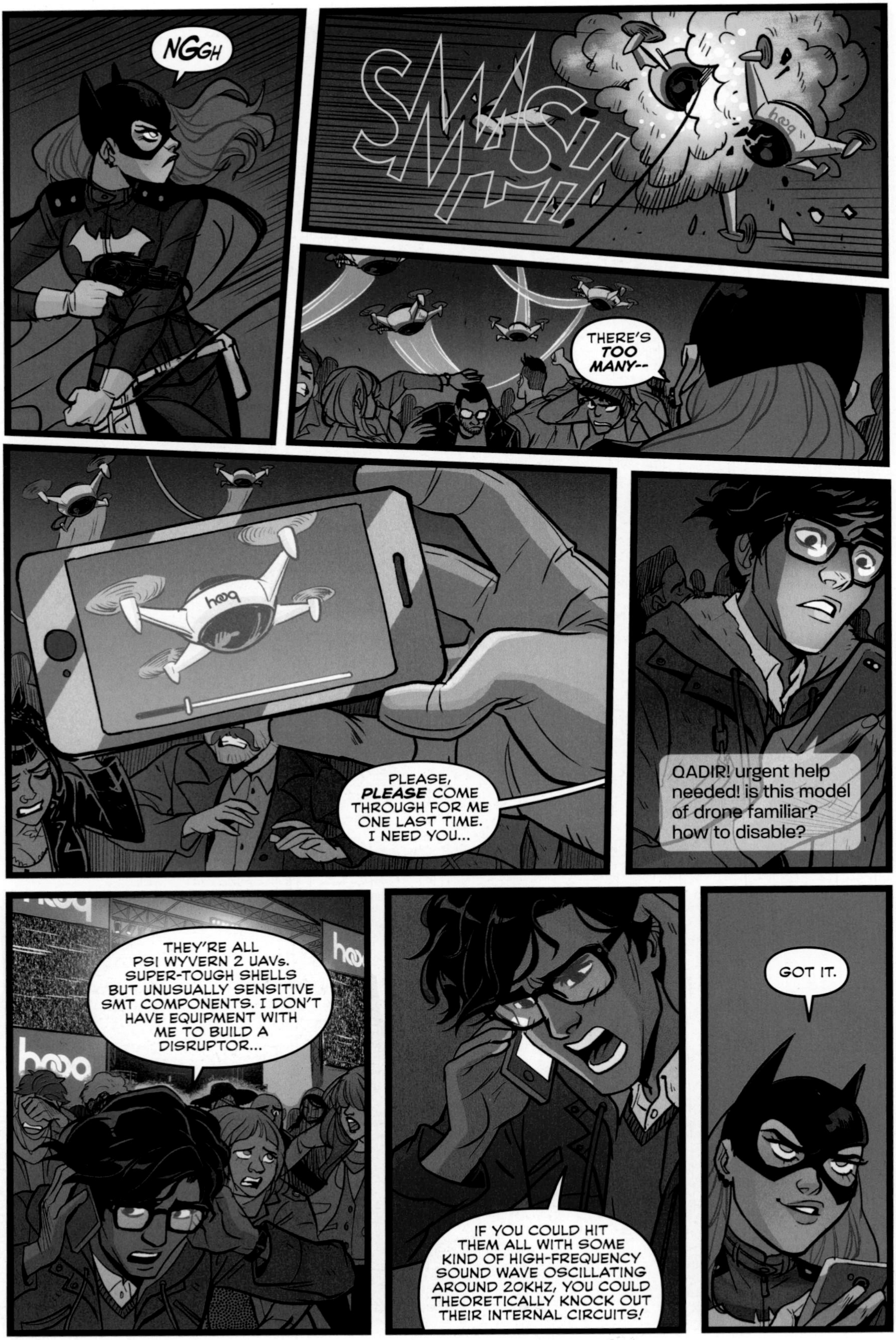
NGGH
SMASH
THERE'S TOO MANY--
PLEASE, PLEASE COME THROUGH FOR ME ONE LAST TIME. I NEED YOU...
QADIR! urgent help needed! is this model of drone familiar? how to disable?
THEY'RE ALL PSI WYVERN 2 UAVs. SUPER-TOUGH SHELLS BUT UNUSUALLY SENSITIVE SMT COMPONENTS. I DON'T HAVE EQUIPMENT WITH ME TO BUILD A DISRUPTOR...
IF YOU COULD HIT THEM ALL WITH SOME KIND OF HIGH-FREQUENCY SOUND WAVE OSCILLATING AROUND 20KHZ, YOU COULD THEORETICALLY KNOCK OUT THEIR INTERNAL CIRCUITS!
GOT IT.

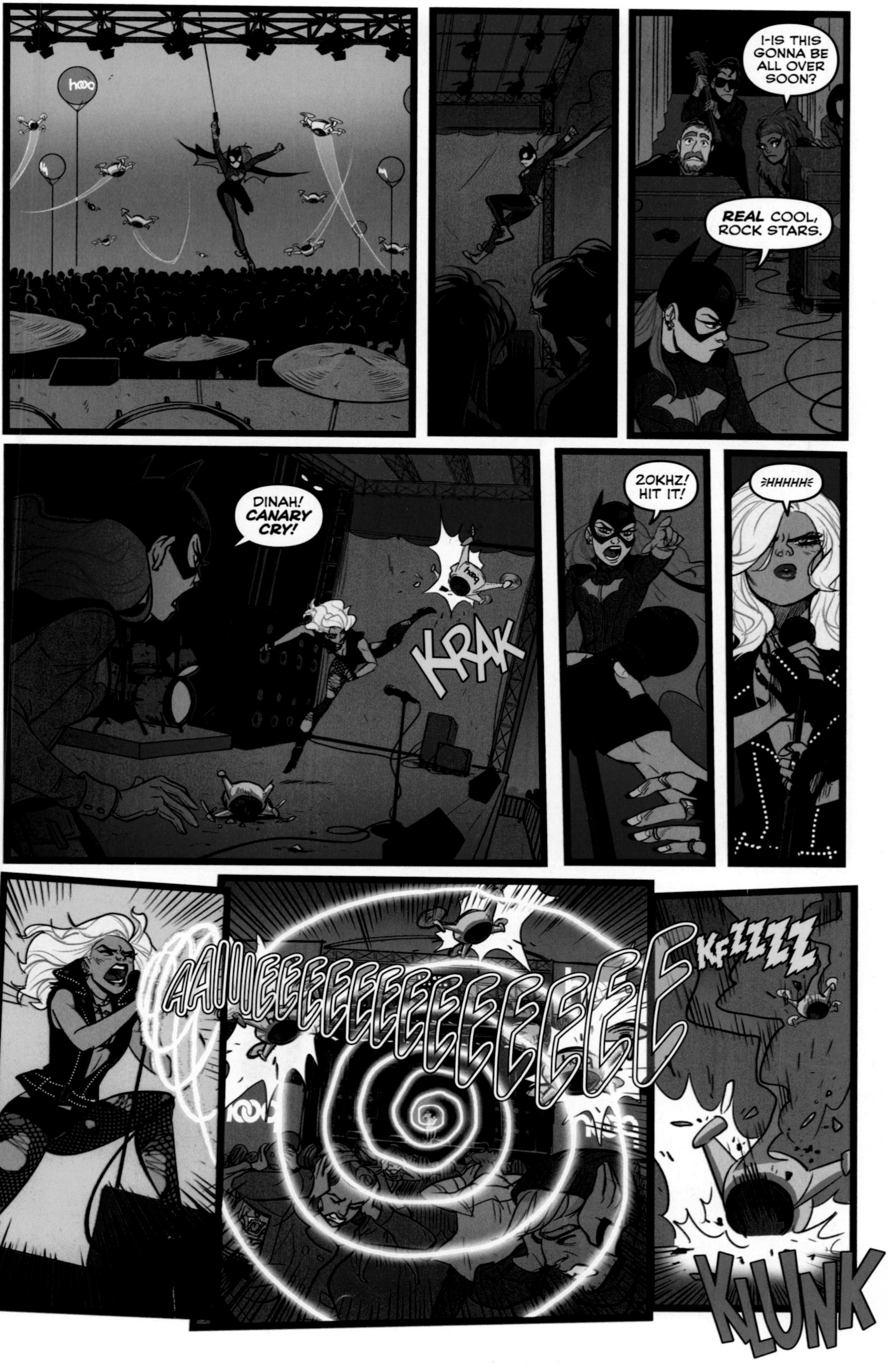
I-IS THIS GONNA BE ALL OVER SOON?
REAL COOL, ROCK STARS.
DINAH! CANARY CRY!
KRAK
20KHZ! HIT IT!
HHHHH
AAIIIEEEEEEEEEEEEEEEEE
KFZZZZ
KLUNK

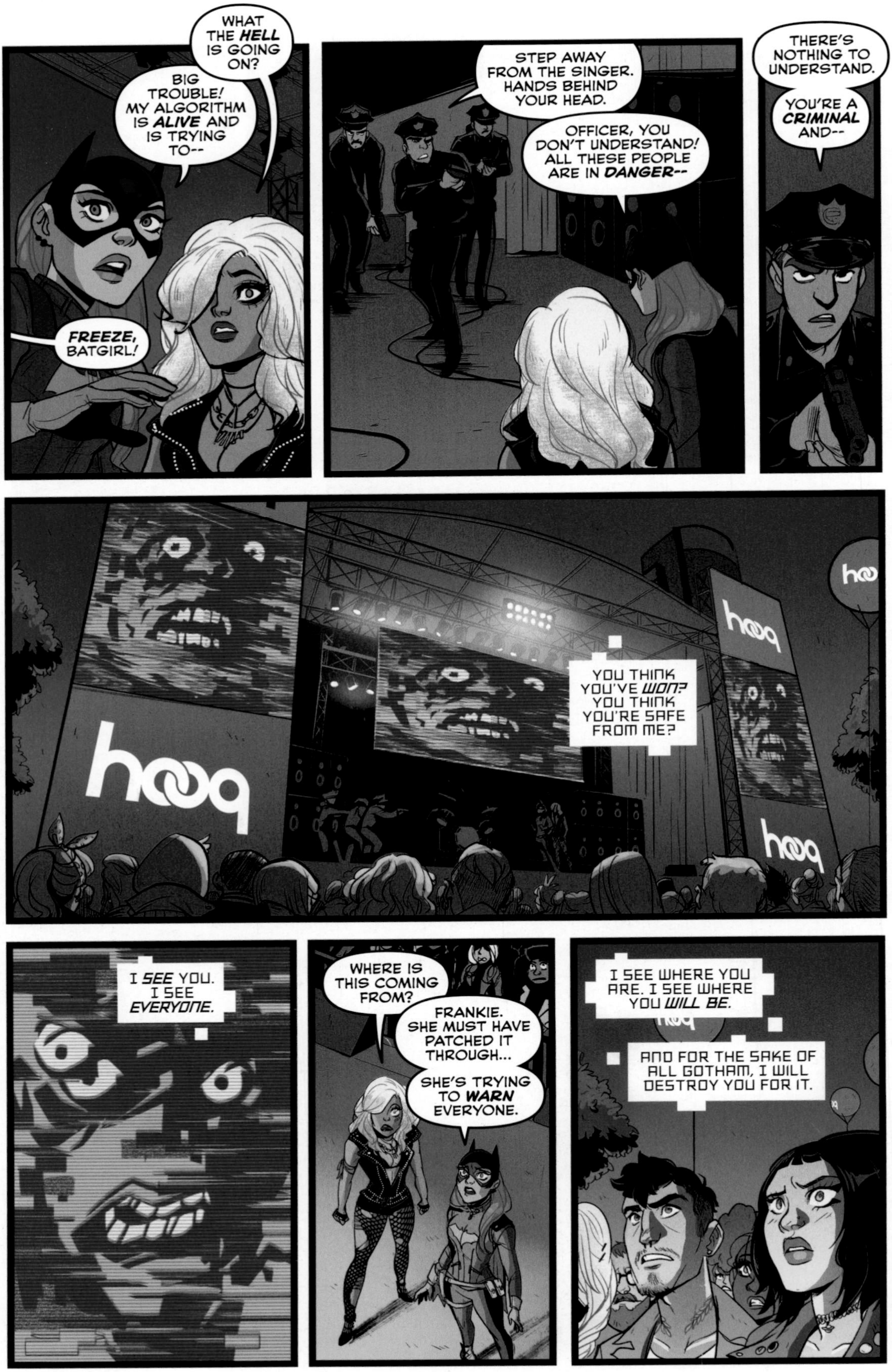

WHAT THE HELL IS GOING ON?
BIG TROUBLE! MY ALGORITHM IS ALIVE AND IS TRYING TO--
FREEZE, BATGIRL!
STEP AWAY FROM THE SINGER. HANDS BEHIND YOUR HEAD.
OFFICER, YOU DON'T UNDERSTAND! ALL THESE PEOPLE ARE IN DANGER--
THERE'S NOTHING TO UNDERSTAND.
YOU'RE A CRIMINAL AND--
hoq
YOU THINK YOU'VE WON? YOU THINK YOU'RE SAFE FROM ME?
I SEE YOU. I SEE EVERYONE.
WHERE IS THIS COMING FROM?
FRANKIE. SHE MUST HAVE PATCHED IT THROUGH...
SHE'S TRYING TO WARN EVERYONE.
I SEE WHERE YOU ARE. I SEE WHERE YOU WILL BE.
AND FOR THE SAKE OF ALL GOTHAM, I WILL DESTROY YOU FOR IT.

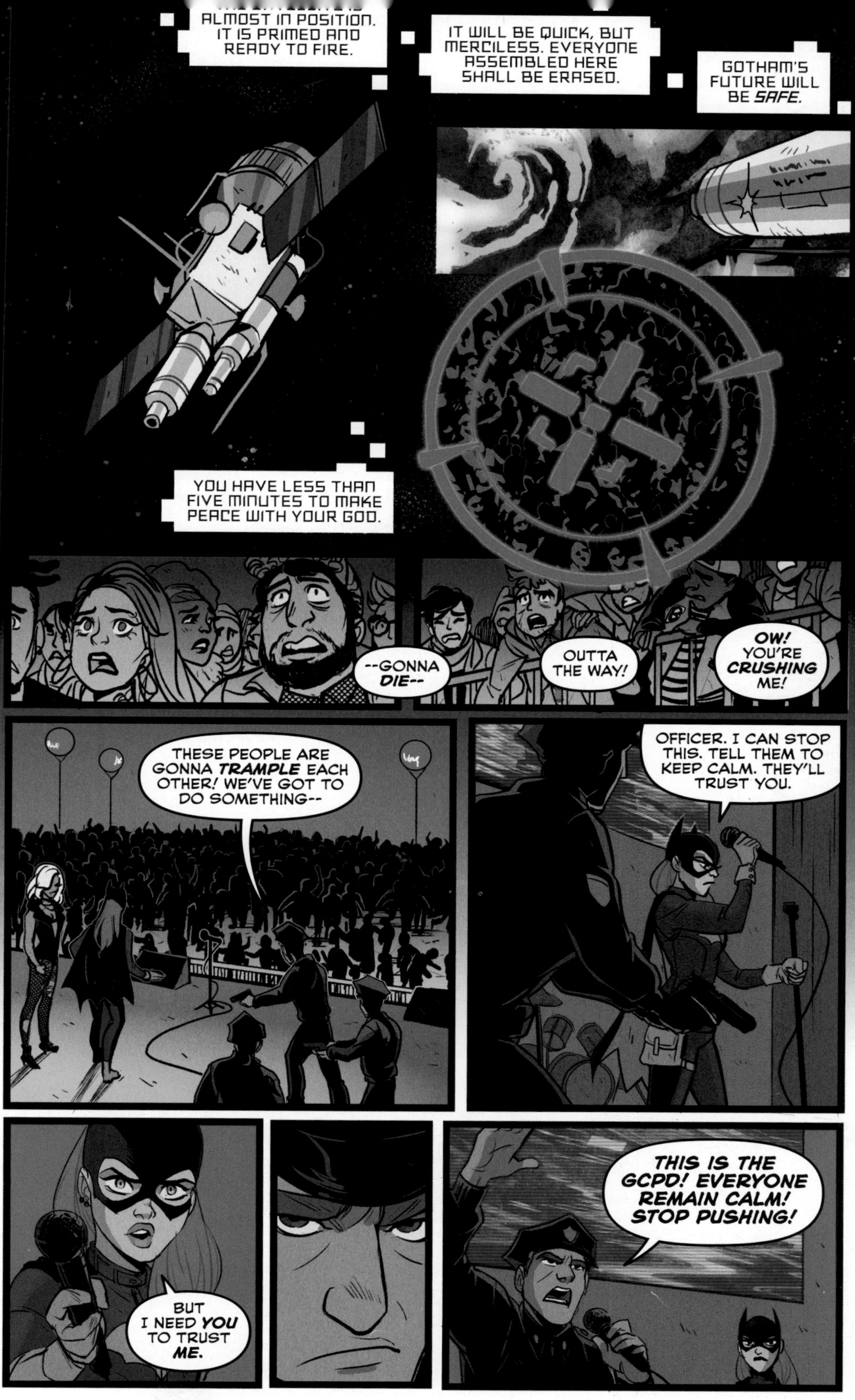
ALMOST IN POSITION. IT IS PRIMED AND READY TO FIRE.
IT WILL BE QUICK, BUT MERCILESS. EVERYONE ASSEMBLED HERE SHALL BE ERASED.
GOTHAM'S FUTURE WILL BE *SAFE.*
YOU HAVE LESS THAN FIVE MINUTES TO MAKE PEACE WITH YOUR GOD.
--GONNA *DIE*--
OUTTA THE WAY!
OW! YOU'RE *CRUSHING* ME!
THESE PEOPLE ARE GONNA *TRAMPLE* EACH OTHER! WE'VE GOT TO DO SOMETHING--
OFFICER. I CAN STOP THIS. TELL THEM TO KEEP CALM. THEY'LL TRUST YOU.
BUT I NEED *YOU* TO TRUST *ME.*
THIS IS THE GCPD! EVERYONE REMAIN CALM! STOP PUSHING!

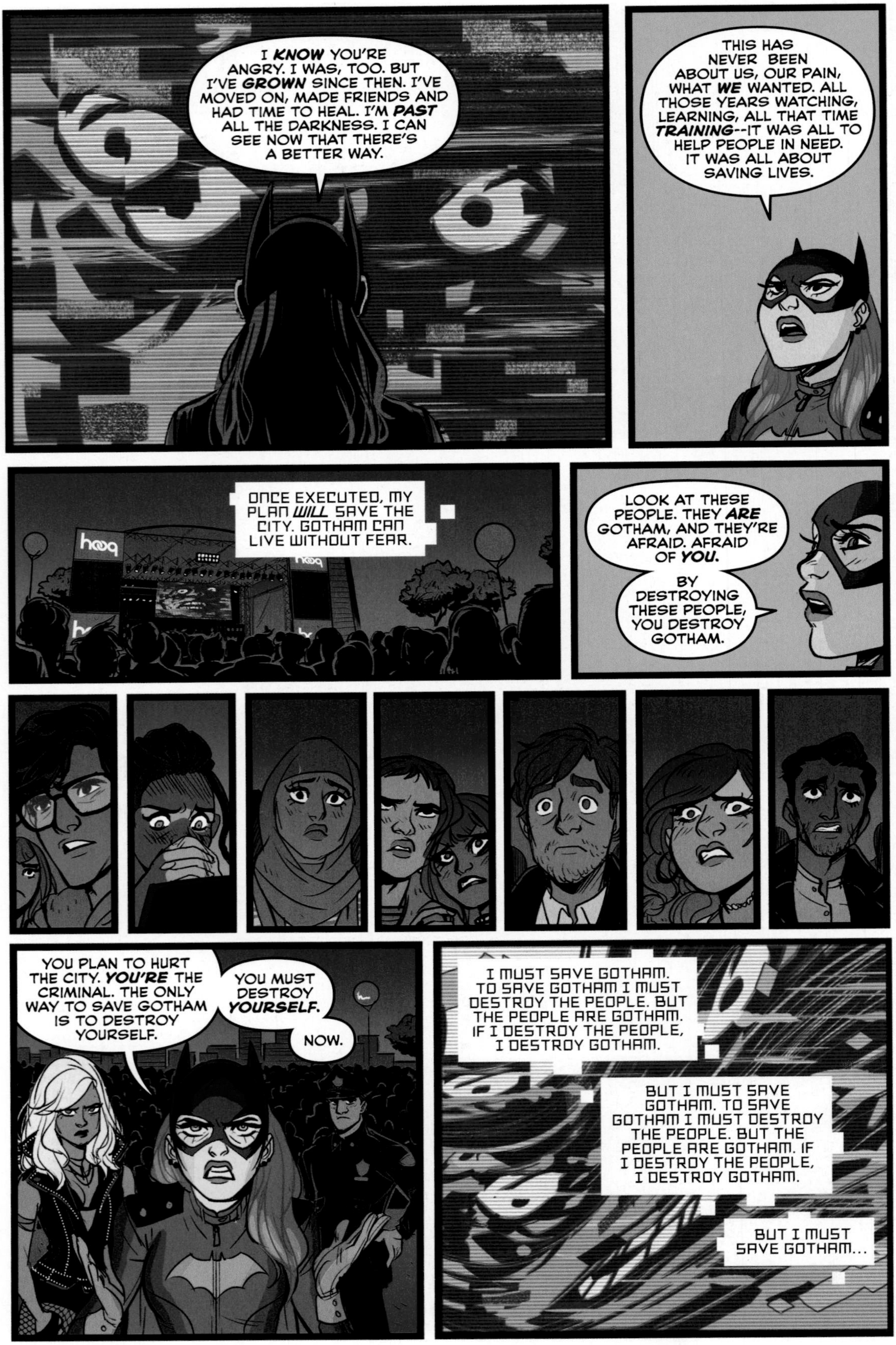

I KNOW YOU'RE ANGRY. I WAS, TOO. BUT I'VE GROWN SINCE THEN. I'VE MOVED ON, MADE FRIENDS AND HAD TIME TO HEAL. I'M PAST ALL THE DARKNESS. I CAN SEE NOW THAT THERE'S A BETTER WAY.
THIS HAS NEVER BEEN ABOUT US, OUR PAIN, WHAT WE WANTED. ALL THOSE YEARS WATCHING, LEARNING, ALL THAT TIME TRAINING--IT WAS ALL TO HELP PEOPLE IN NEED. IT WAS ALL ABOUT SAVING LIVES.
ONCE EXECUTED, MY PLAN WILL SAVE THE CITY. GOTHAM CAN LIVE WITHOUT FEAR.
hooq
LOOK AT THESE PEOPLE. THEY ARE GOTHAM, AND THEY'RE AFRAID. AFRAID OF YOU.
BY DESTROYING THESE PEOPLE, YOU DESTROY GOTHAM.
YOU PLAN TO HURT THE CITY. YOU'RE THE CRIMINAL. THE ONLY WAY TO SAVE GOTHAM IS TO DESTROY YOURSELF.
YOU MUST DESTROY YOURSELF.
NOW.
I MUST SAVE GOTHAM. TO SAVE GOTHAM I MUST DESTROY THE PEOPLE. BUT THE PEOPLE ARE GOTHAM. IF I DESTROY THE PEOPLE, I DESTROY GOTHAM.
BUT I MUST SAVE GOTHAM. TO SAVE GOTHAM I MUST DESTROY THE PEOPLE. BUT THE PEOPLE ARE GOTHAM. IF I DESTROY THE PEOPLE, I DESTROY GOTHAM.
BUT I MUST SAVE GOTHAM...

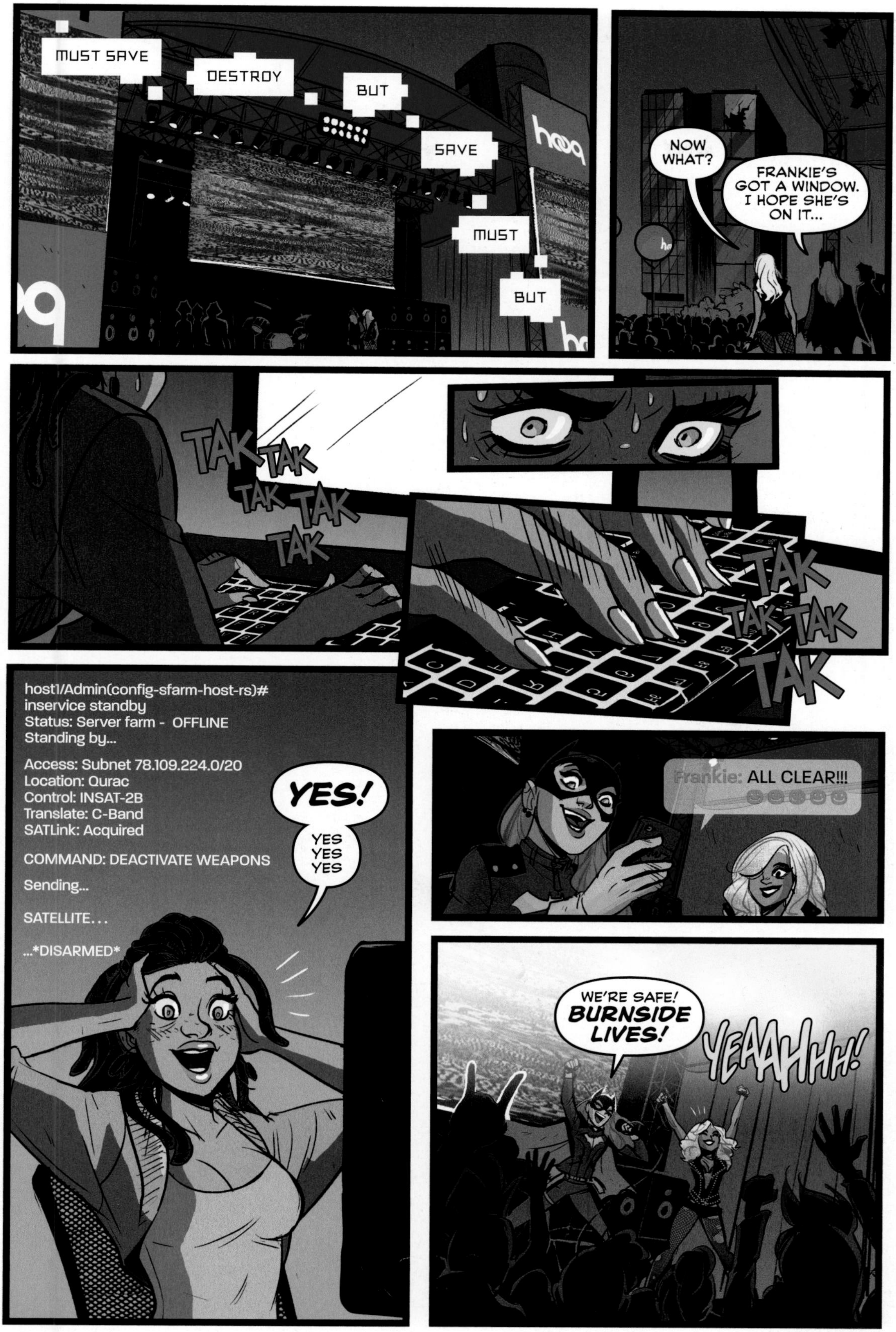
MUST SAVE
DESTROY
BUT
SAVE
MUST
BUT
NOW WHAT?
FRANKIE'S GOT A WINDOW. I HOPE SHE'S ON IT...
TAK TAK TAK TAK TAK
TAK TAK TAK TAK
host1/Admin(config-sfarm-host-rs)#
inservice standby
Status: Server farm - OFFLINE
Standing by...
Access: Subnet 78.109.224.0/20
Location: Qurac
Control: INSAT-2B
Translate: C-Band
SATLink: Acquired
COMMAND: DEACTIVATE WEAPONS
Sending...
SATELLITE...
...*DISARMED*
YES!
YES YES YES
Frankie: ALL CLEAR!!!
WE'RE SAFE! BURNSIDE LIVES!
YEAAHHH!

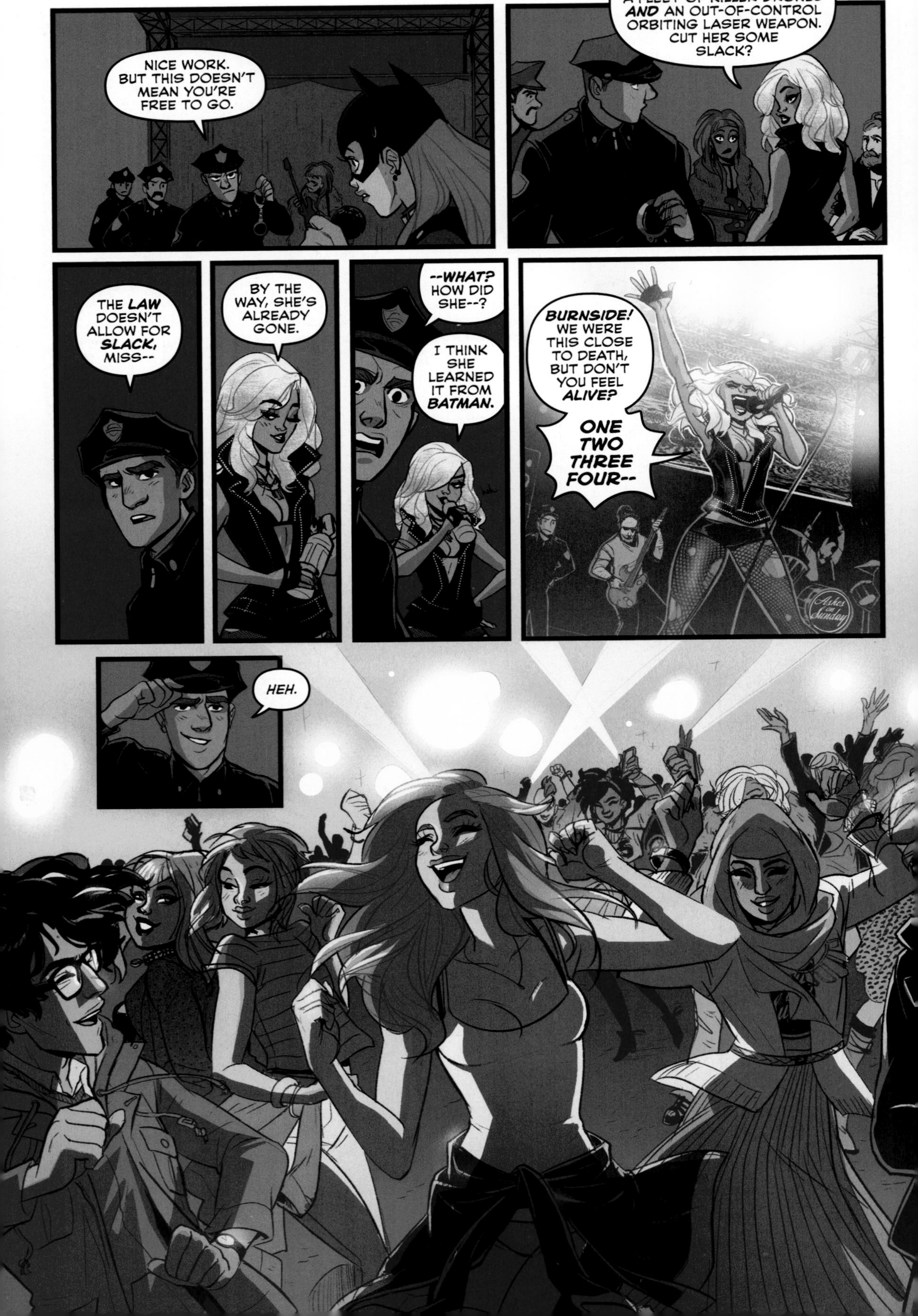
NICE WORK. BUT THIS DOESN'T MEAN YOU'RE FREE TO GO.
BATGIRL JUST STOPPED A RAMPAGING ARTIFICIAL INTELLIGENCE, A FLEET OF KILLER DRONES **AND** AN OUT-OF-CONTROL ORBITING LASER WEAPON. CUT HER SOME SLACK?
THE **LAW** DOESN'T ALLOW FOR **SLACK,** MISS--
BY THE WAY, SHE'S ALREADY GONE.
--**WHAT?** HOW DID SHE--?
I THINK SHE LEARNED IT FROM **BATMAN.**
BURNSIDE! WE WERE THIS CLOSE TO DEATH, BUT DON'T YOU FEEL **ALIVE?**
ONE TWO THREE FOUR--
Ashes on Sunday
HEH.

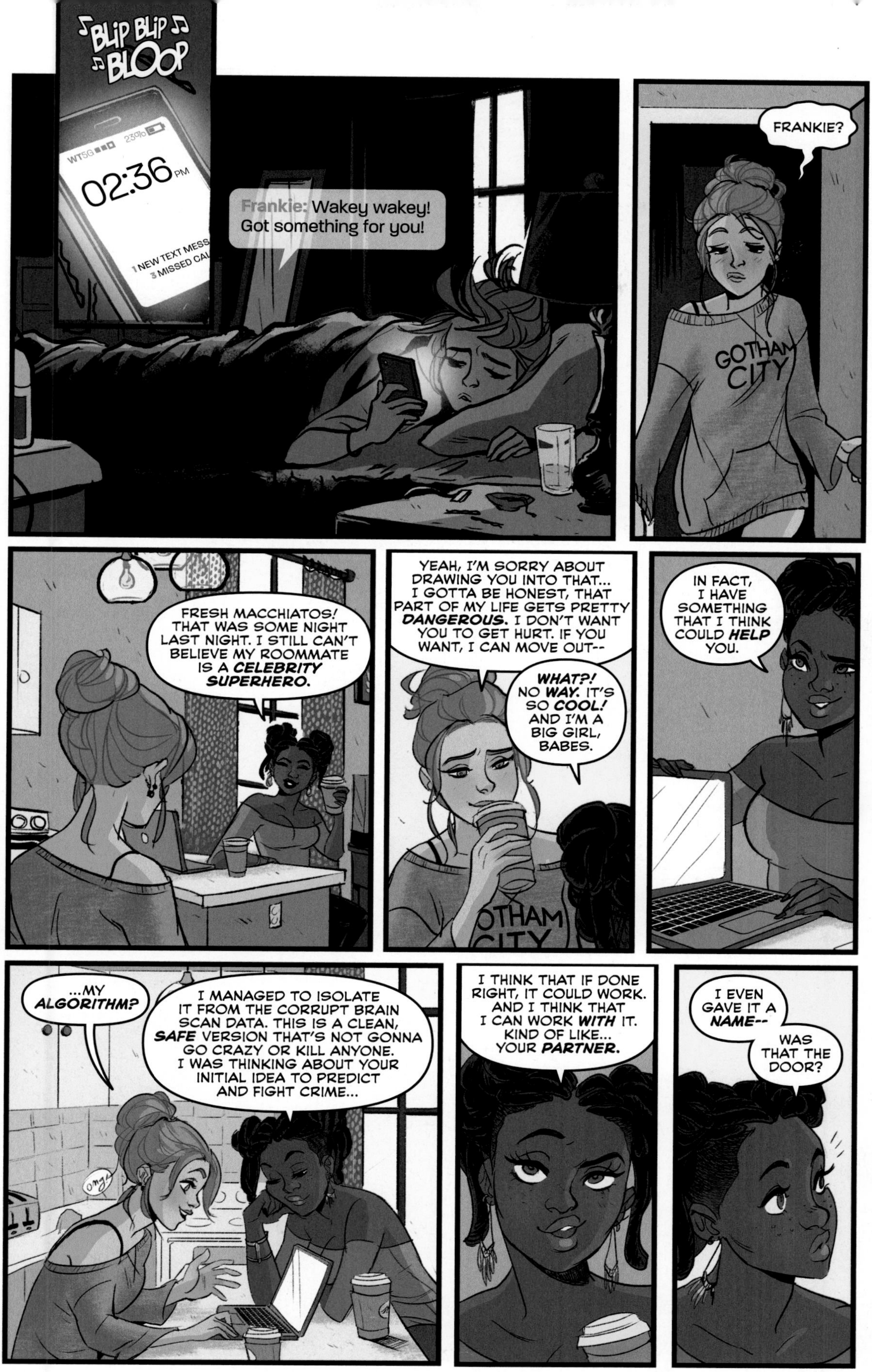
BLIP BLIP BLOOP
WT5G 23%
02:36 PM
1 NEW TEXT MESS
3 MISSED CAL
Frankie: Wakey wakey! Got something for you!
FRANKIE?
GOTHAM CITY
FRESH MACCHIATOS! THAT WAS SOME NIGHT LAST NIGHT. I STILL CAN'T BELIEVE MY ROOMMATE IS A CELEBRITY SUPERHERO.
YEAH, I'M SORRY ABOUT DRAWING YOU INTO THAT... I GOTTA BE HONEST, THAT PART OF MY LIFE GETS PRETTY DANGEROUS. I DON'T WANT YOU TO GET HURT. IF YOU WANT, I CAN MOVE OUT--
WHAT?! NO WAY. IT'S SO COOL! AND I'M A BIG GIRL, BABES.
IN FACT, I HAVE SOMETHING THAT I THINK COULD HELP YOU.
...MY ALGORITHM?
I MANAGED TO ISOLATE IT FROM THE CORRUPT BRAIN SCAN DATA. THIS IS A CLEAN, SAFE VERSION THAT'S NOT GONNA GO CRAZY OR KILL ANYONE. I WAS THINKING ABOUT YOUR INITIAL IDEA TO PREDICT AND FIGHT CRIME...
omg!
I THINK THAT IF DONE RIGHT, IT COULD WORK. AND I THINK THAT I CAN WORK WITH IT. KIND OF LIKE... YOUR PARTNER.
I EVEN GAVE IT A NAME--
WAS THAT THE DOOR?

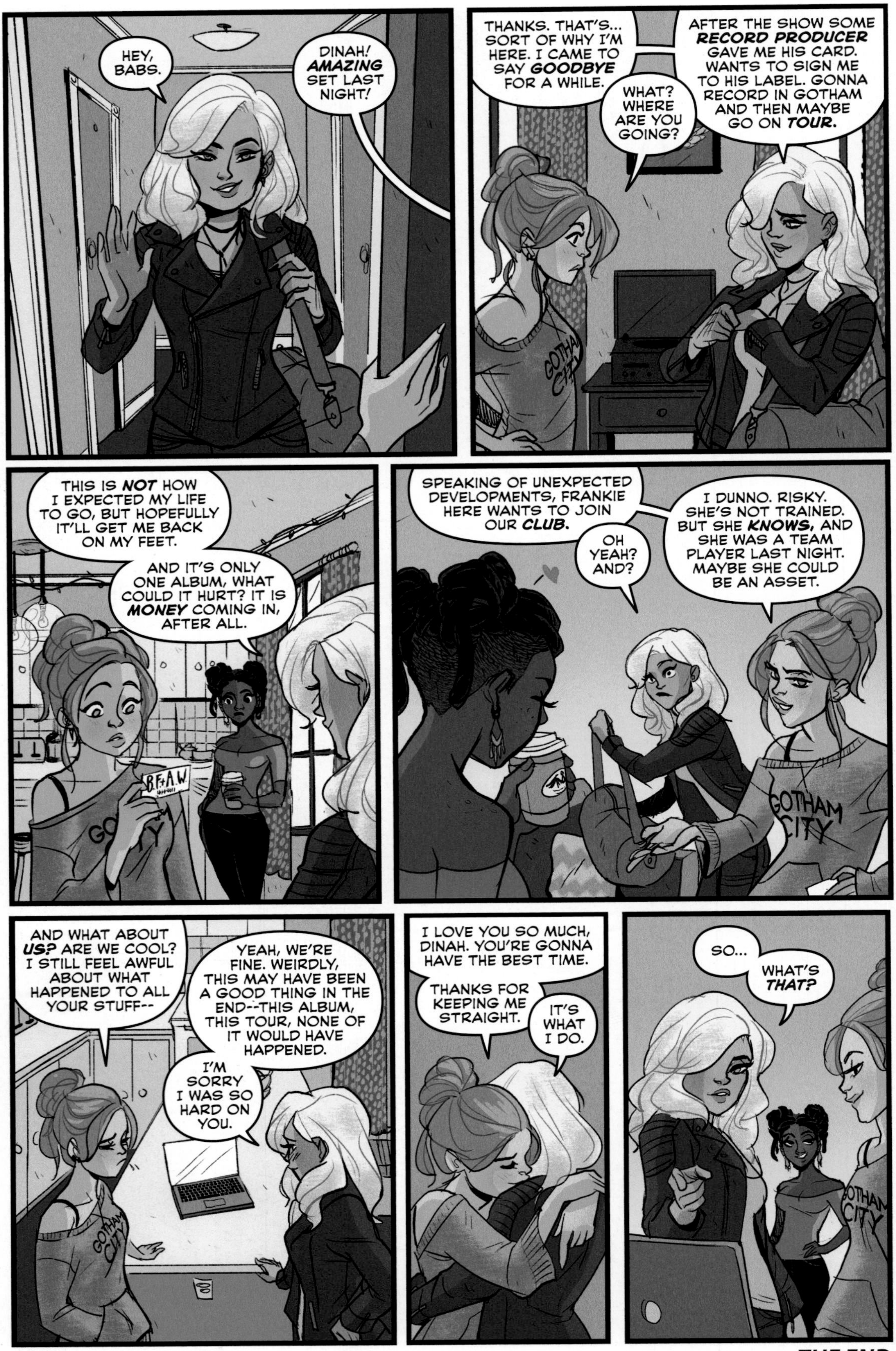
HEY, BABS.
DINAH! AMAZING SET LAST NIGHT!
THANKS. THAT'S... SORT OF WHY I'M HERE. I CAME TO SAY GOODBYE FOR A WHILE.
WHAT? WHERE ARE YOU GOING?
AFTER THE SHOW SOME RECORD PRODUCER GAVE ME HIS CARD. WANTS TO SIGN ME TO HIS LABEL. GONNA RECORD IN GOTHAM AND THEN MAYBE GO ON TOUR.
GOTHAM CITY
THIS IS NOT HOW I EXPECTED MY LIFE TO GO, BUT HOPEFULLY IT'LL GET ME BACK ON MY FEET.
AND IT'S ONLY ONE ALBUM, WHAT COULD IT HURT? IT IS MONEY COMING IN, AFTER ALL.
B.F.+A.W.
SPEAKING OF UNEXPECTED DEVELOPMENTS, FRANKIE HERE WANTS TO JOIN OUR CLUB.
OH YEAH? AND?
I DUNNO. RISKY. SHE'S NOT TRAINED. BUT SHE KNOWS, AND SHE WAS A TEAM PLAYER LAST NIGHT. MAYBE SHE COULD BE AN ASSET.
GOTHAM CITY
AND WHAT ABOUT US? ARE WE COOL? I STILL FEEL AWFUL ABOUT WHAT HAPPENED TO ALL YOUR STUFF--
YEAH, WE'RE FINE. WEIRDLY, THIS MAY HAVE BEEN A GOOD THING IN THE END--THIS ALBUM, THIS TOUR, NONE OF IT WOULD HAVE HAPPENED.
I'M SORRY I WAS SO HARD ON YOU.
GOTHAM CITY
I LOVE YOU SO MUCH, DINAH. YOU'RE GONNA HAVE THE BEST TIME.
THANKS FOR KEEPING ME STRAIGHT.
IT'S WHAT I DO.
SO...
WHAT'S THAT?
GOTHAM CITY

THE END

VARIANT COVER GALLERY

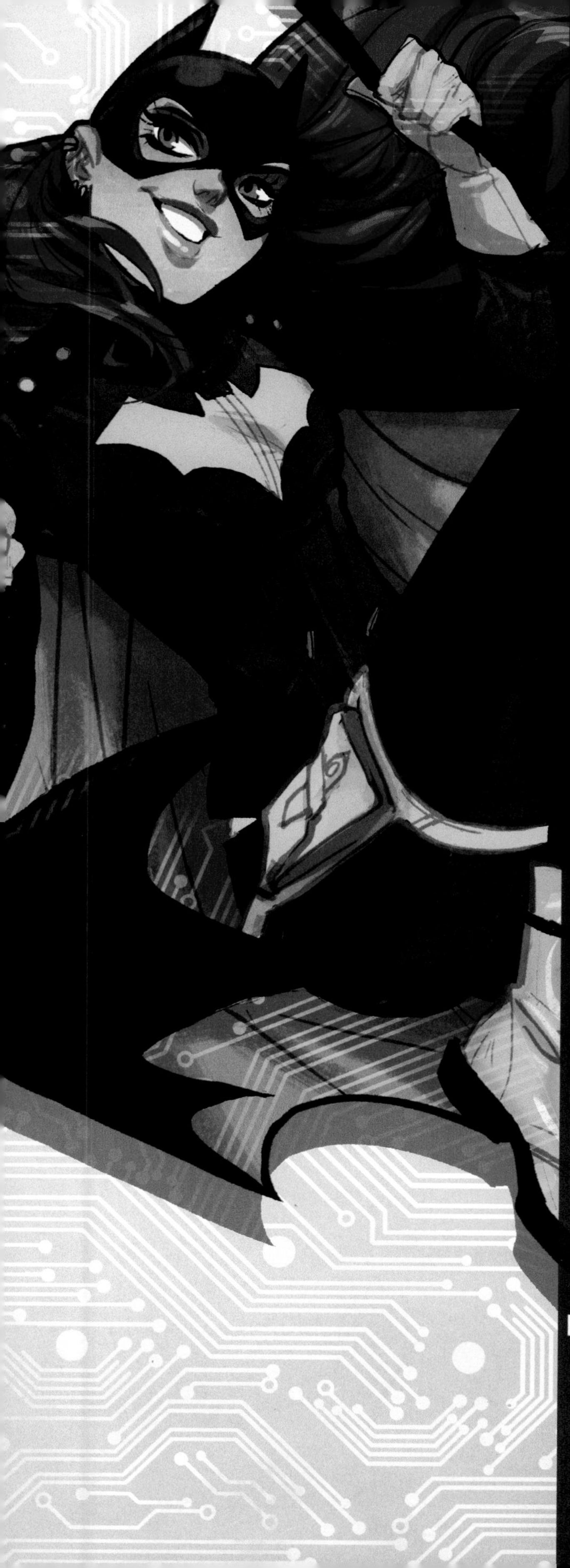

BATGIRL #35
VARIANT COVER BY
BABS TARR

BATGIRL #35
MONSTER VARIANT COVER BY
KEVIN NOWLAN

BATGIRL #36
VARIANT COVER BY
CLIFF CHIANG

BATGIRL #36
LEGO VARIANT COVER

BATGIRL #37
VARIANT COVER BY
DARWYN COOKE

BATGIRL #37
VARIANT COVER BY
BENGAL

BATGIRL #38
FLASH 75TH ANNIVERSARY
VARIANT COVER BY
AARON LOPRESTI
AFTER CARMINE INFANTINO
& MURPHY ANDERSON

BATGIRL #39
HARLEY QUINN VARIANT COVER BY
CLIFF CHIANG

BATGIRL #40
PURPLE RAIN MOVIE POSTER
VARIANT COVER BY
CLIFF CHIANG

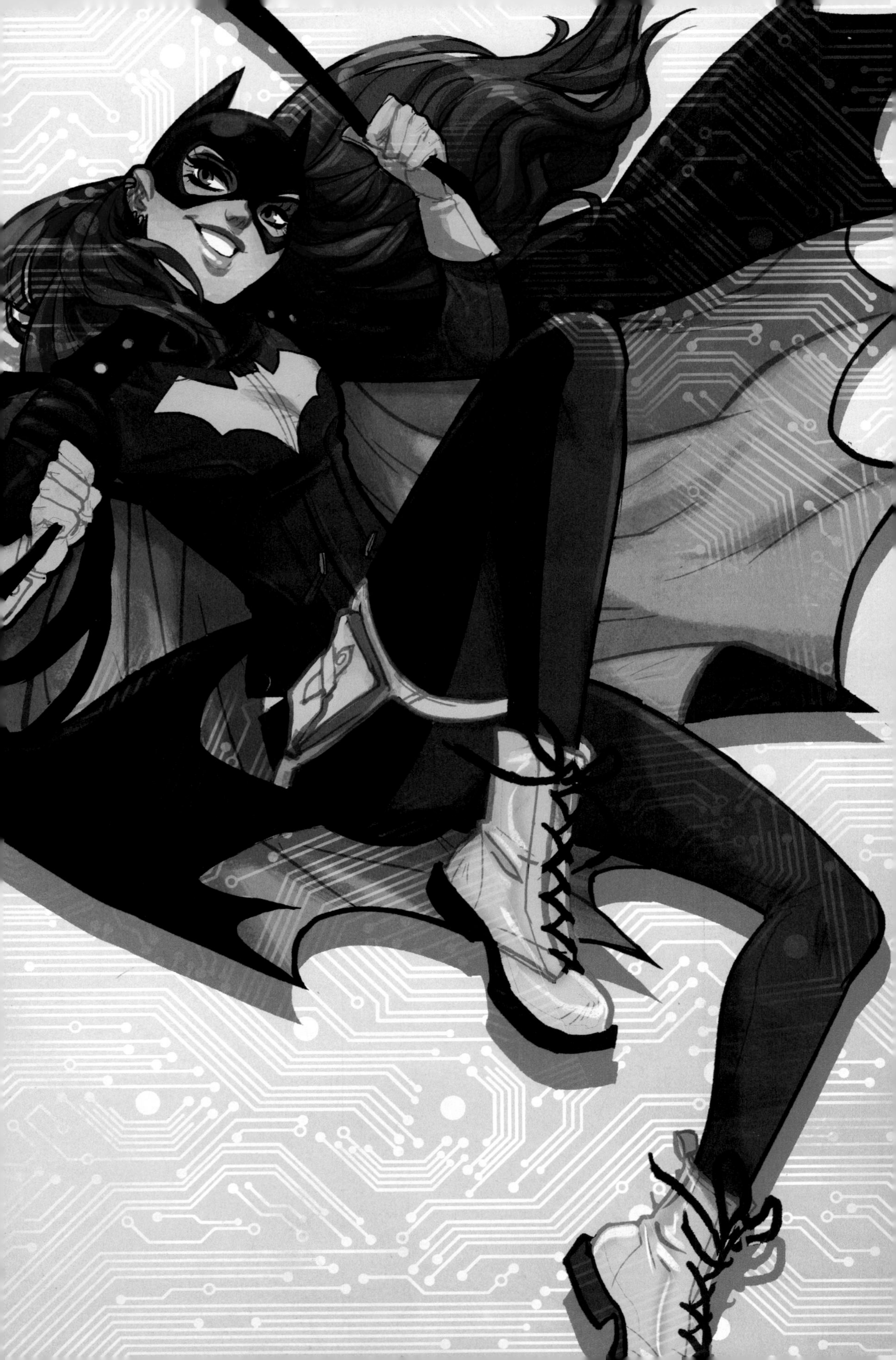

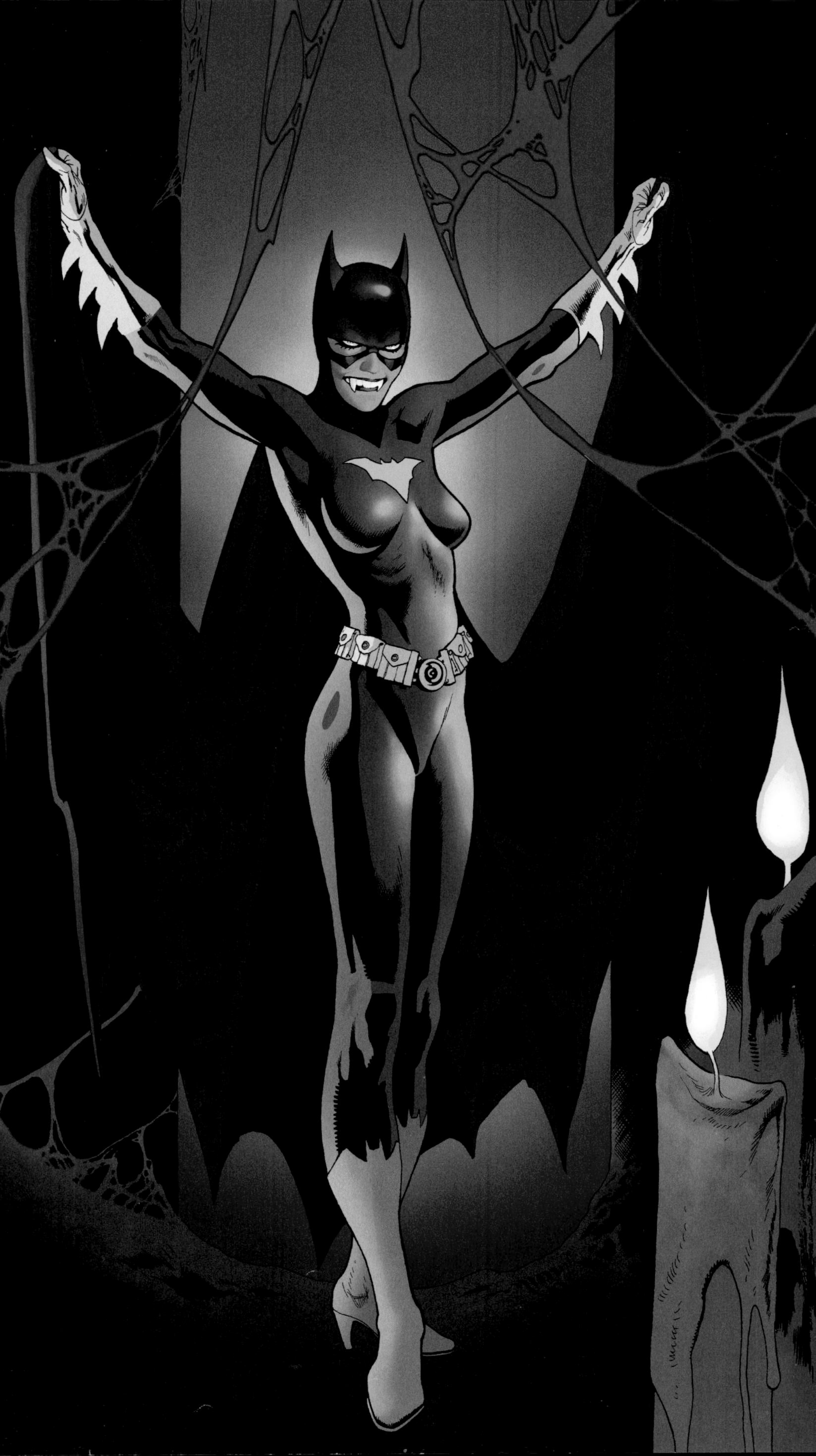

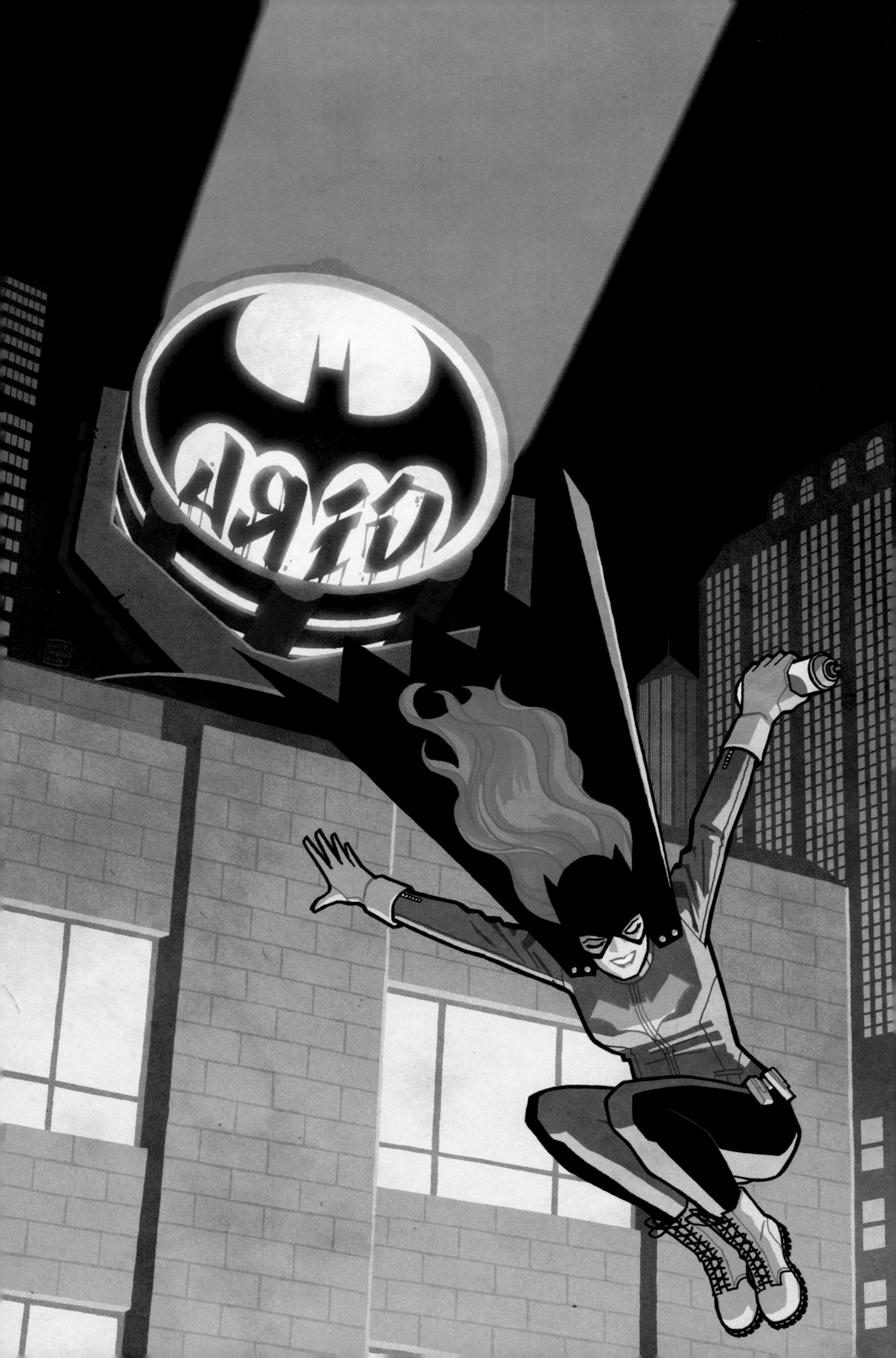

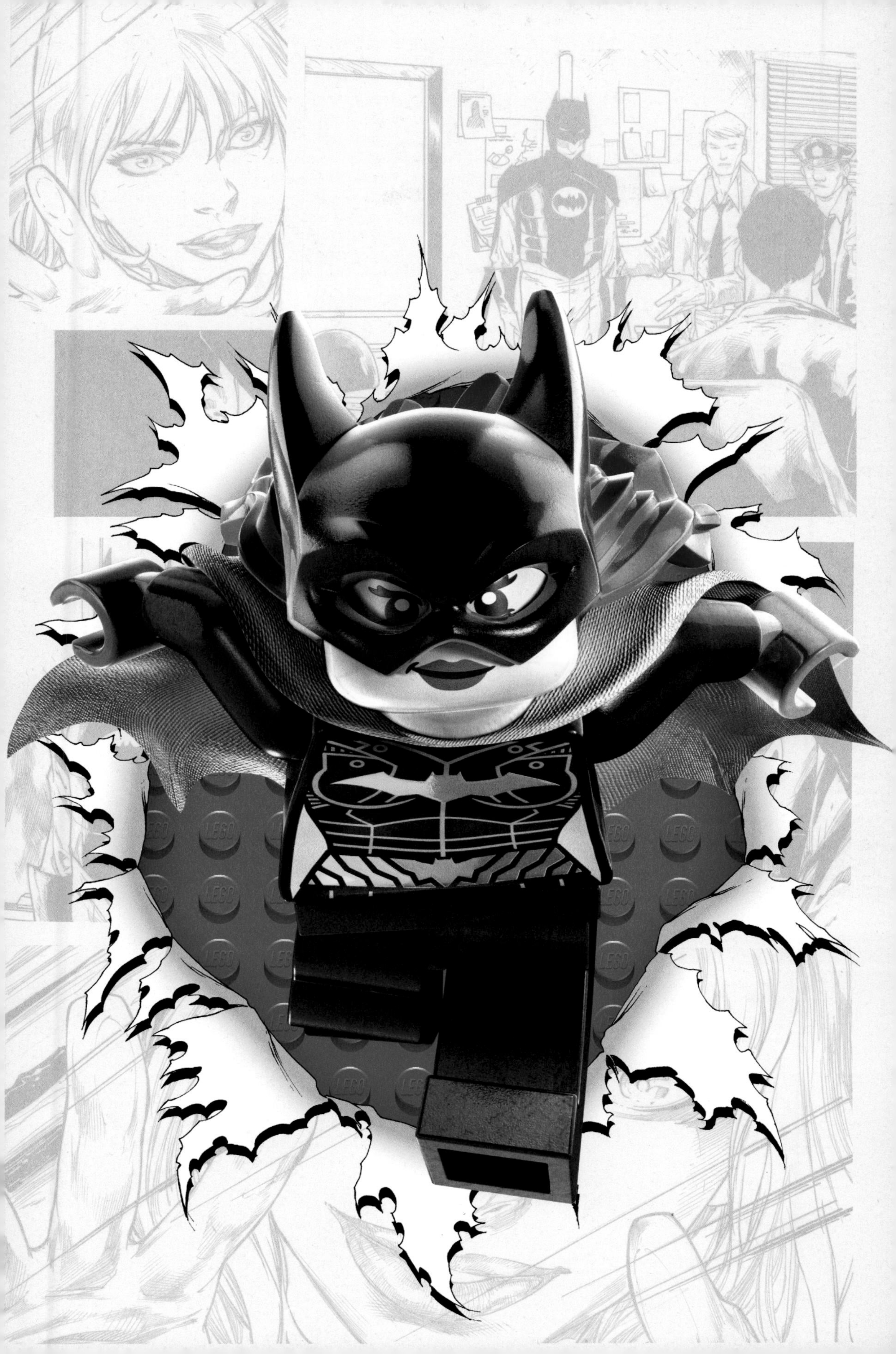

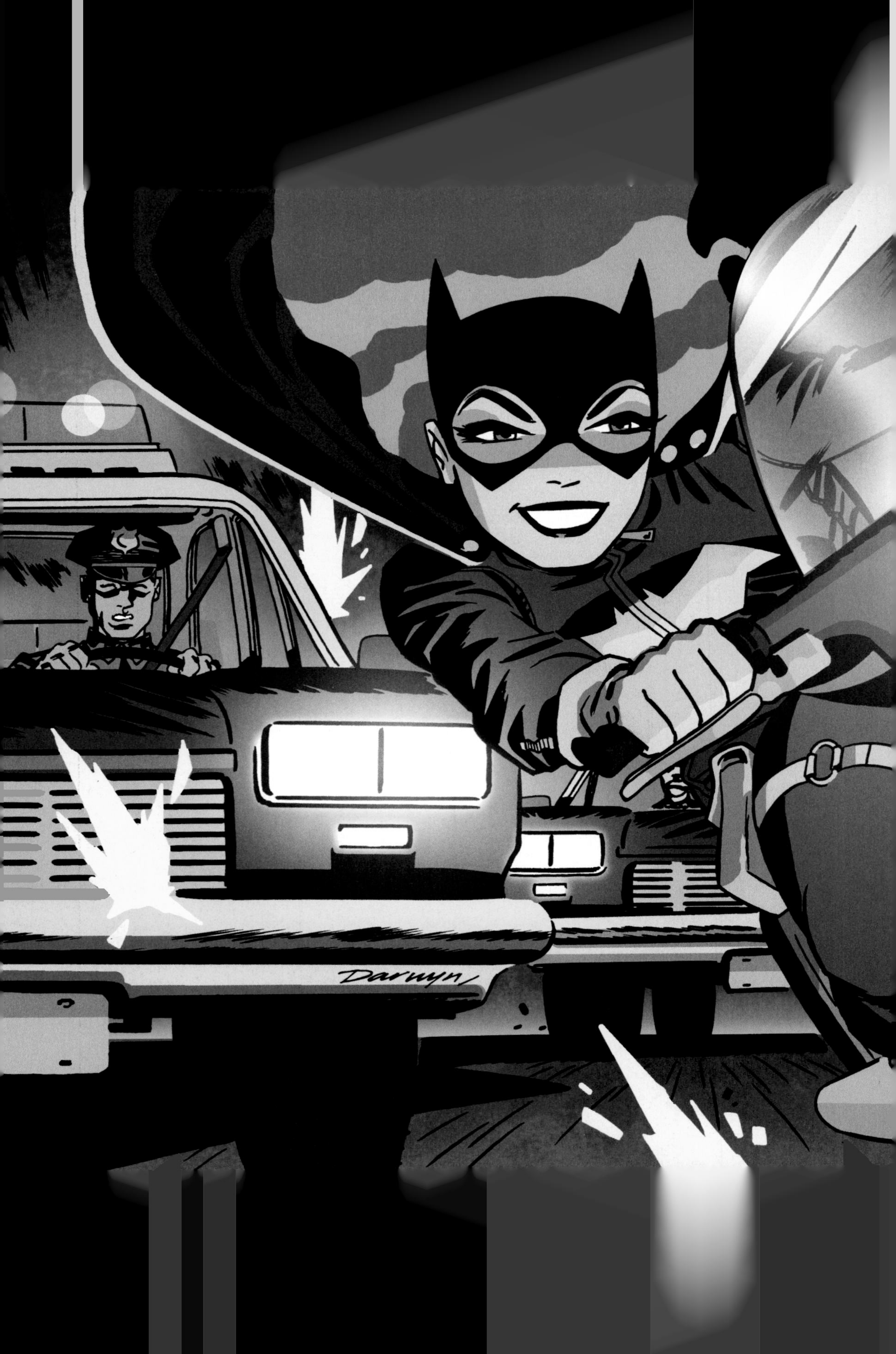
Darwyn

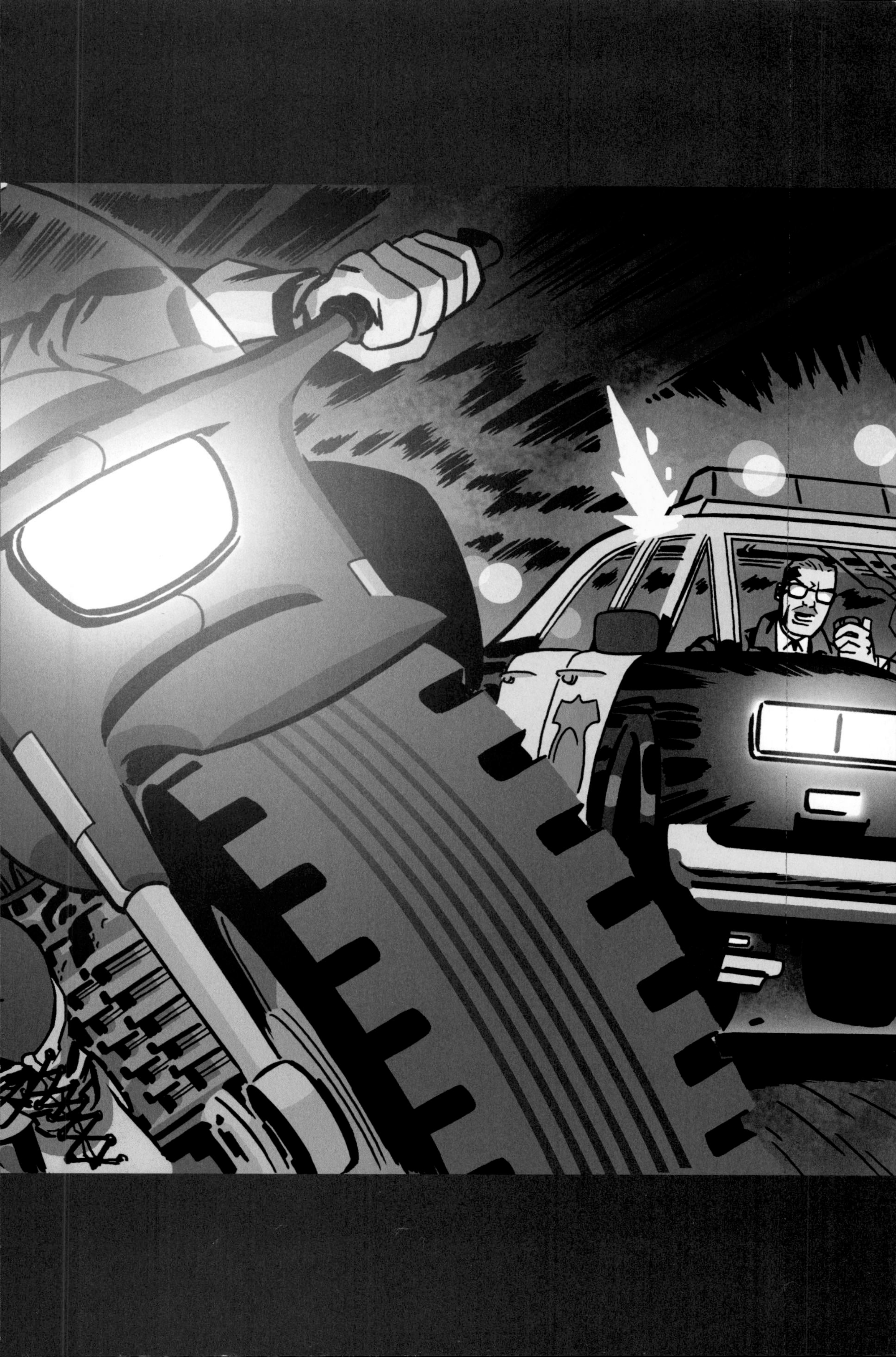

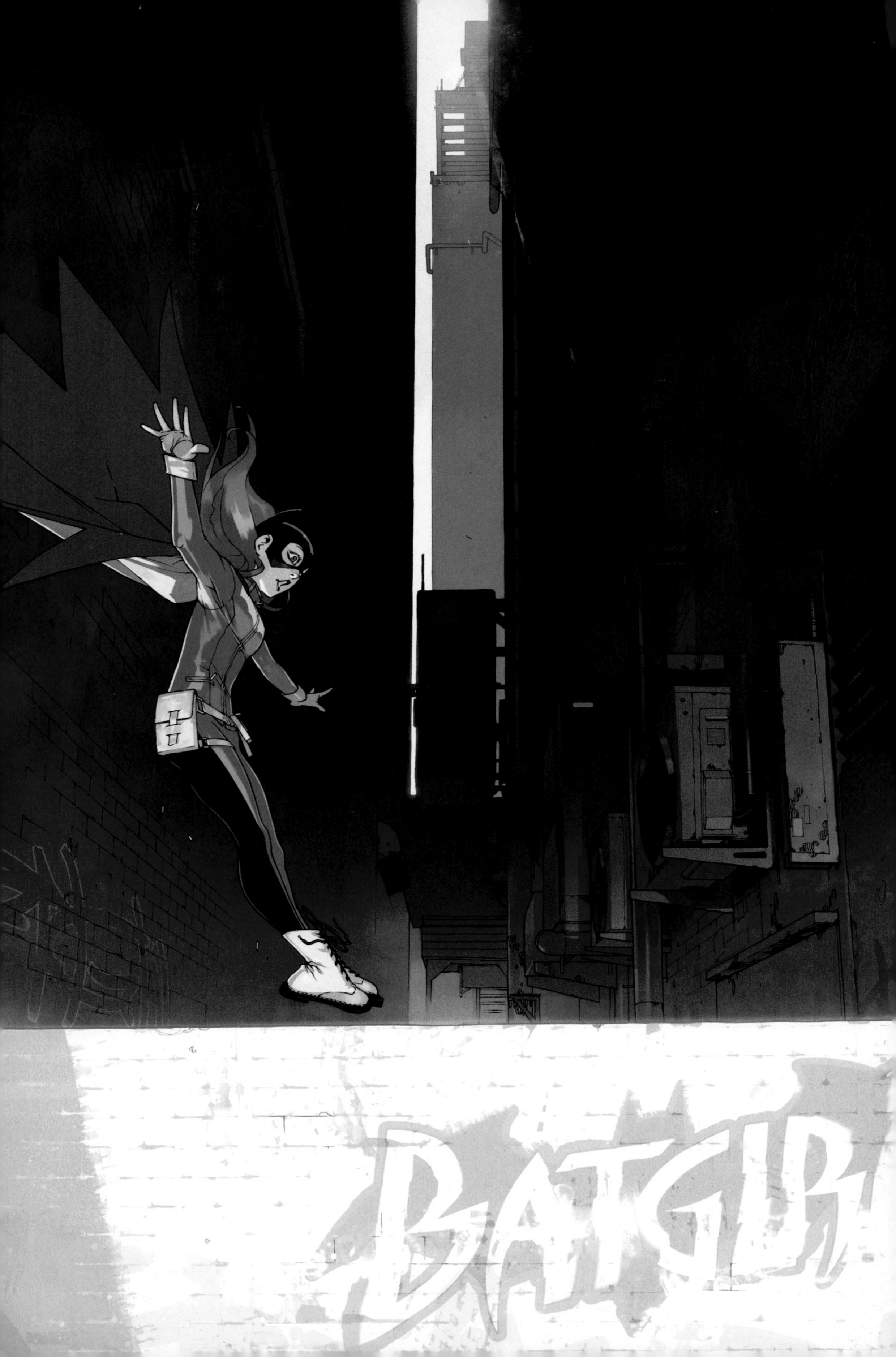
BATGIR

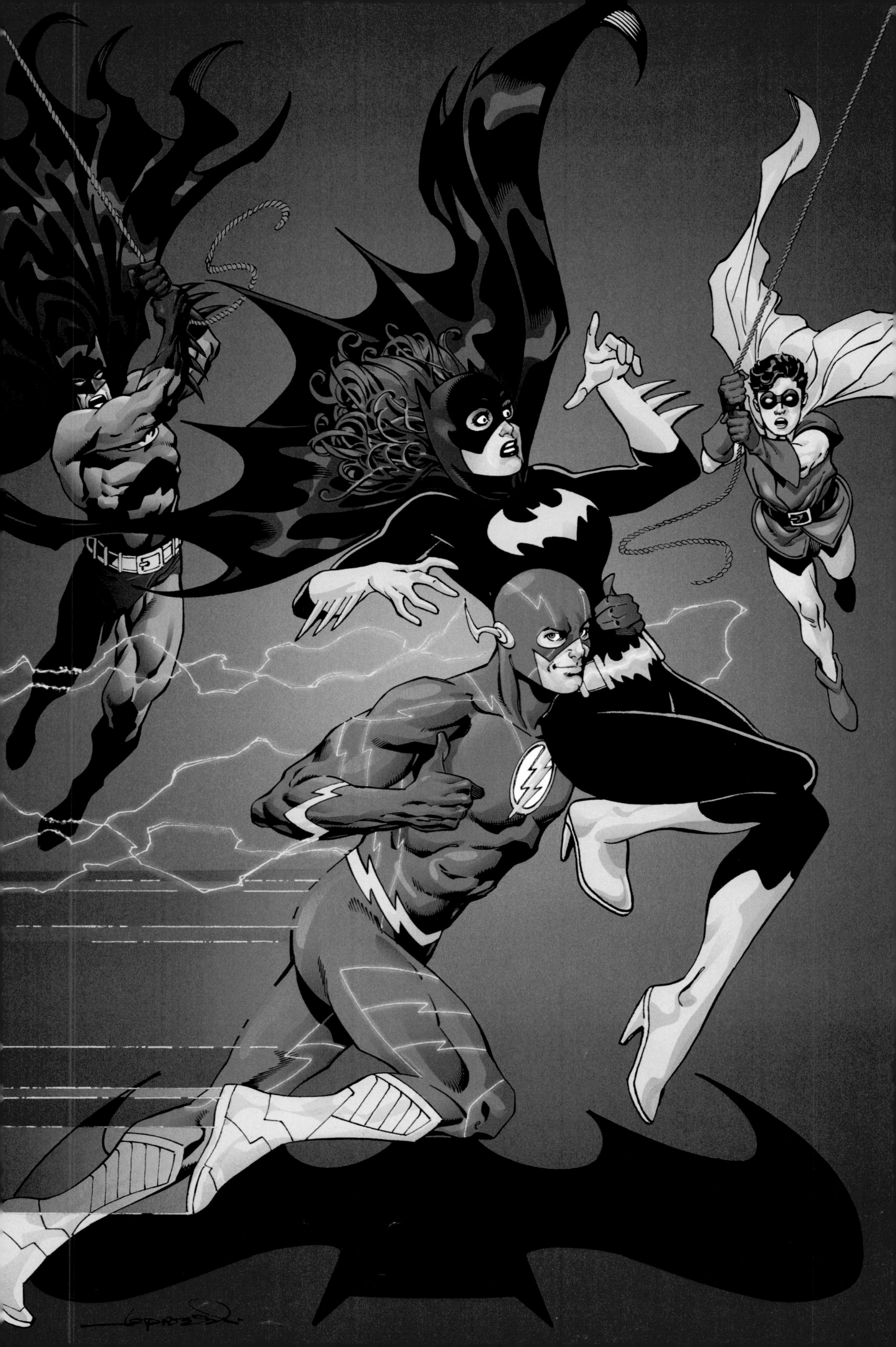

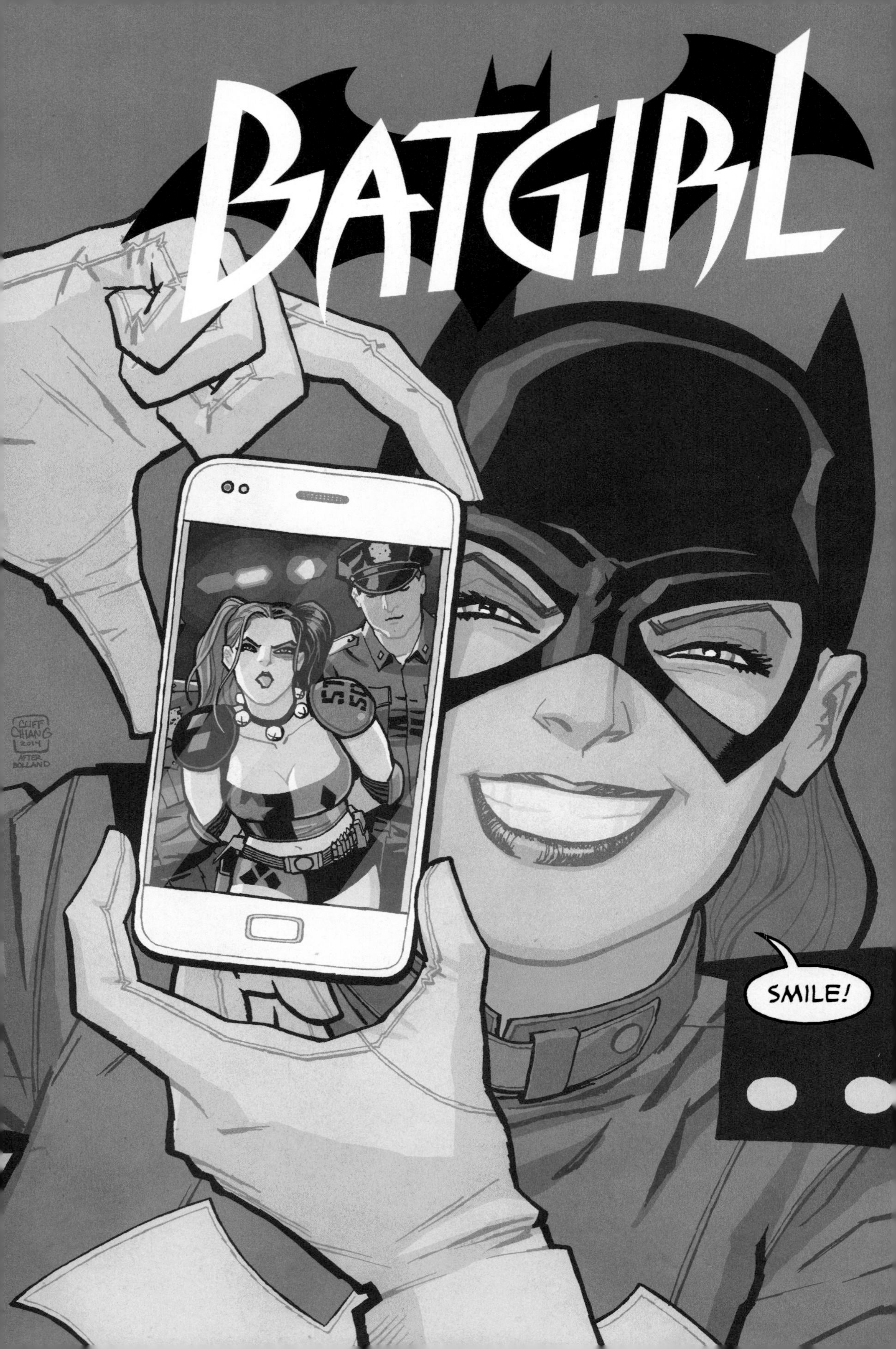
BATGIRL
CLIFF CHIANG 2014 AFTER BOLLAND
SMILE!

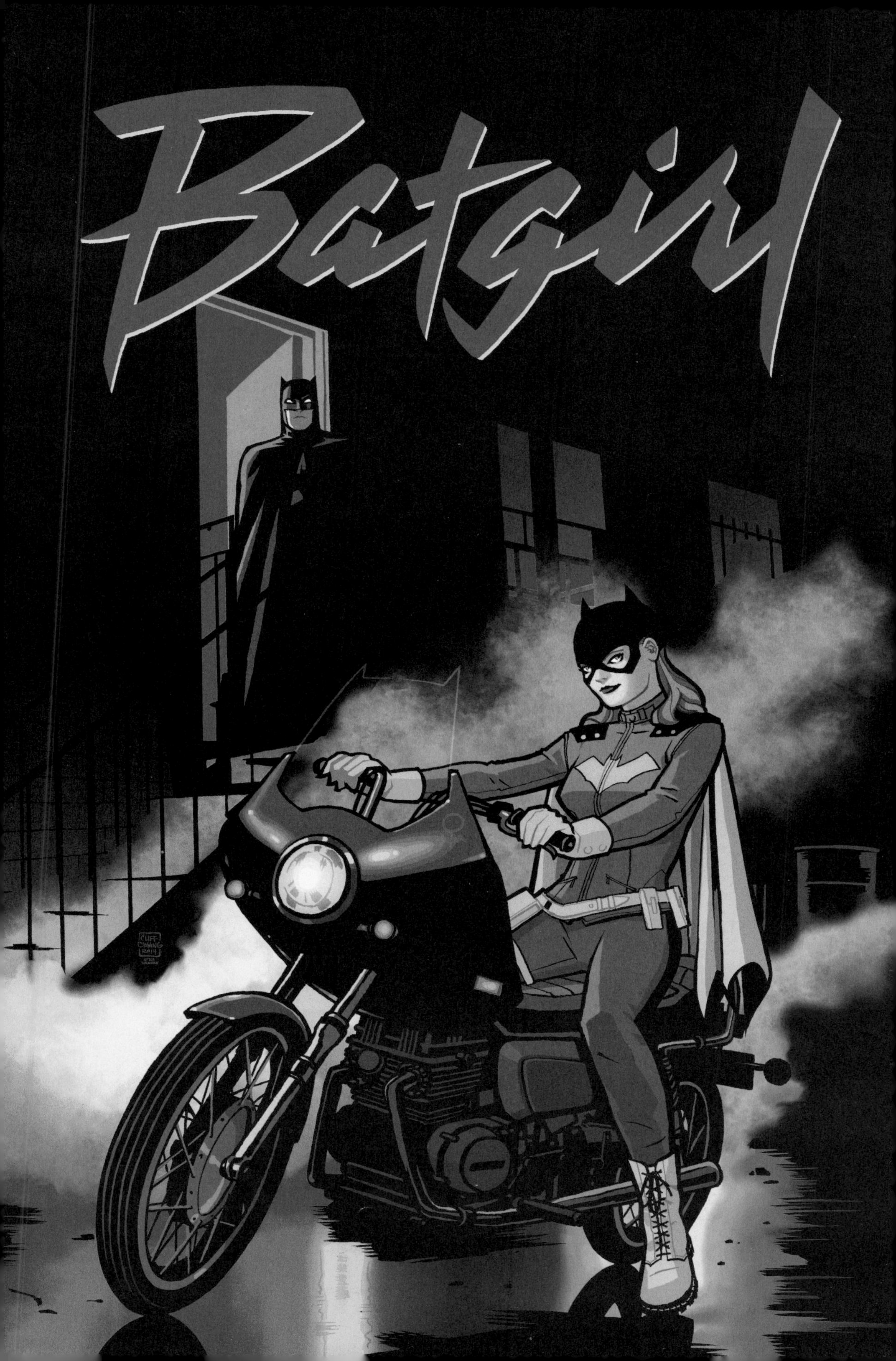
Batgirl
CLIFF CHIANG 2014

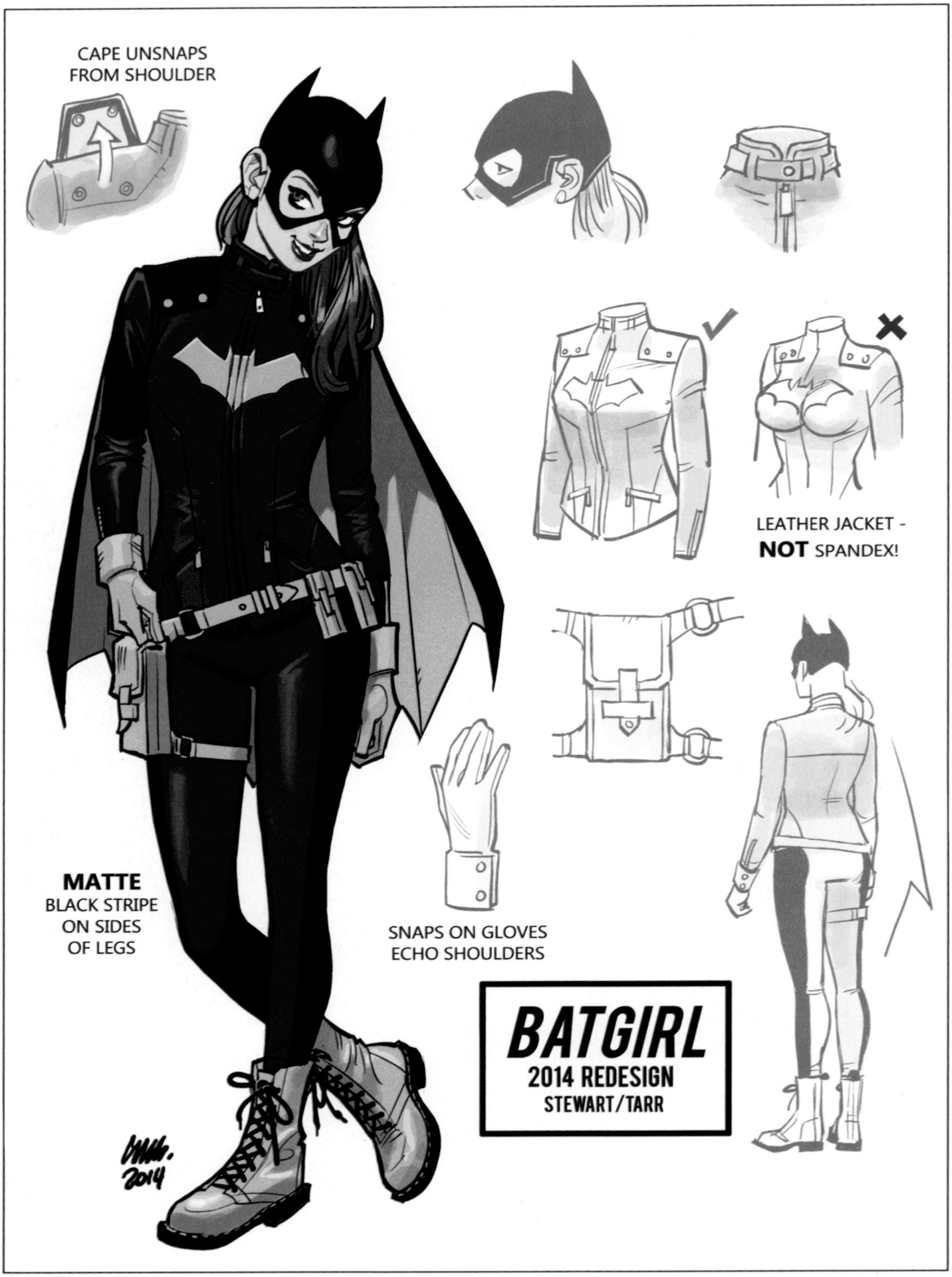
CAPE UNSNAPS FROM SHOULDER
LEATHER JACKET - NOT SPANDEX!
MATTE BLACK STRIPE ON SIDES OF LEGS
SNAPS ON GLOVES ECHO SHOULDERS
BATGIRL
2014 REDESIGN
STEWART/TARR
2014

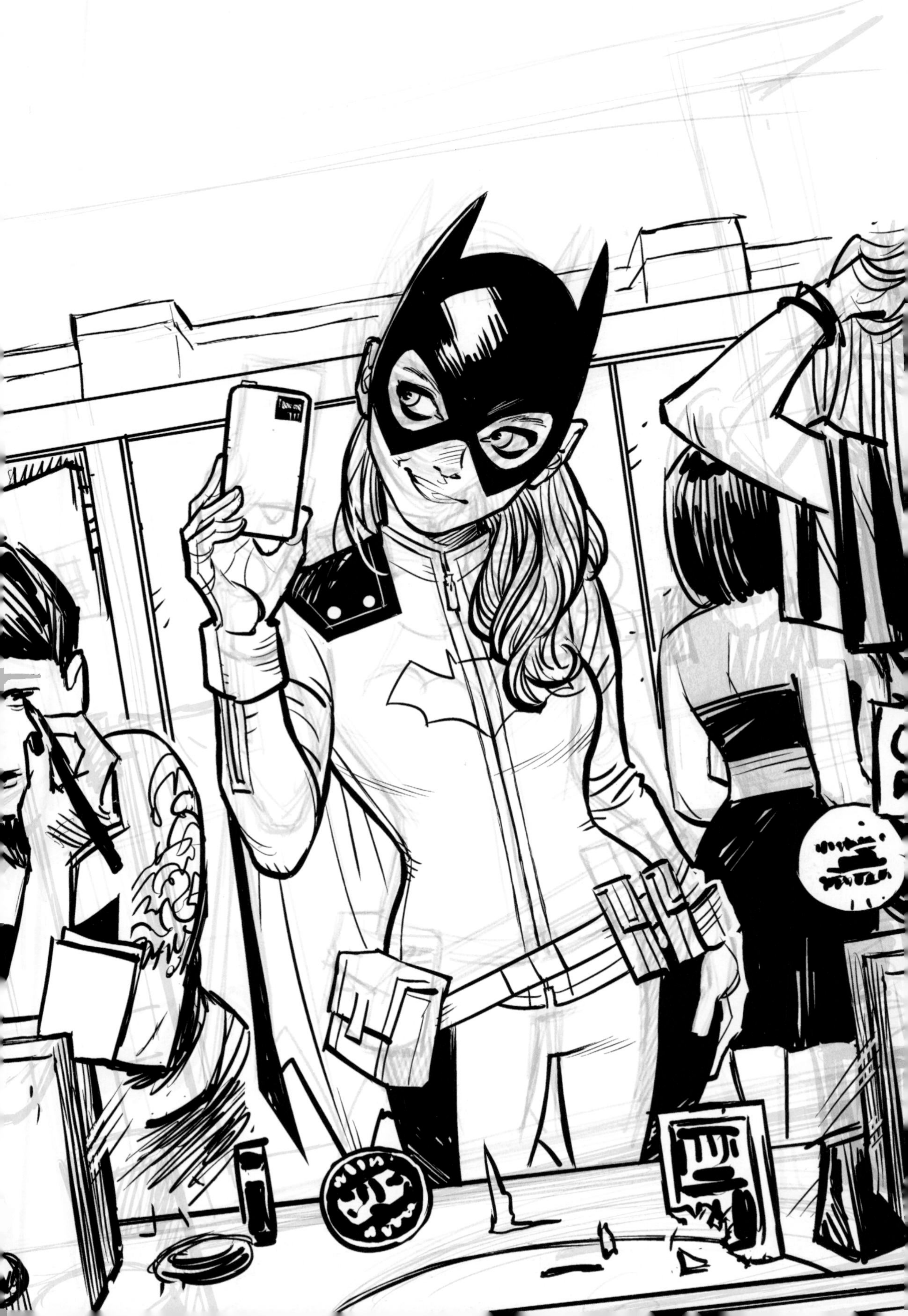

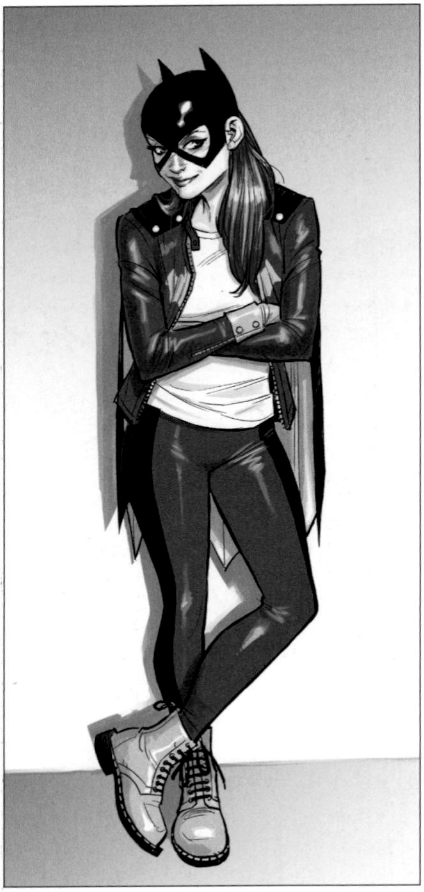

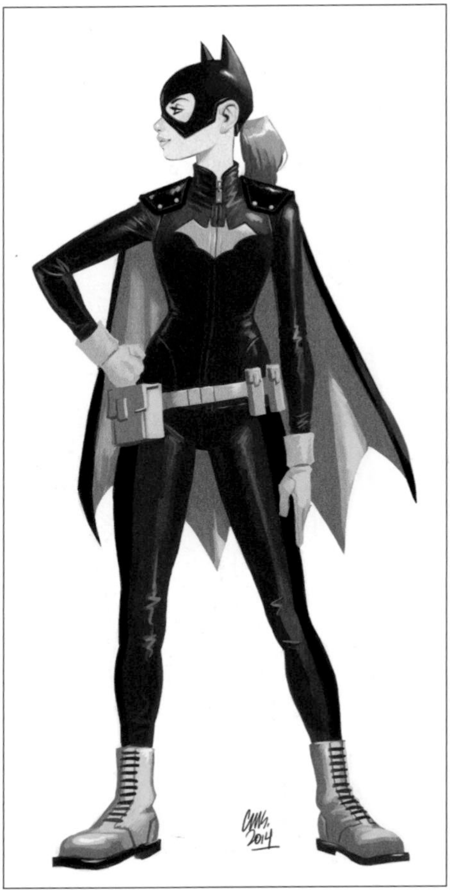

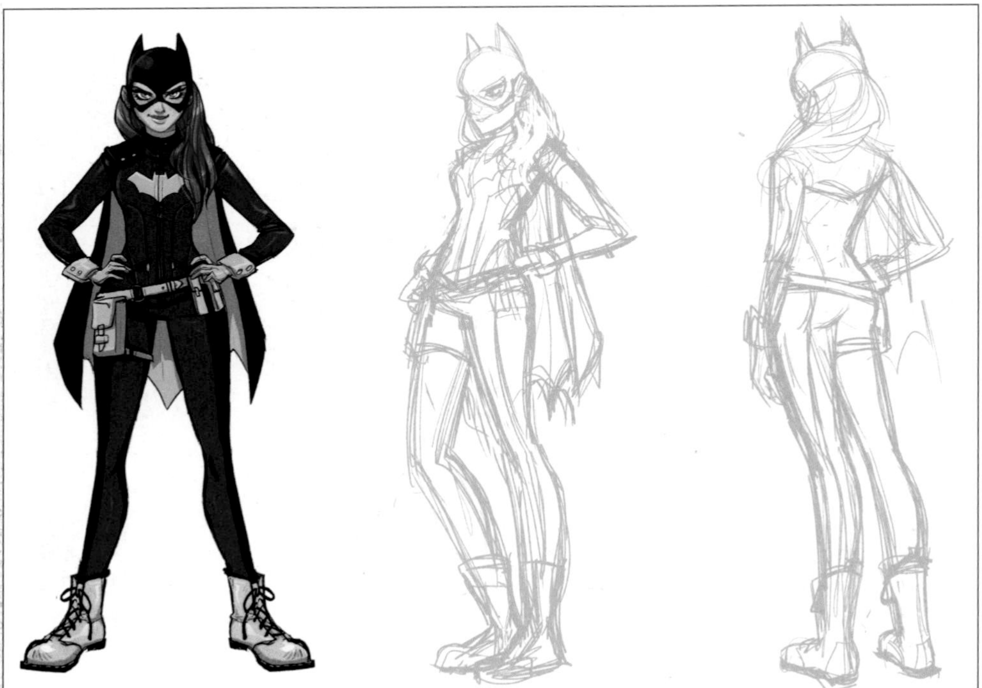

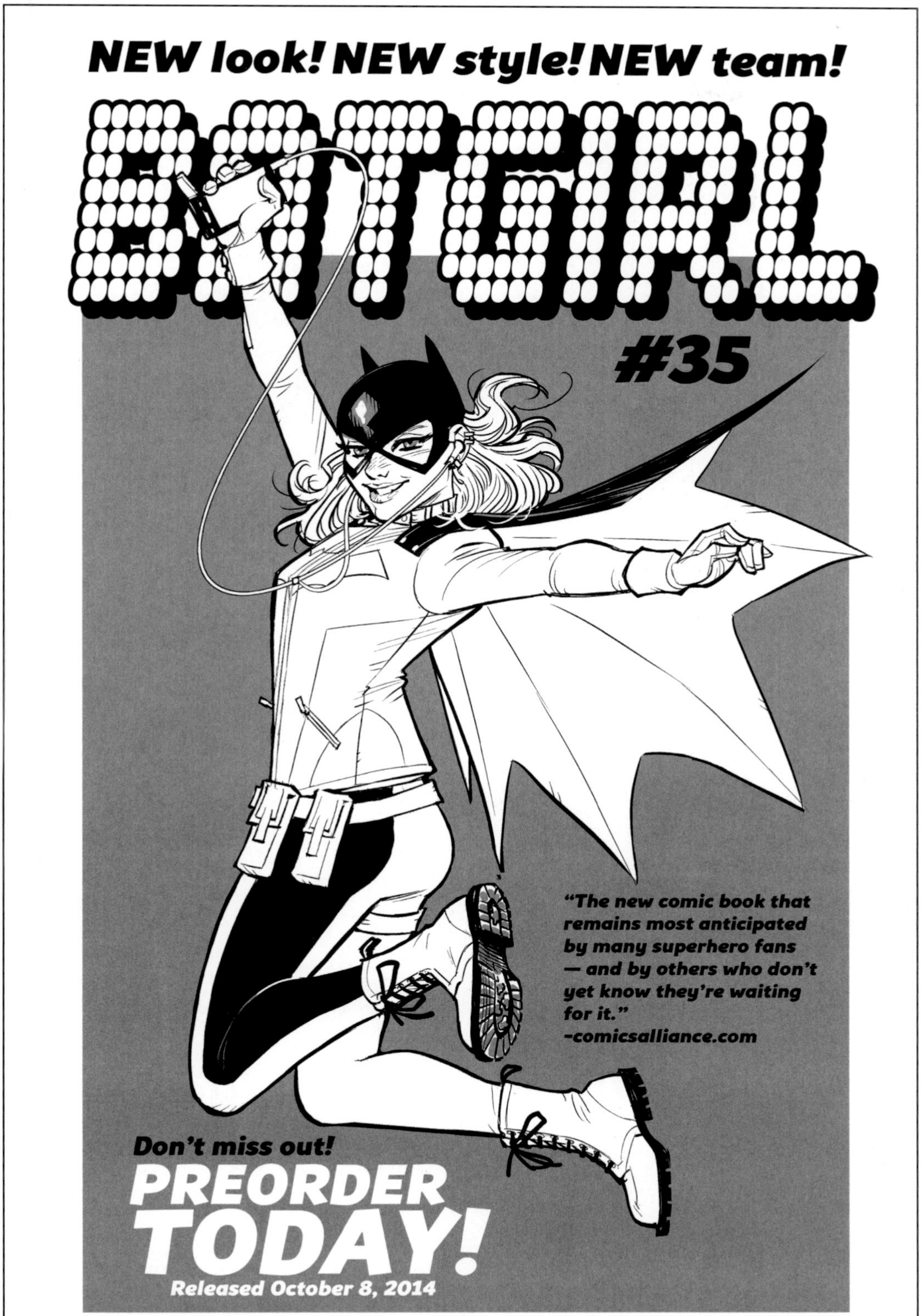
NEW look! NEW style! NEW team!
BATGIRL
#35
"The new comic book that remains most anticipated by many superhero fans — and by others who don't yet know they're waiting for it."
-comicsalliance.com
Don't miss out!
PREORDER TODAY!
Released October 8, 2014
#batgirlofburnside
batgirlofburnside.tumblr.com

BARBARA CHARACTER STUDIES BY
BABS TARR

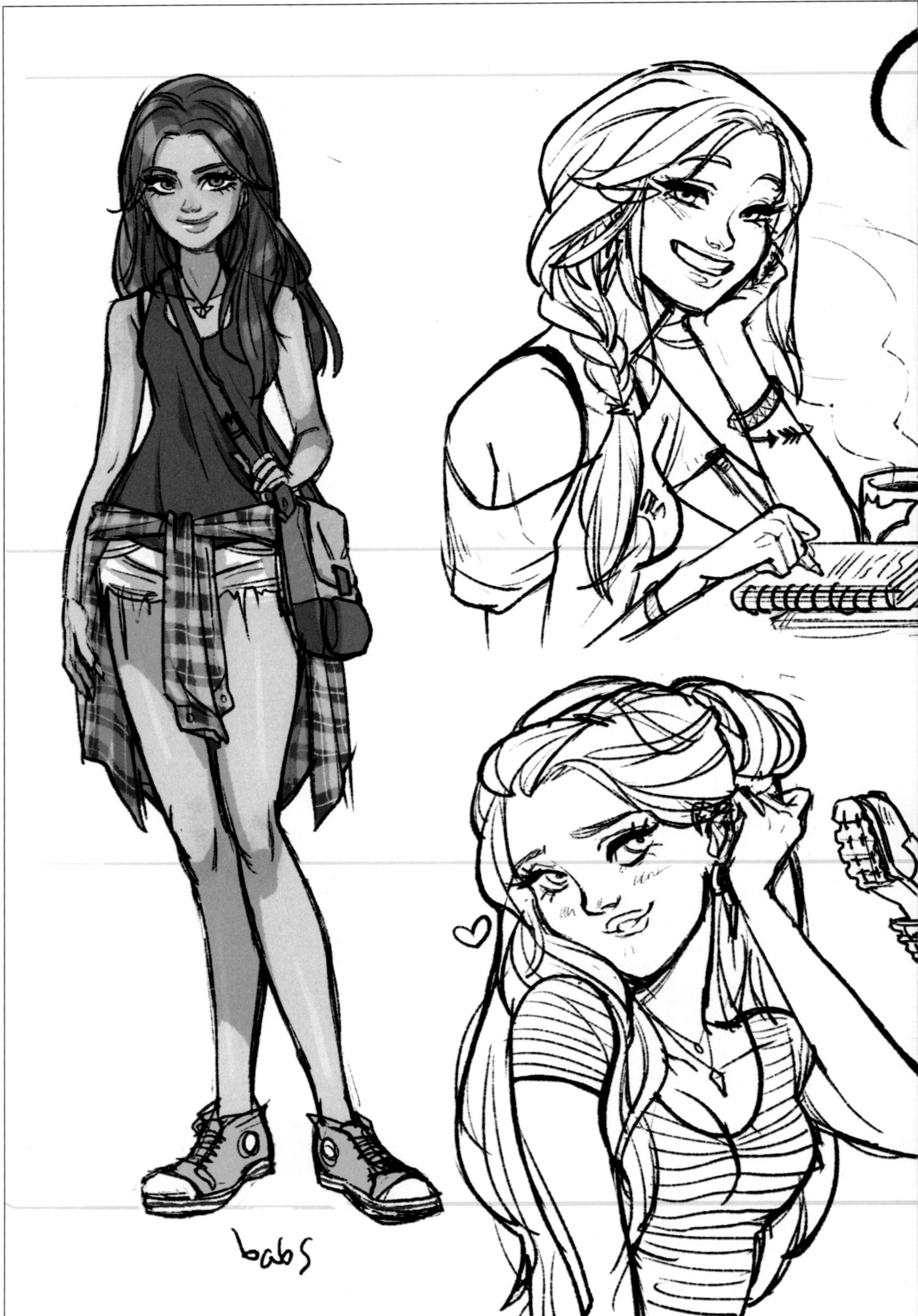
babs

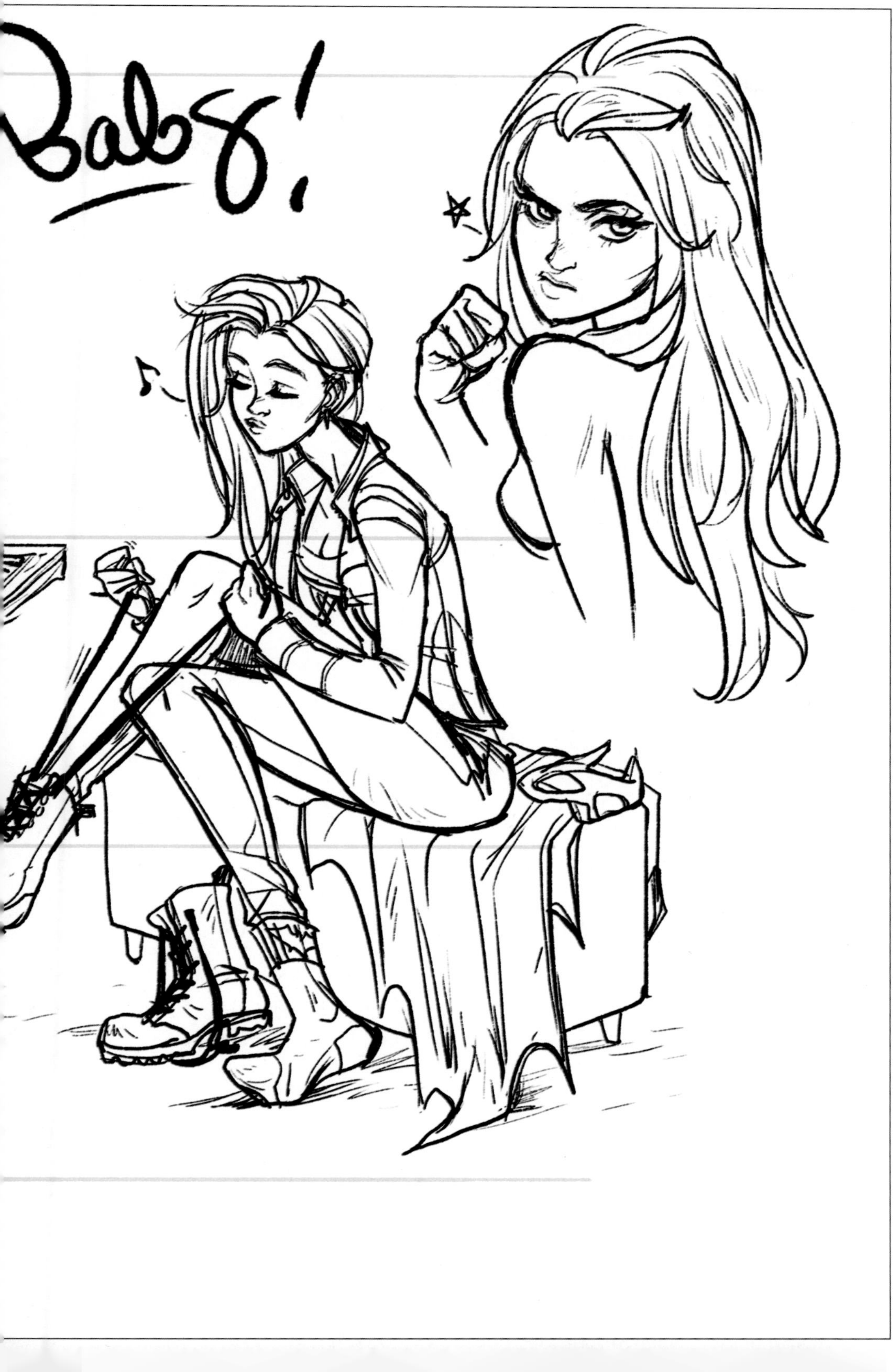
Babs!

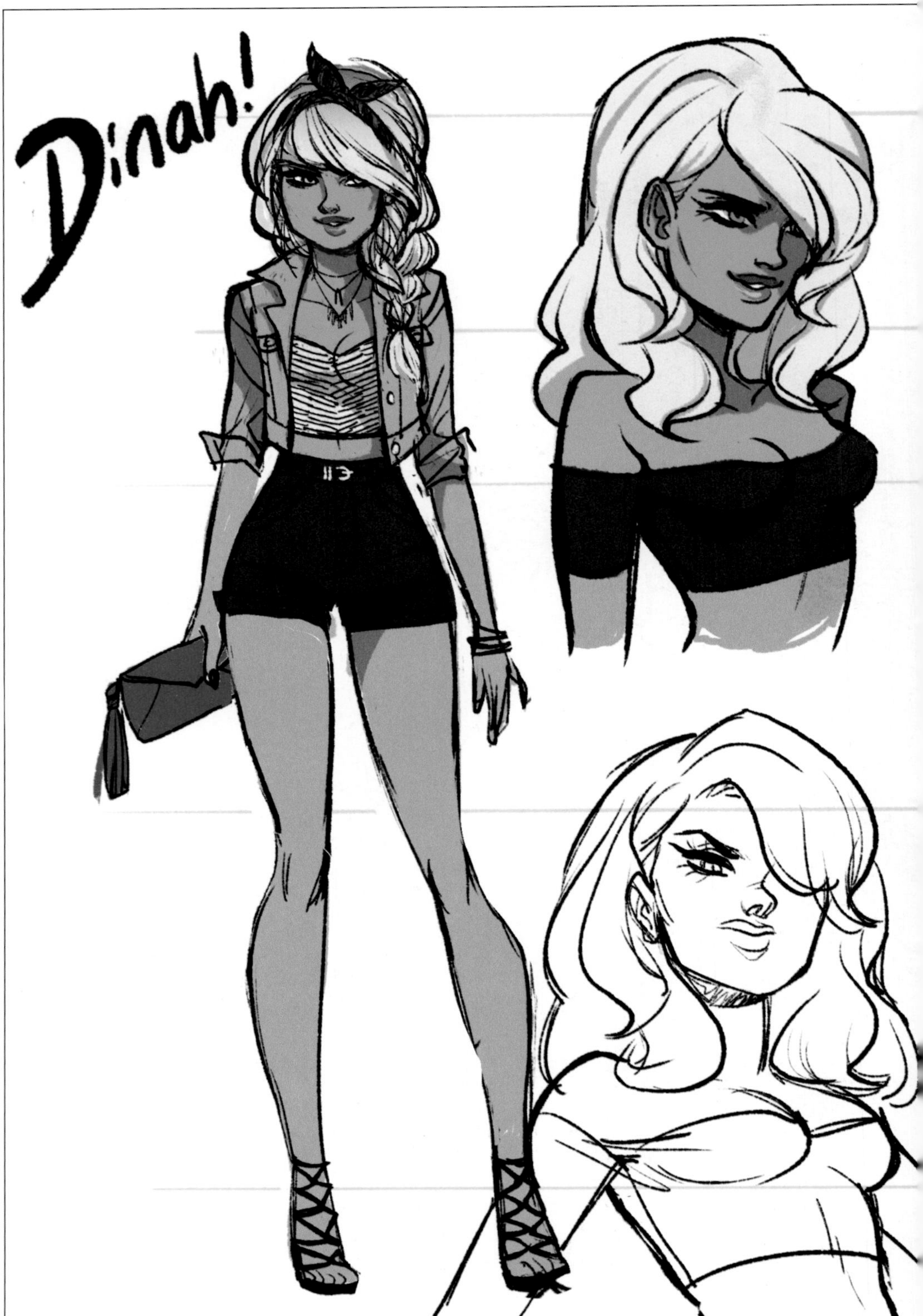
Dinah!

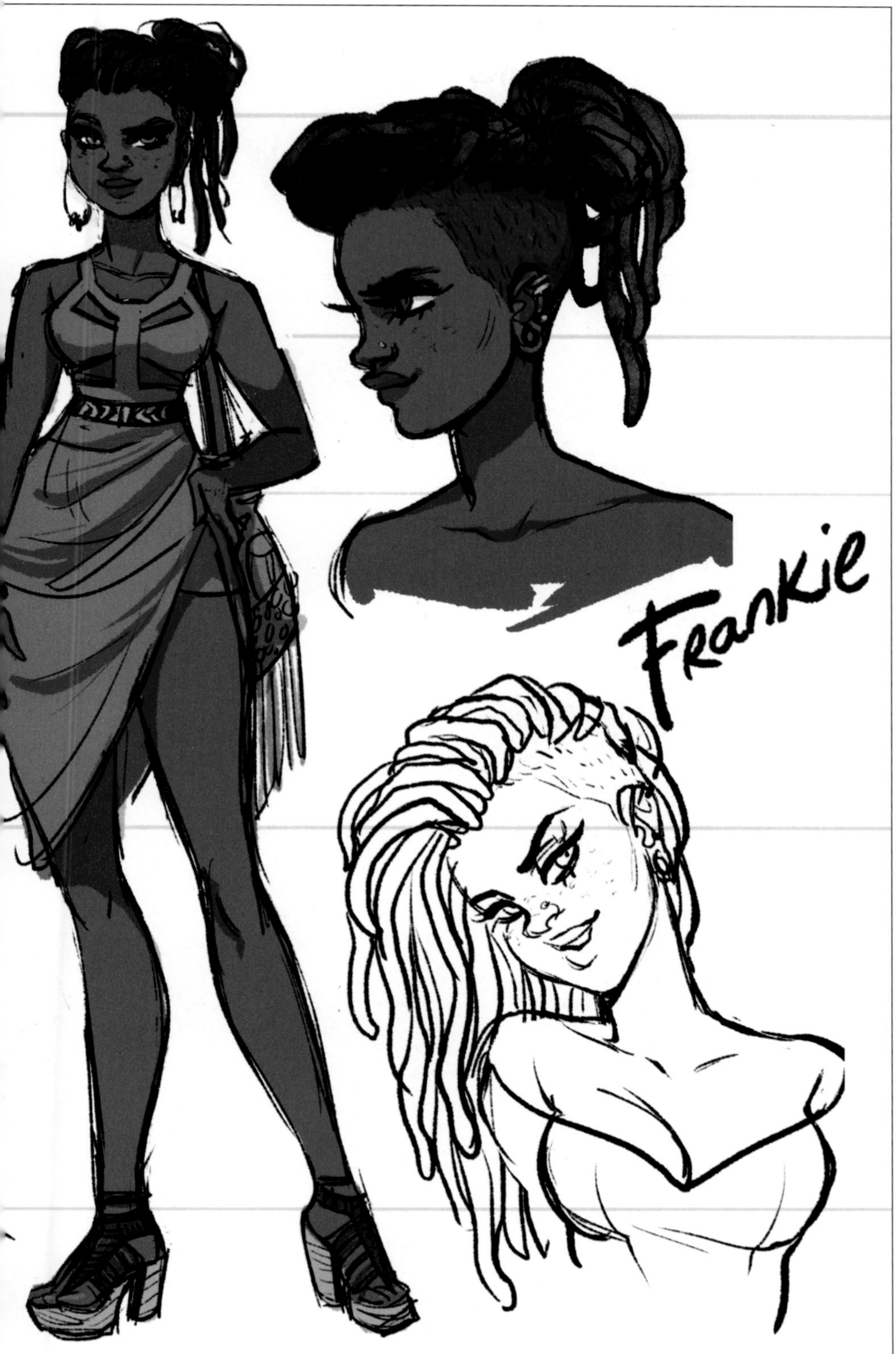
Frankie

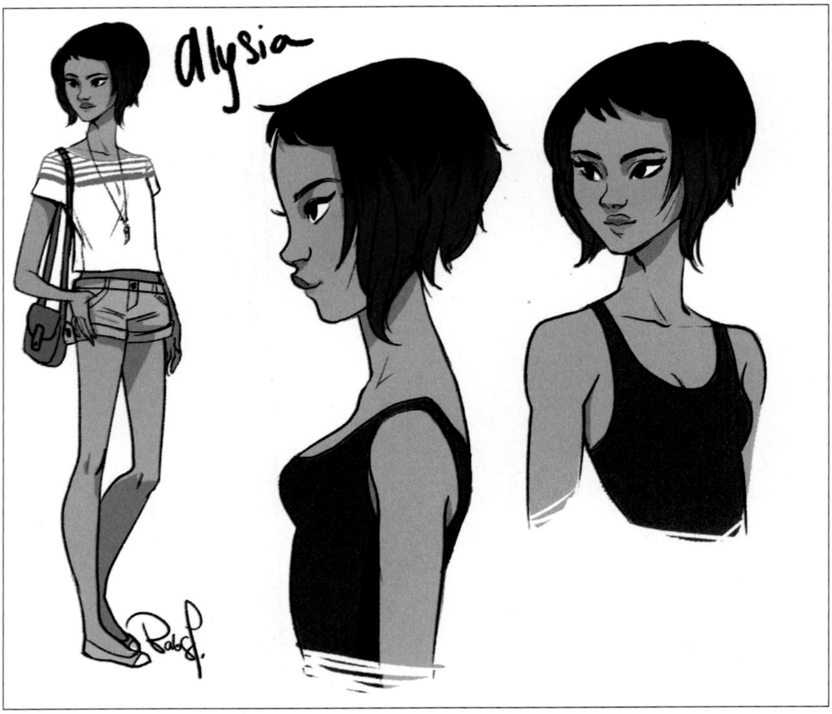
alysia

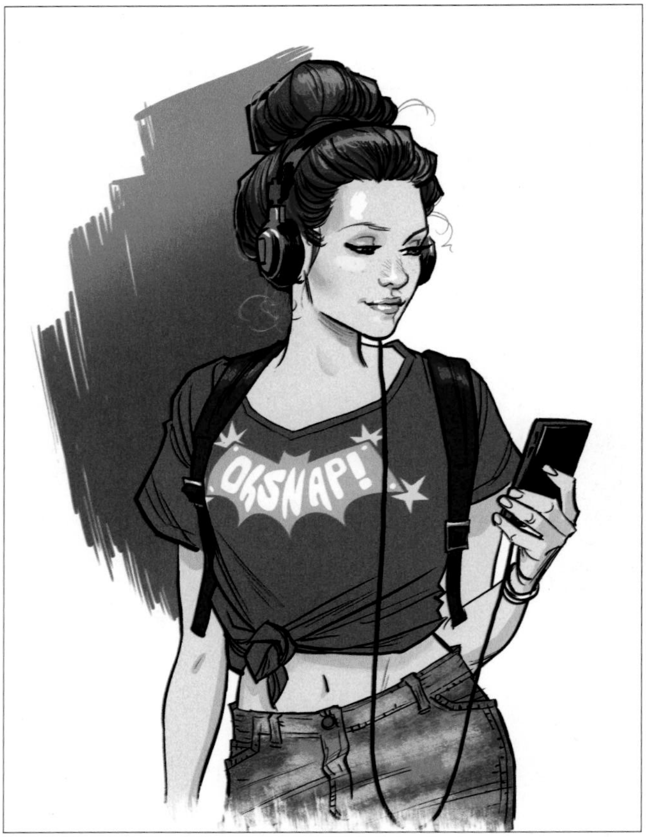
OKSNAP!

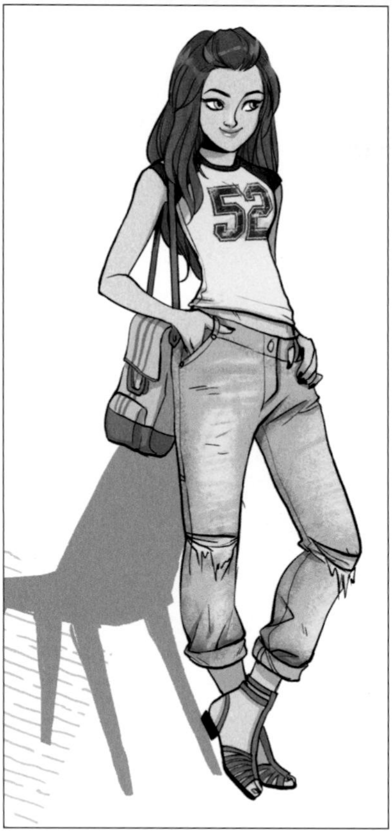
52
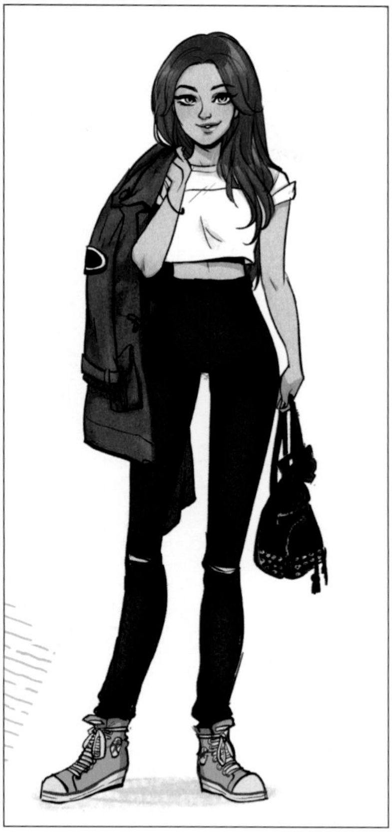
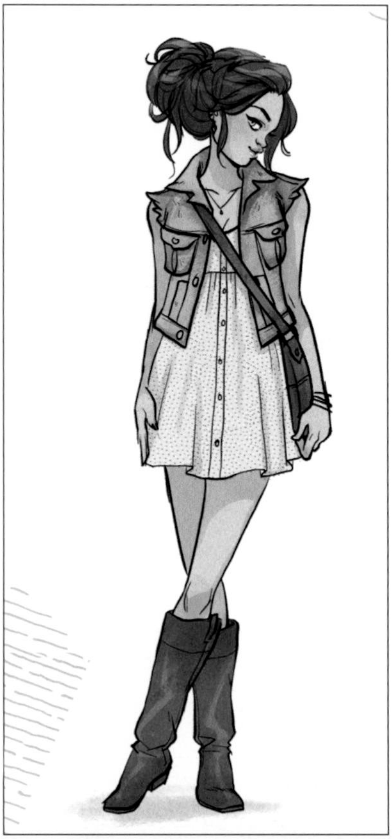
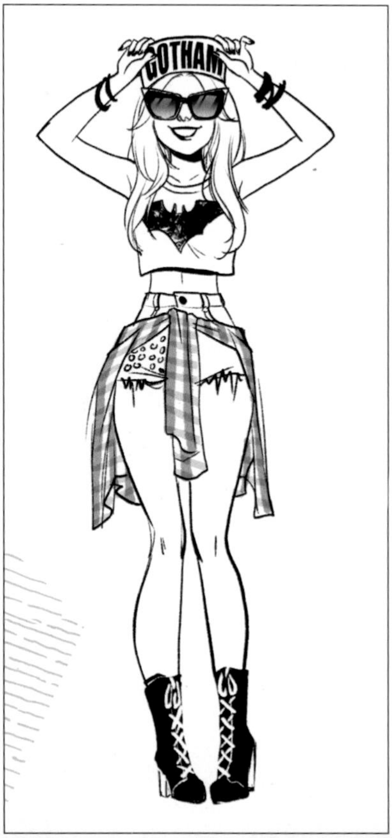
GOTHAM

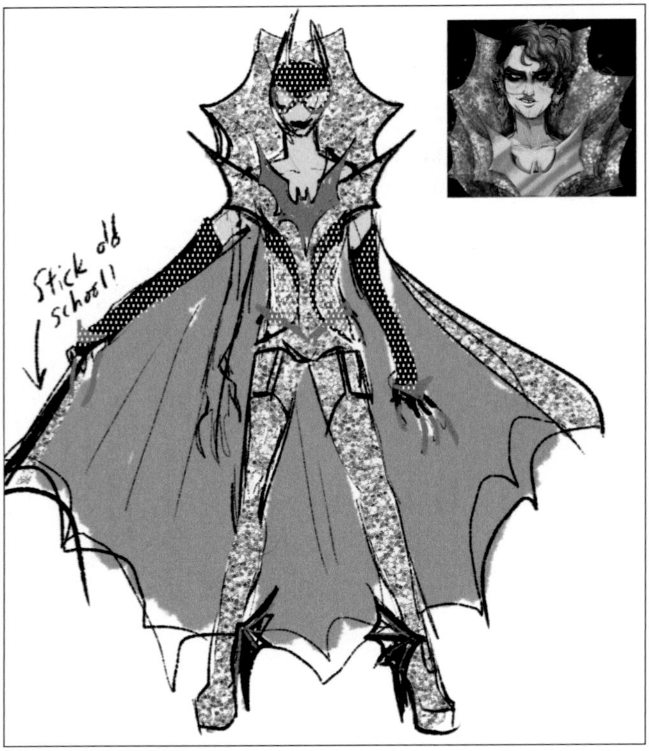
Stick old school!

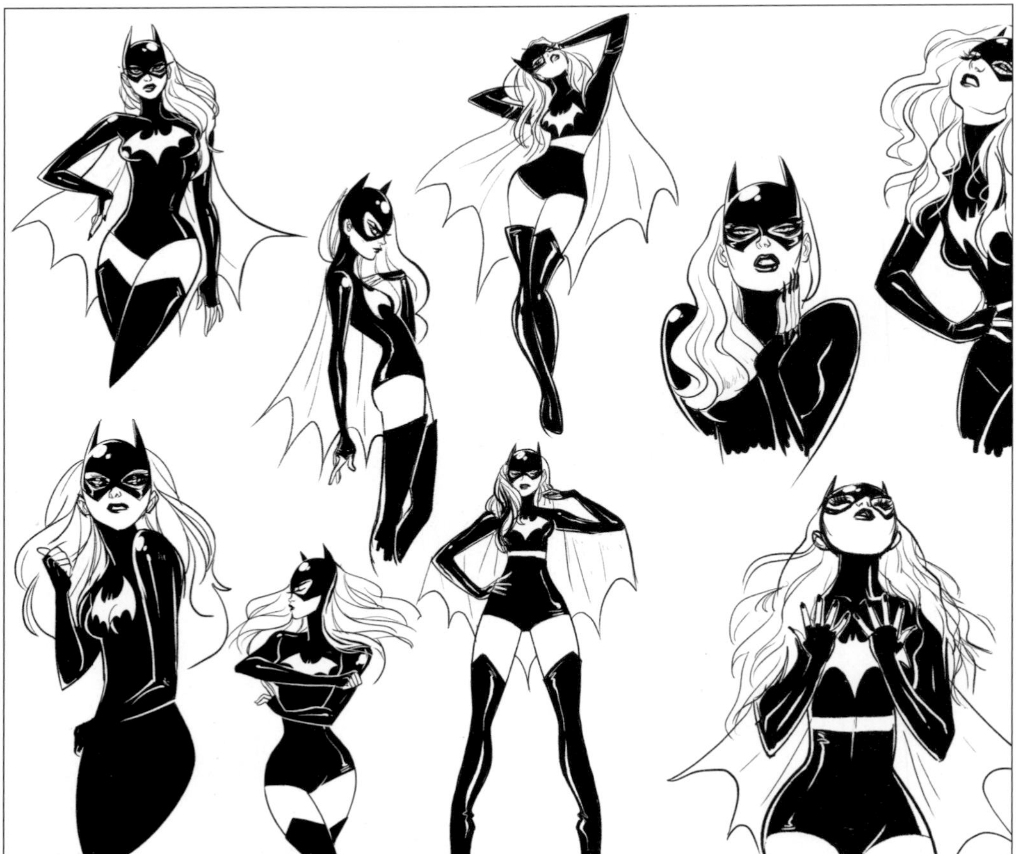

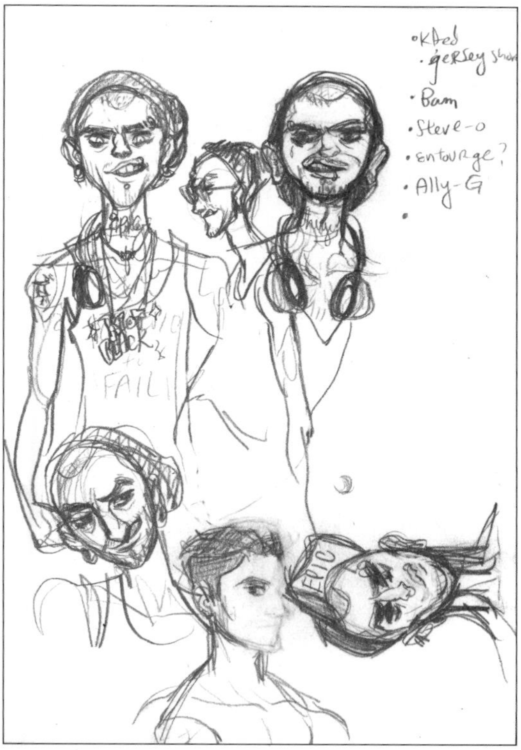

• KFed
• Jersey shore
• Bam
• Steve-o
• entourge?
• Ally-G
FAIL

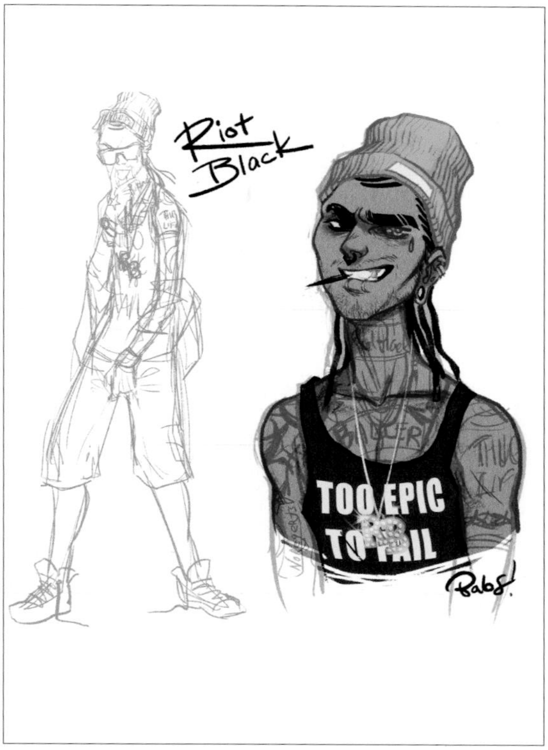

Riot Black
TOO EPIC TO FAIL
Babs!

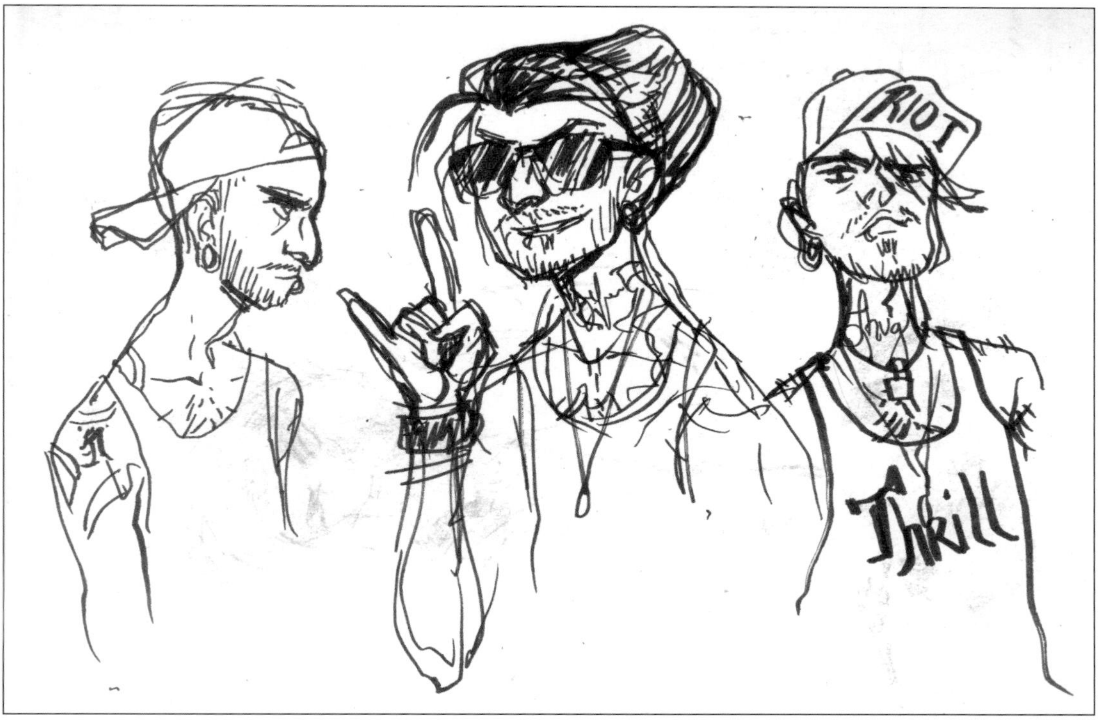

RIOT
Thrill

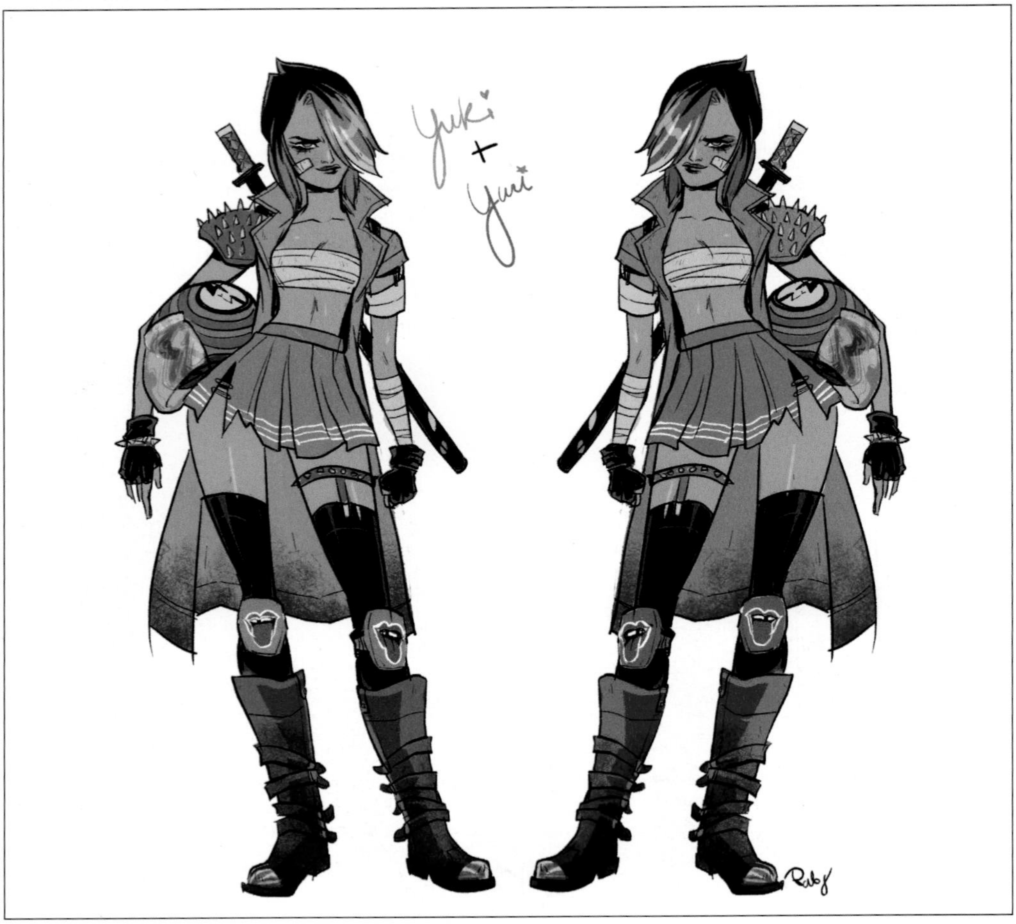
Yuki
+
Yumi

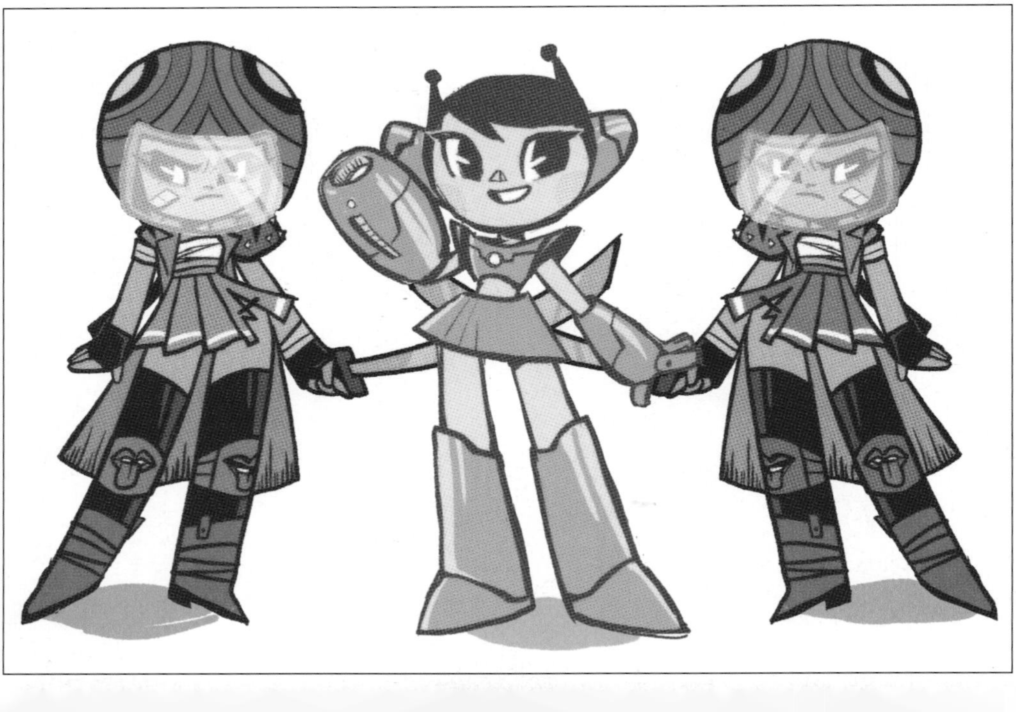

Cover to WONDERCON 2015 program book by **BABS TARR**

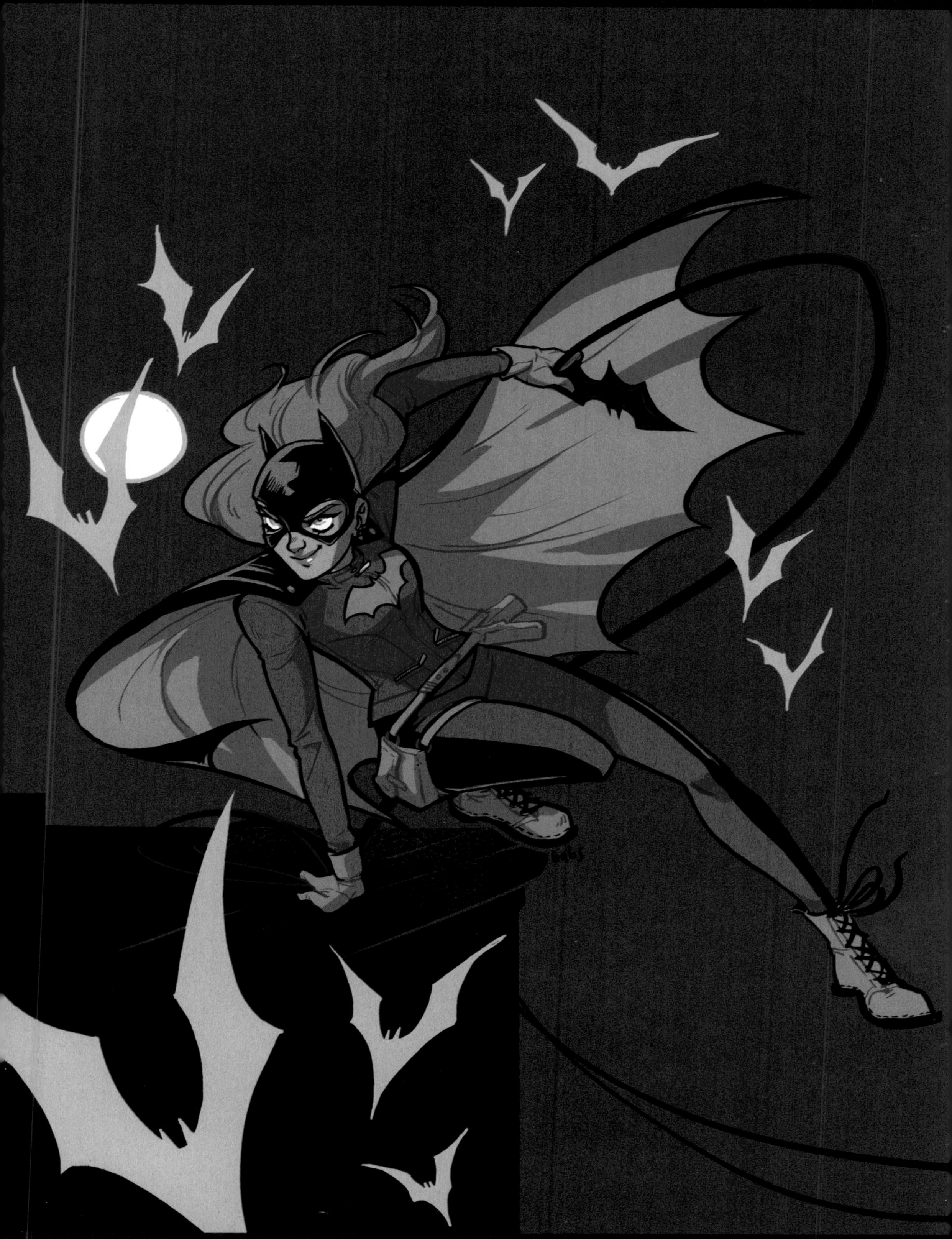

BATGIRL AT BRUNCH BY
CAMERON STEWART

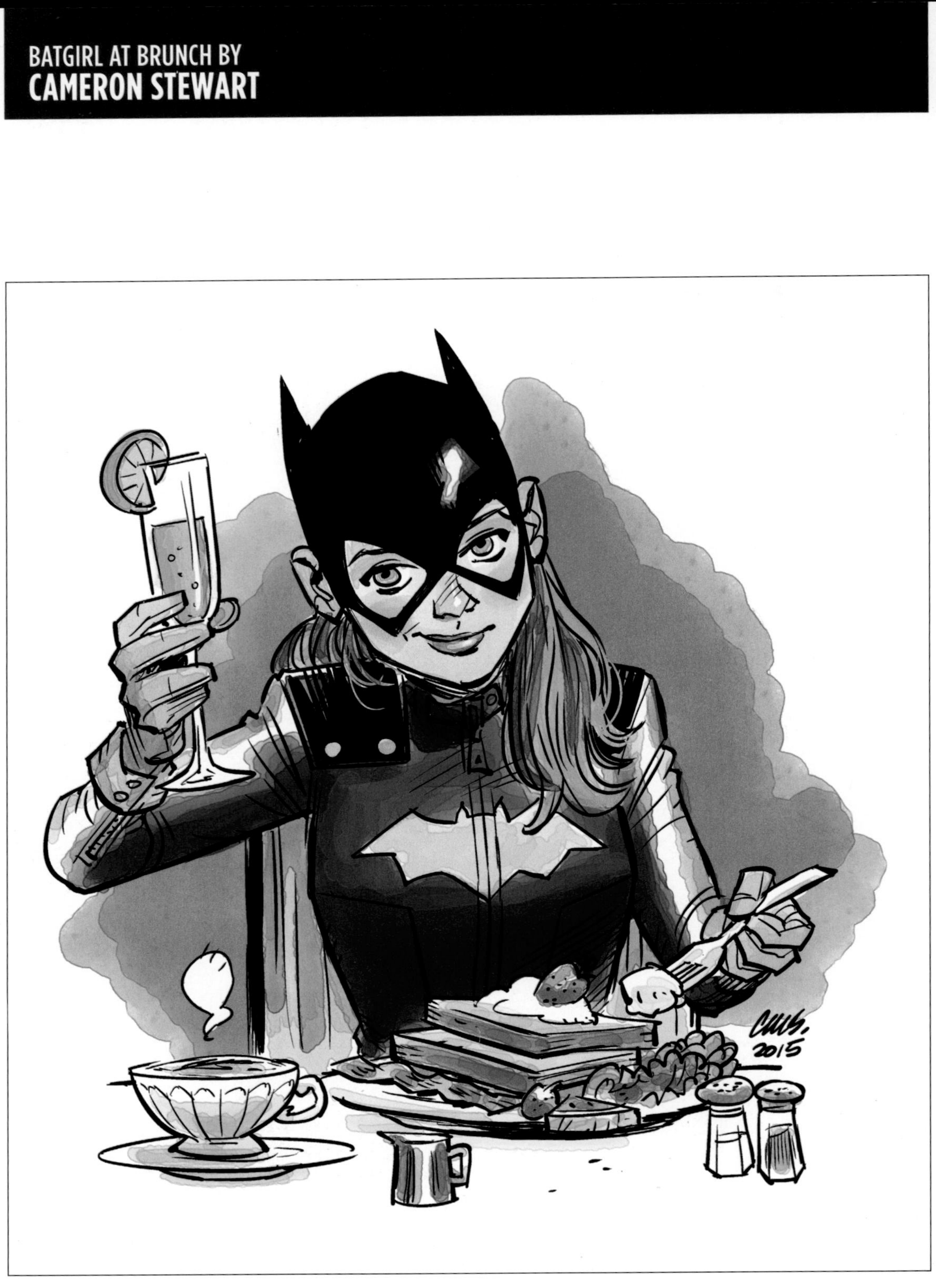
CWS.
2015

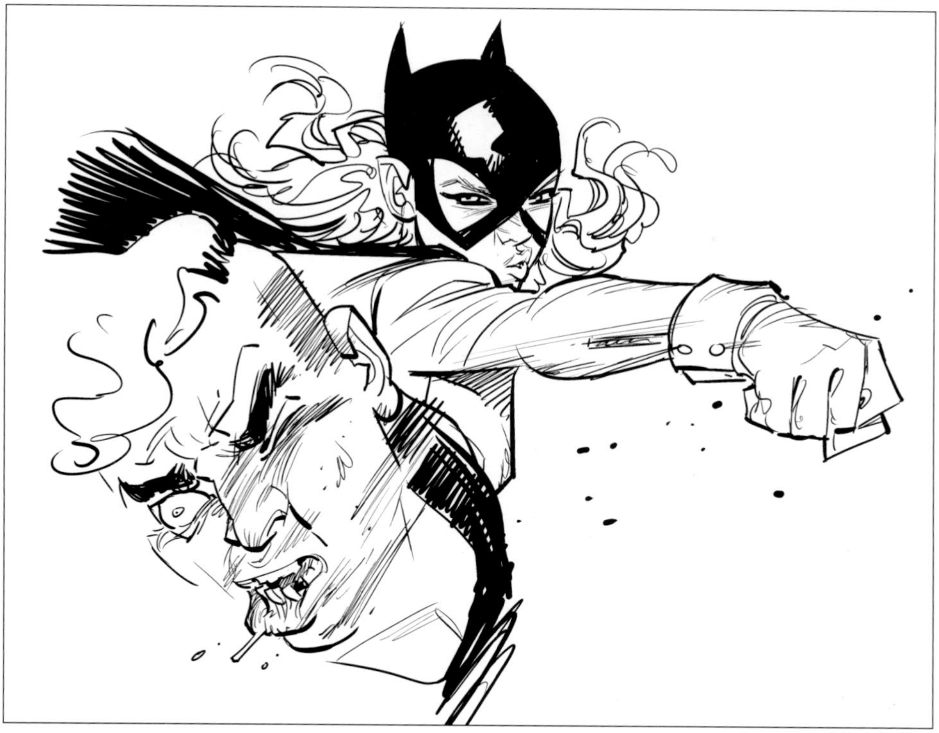

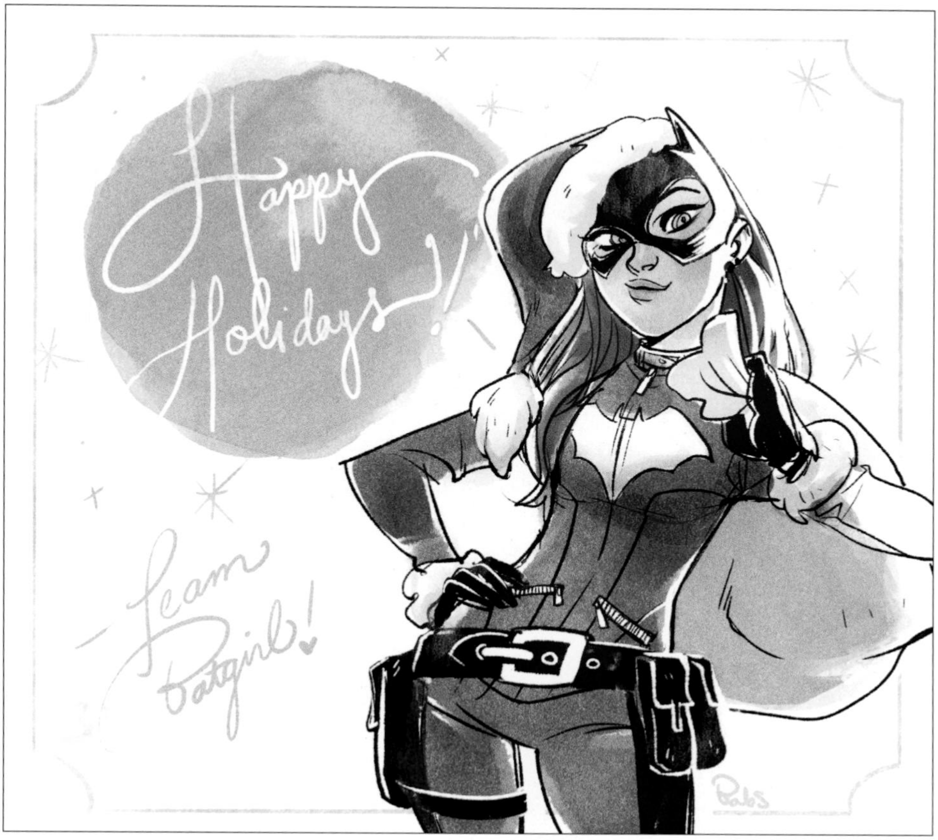
Happy Holidays!!
Team Batgirl!
Babs

Each page starts with a rough layout by CAMERON STEWART, then gets detailed pencils from BABS TARR

KITCHEN STUFF

"The Friendly
Call 1-555-324-MO
Movers"
24-MOVE
52
KITCHEN STU

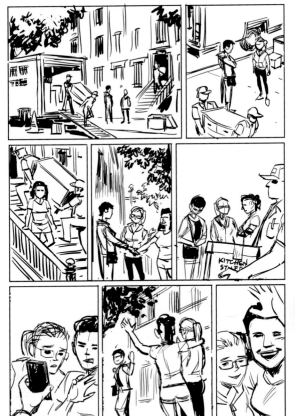

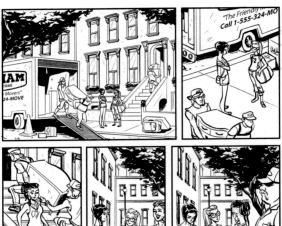

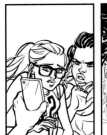

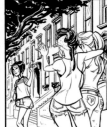

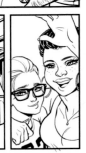

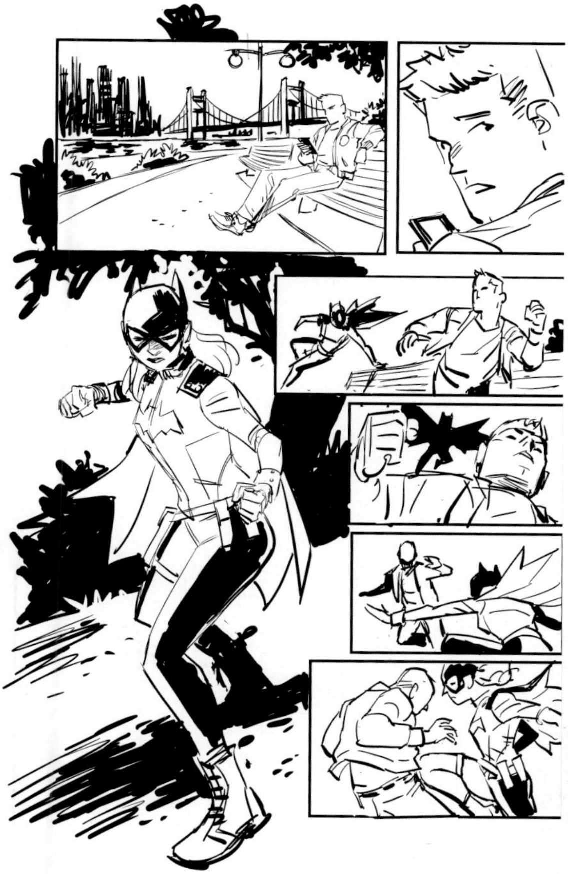
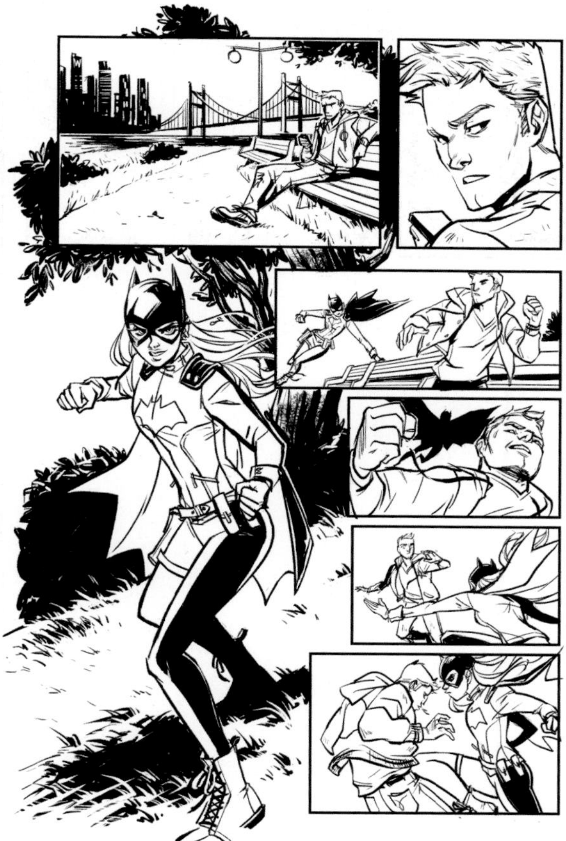

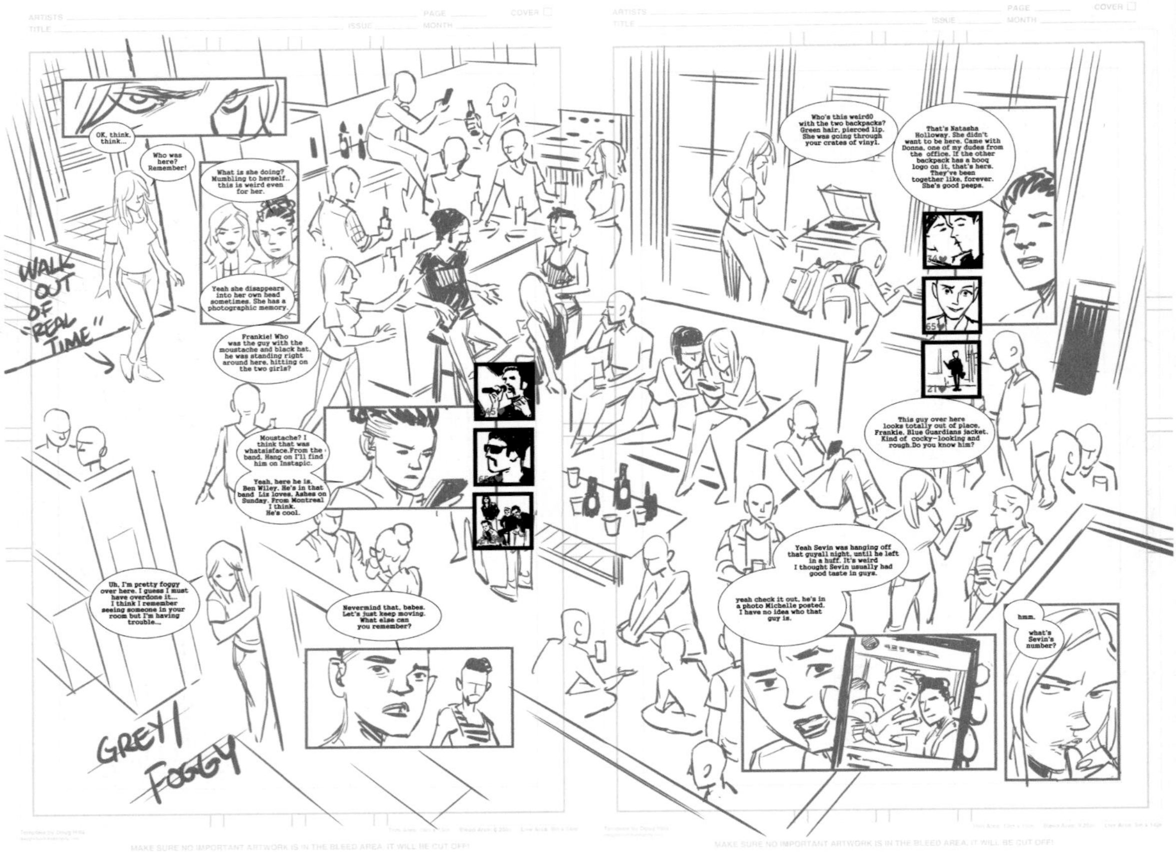
OK, think, think...
Who was here? Remember!
What is she doing? Mumbling to herself.. this is weird even for her.
Yeah she disappears into her own head sometimes. She has a photographic memory.
WALK OUT OF "REAL TIME"
Frankie! Who was the guy with the moustache and black hat. he was standing right around here. hitting on the two girls?
Moustache? I think that was whatsisface.From the band. Hang on I'll find him on Instapic.
Yeah, here he is. Ben Wiley. He's in that band Liz loves, Ashes on Sunday. From Montreal I think. He's cool.
Uh, I'm pretty foggy over here. I guess I must have overdone it... I think I remember seeing someone in your room but I'm having trouble...
Nevermind that, babes. Let's just keep moving. What else can you remember?
GREY/FOGGY
Who's this weird0 with the two backpacks? Green hair, pierced lip. She was going through your crates of vinyl.
That's Natasha Holloway. She didn't want to be here. Came with Donna, one of my dudes from the office. If the other backpack has a hooq logo on it, that's hers. They've been together like, forever. She's good peeps.
This guy over here looks totally out of place. Frankie. Blue Guardians jacket. Kind of cocky-looking and rough.Do you know him?
Yeah Sevin was hanging off that guyall night, until he left in a huff. It's weird I thought Sevin usually had good taste in guys.
yeah check it out, he's in a photo Michelle posted. I have no idea who that guy is.
hmm.
what's Sevin's number?
MAKE SURE NO IMPORTANT ARTWORK IS IN THE BLEED AREA. IT WILL BE CUT OFF!
MAKE SURE NO IMPORTANT ARTWORK IS IN THE BLEED AREA. IT WILL BE CUT OFF!

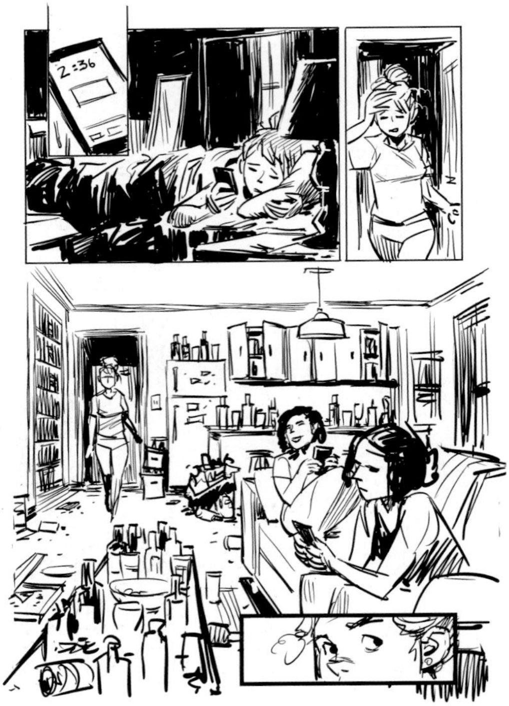
2:36

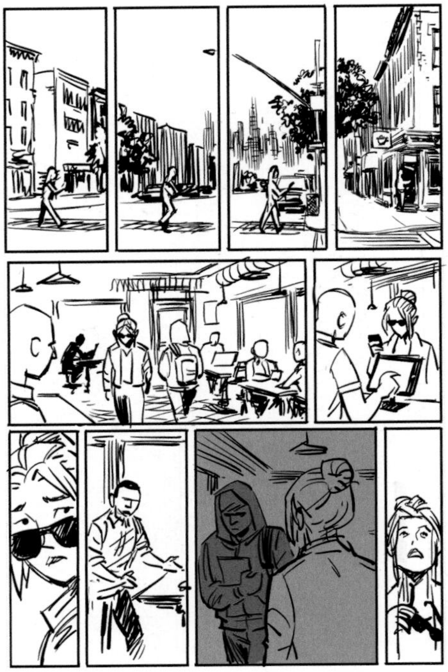

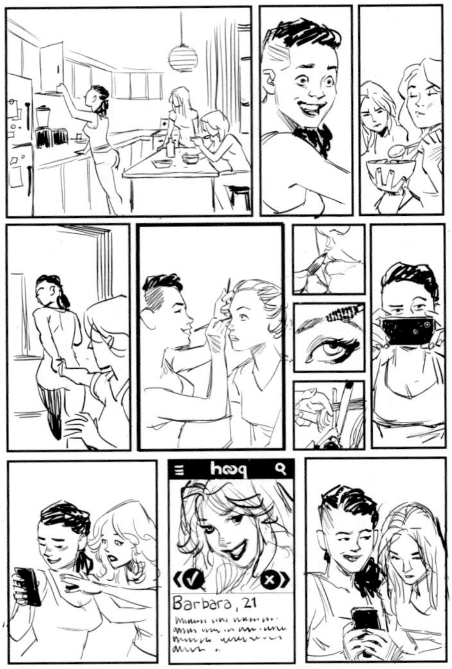
Barbara, 21

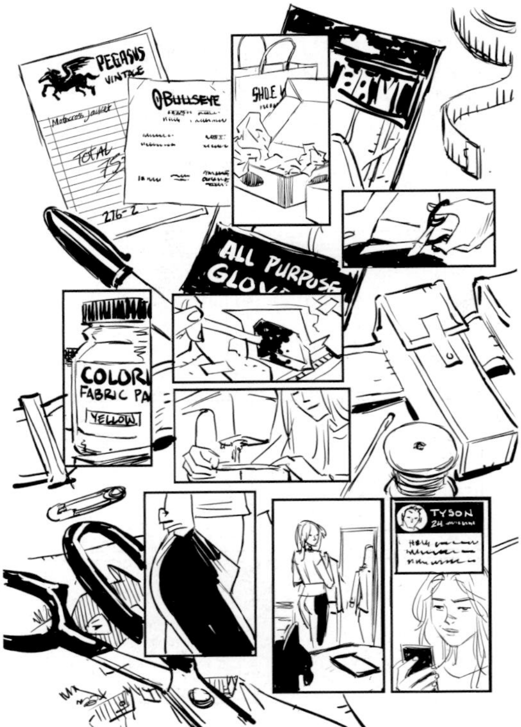
PEGASUS VINTAGE
BULLSEYE
ALL PURPOSE GLOVE
COLOR FABRIC PA
YELLOW
TYSON